INTERIOR DESIGN IN 20th-CENTURY AMERICA

A History

C. Ray Smith

1817

HARPER & ROW, PUBLISHERS, New York
Cambridge, Philadelphia, San Francisco, Washington,
London, Mexico City, São Paulo, Singapore, Sydney

Sponsoring Editor: Fred Henry/Judith Rothman
Text Design: Michael A. Rogondino
Cover Design: Karen Salsgiver
Cover Photos: *Front, top,* Thomas A. Heinz; *right,* © Ezra Stoller/ESTO, 1963;
   bottom, McMillen Inc. *Back, top,* Herman Miller Inc., *left,* Paul T. Frankl,
   New Dimensions (New York: Payson & Clarke, 1928), *right,* © Ezra Stoller/
   ESTO, 1959.
Compositor: Graphic Typesetting Service, Inc.
Printer and Binder: Kingsport Press

INTERIOR DESIGN IN 20th-CENTURY AMERICA: A History

Library of Congress Cataloging-in-Publication Data

Smith, C. Ray.
    Interior design in 20th-century America.

    Includes bibliographies and indexes.
    1. Interior decoration—United States—History—
20th century. I. Title. II. Title: Interior design in
twentieth-century America.
NK2004.S65   1987   729′.0973   86-25674
ISBN 0-06-046322-8

86 87 88 89 9 8 7 6 5 4 3 2 1

Contents

Preface

Interior Design in 20th-Century America is the first book to be concerned *exclusively* with interior design in this century. The opening chapter outlines the foundations of twentieth-century interior design—as received from the legacies of the past. The main body of the book relates the history of interior design from 1900 to the 1980s—decade by decade.

This history surveys the full range of twentieth-century interior design and its influences—not just the Modern movement but also the traditionalist residential designers, the industrial designers, and the space planners who have made recognized contributions in our time. The book provides not only a history of styles and personality designers, but also a history of concepts, plans, materials, functional changes, and technological developments—therefore of our evolving culture.

What has been most popularly seen, understood, and desired in interior design in each decade is compared with both vanguard original invention and the mainstream of design practice and design education. Before the twentieth century, the range of interiors made considerably simpler demands on designers in terms of functional planning. The technologies and processes of each activity and profession were less categorized and specialized. Around the turn of the century, in hospital and laboratory spaces, in courts and prisons, in department stores, and in offices, countless elaborations of procedure brought greater and greater needs for more specific and knowledgeable planning and provision of interior equipment. The interior designer sprung up to focus on these activities, and since then the practice of interior design has witnessed a steady development of increasing specialization.

Today's interior designers are involved in creating a remarkable array of different interiors—not only residences but also seats of government and world headquarters, cathedrals and shrines, corporate office and production complexes, libraries and educational facilities, hospitals and hotels, airplanes and space stations.

Because of this wide activity, interior design is practiced today as a profession by a large variety of people, including interior designers, architects, industrial designers, decorators, furniture dealers, graphic designers, and the design staffs of department stores, corporations, and the federal and state governments. Throughout the book, I refer to interior designers as "designers," whether they classify themselves as architects, decorators, or otherwise.

Other professionals who also actively contribute to interior design include engineers; lighting designers, acoustical and audio-visual specialists; food facilities consultants; behavioral scientists; programmers and planners; draftsmen, detailers, and renderers; exhibit designers; colorists; furniture and textile designers, manufacturers, and suppliers; specification writers; photographers, graphic artists, painters and sculptors; landscape designers, contractors, management consultants, and accountants.

What Is Interior Design? Any study of interior design succeeds or flounders on how much of the subject is considered—on how broad and far reaching its boundaries and limitations are. In the popular mind, interior design is thought to deal mainly with designing furniture and other furnishings. These items have had only a minor part in the success and significance of the best of today's interiors. That part is not unimportant, but it is not the first priority. Instead, concepts and totalities have contributed the greatest achievements in interior design. And it is those overviews and overall interior creations—the designs of interior spaces—along with the designers that created them that have the principal focus in this history.

The history of twentieth-century interiors is essential to a vision of today's practice. Since new professional careers are built on the foundation of past inventive genius, we need to know where the traditions of the field have come from—the events, idioms, and schools that have contributed to design progress and the people, dates, and locations associated with those inventions. In addition, history itself influences the future and provides a basis for aesthetic judgments.

Technical and professional innovations have always been the result of someone's desire to make something beautiful, according to a number of historians. The current thinking is that bronze was developed first of all for jewelry and urns, then used for weapons; that iron was used for the wrought-ironmaker's craft before it became a construction material; that pottery and ceramics were developed for decorative objects before they were used for purely practical purposes. Interior designers can take pride in the fact that their own aspirations reflect these roots of our civilization.

Acknowledgments

This book was made possible by a grant from the Graham Foundation for Advanced Studies in the Fine Arts, under the direction of Carter H. Manny, Jr. To him and to his trustees, I am deeply grateful for having supported an extended final revision of the text.

To Allen Tate, former chairman of the Department of Environmental Design at the Parsons School of Design in New York City, I am indebted for stressing the necessity of surveying twentieth-century interior design history. To many people, that assignment would suggest merely a history of the Modern movement as it affected interior design. My view of the assignment was more inclusive.

To all those designers whose own personal preferences advanced the field of interior design in the twentieth century—as well as to their associates, friends, and families who opened their files, records, and memories to make this history more accurate, complete, and understandable—I am deeply indebted.

To all the scholars and historians whose previous research and evaluations about individual designers and movements have informed my work, I am fundamentally indebted. Many of their works appear in the Suggested Reading lists that follow each chapter. I am fundamentally indebted to Edgar Kaufmann, Jr., whose learned scholarship in interior design and architecture has been an unattainable model.

To all the magazine editors and journalists who reported on the works of their day, I am, like succeeding historians, indebted. For, maligned by historians as journalists often are, their daily reporting is among the first-source research material of history.

To all the photographers who recorded the work of interior design, along with the many manufacturers and museums that provided photographs, I am both indebted and in admiration; for without them, the designs of this ephemeral art would be virtually lost. I especially appreciate Erica Stoller's professional management of ESTO, and the cooperation of August Lotito and the Hans van Nes Studio.

Among the interior designers and architects who extended readings and interviews and who shared their knowledge and memories most generously are Peter Andes, Benjamin Baldwin, Richard Callahan, Jack Conner, Michel B. de Turck, Roger Ferri, Albert Hadley, Anthony Hail, Robert D. Kleinschmidt, George Nelson, William Pahlmann, Mrs. Henry Parish II, Charles Pfister, Edward J. Wormley, and Edward Zajac.

Among the educators and historians who read sections in different stages and versions and for whose special care in directing sensitive emphasis and avoiding egregious errors I express gratitude, are Stanley Barrows, David G. De Long, Kerwin Ketler, Aristeides Papadakis, Guido Stockmann, and Christopher Wilk.

Other readers gave extended time, insight, and knowledge, and dealt with suggested corrections with experience, charm, humor, and perspective. To them and to a host of others—friends, professional associates, librarians, and many more—I am indebted for assistance in opening their funds of information to me and providing much-appreciated support and encouragement along the seemingly unending way: Alexandra C. Anderson, Suzanne Stephens, Everett Brown, Lyman Martin, Luiz Rey; Roger and Edith Tuckerman, Carol and Richard Selle, Lester Grundy, John B. Wisner, John Fitler-Ellis, Carleton Varney; Melanie Kahane, Mary Jean Alexander, Harriet Morrison, Marion Gough, Jacqueline Beymer, and Anita Welch of the Decorators Club of New York; James Amster, Arthur E. Smith, Mrs. Charles Gleaves, Robert Modaff, Ann Wright, Peter Keibel; Ralph Caplan, George Finlay, James Wines, Gerard F. McCauley, Channing Blake, Sherman B. Emery, Stanley Abercrombie, James Earl Jewell, Howard B. Leighton, Ralph Cutler, Eileen Seidelbach, Ariane Breitling, Abigail Sturges, Mr. and Mrs. James F. McClelland, Jr.; Elaine Kirkland and Jacquelyn Kavanaugh of the Atlanta Historical Society; Sarah Cecil, DePuy Warwick Reed, Katherine E. Boyd; Michael Vincent, Ruth Weinstein, Louis Tregre, John H. Timothy, Stephen Kirschenbaum, Paul Blyth Hill, Kathleen Kirk, Claiborne Jones, Charlotte Sunday, Richard Oliver, Ricardo Regazzoni, Christine Rae, David Pelt, Nicole Richards, John-Michael Amato; Thomas A. Heinz, Herbert E. Walker, Leo Goldsmith, Jr.; the librarians at the Parsons School of Design: Sharon Chickanzeff, Catherine Fukushima, Claire Petrie, Howard Wood; Lisa Taylor, Peter Scherer, Eileen White, Katherine Martinez, and the Cooper-Hewitt Museum Library; Elaine Greene, Denise Otis, and the librarians at *House & Garden*.

And especially I express my gratitude and appreciation to those who worked directly with me and for long periods on the task: my research team—Marian Page and Timothy G. Morrell; those who collected photographs for me—Janet Marks, Stephen Jones, Jill Sanchia Cowan, and Elizabeth Childs-Johnson. The text was written entirely on an Osborne 1 computer, without which the task would have been insuperable. Michael Dembo expedited my learning to write on the Osborne. Karl Sandin and Diane Moran at Harper & Row offered many generous acts of assistance. Pearl C. Vapnek's shepherding of the text through the production process has been invaluable. To all these mainstays I offer my sincerest and most indebted expression of gratitude.

Finally, I express my thanks to Marcel and Jean Grignon, in whose house the original chance connection with Harper & Row was made, and to my son Scott, who patiently and genially gave up hours of our recreation time together.

C. Ray Smith

Chapter 1

Before 1900: Precursors of the Twentieth-Century Interior

In 1851 the Great Exhibition of the Works of Industry of All Nations spread out, in London's Crystal Palace, the glorious accomplishments of the Industrial Revolution. As the first international exposition, it was a vast array of industry's products, including its decorative and artistic achievements. Some of them were wonderful and beautiful, some bizarre and hideous. For many Victorians it was the first glimpse of the furnishings, appointments, and interior design that could be produced by industry. For nearly everybody it was the first view of the architecture and interiors of metal and glass, which Joseph Paxton (later knighted for his work) demonstrated in the Crystal Palace itself.

The Industrial Revolution

To this day many people believe that the Great Exhibition signifies the beginning of the Industrial Revolution, and therefore the beginning of the modern world. It was not the actual beginning—either of the Industrial Revolution or of Modernism; the Industrial Revolution had already been in effect for at least a hundred years. Mere logic is sufficient documentation of this statement: In order to fill so vast a hall as the Crystal Palace—it was nearly 1,851 feet long—with industrially made objects, there had to have been considerable industrial activity in advance. As with any anthology of literature, the writing must have been produced before the anthology could have been assembled. So too, the many production techniques exhibited at the Crystal Palace had been available before—though many new products were introduced at that time. To the vanguard innovators it was—like most expositions and compendiums—a summary. To the uninitiated it was a revelation of the new.

Above all, the Crystal Palace Exhibition served as a signal and a symbol: It demonstrated that the world had changed. From then on there would be a greater availability and a greater possibility for greater numbers of possessions—regardless of aesthetic quality—by greater numbers of the population than ever before. It also signified the arrival of the masses as a new force in the population, certainly as a new force in design. Now they were wage earners and product buyers.

For that is what the Industrial Revolution meant: not only that machines had arrived; but, more important, that the masses of population now had more possibility to acquire things that would make their lives healthier, happier, safer, and wider-reaching than ever before in the history of humankind.

All this came with more than a few curses, of course. The Industrial Revolution from 1750 onward had brought smoke and pollution, causing the loss of natural daylight behind new manmade clouds. It had brought excesses and abuses of child labor. Long work hours and hazardous conditions brought many accidents and illnesses to workers. Coal-gas poisoning was a common occurrence. The concentration of factory workers had brought urban crowding, to the degree that there was a complete redistribution of population. In England, for example, before 1800, two-thirds of the population lived in rural areas; after 1856 half the population lived in towns and cities.[1]*

The Industrial Revolution also brought an inevitable decrease in handcraft, as more things were made by a greater number of inexperienced people in less time. It brought a greedy and insensitive use of natural materials to the production of manmade objects. Before the arrival of industrial production, true beauty had always "been based on the balance between purpose, process, and the property of the material," as the contemporary metallurgist Cyril Stanley Smith has written.[2] Beauty still means that today, though the effects of the Industrial Revolution and the clouds it produced have been hard to see through. A reform movement was soon to come.[3]

Nevertheless, the Industrial Revolution had brought a whole new world, and the Crystal Palace Exhibition proclaimed that fact for all the world to see. It exhibited the major developments—the precursors—that were leading to modern thinking, modern living, and modern interior design. The exhibition had not brought those developments about. Rather, it announced the possibility that interior design, along with the other advantages of world civilization, was no longer available only to the privileged—to kings and princes, to the aristocracy and successful merchants. Now interior design and furnishings design—the decorative arts and home furnishings—were within the grasp of a broad range of the population. To students of interior design, therefore, the London Crystal Palace Exhibition of 1851 signifies the first possibility for the creation of the modern form of their profession—interior design.

What Led Up to All This?

It had been long in coming—at least four hundred years, if we count Gutenberg's printing of the Bible around 1454. What Gutenberg did was to put together all the basic components of mass production.[4] His first successful use in the West of movable, reusable type for printing contained all the components: (1) mass production of (2) prefabricated (3) multiples that are (4) assembled to (5) form a system

---

*Notes will be found at the end of each chapter, following the list of books and articles for suggested reading.

for (6) communication, convenience, or comfort. It was a soaring commencement. Prefabrication and assembly made it possible for work to be done by different people. This became known as the division of labor.

Gutenberg's achievement not only initiated mass production; it also led, in due course, to the spread of literacy, literature, and scholarship beyond the confines of the ecclesiastical community.[5] This revolution from script to print led to the founding of many new and great universities in the next century.

From Gutenberg onward, the course of history was set on an unswerving, if occasionally halting, course. Mass production reached its culmination, perhaps, in the machine aesthetic of the Modern movement (see Chapter 4). To that way of thinking the goal of design and production was not only the actuality of machine production, but also the mere image of the machine or the aesthetic suggestion of the machine-made. By 1851 the machine had made its breakthrough and was a pervasive force that affected the life of everyone in the Western world.

Among the factors and developments that contributed to this progress were the increase in population between the fourteenth and eighteenth centuries, the intellectual and scientific revolutions of the seventeenth century, the democratic revolution of the eighteenth century, the technological revolution of the eighteenth and nineteenth centuries, and the development of materials for shelter and protection that the latter brought.

An Increase in Population

Between 1300 and 1350, as the contemporary French historian Fernand Braudel reads the statistics, the population of the world was between 250 and 350 million.[6] By 1780 it had increased to between 836 and 1,380 million. That increase represented a growth of somewhere between 138 percent and 400 percent in 400 years. Whichever remarkable figure is accurate, the population of the entire world, not just Europe, probably doubled during this period. Among the causes of that increase were:

1. Scientific and medical advances against disease, plague, and death. Due to scientific developments in the eighteenth century, disease was markedly brought under control, and the mortality rate—particularly infant mortality—was decreased. As a result, longevity was also increased.

2. Agricultural advances. Due to the migration of populations to newly available arable lands such as the New World, with its more efficient crops of corn and potatoes, the production of food was greatly increased by 1800. Consequently, famine was considerably decreased.

3. Better trade communications. Accompanied by the spread of international banking and credit, which had been established by the Florentines in the fourteenth century, trade between countries began to make necessities more available.

4. A change in moral outlook toward money. In the seventeenth century, production for profit was accepted as an honorable pursuit. No longer was it considered good merely not to waste labor on luxury; now the accumulation of money was also an acceptable goal.

An Intellectual and Scientific Revolution

During the seventeenth century the intellectual revolution, ongoing since the Renaissance, began to free Western thinking from dependence on previous authorities, assumptions, religions, and superstitions.[7] Based on contemporaneous scientific discoveries, it proffered the ultimate reliance on observable fact and on the courageous fusion of data-gathering with deductive theory. This put everyone in the position of being able to question his or her own destiny—and essentially of coming closer to controlling it. Before, one's lot had been generally considered as governed by religion and death, work and taxes, obligation and servitude. The intellectual and scientific revolutions brought the possibility of self-reliance, challenge, and desire.

Among the milestones of that intellectual and scientific progress were (1) René Descartes's examination of Nature and observable fact for proof of reasoning. From that viewpoint he proclaimed in his *Discourse on Method,* "I think, therefore I am" (1637); (2) Isaac Newton's publication of the *Mathematical Principles of Natural Philosophy* (1687); and (3) John Locke's philosophical justification of revolution and independence in his "Letter on Toleration" and "Two Treatises on Government" (1688).

This intellectual revolution led, during the seventeenth century, to Rationalism—including rationalism in design. Rationalism observed, accepted, and applauded the specific functions of each design of nature—each plant, each animal—for its own peculiarities. This was the Age of Reason; its attitudes were the intellectual foundation of functionalism in the twentieth century (see Chapter 3).

A Democratic Revolution

From the third quarter of the seventeenth century onward, revolution by force gradually brought greater political power and greater social independence to the population:[8] (1) beginning with the Glorious Revolution in England (1644); (2) then, notably, in the United States (1776–83); (3) next, in France (1789–92); (4) and again in France, though less successfully, and throughout Europe (1848); and (5) finally, the gradual abolition of slavery throughout this period.

All the democratic revolutions aimed to change the ancient regime that guaranteed position, power, and money by birthright alone. No longer could kings, the nobility, and the clergy rule by divine right. Instead, ever afterward, the democratic revolutions offered, in the battle cry of the French Revolution, a greater degree of liberty, equality, and fraternity to everyone.

A Technological Revolution

Major discoveries and inventions altered the sources of power, changed machinery, and ultimately produced new materials. The source of power to run machines changed at the end of the eighteenth century. From 1650 to 1800 water and wind had been the primary power sources of the Western world.[9] From 1800 to 1900 steam (produced by burning coal or wood) took precedence as the primary source of power. The availability of coal as opposed to wood was to give a lead to whichever region or country had the most. The discovery of petroleum deposits in northwestern Pennsylvania in 1860 added petroleum to the list of fossil fuels. Then the fossil fuels, coal and oil, became the principal power sources.

The development of the factory system from 1800 onward meant that production no longer had to rely on individual craftsmen working at home from beginning to end. The centralization of work activity and the subdivision of labor into a process, where prefabricated parts or components were assembled, produced widespread mass production. Contributing to this process were the use of iron, as opposed to wood, for the construction of machinery; the transformation of the textile industry; James Watt's invention of the steam engine (1769); Robert Fulton's first steamboat run from New York to Albany (1807); and George Stephenson's first railroad run in England (1825).

The essential fact is that, beginning in the mid-eighteenth century, power-driven machines transformed industry and transportation, trade and communications, and therefore politics and society. People moved to be near the new factory system that used those machines. Thereby numerous new cities were formed, with concomitant disadvantages as well as advantages. This was the Industrial Revolution that was to be proclaimed as a success, however qualified, in the Great Exhibition at the Crystal Palace a hundred years later.

New Materials for Interiors

In the course of these many discoveries, new materials for building and furnishing were developed that made possible our modern interiors. Among them were the building and construction materials of which room envelopes are made, as well as the materials used in the manufacture of furnishings: iron and steel, glass, ceramics and concrete, textiles and carpets. The new materials were outgrowths of basic and ancient industries that go back to the historical origins of our species. But the methods of manufacture and the new uses and applications of these materials became more abundant and more accepted.

Iron and Steel

Iron and steel have made possible our buildings and interiors of metal and glass—from the Crystal Palace to the Seagram Building (see Chapter 7). Yet iron and steel were first considered as "base" and "unfinished" materials that were acceptable only for their practical strength. Only gradually did they become accepted as materials that could be visible and make aesthetic contributions.

The technological possibility was initiated in the fifteenth century, when the blast furnace was first used in the West to produce liquid cast iron. A second major change in this development occurred around 1860, when it became possible to melt large quantities of low-carbon iron and cast it into relatively homogeneous ingots, purifying it of the slag that had previously always been present.[10] This produced steel, which is a simple alloy of iron with carbon. Henry Bessemer's 1856 patent for manufacturing steel from cast iron began this new phase of availability and construction.

In the beginning of this progress, iron was used mainly for fittings, machinery, and equipment, including weapons. Wrought iron or hand-hammered iron art had had an honorable heritage as railings, screens, and ornaments; but pots, pipes, and firebacks were more typical of the thinking of artisans through the seventeenth century about the proper status and use of cast iron.

In the eighteenth century the use of iron increased markedly through the designs of engineers as a purely practical material. The early eighteenth-century architectural uses of iron were for bridges, as Nikolaus Pevsner traces its development.[11] An iron chain bridge was built over the River Tees in the north of England between 1740 and 1742. The earliest all-iron bridge was designed by T. F. Pritchard and built by Abraham Darby at Coalbrookdale, England, in 1775. In America, James Finley built nine iron suspension bridges between 1801 and 1811.

Cast iron was used in the construction of mills in England in 1780. In the same year the Grand Salon of the Louvre was roofed with an iron construction; and that was followed by the iron roof of the Théâtre Français between 1787 and 1790. The first known structure of exposed cast-iron columns and beams was in a flax-spinning factory at Ditherington, Shrewsbury, designed by Benyon, Bage & Marshall in 1796.

Still, in these uses the material was considered for its practical strength alone, essentially, as utilitarian engineering, and therefore concealable or at least not focal. During 1790–92 iron columns in St. Chad's Church, Shrewsbury, by George Steuart, were encased in wood. Then, during 1808–09, Smirke's Covent Garden Theatre in London used iron unconcealed to support the balconies. That was followed by the earliest known example of a metal-and-glass dome—at the Halles au Blé in Paris, designed in 1809 and built in 1811. Shortly thereafter (1815) John Nash designed his renowned all-iron staircase for the Royal Pavilion at Brighton and used iron columns (with copper palm-tree capitals) in the kitchen (1818–21). This was, as Pevsner says, "the first appearance of unmasked iron in connection with royalty"[12] and it signaled the ultimate acceptance of the material.

Iron, then, first appeared on the exterior of buildings for its structural properties, from 1837 on, in cast-iron fronts of commercial buildings in New York City.[13] From 1843 to 1850 Henri Labrouste designed his celebrated Bibliothèque Ste. Geneviève in Paris with iron columns and iron arches, as Pevsner points out, "exposed as frankly as if he were concerned with a factory or a railway station,"[14] in contrast to being concerned, as Labrouste was, with an elegant municipal interior.

Many other buildings followed in a steady succession: the London Coal Exchange, with both its structure and decorations in iron by Bunning (1847–49); cast-iron fronts on warehouses in St. Louis (1850–77); and, bringing us to the first prominent public building almost entirely of metal and glass—Joseph Paxton's Crystal Palace in London (1851). From then on, spurred by the advocacy of, among others, James Bogardus in America—by his building for Harper Bros. in New York of 1854 and especially by his pamphlet "Cast Iron Buildings" of 1856—and by Viollet-le-Duc in France (especially his lectures of 1863–64), the acceptance of iron structures and decorations grew rapidly.

After 1860 construction was further improved by the use of steel, which made possible both wider spans between columns and higher buildings. After the completion of the Brooklyn Bridge (1883) and the Eiffel Tower (1889), no construction could overlook the possibilities and availabilities of iron and steel.

Glass

The ancient craft of glassmaking changed drastically in the late seventeenth century with the development of plate glass. Today, it is plate glass that opens our interiors to daylight and relates them to the openness of outdoor space. Glass is, perhaps, the most dramatic component of the modern interior.

Blown glass had reached a peak of performance in sixteenth-century Venice; but glass for windows and mirrors was not much used until the seventeenth century.[15] Sash windows were invented in Holland in the 1680s, and the first recorded use of sashes in England was in 1685 as replacements in Inigo Jones's Banqueting House at Whitehall Palace (1619–22).[16] Afterwards, sashes rapidly replaced casement windows in all but the smallest houses. Still, when glass was used in them in these early days, it was roundels of blown glass held in by lead cames.

Around 1680 the process for casting glass was invented in France. This new plate glass was developed to achieve perfectly parallel surfaces, and consequently provided almost pure translucency. It was then that larger and clearer panes of glass were used for the orangerie-like windows in the Galerie des Glaces at Versailles and for its inner wall of mirrors. The Galerie des Glaces was therefore something of a technological milestone—as well as one of the truly great rooms of Western civilization—when it was built (1678–84). France led in the production of plate glass for many years afterward.

In the course of the eighteenth century the panes of glass in windows became larger, and the glazing bars or muntins became thinner. This progress shows as New England's 24 panes over 24 panes was reduced to the early nineteenth-century common variety of 6 over 6. But not until the mid-nineteenth century did the ready availability of large panes of sheet glass allow the muntins and transoms to be abandoned—first reducing the number of panes to 2 over 2 (the late-Victorian standard), then reducing that number to a single large pane per sash as the nineteenth century drew to a close.

Using this new plate glass between 1837 and 1840, Joseph Paxton, in his capacity as landscape gardener and horticulturalist to the Duke of Devonshire, built a metal-and-glass conservatory to house the Duke's plants at Chatsworth. In 1845 Decimus Burton and Richard Turner designed the conservatory for Kew Gardens outside London. Other prototypical metal-and-glass buildings accompanied this development.

Then Paxton built the Crystal Palace for the Great Exhibition in London, using 900,000 square feet of sheet glass. The design utilized the largest pane of glass then available, which was 49 inches by 10 inches. Paxton had achieved an astonishing feat of mass production, since all the components of the Crystal Palace were prefabricated in factories and assembled on the building site; and he had brought metal-and-glass construction into the public recognition as a major building system.

From then on an irresistible force moved the glass industry headlong toward the glass-paneled curtain walls of the 1950s and 1960s, and to the twentieth century's glass-pavilion-like houses and interiors with their sliding glass doors, and their (essentially) walls of glass (see Chapters 6 and 7).

Concrete

The third ancient material to be developed further to affect the twentieth-century interior was concrete. Imperial Rome had achieved considerable sophistication in concrete construction, but concrete technology lapsed until its rediscovery in the late eighteenth century.[17] Present-day concrete is a mixture of cement (made from a mixture of limestone and clay), sand, crushed stone (aggregate), and water. This manufactured stone has the supporting or "compressive" strength of natural stone.

The first modern use of concrete was in 1774 for the construction of the Eddystone Lighthouse in England by John Smeaton.[18] Smeaton had used a mixture of lime, clay, sand, and crushed iron-slag. Then, in 1824, Joseph Aspdin produced the first cement that hardened with water. Named for the Isle of Portland, where the limestone was obtained, Aspdin's durable mixture is still called portland cement. A concrete flooring system developed in 1829 used concrete as a filling between iron girders. The first extensive use of concrete occurred in 1867 in the main building of the Paris Exhibition.

Reinforced concrete also was known by the Romans in the form of iron clamps over masonry joints.[19] The method of increasing the strength of concrete by incorporating metal reinforcements in the concrete while it is still wet came about in the 1850s and 1860s in England and France. The first patent for its application was taken out by Joseph Monier for use in making plant pots in 1868; he used a wire network to reinforce his concrete tubs. This was the ancestor of concrete reinforced with steel bars, which made its general appearance by the end of the nineteenth century. Steel reinforcing added the tensile strength of steel to the compressive strength of concrete.

In the 1890s reinforced concrete frame construction for buildings began to be used in America by the Englishman Ernest Leslie Ransome and in France by François Hennebique, who patented a process for it in 1892. In 1894 Anatole de Baudot began work on the first church to have a reinforced concrete skeleton and a thin-walled enclosure—St. Jean de Montmartre, Paris. But it was Auguste Perret at this same time who realized the first complete architecture of reinforced concrete in the design of apartment houses and other buildings in France. Reinforced concrete was to become a key material in the development of twentieth-century building.

Textiles

The textile industry, too, was transformed from the ancient home craft of the distaff side—since the ancients considered it women's work at home—into factory production. In the eighteenth century the methods and equipment for the production of fibers into textiles changed drastically. This was an essential part, if not the spearhead, of the Industrial Revolution. This industry turned out the miles of upholstery, drapery fabrics, and carpets that the Crystal Palace enthroned.

Some of the inventions that aided the development of textile production were the flying shuttle of John Kay (1733); the parallel drawing rollers of Lewis Paul (1738); the spinning jenny of James Hargreaves (1767); the roller spinning frame of Richard Arkwright (1769 and 1775); and the spinning mule of Samuel Crompton (by 1779). Edmund Cartwright's power loom (1785) mechanized weaving; and Eli Whitney's cotton gin (1793) brought America precedence in the production of cotton goods.

The world of textiles was never to be the same. In 1780 nine-tenths of English textile workers labored at home; by 1850 nine-tenths were employed in factories. The factory of Jouy-en-Josas, near Versailles, was started in 1760 and continued to produce *toiles de Jouy*—those cottons printed with designs of landscapes and figures, primarily in monotones of rust, blue, or gray. They remain popular after two centuries. At the same time, English chintzes were having a parallel development from 1760 to 1780.

At Jouy, in 1797, Oberkampf introduced cylinder printing to the factory. He claimed that one machine could do the work of forty hand-block printers. Improving on the perforated-card loom attachments of M. Falcon (1728) and Jacques de Vaucanson (1745), Joseph-Marie Jacquard had, by 1801–05, developed the loom that bears his name. It made possible the machine production of elaborate textures and patterns—tapestries, brocades, and damasks.

Subsequently, the carpet industry underwent a similar transformation as Axminsters and broadlooms were produced on new larger looms in vast quantity. This was made possible after the French Revolution broke up the prohibitive regulations and rules that had been set up by local corporations and guilds. At the Crystal Palace Exhibition all these new carpetings were to be seen, seemingly by the mile. Not until a century later, in the early 1960s, was the carpet industry to see such a marked advance again (see Chapter 8).

In this way the materials for interior construction and finishing were developed. It can be a source of some justifiable pride for interior designers that the development of these interior furnishing materials was often synonymous with the development of the Industrial Revolution itself.

Only two now widely used materials remained to be added to the twentieth-century interior designer's palette: aluminum and plastics. Aluminum was discovered and first demonstrated around 1890. Celluloid, the first acknowledged plastic, was introduced in 1862. The plastics of the twentieth century, including synthetic fibers, were first developed in the 1920s, but only came into widespread usage after World War II (see Chapters 5 and 6).

The Modern Interior

In addition to the effects and new materials made available by the Industrial Revolution, a number of other developments contributed to the twentieth-century interior. From the late seventeenth century and the early eighteenth century—although there were variations in degree from country to country (especially between England and the Continent, which developed differently and somewhat more slowly away from ceremonial hierarchy) and from palace to farmhouse—new types of buildings and new types of interiors came about; privacy and informality increased; comfort and convenience gained new meaning; heating and sanitation were improved; and electric lighting was added.

New Types of Buildings and Rooms

From the late seventeenth century onward, interiors proliferated in many new forms for many new functions. No longer were interiors limited to palace, church, town hall, fortification, and private house. This proliferation accompanied the increase in the new types of buildings that developed to accommodate the daily use of a wide new spectrum of ever more active and independent citizens.[20]

Those new buildings included the hospital and asylum, which were developed in the eighteenth century. In the nineteenth century came public libraries and museums; railway stations; university and school buildings; banks and department stores; hotels and more elaborate hospitals; large theaters and concert halls; and offices for government, municipal, and private or corporate use. What had been perceived as standard plans for some of these buildings since the Middle Ages, and perhaps before, now came to be reanalyzed and reconsidered in light of special functions for new societal changes.[21] This was the beginning of functional interior planning.

In addition, the poverty that had been everywhere and for all peoples, except for the few very rich, gradually began to disappear. Increasing numbers of people had more money to acquire the advantages that were made available by the discoveries, inventions, and advances of the Industrial Revolution.

As a corollary, this ultimately meant that fewer people had less money. There was a decrease in slaves and servants as more people became their own masters, and as industrial production required a more flexible, mobile, and educated working force. This change affected not only modern social conditions, but also the way that interiors could be used or operated—and, consequently, the way they were designed.

Like the traditional Japanese house since the tenth century or earlier, the interiors of the Western world had been operated by uncounted servants. They moved things, arranged things for use, rearranged, and generally transformed interiors at the desires and commands of their employer-masters.[22] They made possible the constant rearranging that was required to turn any palace chamber into a dining room, game room, or, indeed, bathroom. This is the way persons of considerable means operated their houses until the eighteenth century. This is also the way most nonresidential interiors were operated until the end of the eighteenth century.

Specialized Rooms

With the availability of more objects—furniture, furnishings, and all their complement—and with the decreasing availability of servants, rooms became more specialized in the eighteenth century.[23] That is, rooms in residences, as well as in the new public buildings, were designed and furnished specifically for single major functions—distinct from the ceremonial hierarchies they had reflected. No longer did the servants cart in a table and chairs, lay the table, and light the candles in the salon or bedroom. No longer was a single major hall used as a hospital ward along with other hospital functions.

It is hard for us to envision that in the main—in most palaces and houses before the seventeenth century—there were few specialized rooms except for the great halls and kitchens, state bedrooms, and rooms for walking and gaming, like the long galleries in England and France. The long galleries of English Renaissance houses such as Hatfield House, Syon House, Wollaton Hall, and the like were designed specifically for strolling during inclement weather and for playing games such as badminton. In this tradition, also, the gallery of François I was built at Fontainebleau.

Otherwise, most early palaces as well as small houses had multipurpose changeable spaces like those in the houses of ancient Japan. The principal space in any dwelling was designed as a reception room. In it the household also gathered for meals; nearby, as late as the early eighteenth century in Europe, was the heavily curtained bed, which was customarily next to the fireplace.

The eighteenth century changed all that and brought specialized rooms to houses and palaces, and to all the new nonresidential building types. In the eighteenth century a separate room was set aside for dining—permanently set up with a table and chairs—in more and more homes of the new bourgeoisie as well as people of greater means. The bedrooms were set off from the other rooms, usually by moving them upstairs or, in palaces, to other parts of the building.[24] Similarly, specialized interiors were developed for specific nonresidential functions. This specialization continued throughout the nineteenth century, in ever-increasing subcategories. Specialized rooms are a fundamental component of today's interior.

Privacy and Informality

Specialization and the permanent placement of furnishings were not the only results that this idea of separation brought to interior design. It also brought an aspect of life that was virtually an invention of the eighteenth century: privacy.[25] Since living was dependent on servants, one was never alone, never able to go off by oneself. The servants were always there—moving, rearranging, helping, eavesdropping, prying, spying. When the eighteenth century brought separate rooms for separate functions to more residences, it also brought the modern sense of privacy with it.

The development of the corridor in the seventeenth century fundamentally changed the possibility of attaining privacy.[26] Before, most palaces and mansions had been planned as series of interconnected suites of rooms—room joined to room and anteroom in an enfilade without corridors. There was no way to get from one room to another without going through someone else's room—bedrooms included—at any hour of day or night. Servants made the most of this opportunity. The new corridors, however, permitted privacy as well as aiding heating and ventilation. The use of the dumbwaiter made private dining possible. The increasing inclusion of back stairs also led to the separation of servants and masters. This new privacy led to the expression of individualistic behavior.

Informality was a natural result. It gradually supplanted pomp and display, formality and ritual, in daily life in the West. During the eighteenth century the pursuit of happiness for the individual, the acceptance of personal preference and ambition, of desire and challenge, constituted a shift in the system of values to a new set of psychological attitudes. The resultant personal and informal approach to human life and relations was a keynote of the Romantic movement in the early nineteenth century. Privacy and informality are fundamental aspects of the twentieth-century interior.

Comfort and Convenience

In the eighteenth century one additional fundamental component of the twentieth-century interior was established in its present form: the requirement for comfort. Historians have generally claimed that the idea of comfort was born in the eighteenth century;[27] but that may need a bit of modification.

Humankind has generally yearned to make life more comfortable and easy, both at work out in the field and at home back in the cave. This ideal has suffered numerous setbacks, such as the loss of Roman luxuries after the fall of Rome, as well as self-deprivation by monks, and other social standards, including the supremacy of pomp and formality before the eighteenth century. But the emotional need or desire has surely been with the human species from the beginning. In the eighteenth century, however, that quest for comfort as convenience began to seem realizable—possible and available. What was required to produce that comfort, however, began to be more complicated.

Heating   Most important to that sense of comfort was the improvement of heating—and the return of central heating, which had been virtually forgotten since the days of the Romans. Before the eighteenth century, fireplaces and chimneys, which were designed on the medieval model as cooking fireplaces, provided the only heat in some European countries.[28] Coal braziers supplemented them in other rooms—and they caused frequent cases of coal-gas poisoning. Stoves of ceramic tile and, in the late eighteenth century, of iron were used in Northern and Eastern European countries. Until that time, things and people froze—including wine at the king's table in winter. People who could afford to do so wore furs indoors to keep warm.

But, around 1720, that too changed. "The hearth of the chimney was made narrower and deepened," as Fernand Braudel tells us, "the mantel lowered, the chimney shaft curved."[29] The latter prevented it from smoking. With this better chimney construction, there was less heat loss and it became possible to heat domestic-scaled rooms. It was a revolution in heating, and the number of fireplaces and chimneys increased markedly over the next decades—leading to the smoke and pollution problems of the Industrial Revolution as well as to greater comfort. In the nineteenth century, heating systems began to be widely used for necessary industrial and factory production. Today, in cold-winter climates, adequate heating—60 to 65 degrees Fahrenheit—is unquestioned.

Sanitation and Ventilation   Even the eighteenth century, however, did not make much progress in that other component of the twentieth-century interior—sanitation and plumbing.[30] Inside, sanitation was deplorable by our standards, and ventilation primitive in its reliance only on open windows and doors. At the end of the eighteenth century chamber pots were still the norm, despite the fact that the water closet had been invented by Sir John Harrington in 1596. People had not learned from medieval castles, with their privies perched up high in turrets, or from sailing vessels with privies hanging out over their sterns. Far into the nineteenth century chamber pots, sometimes modestly hidden in a *chaise percée*, continued to be dumped out of windows and onto the open sewers of the street.

A separate bathroom was rare in Western Europe until the late eighteenth and early nineteenth centuries. Legendary are the tales about Versailles in the seventeenth century concerning the use of any available interior area for these human functions, even under the Queen's Staircase. But this changed in the eighteenth century. Water and plumbing had become available indoors as water technology developed from 1650 to 1800. Indoor fountains and rainwater cisterns provided water for kitchen use as well as for washing and bathing. But it was expensive and generally unavailable except to the very rich—besides, not all the rich considered these amenities priority items. Personal cleanliness and hygiene were limited at best.

By the early eighteenth century, however, a new attitude of personal cleanliness began to spread throughout the West. It was associated psychologically with the new personal privacy. The body, its wastes, and its odors were to be withdrawn from physical contact with others. Forks, handkerchiefs, and nightdresses came into wider use at this time. Washing the body became the expected norm in upper-class families in the late eighteenth century, when washbasins and portable bathtubs began to be used.[31]

In the nineteenth century, sanitary conditions were improved in the towns. A less expensive water closet had been patented by Joseph Bramah in 1778; the shower bath was invented; and bathtubs replaced the pool-like baths and the portable tubs of the eighteenth century. Benjamin Latrobe is credited with designing the first complete bathroom in America in 1810;[32] but the outhouse lingered in the rural areas until the mid-twentieth century.

American cities did not begin to have water systems until 1820, by which time Philadelphia had acquired reservoirs, pumping stations, and wood water mains. New Orleans, Cincinnati, and New York were to follow before the middle of the nineteenth century.[33] But until the industrial production of steel piping and fittings for such systems, they—along with bathtubs, toilets, kitchen sinks, and laundry tubs—were not common until decades after 1850.

Electric Lighting   One other component of the twentieth-century interior waited until the late nineteenth century to be developed—electric lighting, the "victory over night." Until the sixteenth century most interiors were as dark as caves. Daylight was admitted to residential interiors only through open, wood-shuttered windows—seldom open in winter, probably never at night—or through parchment, oiled paper, or cloth treated with turpentine.[34]

Then, in the early sixteenth century, white glass appeared, still in a form more translucent than transparent. It was never sunny inside, except in streaks. By the late eighteenth century plate glass windows were common in workers' houses in Paris, though less available elsewhere. The new practice of whitewashing ceilings also began to change interior light levels.

Candles had begun to be widespread in the sixteenth century. Oil lamps—with a history of different types of oil that included the increasing use of whale oil—continued to dispel the shades of evening indoors. Around 1808, gas lighting appeared.

But it was the incandescent electric light that made the ultimate and elemental contribution to modern interior lighting. Briefly, the history of electricity in this achievement is as follows:

- 1752: Benjamin Franklin discovers the possibility of channeling electricity.

- 1841: Michael Faraday discovers how to induce an electric current by rotating a wire around a magnet.

- 1844: Samuel F. B. Morse demonstrates his electric telegraph before the U.S. Congress.

- 1878: Thomas Alva Edison develops the first practical electric light.

- 1879: Edison develops the incandescent electric light.
- 1881: Edison helps to build the first public electric-light power plant.

Components of the Twentieth-Century Interior

This, then, is our twentieth-century interior: an interior space composed of walls—in plan either rectangular, circular, elliptical, triangular, or some irregular shape—with a floor and a ceiling as well as windows and doors. To this traditional and ancient assemblage, the eighteenth century added specialized rooms, privacy, and heating as well as comfort of the kind we know today. In the nineteenth century sanitation, plumbing, and ventilation were added along with electric lighting.

These are the fundamental components of the modern interior that had been developed when the twentieth century opened. What succeeding twentieth-century generations have done to vary, alter, transform, improve, elaborate, and minimalize is the subject of the following history of twentieth-century interior design.

In the second half of the nineteenth century, America, with a newfound independence and brilliance, pioneered in construction techniques that permitted interiors to be stacked one on top of the other to unprecedented heights: It was the development of the skyscraper. That building type is rightly acclaimed as the twentieth century's wonder of the world, its Pyramid of Cheops, and more surely as the building achievement of the twentieth century that most captured the modern romantic imagination.

But the skyscraper is not only indicative of our reach for the skies; it is also a compendium of the technologies that were made possible in the second half of the nineteenth century. Then, from 1860 onward, and especially after the great Chicago fire of 1870, when real estate speculation and the growth of large corporations fostered them, skyscrapers put together into one new type of building all the technologies discussed above.

Among them were (1) steel-frame construction; (2) glass; (3) the elevator—made safe by Otis in 1852, and electrified by Siemens in 1880; (4) high-pressured plumbing and sanitation systems; (5) efficient heating systems; and (6) electric lighting and communication systems. These, when combined in a building of ten to fourteen stories, came to be defined as a skyscraper. Among the pioneer skyscrapers were William Le Baron Jenney's Home Insurance Building in Chicago (1884–85); Holabird & Roche's Tacoma Building (1887–88); and Louis Sullivan's achievement of the first expressive skyscraper form in the Wainwright Building in St. Louis (1890).

Interior decorators and designers did not have much involvement in skyscrapers—except in lobby decorations—until the middle of the twentieth century. Before then, office interiors were almost exclusively the province of the office manager and the furniture supplier, except in rare projects by exceptional architects. By the middle of the twentieth century, however, interior designers had developed an expertise that was to make them indispensable in office design in skyscrapers and elsewhere.

Design Education

Design education grew along with other educational institutions. To further the improvement of design in this country, new schools and programs had been initiated throughout the nineteenth century. First came art schools such as the Maryland Institute of Art in Baltimore, founded in 1826, and the Moore College of Art in Philadelphia, founded in 1844; but they did not add design courses or programs until much later.[35] The Massachusetts Institute of Technology (MIT) was the first school of architecture on these shores; founded in 1865, MIT's program was followed by other architecture schools in due course.

Shortly thereafter, specialized design schools began to be established: the Minneapolis College of Art and Design in 1867, the Art Institute of Chicago in 1869, the Columbus College of Art in 1870, the Philadelphia College of Art in 1876. University programs were started at the University of Cincinnati in 1870 and at Syracuse University in 1870, among others. Soon other design schools and programs were initiated: the New York School of Decorative Arts in 1877, the Rhode Island School of Design in 1877, the Cleveland Institute of Art in 1882, the Kansas City Art Institute in 1882, and Pratt Institute in Brooklyn, New York, in 1887.

Most of these design programs seem to have been directed toward art and graphic design and to painted decoration rather than to overall interior design. Education in that broader sphere began in the twentieth century in America. Together, all these factors combined to bring about the existence of educated interior designers as a new and necessary twentieth-century profession.

Suggested Reading

Banham, Reyner. *The Architecture of the Well-Tempered Environment*. London: The Architectural Press, 1969. Chicago: University of Chicago Press, 1969.

Benevolo, Leonardo. *History of Modern Architecture*. Cambridge: MIT Press, 1971 (especially Chapter 7).

Braudel, Fernand. *Afterthoughts on Material Civilization and Capitalism*. Baltimore: Johns Hopkins University Press, 1977.

———. *The Structures of Everyday Life*. New York: Harper & Row, 1981.

Cowan, Henry J. *Design of Reinforced Concrete Structures*. Englewood Cliffs, NJ: Prentice-Hall, 1982.

Eisenberg, Elizabeth. *The Printing Press as an Agent of Change*. Cambridge: Cambridge University Press, 1979.

Fitch, James Marston. *American Building*, Vol. 1: *The Historical Forces That Shaped It*. Boston: Houghton Mifflin Company, 1947, 1966 (see Chapter 4).

Foucault, Michel. *The Birth of the Clinic*. New York: Pantheon Books, 1973.

———. *Discipline and Punish: The Birth of the Prison*. New York: Pantheon Books, 1977.

Giedion, Sigfried. *Mechanization Takes Command*. Oxford: Oxford University Press, 1948. New York: W. W. Norton, 1975.

———. *Space, Time and Architecture*. Cambridge: Harvard University Press, 1941, 1954, 1976.

Girouard, Mark. *Life in the English Country House*. New Haven: Yale University Press, 1978. Baltimore: Penguin Books, 1980.

Hitchcock, Henry-Russell. *Architecture in the Nineteenth and Twentieth Centuries*. Baltimore: Penguin Books, 1958–82.

Kaufmann, Edgar, Jr. "Interior Design: Architecture or Decoration?" *Progressive Architecture*. October 1962, pp. 141–44.

Palmer, Robert R. *Age of Democratic Revolution: A Political History of Europe and America*. Princeton: Princeton University Press, 1970.

———, and Joel Colton. *A History of the Modern World*. New York: Alfred A. Knopf, 1966, 1977.

Pevsner, Nikolaus. *Pioneers of Modern Design*. New York: The Museum of Modern Art, 1949.

———. *An Outline of European Architecture*. Harmondsworth, England: Pelican Books, 1943. Baltimore: Penguin Books, 1972.

Praz, Mario. *The House of Life*. New York: Oxford University Press, 1964.

———. *An Illustrated History of Interior Decoration from Pompeii to Art Nouveau*. New York: Braziller, 1964. New York: Thames and Hudson, 1982.

Pulos, Arthur J. *American Design Ethic: A History of Industrial Design to 1940*. Cambridge: MIT Press, 1983.

Smith, Cyril Stanley. *A Search for Structure*. Cambridge: MIT Press, 1981.

Stone, Lawrence. *The Family, Sex and Marriage in England: 1500–1800*. New York: Harper & Row, 1979.

Thornton, Peter. *Authentic Decor: The Domestic Interior 1620–1920*. New York: Viking, 1984.

Notes

1. Robert R. Palmer and Joel Colton, *A History of the Modern World* (New York: Alfred A. Knopf, 1966), pp. 426f., 563; M. Chambers et al., *The Western Experience* (New York: Alfred A. Knopf, 1979), p. 773.

2. Cyril Stanley Smith, *A Search for Structure* (Cambridge: MIT Press, 1981), p. 308; noting Soetsu Yanagi, *The Unknown Craftsman: A Japanese Insight into Beauty*, ed. and trans. Bernard Leach (Tokyo and Palo Alto: Kodansha, 1972).

3. The Crystal Palace, like most such exhibitions later, was not so much a demonstration of vanguard design vision as it was the sanction of official taste made available to the general public. So appalled by many of the objects were vanguard designers that a sweeping aesthetic reform movement began. See the section "The Arts and Crafts Movement" in Chapter 2.

4. Smith, op. cit., p. 144f.

5. Elizabeth Eisenberg, *The Printing Press as an Agent of Change* (Cambridge: Cambridge University Press, 1979).

6. Fernand Braudel, *The Structures of Everyday Life* (New York: Harper & Row, 1981), p. 41.

7. Palmer and Colton, op. cit.

8. Robert R. Palmer, *Age of Democratic Revolution: A Political History of Europe and America* (Princeton: Princeton University Press, 1970).

9. Braudel, op. cit., pp. 353ff.; see also Palmer and Colton, op. cit.

10. Smith, op. cit., p. 96.

11. Nikolaus Pevsner, *Pioneers of Modern Design* (New York: The Museum of Modern Art, 1949), pp. 70ff.; Nikolaus Pevsner, *An Outline of European Architecture* (Harmondsworth, England: Pelican Books, 1943; Baltimore: Penguin Books, 1972), p. 389.

12. Pevsner, *Pioneers of Modern Design*, p. 74.

13. Ibid., p. 69; Sigfried Giedion, *Space, Time and Architecture* (Cambridge: Harvard University Press, 1941, 1954), p. 200.

14. Pevsner, *Pioneers of Modern Design*, p. 76.

15. Braudel, op. cit., p. 296f.; Leonardo Benevolo, *History of Modern Architecture* (Cambridge: MIT Press, 1971) p. 20.

16. Nikolaus Pevsner, John Fleming, and Hugh Honour. *A Dictionary of Architecture* (Woodstock, NY: The Overlook Press, 1976), p. 545.

17. Henry J. Cowan, *Design of Reinforced Concrete Structures* (Englewood Cliffs, NJ: Prentice-Hall, 1982), pp. 13ff.

18. Ibid., p. 13; Benevolo, op. cit., p. 321f.

19. Cowan, op. cit., p. 17.

20. Pevsner, *An Outline of European Architecture*, p. 382.

21. Ibid., p. 383.

22. Lawrence Stone, *The Family, Sex and Marriage in England: 1500–1800* (New York: Harper & Row, 1979), pp. 169, 245.

23. Braudel, op. cit., p. 307; Mark Girouard, *Life in the English Country House* (New Haven: Yale University Press, 1978. Baltimore: Penguin Books, 1980), pp. 126, 230f.; Mario Praz, *An Illustrated History of Interior Decoration from Pompeii to Art Nouveau* (New York: Braziller, 1964; New York: Thames and Hudson, 1982), p. 152f.

24. Stone, op. cit., p. 246; Braudel, op. cit., p. 308; Girouard, op. cit., pp. 194, 230f.

25. Braudel, op. cit., p. 308; Stone, op. cit., p. 245f.; Girouard, op. cit., pp. 143f., 214ff.

26. Braudel, op. cit., p. 308; Stone, op. cit., pp. 169, 245f.; Girouard, op. cit., pp. 114, 123.

27. Braudel, op. cit., passim; Sherrill Whiton, *Interior Design and Decoration* (New York: J. B. Lippincott, 1937, 1974), p. 156f. Sigfried Giedion, *Mechanization Takes Command* (Oxford: Oxford University Press, 1948; New York: W. W. Norton, 1975), pp. 305–28; Praz, op. cit., pp. 56–59, 152–67.

28. Braudel, op. cit., p. 298f.; James Marston Fitch, *American Building*, Vol. 1: *The Historical Forces That Shaped It* (Boston: Houghton Mifflin Company, 1947, 1966), pp. 15f., 116ff. Girouard, op. cit., p. 263.

29. Braudel, op. cit. p. 299.

30. Ibid., p. 310; Fitch, op. cit., pp. 22, 113f.; Girouard, op. cit., pp. 246ff., 265ff.

31. Stone, op. cit., p. 169; Girouard, op. cit., p. 256.

32. Talbot Hamlin, *Benjamin Henry Latrobe* (New York: Oxford University Press, 1955), p. 342f. Hamlin observes that Latrobe's sketch, dated January 23, 1810, for rearranging the bathroom of the Markoe house in Philadelphia is "perhaps the earliest existing American drawing of a complete bathroom."

33. Benevolo, op. cit., Chapter 7; Fitch, op. cit., p. 113.

34. Braudel, op. cit., pp. 296f., 310; Fitch, op. cit., p. 21.

35. Arthur J. Pulos, *American Design Ethic: A History of Industrial Design to 1940* (Cambridge: MIT Press, 1983), p. 157.

Chapter 2

1900–1910: Pioneers of Twentieth-Century Interior Design

When the twentieth century opened, interior design presented two different directions, or basic approaches, for designers to take. One was the ages-old evolutionary direction that closely followed, built upon, and gradually advanced the historical traditions of the past. This conservative direction led to a concentration on refinements of visual style—to a predominant concern with surface and ornament, color and texture, furnishings and accessories.

The other direction aimed to explore innovation and invention, the future and the new. This more radical approach looked at all aspects of interior design as potential candidates for experiment and improvement. It investigated the shapes of spaces, their structural and construction systems, their functional activity patterns, the use of new materials, new manufacturing processes, and any other aspect of interior design that was of immediate interest. That included walls, ceilings, floors, furniture, and objects. This direction led to an ultimate concern for the integration of all these elements to achieve total design consistency.

The two approaches were distinguished by breadth of concern, scope of interest, and degree of detail. One was concerned more with the way things look; the other was concerned more with the way things work. Their differences may have been matters of emphasis and scope; nevertheless, in the twentieth century their existence led to the division of interior design into two separate professions.

The conservative approach was carried to new prominence in the first decade of the twentieth century by the work of Elsie de Wolfe. She began twentieth-century decorating, both as a style and as a profession. The other direction at that time was epitomized by the work of Frank Lloyd Wright. He brought early Modernism to interior design during that same first decade of the twentieth century. The disparate nature of their approaches and of their activities set the world of interior designers onto two distinct—and often controversial and conflicting—courses for the entire century.

Elsie de Wolfe: The Birth of Professional Decorating

Elsie de Wolfe (1865–1950) called herself America's first woman professional decorator. To a degree, she was justified. Before her there were no independent interior decorators who were considered professionals. It was not that the activity of decorating interiors was new. That had been engaged in at least since prehistoric cave painting. It was new, however, for a woman to practice it as a profession.

The sculptors, architects, and other artisans who had also designed interiors were considered artists or craftsmen. The linen drapers, upholsterers, and painters who traditionally had provided interior furnishings—along with the cabinetmakers-turned-manufacturers of the nineteenth century—were considered shopkeepers. In France these latter were called *ensembliers*, since they assembled all the necessary furnishings for an interior.

Ensembliers and shopkeepers, however, were tradesmen and craftsmen who supplied specific materials. They were not professionals whose primary province was an intellectual or aesthetic discipline. No matter how refined their sensibilities as artists, such firms as Louis Comfort Tiffany's studios, John La Farge's firm, and Herter Brothers were considered among the *ensembliers* that provided services in the craftsman and shopkeeper tradition. Other such firms at this time included William Baumgarten & Company, the Zimmerman Brothers, and the Rambusch Company, all of New York; as well as the Niedecken-Walbridge Company of Milwaukee, Wisconsin. Nevertheless, theirs was not the status of the new professional decorator.

In addition to these purveyors of diverse crafts, antique dealers and art gallery owners plied a similar trade. Knoedler and Duveen Brothers, the most celebrated among them, offered paintings and sculptures by the great Gothic and Renaissance masters along with important furniture from the past. As tastemakers themselves, they recommended interior design schemes and the architects and craftsmen to carry them out. The end of the nineteenth century through the first quarter of the twentieth century was the age of the great collectors.

Elsie de Wolfe, in contrast to this tradition, did not practice as a craftsperson. She was a supervising designer and, consequently, called herself a professional. In so doing she gave an initial stance of independence and social standing to the twentieth-century activity of interior design.

Elsie de Wolfe was born in New York City of parents from Nova Scotia. She was sent off to finishing school in Scotland, and at the age of twenty was presented to Queen Victoria and London society. This event focused her vision of life on elegance, refinement, good living, and good taste. In 1890 she began a fourteen-year career as a professional actress—from the age of twenty-five to thirty-nine. Her reviews were never entirely favorable, but her acting made it economically possible for her to spend summers in France, where she commissioned the clothes that she wore on stage. She first became known for her sense of style in clothes.

During this period she set up housekeeping in New York City with Elisabeth Marbury, who established herself as the foremost theater and literary agent of her day. It was in their house on Irving Place—the house that author Washington Irving had once owned—that Elsie de Wolfe laid the foundation of twentieth-century decorating. She transformed its interiors from those of a dark Victorian dwelling into the prototype of twentieth-century decoration. From it she launched her career as the first American woman professional interior decorator.

The Turn-of-the-Century Interior

Before Elsie de Wolfe made her first foray into the world of interior design, the average American residential interior was almost universally cast in the image of the dark, stuffy, and cluttered late-Victorian art gallery, or as a scrapbook of mementos collected over years of travel. From the homes of the middle class to the monumental interiors of such magnates as the Vanderbilts and J. P. Morgan (see Figure 1), the goal seemed to be to fill rooms with collections—paintings, sculptures, tapestries, manuscripts, and furnishings from the past. Dark, somber rooms were considered evocative of the Gothic age, the Greco-Roman classical inspiration, and the Italian Renaissance summation of both. Antique furnishings were therefore the keystone of this direction.

In average houses, walls—or what could be seen of them beneath their patch-work of gilt-framed paintings, lithographs, and engravings—were papered or

1. McKim, Mead & White. The Pierpont Morgan Library. New York City. 1903–06. *Photograph courtesy The New-York Historical Society, New York City.*

upholstered in heavy, dark patterns. Tables were covered with tapestries, overlaid with embroidery, crewelwork, or handworked linen. Crocheted doilies helped to protect those table coverings from the footprints of countless pictures, bronze statues, vases of china or cloisonné, and whatever bric-a-brac might be acquired in travel or from auction houses. At the windows, multiple layers of shutters, roller shades, lace curtains, and heavy overdraperies helped to sequester this romantic mood. By the late 1890s, however, some exceptions to this general design approach had begun to emerge, and Elsie de Wolfe's house was one of them.

The original interiors of the de Wolfe–Marbury house on Irving Place were typical of the average clutter, stuffiness, and confusion. In the dining room (see Figure 2A) the heavy Victorian moldings, doorjambs, and doors, like the paneled wainscoting and the capitals and bases of two columns flanking the window bay, were all varnished dark brown. A striped wall covering was overlaid with hanging plates, tapestry, and paintings in gilt frames. The chimney breast was layered with a dark panel instead of the striped wall covering; and on top of that panel a collection of plates was hung in a circle around a Rococo gilt-framed mirror. The mantelpiece itself displayed a bowl and four ceramic swans as well as four shaded candlesticks. A grandfather clock stood nearby.

Over the sideboard, which was laden with silver spread out on a cloth runner, was a two-level rack of plates hung in front of a tapestry panel. More plates were hung above this tapestry as well as over the doors to the room. The furniture was dark-finished, the table draped in damask that revealed only the reeded bulbous feet. Above it was a metal chandelier with round glass globes. The chairs, of Chippendale appearance, were upholstered with patterned damask edged with fringe, and had separate fringed back pillows. All this rested on a floor overlaid with oriental carpets and runners with contrasting patterns and colors.

The Elsie de Wolfe Style

Elsie de Wolfe redecorated that dining room in 1898 (see Figure 2B). The striped wall covering remained the same, but the woodwork—wainscoting, doors, ceiling molding, as well as the bases and capitals of the columns—were all painted white. The chandelier, the tapestry, the clock, the easel-mounted portrait, and all the plates were removed. The chairs were replaced with a cane-back Louis XVI model that had a light-colored frame. On the table the same dark damask was lightened by a linen runner, on top of which was a sheet of glass. All the oriental rugs were replaced by a single plain carpet. Over the mantelpiece the dark panel had come down, along with the Rococo mirror and the plates. It was replaced by a single large, paneled gilt mirror that filled the same space. On the mantelpiece the shaded candlesticks remained, but the swans were superseded by a white Louis XVI–vintage bust. Additional wall sconces were mounted against large white-framed mirrors. And at the windows were simple shades and half-curtains of white muslin. The influence of electric lighting on vision was everywhere. It was, in the words of one visitor, "a model of simplicity . . . gold and white."[1]

In the drawing room Elsie de Wolfe wrought a similar transformation. The Turkish cozy corner, which had been hung with fabric, layered with pictures, and piled with pillows covered in a dozen different fabrics, was swept away. Along with it went a mass of chests and tables stacked with brass jardinieres for potted palms, aspidistras, and fronds of pampas grass. In their place she filled the bay window with flowers and let the light come into the room. The heavy furniture was replaced by French pieces. She banished the fabric that had draped the mantelpiece, and stripped away the ornaments and collections of fans, portraits, and bric-a-brac.

In the bedrooms, too, Elsie de Wolfe painted the woodwork and furniture the same shade of ivory. Then she covered the beds, chairs, windows, often the walls,

2A. Elsie de Wolfe. Own dining room, Irving Place. New York City. 1896. *Photograph from The Byron Collection, The Museum of the City of New York.*

2B. Elsie de Wolfe. Own dining room, Irving Place. New York City. After 1898. *Photograph from The Byron Collection, The Museum of the City of New York.*

and even the wastebaskets with a single pattern of chintz (see Figure 3). For a city house, such country simplicity was virtually unheard of.

The entire transformation was, to the eyes of her contemporaries, dazzling. Elsie de Wolfe stripped away the many overlays of *things* that the Industrial Revolution had made possible by 1851. Instead of the dark Renaissance and Queen Anne imagery that had been popular for decades, Elsie de Wolfe had adopted the 1890s preference for Neoclassicism—the elegant eighteenth-century French furniture of Louis XV and of Louis XVI. These she brought back from her summers in Versailles, along with the comfortable chintzes she had seen on visits to English country houses. While Americans were still cherishing their newly rediscovered Colonial interiors and furniture, Elsie de Wolfe offered French eighteenth-century pieces (see Figure 4).

Elsie de Wolfe had begun to redecorate the house on Irving Place sometime between the fall of 1897 and the end of 1898. Elisabeth Marbury's theater and literary connections brought celebrated European visitors to the house such as Sarah Bernhardt, Oscar Wilde, and Beerbohm Tree. New York and Boston society leaders came on invitation to see them—the architect Stanford White, Henry Adams, Isabella Stewart Gardner, William C. Whitney, and Mrs. William K. Astor, the capacity of whose ballroom prompted the epithet "The 400" for the select echelon of New York "society."

To all visitors Elsie de Wolfe's sense of style in decorating was established—just as her sense of style in dressing had first been established on the stage. So she had cards printed, announcing that she was available to supervise the arrangement of other people's houses. Business came in immediately. She had established herself as a professional interior decorator by the turn of the century.

Antecedents of the de Wolfe Style

Elsie de Wolfe was not the first to object to the darkness and clutter of the interiors of her day, nor the first to do something about them. Her protest was part of a quest for "light, air, and comfort,"[2] as she wrote, that became a popular desire

3. Elsie de Wolfe. Elisabeth Marbury's bedroom. New York City. After 1898. *Photograph from Elsie de Wolfe,* The House in Good Taste *(New York: The Century Co., 1913).*

4. Elsie de Wolfe. Own living room, Irving Place. New York City. After 1898. *Photograph from Elsie de Wolfe,* The House in Good Taste *(New York: The Century Co., 1913).*

5. C. F. A. Voysey. Own house, The Orchard. Chorley Wood, Hertfordshire, England. 1900. *Photograph from Karl Mang,* History of Modern Furniture *(New York: Harry N. Abrams, 1979).*

around the turn of the century. All-white rooms had been designed by Boffrand and Gabriel in the eighteenth century, when lightness had also been a goal. After the dark-brown decades of the late-Victorian period, lightness was revived in the 1890s in England by architect C. F. A. Voysey (see Figure 5) and in Scotland by architect Charles Rennie Mackintosh (see Figure 6) and his colleagues, the MacNairs. Their house designs and their restaurant designs had made similarly dramatic effects with light-colored paints and enamels. Their work had influenced the designers of Vienna's Secession movement, including architect Josef Hoffmann and designer Koloman Moser, who also took up the vogue for white.

6. Charles Rennie Mackintosh. Entry hall, Hill House. Helensburgh, Scotland. 1902–03. *Photograph from Karl Mang,* History of Modern Furniture *(New York: Harry N. Abrams, 1979).*

Though she probably knew little of this European work, Elsie de Wolfe adopted the penchant of the 1890s for lightness—beige, ivory, and white. Along with this came the new and brighter electric light that greatly influenced interior design by the turn of the century. She further lightened her schemes with mirrors and glass; the absence of bric-a-brac refreshed and brought air to her work.

Edith Wharton and Ogden Codman   In December 1897 the book *The Decoration of Houses* by Edith Wharton and architect Ogden Codman appeared in America. Edith Wharton, not yet the celebrated novelist she would become, claimed that the book was the only study of house decoration as a branch of architecture that had been published in the past fifty years. *The Decoration of Houses* set out to sweep away the confusion and clutter of "a superficial application of ornament" and to supplant, instead, architectural proportions, harmony of style, and classical European furnishings. Wharton and Codman stressed the importance of "repose and distinction" over the ostentatious display of bric-a-brac. Simplicity, suitability, and, perhaps above all, authenticity were tenets that the book generally established.

The Decoration of Houses is authoritative, enthusiastic, and convincing. Although Elsie de Wolfe never acknowledged her familiarity with it, the evidence strongly suggests that it had influenced her first venture into interior design in her Irving Place house.

Elsie de Wolfe may also have known the interior designs by Ogden Codman, who had opened a Boston office in 1891, one in Newport in 1893, and then another in New York. Among his most important commissions was the decoration of the upstairs bedrooms in Cornelius Vanderbilt's Newport house, The Breakers; they have been restored and stand as a clear example of Codman's work. He had transformed Edith Wharton's Newport house, adding to it "a certain dignity," as she later wrote, and revealing the common "dislike of sumptuary excesses"[3] that led them to collaborate on *The Decoration of Houses*.

Education and Journals   Another source of Elsie de Wolfe's inspiration must have been an article by Mrs. Candace Wheeler, who had been a design partner with Louis Comfort Tiffany in the Associated Artists around 1880 and who had founded the Society of Decorative Art in New York. Mrs. Wheeler's article, "Interior Decoration as a Profession for Women," was published in *The Outlook* magazine in 1895. But her suggested qualifications for women decorators—"much special *training*" and "work in an architect's office"[4]—seem to have given Elsie de Wolfe no hesitation. Besides, such experience was not easy for women to come by in the late nineteenth century.

Education in interior design was not readily available through American schools at this time. Art schools across the country continued to expand their programs in the arts and crafts. Not until after 1904, however, did the New York School of Fine and Applied Arts, which had been established as a school for painting in 1896, begin to offer courses in interior decoration. Those courses were initiated after the arrival of Frank Alvah Parsons, by which time there appeared to be a sufficient number of interested students.

For the general reader *Ladies' Home Journal* (founded in 1883), *House Beautiful* (founded in 1896), and *House & Garden* (founded in 1901) kept readers abreast of the newest developments, including the work of Frank Lloyd Wright. Of the trade journals at this time, *Decorative Furnisher*, *Arts & Decoration*, and *Good Furniture* were forward-looking; but *The Upholsterer* was published for the audience that indicated the actual early status of the profession.

Stanford White   The real father of the Elsie de Wolfe style and approach was Stanford White (1853–1906). By the 1890s he was the leading American designer of interiors. As a partner in the architecture firm of McKim, Mead & White since 1879, he had gradually begun to change the American interior from one of dark and heavy Victorian dinginess into one that was lighter, more delicate in detail, and more graceful in character.

Buildings were embellished, under his hand, by delicate friezes and moldings in the Florentine style—swirls of vines interspersed with seated griffins and the like. Pale and gilded mosaics, intarsia designs, and carvings further enhanced his schemes. In his country houses a recall of Louis XIII splendor within Adamesque white fluted columns and other trappings of the classical revival created interiors that were, for all their decorative features, lighter and freer than what had gone before (see Figure 7).

In 1905 he effected another change—in both the look of interiors and the profession of interior design—when he secured the commission for Elsie de Wolfe to furnish his new building for the Colony Club. The club was a new women's organization for which he had designed the building at 110 Madison Avenue in New York (now the home of the American Academy of Dramatic Arts). Fortunately for Elsie de Wolfe, Elisabeth Marbury was a founding member along with their new friend Anne Morgan, J. P. Morgan's daughter. Stanford White was to say to the club's planning committee, "Elsie knows more than any of us." Thereafter Elsie de Wolfe had carte blanche for her first big project.

At the Colony Club (1905–07) Elsie de Wolfe adapted the style of her Irving Place interiors to the realm of nonresidential interiors, which were later to become known as "contract interiors." On the entrance floor she lined the rough gray

7. Stanford White. Adamesque living room, C. D. Gibson House. New York City, 1903. *Photograph courtesy The Museum of the City of New York.*

plaster walls and ceiling with green trelliswork and trained ivy to grow up it; there too, she installed a fountain and urns, along with garden furniture that had a Gothic-cottage feeling (see Figure 8). This garden-pavilion scheme had been seen in country houses in Newport and at society balls, but never before in city institutions. In another room she designed there were green-and-white striped walls, white woodwork, dark mahogany furniture, and gold-framed mirrors.

Elsewhere in the Colony Club Elsie de Wolfe installed wallpapers with a chinoiserie feeling; she used chintz both in the bedrooms and in the sitting rooms.

8. Elsie de Wolfe. Trellis Room, Colony Club. New York City. 1905–07. *Photograph from Elsie de Wolfe.* The House in Good Taste *(New York: The Century Co., 1913).*

Bedrooms had simple painted furniture—including a writing table, chaise longue, and chest of drawers with a mirror above it; chintz was used as window coverings and for the bedspreads. She ultimately became known as "the chintz lady." In this way de Wolfe brought light and air—as well as the French style and country chintz—to the nonresidential interiors of her day.

By this activity she made interior design and decorating a professional endeavor, as opposed to an activity of craftsmen, tradesmen, or shopkeepers. She also made interior design and decorating a suitable occupation for a woman. In 1910 she began to recapitulate this achievement in a series of lectures and magazine articles. They promulgated her style and her activity, sponsored her first competitor, and spawned the next generation of American professional interior decorators.

Frank Lloyd Wright: Pioneer of Modern Interiors

What Elsie de Wolfe did to lighten the surfaces and textures of American interiors in the first decade of the twentieth century, Frank Lloyd Wright had already achieved with the core, the plan, and the basic forces of interior spaces.

Frank Lloyd Wright (1867–1959) is generally acknowledged to be the greatest American architectural genius of the twentieth century. His innovative vision helped to transform American interiors, as well as American architecture. His original inventions affected the basic plan, the construction, the spatial character, and the connotative meanings of interiors. He gave his residential interiors a wholly American identity and context. He brought drama and mythic meaning to the hearth and the fireplace, to the great hall and the inglenook. He composed nonresidential interiors of interrelated, interlocking complexity such as had not been created since the Baroque and Rococo churches of Europe. In all his work, space as a single flowing entity was the primary goal on which all materials, technologies, and ornamentation were focused.

The designs of Frank Lloyd Wright are integrated at every level. His planning relates to his siting; his spatial geometry reflects his structural invention; his fenestration and lighting reinforce his spaces; his furnishings reiterate his linear schemes and his construction materials; and his every ornamental detail is integrated with his larger concerns. More than any American designer before him, more than most after him, Frank Lloyd Wright achieved an integrated consistency for the totality of his schemes. He called this integration "organic design."

Frank Lloyd Wright had developed his artistic maturity by 1900. He became the first fully independent American architect—independent of reliance on European traditions. In this regard he surpassed his great predecessors Henry Hobson Richardson (1838–86) and Louis Sullivan (1856–1924), who had begun to develop a truly American architecture. Frank Lloyd Wright developed one around 1900.

The first decade of this century was Wright's golden age, certainly his most active and perhaps the greatest decade of his seventy-year career. During those ten years he designed a half-dozen of his greatest masterpieces. Among them were the Susan Lawrence Dana House in Springfield, Illinois (1903); the Darwin D. Martin House in Buffalo, New York (1904); the Larkin Building in Buffalo (1904); Unity Temple in Oak Park, Illinois (1906); the Avery Coonley House in Riverside, Illinois (1908); and the Robie House in Chicago (1909).

Wright's preparation for his career as an architect followed a direct and virtually single-minded path. He was born in Richland Center, Wisconsin, in 1867, and his mother hoped from the beginning that he would become an architect. During his infancy she introduced him to the process of building through the Froebel kindergarten blocks—a kit of geometric building blocks. To them he later gave credit for his interest in the systematic building up of geometric forms in his concepts, plans, and detailing. His father had played music to him, and from it he recognized the relationship between composition and expression. Another early influence was his summer experience working on his uncle's farm. There he gained his appreciation and respect for the land, for nature, and for natural materials. He recognized that architecture was integrally related to life and to the whole of nature. As historian Edgar Kaufmann, Jr., has written, Wright had "a faith in architecture as the natural link between mankind and the environment."[5]

His technical training was brief. From 1886 to 1887 he took courses in mechanical drawing and basic mathematics at the University of Wisconsin. Then he went off to Chicago—already the center of skyscraper construction—and worked for several months in the architectural office of J. Lyman Silsbee.

Wright's real apprenticeship, however, was in the office of Adler & Sullivan from 1887 to 1893. Louis Sullivan was then the leading innovator in skyscraper development and, with Richardson and Wright, one of the three great American pioneers of twentieth-century design. Dankmar Adler was the engineering genius of his day. Those were the years when the Adler & Sullivan office was working on the Chicago Auditorium, the Wainwright Building in St. Louis, and the Transportation Building for Chicago's World's Columbian Exposition of 1893. What Wright learned from Sullivan about the honest expression of building concepts and about architecture as an expression of the goals of society laid the foundation for his dramatic and innovative career.

In 1893 Wright established his own practice, and spent the next decade developing the Prairie houses that immediately established his independent imagination and his place in the history of interior design and architecture. In his early houses and public buildings during that first decade of the twentieth century, Frank Lloyd Wright revolutionized the design of interiors.

The Prairie Houses

By 1900 Wright had developed a clear relationship between his houses and the context of the prairie region—the region from Ohio to Wisconsin and westward

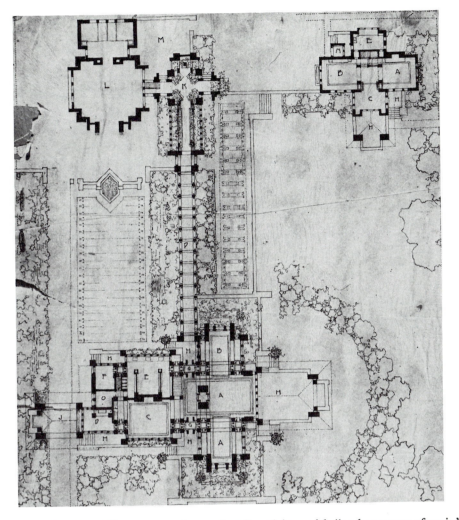

9. Frank Lloyd Wright. Plan, Darwin D. Martin House. Buffalo, New York. 1904. *Illustration © Frank Lloyd Wright Foundation, 1942.*

to the Rockies. Those states of sweeping flat plains, with "amber waves of grain" divided into vast hectare tracts, provided the contextual imagery of Wright's early houses. To relate them to this terrain in Oak Park and Riverside—suburbs west of Chicago that had until recently been flat farmland on the edge of the prairie—Wright devised long low horizontal forms, long low pyramidal roofs, sweeping cantilevered eaves, and rows of windows overlooking the wide views. The parallel roof lines and extended eaves of the Robie House sum up this direction.

Wright built with narrow brick and roof tiles in tones that echoed the soil. He brought the landscape up to the house in urns and other planters, and extended the house into the landscape by means of projecting walls. He thereby created an interpenetration of interior and exterior space. By these means Wright related his houses specifically to their midwestern terrain—to its landscape, to its recent Chicago-school structural invention, to its local materials—and to early twentieth-century domestic lifestyle. He made his Prairie houses entirely American.

Wright's Prairie House plans were centered on a massive core, usually comprising fireplace—sometimes a double fireplace—and stove chimney, which was also integrated with the heating plant (see Figure 12). This was in the manner of his day, which had been popularized in 1869 by Catherine Beecher's *American Woman's Home.* By the manipulation of adjacent ceiling heights and the inclusion of adjacent benches, Wright often created cozy inglenooks in which people could cluster around the fire. At the same time he augmented the practical value of his fireplaces with perimeter heating systems and clerestory ventilation, which were being used in industrial and commercial buildings at the time. Only by incorporating such central heating systems could Wright liberate the American house from its dependence on multiple fireplaces and stoves and on the servants to keep them burning. Wright later explained that hot-water heating systems and low ceilings had made it possible for him to spread his plans into organic blocks and to open up the windows to light and air. For these plans Frank Lloyd Wright went back to the fireplace as symbol and heart of the house.

Wright specified his fireplaces to be constructed of the same stone or brick as the exteriors of his houses. He left these materials exposed, rather than plastering or paneling them over. The effect was to bring the terrain—the prairie itself—into the center of the house and to give the house an actual as well as symbolic anchor to the soil.

The fireplace in the Robie House in Chicago (1909) was freestanding, central to the principal living spaces, and incorporated with the main stair so that one experienced it as pivotal to the entire house (see Figures 10A and B). The Darwin D. Martin House (1904) in Buffalo had a fireplace that was freestanding between the living room and the entry (see Figure 9), where it originally presented an ornamental gilt panel as a welcome. In the Avery Coonley House in Riverside, Illinois (1908), the brick fireplace had an opening that was low and wide, and the stone lintel was as wide as the chimney breast (see Figure 11). The composition seemed to encompass the whole wall, engulfing, welcoming with outstretched arms the surrounding space and the surrounded family. By all these means Wright reinforced the symbol of the hearth as the heart of the home. It was a dramatization of domesticity, a celebration of the strength of the household and of the American way of life.

Around these cores, and on platforms set on the ground without cellars, Frank Lloyd Wright conceived his houses as composed of blocks of rooms. He based his most innovative plans on this additive "unit" system of composition (the word is Wright's) that recalled his childhood building blocks. The most original of his plans were composed in two ways. In the first way, a living room, dining room, and study were arranged in line and essentially open to each other, with the fireplace on an inside wall backed by service areas. In the second way, living room, dining room, study, and main entry hall were spread out from the core as separate

10A. Frank Lloyd Wright. Plan, Robie House. Chicago, Illinois. 1909. *Illustration © Frank Lloyd Wright Foundation, 1983.*

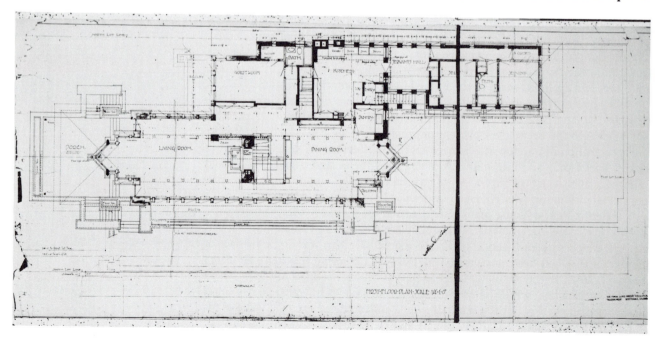

10B. Frank Lloyd Wright. Dining room, Robie House. Chicago, Illinois. 1909. *Photograph © Frank Lloyd Wright Foundation, 1983.*

11. Frank Lloyd Wright. Living-room fireplace, Avery Coonley House. Riverside, Illinois. 1908. *Photograph by Thomas A. Heinz.*

12. Frank Lloyd Wright. Plan, Ward W. Willits House. Highland Park, Illinois. 1902. *Illustration © Frank Lloyd Wright Foundation, 1983.*

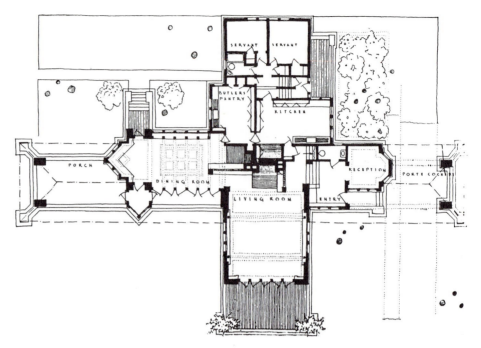

pavilions. The pavilions, expressed as separate units on the exterior also, composed L-, T-, and cross-shaped plans.

The Darwin D. Martin House was the largest of the T-shape plans. It offered a long horizontal interior vista. Of the cruciform plan houses, the Ward W. Willits House in Highland Park, Illinois (1902) (see Figure 12), and the Isabel Roberts House (1908) in River Forest, Illinois, both focused on central fireplaces with the living, dining, and porch/reception areas forming the arms of a cross.

Inside, however, Wright worked to free his spaces from this box-like "unit" derivation. He made the openings between principal spaces wider, though usually separable by portieres, thereby merging and interlocking the adjacent spaces. The effect was that his interiors offered long vistas and seemed to flow outward in horizontal outreaches like the open prairie. He made living rooms two stories high with balconies over the fireplace and inglenook. And he inserted long bands of windows—sometimes as clerestories that inflected the view upward—and created an interpenetration of inside and outside. To reinforce this he extended the supporting walls out beyond his spaces and beyond the roofs. Walls thereby seemed to become independent screens; roofs seemed to hover above the clerestories.

Interior space, though defined for different functions by specific furnishings, appeared not as enclosed, but as a single flowing entity. He stepped floors and ceilings so that there were different areas within a single room and spatial variety was achieved, yet openness was not impeded. Corners were often designed as if open. Other openings were semitransparent through ornamental leaded-glass panels. Wright often called these devices "breaking the box."

Wright's plans interrelated one space with another, bringing about an interpenetration of the one with the whole. With his variations on openness, he created the free-flowing space. In this, perhaps influenced by his admiration for the traditional Japanese interior, Wright returned somewhat to the multipurpose interior concept that preceded the eighteenth century's separation of specialized rooms. Such plans were virtually unknown before Wright's work, though there had been some intimations or probings in the area of open planning by the preceding generation of Shingle Style architects in New England. Other forward-looking architects in the Chicago area who shared similar aims came to be called the Prairie

School. None was so dedicated to advancing spatial expression as Frank Lloyd Wright. His free-flowing space, in fact, was the progenitor of the "free plan" of the later Modern movement. This was all part of Wright's consistent view of architecture and the site, of architecture and human life as integral and organic. It was also part of his view of the turn-of-the-century American lifestyle as assertively informal and democratic.

Wright's genius reinforced the fundamental functions and underlying meanings and symbolism of a house. He expressed, afresh for our century, elemental statements about "house" that evoked our ancient myths of shelter, that related to our subconscious connotations of nest and fortress. For this and for his respect of the land and its materials, as well as for the informal strength of his house plans, Frank Lloyd Wright is considered the quintessential American architect.

The Larkin Building

The Larkin Company Administration Building (1904) in Buffalo, New York, was the first monumental scheme of Frank Lloyd Wright to be constructed (see Figures 13A and B). An office building for the Larkin mail-order firm, the rectangular-plan building (demolished 1949–50) had a five-story-high skylighted central atrium (see Figure 14) surrounded by tiers of balconies. Brick was used consistently inside as well as on the exterior, although the exterior was of red brick and the interior of cream-colored brick.

On the top level was an employee restaurant and rest area; the other levels were, in the main, open office space—a concept that had recently begun to be

13A. Frank Lloyd Wright. First-floor plan, Larkin Building. Buffalo, New York. 1904. *Illustration © Frank Lloyd Wright Foundation, 1985.*

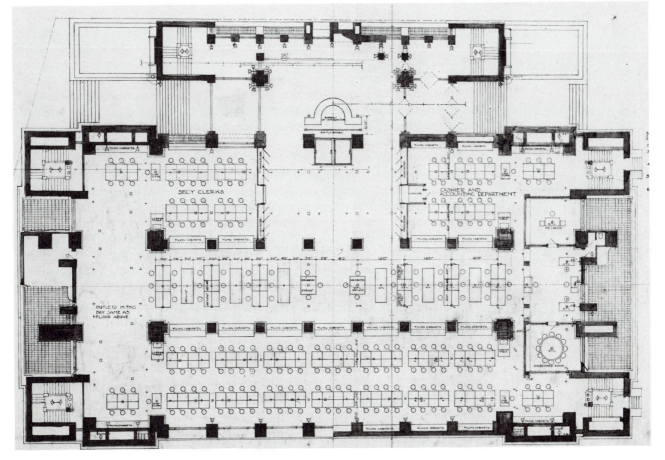

13B. Frank Lloyd Wright. Section, Larkin Building. Buffalo, New York. 1904. *Illustration © Frank Lloyd Wright Foundation, 1985.*

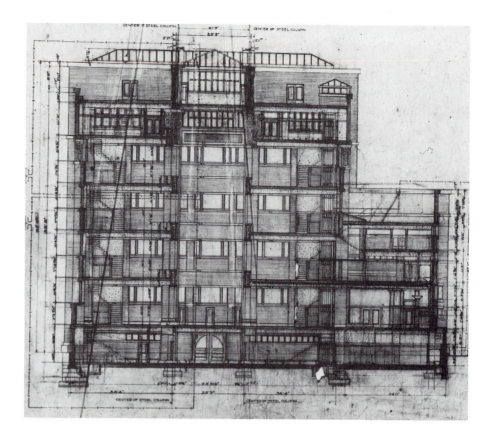

adopted by American businesses. This included open space for executives on the ground level. It was, again, democratic and American. All levels opened onto and therefore shared the large space of the atrium. Mechanical systems such as conditioned air and fire stairs were housed in windowless corner piers. The cubic forms, therefore, stretched out the interior space both horizontally and vertically. Each element clearly expressed its function. It was a major achievement.

The interiors of the Larkin Building demonstrate Wright's skill and subtlety in building up units. He used them to compose his interior elevations as well as his plans. Inside the perimeter walls (see Figure 15) rectangular blocks of built-in file cabinets (in variable and versatile grids) were beneath rectangular windows. On the atrium elevations, rectangular brick balustrades formed a grid with the rectangular openings to the atrium; on the workspace side the balustrade was composed of a long bank of built-in file drawers. His alternation of rectangles of different dimensions, and of horizontal and vertical ones, and his formation of grids—articulated by the exposed brick piers—showed his mastery of the principle of repetition. It created great rhythm in the Larkin interiors and produced a working space of power, strength, and dignity.

Furnishings and Objects

For all of his projects Wright designed as much of the required furnishings as his clients were prepared to pay for. He designed sofas and chairs, tables and bookcases—piano cases, even. He designed lamp fixtures and stained glass, carpets and textiles, desk appointments, metal urns and vases, andirons and fire tools, china and glassware, and other objects and equipment. In his office, Wright was assisted in his furniture designs by the architects Marion Mahony and her husband Walter Burley Griffin.

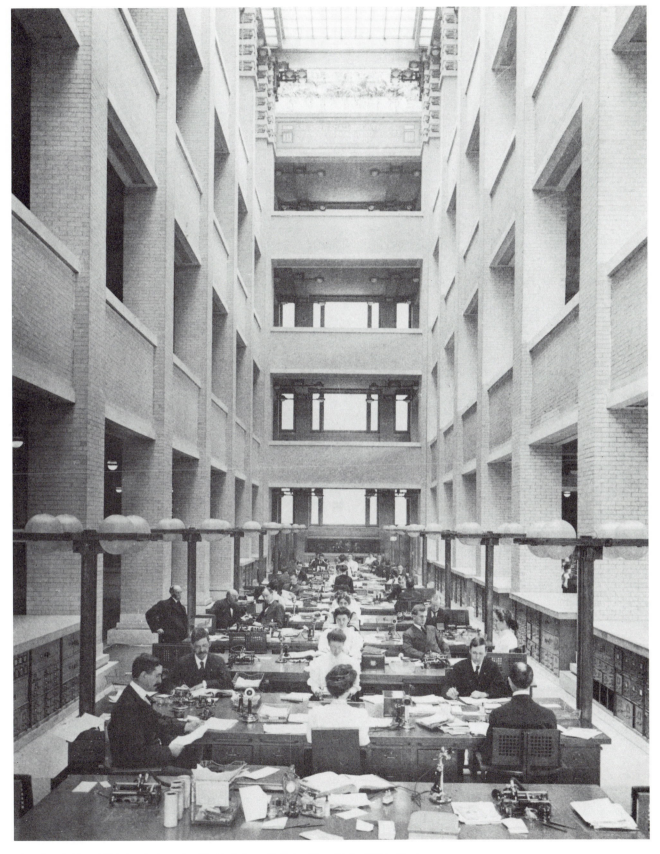

14. Frank Lloyd Wright. Atrium, Larkin Building. Buffalo, New York. 1904. *Photograph from the Buffalo and Erie County Historical Society.*

15. Frank Lloyd Wright. Perimeter wall, Larkin Building. Buffalo, New York. 1904. *Photograph from the Buffalo and Erie County Historical Society.*

For the Larkin Building he designed all the furniture and appointments, making a number of innovations. It was the first metal furniture of the century to express its material and construction so honestly. Manufactured by the Van Dorn Iron Works Company of Cleveland, Ohio, the Larkin desks and three chairs were among the earliest metal office furniture.

The desk chair (see Figure 15) was on a cantilevered metal arm; when the seat back was folded down onto the seat, the arm automatically returned the seat to the knee-space under the desk to facilitate floor cleaning. The two executive armchairs were framed with tubular metal, prefiguring the tubular chairs of two decades later. One version had a swivel seat on a four-legged base, which was elevated on casters. The adjustable back panels of these two armchairs were made as double-layered boxes of metal; for air circulation and visual detail the back panels were perforated in a gridded square pattern. This grid pattern was similar to the detailing of Charles Rennie Mackintosh in Scotland and of Josef Hoffmann in Vienna about this same time. The furnishings of the Larkin Building were innovative and also achieved a degree of consistency that was a model of "total design."

Ultimately, Frank Lloyd Wright's monumental achievement was his consistency, his unity of design. His interiors were inextricably integrated with the massing and structural systems of his buildings. In his interior elevations he made a

16. Frank Lloyd Wright. Armchair, Larkin Building. Buffalo, New York. 1904. *Photograph by Thomas A. Heinz.*

constant effort to relate walls to ceilings, windows to doors, benches to lowered soffits and clerestory windows. Oak-banded panels in ceilings reiterated the rectangular forms of windows and doors. Rectilinear clerestory windows were balanced, were almost symmetrical with long benches beneath them. His furnishings and appointments were unified with his interior spaces, and furniture functions— regardless of their varying success at providing comfort—were integrated with each other: Sofas were combined with occasional tables; electric lighting or candle stands were joined to dining-table corners. Yet, for all that doubling up or interrelating of functions, Wright's furniture designs retained a simplicity of purpose and of line. "Simplicity and repose," Wright wrote, "are the qualities that measure the true value of any work of art."[6]

Unity Temple

The supreme example of Wright's achievement of those values is Unity Temple (see color plate 1), the sanctuary building of the Unitarian Universalist Church complex, which Wright designed and built in Oak Park (1906). It was his first exposed reinforced-concrete public monument, and perhaps his best-integrated, most organic early work. The temple has a square plan with stairs rising in blank corner piers (see Figure 17A). The remaining cruciform interior space has two tiers of balconies on three sides. On the focal fourth side is the pulpit, with the organ behind it. Over the central square of the cruciform, a coffered roof is skylighted at the top with clear glass. Clerestories of amber glass atop the balcony walls further lighten the roof and make it appear almost weightless. The floor of the temple is higher in the central square than in the surrounding passageways under the balconies, producing a more complex section than one anticipates (see Figure 17B).

17A.   Frank Lloyd Wright. Plan at auditorium level, Unity Temple. Oak Park, Illinois. 1906. *Illustration © Frank Lloyd Wright Foundation, 1983.*

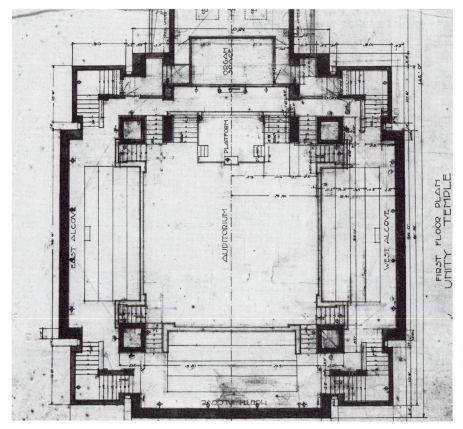

17B.   Frank Lloyd Wright. Section, Unity Temple. Oak Park, Illinois, 1906. *Illustration © Frank Lloyd Wright Foundation, 1985.*

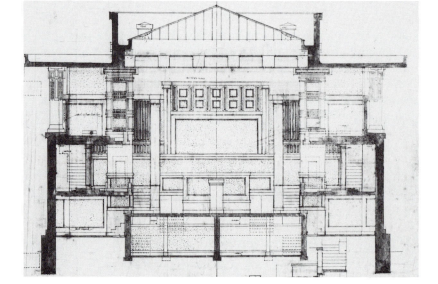

The space flows in, over, and under the balconies, around the great square piers supporting them, and around pendant light fixtures. The eye is led through this constantly flowing space by linear ornament of oak trim banding. That banding merges the two-dimensional with the three-dimensional elements and sends the eye along its raceways to discover the interlocking space and, at the same time, it coalesces the space, bringing it all back together to the center. That center is the acceleration or concentration of oak battens screening the organ box above the speaker's rostrum. The entire composition is a masterly interweaving of major space and circulation passageways with structure, lighting, furnishings, and ornamentation.

In Unity Temple the integration of all elements is unified to a degree unparalleled in American interior design—perhaps from that day to our own. Wall and window are one; ceiling and skylight are one; furniture is part of the walls; ornament is wall. Only the lighting fixtures stand apart as separate sculptural elements. Yet even they are treated in the linear vocabulary of the total design. As a metaphor of the temple itself, as well as a culmination of Frank Lloyd Wright's work to that date, the unity of this design is absolute. And if ever in twentieth-century interior design one can be elevated to transports of the sublime, it is in Unity Temple.

In 1910 the decade was recapitulated by Wright in the pair of portfolios of his work published in Berlin by Ernst Wasmuth. Wright had spent more than a year in Europe preparing the one hundred large lithographs of his projects. The Wasmuth Portfolios and the companion paperbound volume of illustrations and plans were avidly read by the European progenitors of the Modern style in architecture and interior design, including Berlage, Gropius, Mies, and Le Corbusier. The publications established Wright as the American pioneer of the Modern movement for the next two decades.

The Arts and Crafts Movement

Wright had not been alone of his generation to seek the goals of simplicity, total design, and an American way. Simplicity had been gaining adherents throughout the nineteenth century, and Wright was the direct heir of its tradition. A reform movement against the excesses and disadvantages of the Industrial Revolution (see Chapter 1) was spearheaded in England by the mid-1800s. With Ralph Waldo Emerson and Walt Whitman as inspiration, these reformers railed against these excesses—the evils of the machine and the morally "dishonest" ornamentation it produced when used to imitate handcraft. The development of the Modern movement can be seen as the battle for and against the machine. From the early nineteenth-century reformers until the birth of the Modern movement in the second decade of the twentieth century, pioneer after pioneer, and designer after philosopher, contributed to a shifting statement and sentiment—first against the machine, then accepting it, and finally celebrating it.

The recommended paths to improvement were different for each reformer. A. W. N. Pugin (1812–52) believed in the superiority of the Middle Gothic age. John Ruskin (1819–1900) praised the ideals and models of North Italian and Venetian Gothic. William Morris (1834–96) advocated a medieval model. All equated handcraft with regenerative good and with moral honesty in design. William Morris was the first to return to such a handcraft activity, banning the machine and designing and producing handmade furnishings on a communal basis in a simplified medieval style. The furnishings of Morris & Company were the basis of inspiration for much of the Arts and Crafts furniture that followed.

By the 1890s the Arts and Crafts movement had been spread in America through the writings of Charles Locke Eastlake (1836–1906). Eastlake's *Hints on*

Household Taste of 1868 advocated stripping away heavy Victorian trappings and returning to the simple lines of Tudor England. He acclaimed honest construction "without sham or pretense"; he felt, as previous reformers had, that machine carving should not look like hand carving. Simplicity was the keynote. The lecture tour of Oscar Wilde throughout America in 1882–83 helped spread the movement, and in 1888 the Arts and Crafts Exhibition Society was founded in London, marking the first use of the term. Throughout the 1890s numerous arts and crafts societies, workshops, and salesrooms were founded in Chicago and throughout America.

In 1901 Frank Lloyd Wright had delivered his provocative and influential lecture "The Art and Craft of the Machine" at Chicago's Hull House. From 1901 to 1916 designer Gustav Stickley (1857–1942) published his *Craftsman* magazine, which was the chief platform for Craftsman designers and a strong influence on the public. *House Beautiful*, which was initiated in 1896, also gave space to craftsmen and the Craftsman tradition; as did *Ladies' Home Journal*, which published the work of Frank Lloyd Wright at the beginning of the century. Other publicizers of the movement included a number of professional publications about architecture and building.

The first sixteen years of the twentieth century were the years of the Craftsman movement. The decorative arts—furniture, glass, and art pottery—were produced in a new handcraft idiom; and a whole generation of designers established a sturdy, straightforward, simple style of furnishings, objects, and ornamentation. Theirs was a dedication to quality of design and craftsmanship in every aspect of life. This approach was the correspondent of the wholesome, strenuous, and back-to-nature life that the Craftsmen believed in. For many of them Theodore Roosevelt was the public symbol. They believed that original, handcrafted, honest designs would bring a new social utopia. That search for a spiritual and physical utopia pervaded the first two decades of the twentieth century.

Among the most prominent of the Craftsmen designers was Gustav Stickley, who designed and produced hefty, foursquare oak furniture in his Craftsman Workshops in Eastwood, a suburb of Syracuse, New York, between 1900 and 1916 (see Figure 18A). Two of his brothers, Leopold and J. George Stickley, produced similar furniture in nearby Fayetteville, New York. Elbert Hubbard (1856–1915) worked in this reform tradition at his Roycroft Shops in East Aurora, near Buffalo, New York, from 1901 until his death. He also published his furniture designs, which were among the best in the Arts and Crafts tradition—simple and heavy, of oak and mahogany (see Figure 18B). And George Niedecken of Milwaukee, who had made some of Frank Lloyd Wright's furniture for his houses, went on to design and produce Craftsman designs of his own.

This furniture came to be popularly known in America as Mission Style. Usually of simple, sturdy golden oak and fumed oak, it was the popular version of the prototype furniture that Frank Lloyd Wright designed for his Prairie houses. When his clients could not afford complete furnishings of his own design, Wright encouraged them to purchase harmonious pieces from the Stickleys.

Wright's furniture designs, like his architecture and interior spaces, were a summation of this reform tradition. His designs gave the authority of genius to the movement, and a whole Prairie School of design—based on the Arts and Crafts tradition—sprang up on this basis in Chicago, Minneapolis, Detroit, Cleveland, and St. Louis. Most of these midwestern cities had art schools that offered programs in arts and crafts. There, too, architects and interior designers emphasized "the unity of interior and exterior, the desire for simplicity, a respect for natural materials, an interest in Japanese art, and a geometric rectilinear style,"[7] as the movement has been summarized.

18A. Gustav Stickle, Reclining armchair, white quarter-sawn oak with leather spring seat and cushion, by Craftsman Workshops. Eastwood, New York. Circa 1909. *Photograph courtesy Jordan—Volpe Gallery, New York City.*

18B. Elbert Hubbard. Drop-front desk, white quarter-sawn oak with copper hardware, by Roycroft. East Aurora, New York. Circa 1910. *Photograph by H. Peter Curran, courtesy Jordan—Volpe Gallery, New York City.*

19A. Greene & Greene. Dining room, David B. Gamble House, Pasadena, California. 1908. *Photograph by Marvin Rand.*

Wright himself had first gone to Japan in 1905 but, like the rest of his contemporaries, he had long admired Japanese art. It had been a totem of his era since at least the 1880s, when Gilbert and Sullivan parodied the penchant for "things Japanese." For Wright, Japanese art and architecture had set an exemplar for his dictum, "Bring out the nature of materials, let this nature intimately into your scheme."

Other Prairie School practitioners produced interior design work that followed this precept. Harvey Ellis (1852–1904), in the last year of his life, produced some of the best designs in Gustav Stickley's catalogue, giving the Stickley operation a fresh lift and perhaps its best designs. George Grant Elmslie (1871–1952), like Wright, worked with Adler & Sullivan before starting his own architecture practice; a number of his Prairie-style interior furnishings show the influence of Sullivan's ornament. Will Bradley (1868–1962) designed Arts and Crafts furniture and interiors in the idiom associated with Charles Rennie Mackintosh in Scotland and its development in Vienna.

Contemporary with Wright in California were Greene & Greene—brothers Charles Sumner Greene (1868–1954) and Henry Mather Greene (1870–1957)—whose work combined the Arts and Crafts tradition with Shingle-Style architecture and Japanese detailing and decoration. They redefined and refined the bungalow for its California setting and thereby ultimately influenced popular taste for the

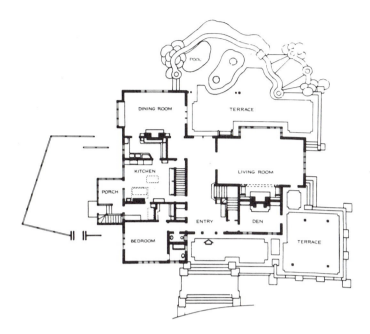

19B. Greene & Greene. Plan, David B. Gamble House. Pasadena, California. 1908. *Illustration from Esther McCoy,* Five California Architects *(New York: Reinhold, 1960).*

next decade. Their masterpieces, built between 1907 and 1909, were the Robert R. Blacker House and the David B. Gamble House (see Figure 19B), both in Pasadena; the Charles M. Pratt House in Ojai; and the William R. Thorsen House in Berkeley. The craftsmanship of Greene & Greene's interiors and furnishings is consummate (see Figure 19A). Bernard Maybeck, Irving Gill, and Julia Morgan, who was the first woman architect registered in California, also worked in this tradition during this time. Lucia and Arthur F. Matthews provided many designs and executed furnishings in the Craftsman idiom for their California contemporaries.

Also influential in this vein was Wallace Nutting, a furniture collector and dealer who focused on seventeenth- and early eighteenth-century unpainted wood pieces. As historian Edgar Kaufmann, Jr., has written, Nutting's was "a brusquer attitude . . . and to him, more than anyone, the tradesmen of the United States owe the sempiternal vogue for 'Early American maple.'"[8]

European Directions

Art Nouveau

Fashionable as Art Nouveau was in Brussels and in Nancy, and fascinating as it has been to mid- and late-twentieth-century observers, it had little stylistic effect on American interior design. Art Nouveau held the design stage of Europe from the early 1880s until around 1900, then was popularized by numerous commercial examples. Largely curvilinear with whiplash curves and flower-and-plant-derived decoration, it was the first stylistic development since Gothic that was not directly imitative of previous historical styles. But it was almost purely a design approach that focused on ornamental effects in interior design. Its influence spread to Italy, where it was called the Stile Floreale and the Stile Liberty—after the fabrics and metalwork sponsored by the Liberty of London store. In Germany and Austria it came to be known as Jugendstile.

Among the rare American Art Nouveau contributions are the glass and metal work of Louis Comfort Tiffany; the book illustrations and posters of Will Bradley; the furniture of Charles Rohlfs; and some of the decorative details of Harvey Ellis, which are in the tradition of Mackintosh. The Arts and Crafts reform movement was in direct opposition to design approaches that focused on surface finish, visual effects, and ornamentation. It was, therefore, in direct opposition to the fantasy ornamentation of Art Nouveau, however antihistorical the aims of that late-nineteenth-century movement.

The early popularity of the Arts and Crafts tradition in America was, perhaps, responsible for the lack of success and the paucity of American practitioners in the Art Nouveau idiom. Art Nouveau did, however, have a profound effect on the ideologies that shaped the Modern movement in providing the other foundation of that movement along with the belief in the machine. That foundation was that contemporary work should be of the day, for the times, and therefore nonhistorical.

The Wiener Werkstaette

At the turn of the century the reformers were joined, in Vienna, by Josef Hoffmann, Adolf Loos, and the Wiener Werkstaette. Inspired by England's Guild of Handicraft, the Wiener Werkstaette (Vienna Workshop) was founded in Vienna in 1903 by Josef Hoffmann (1870–1956) and Koloman Moser to make handcrafted utilitarian objects that would be as aesthetically significant as the work of fine artists. The goals of the Werkstaette were to produce—by handcraftsmanship and the proper treatment of materials—total works of functional art and a "style of today."

The Werkstaette "Work Programme" of 1905 again lashed out against the machine: "The boundless evil, caused by shoddy mass-produced goods and by the uncritical imitation of earlier styles, is like a tidal wave sweeping across the world." Instead, the Werkstaette Programme proclaimed, "We wish to create an inner relationship linking public, designer, and worker, and we want to produce good and simple articles of everyday use. Our guiding principle is function, utility our first condition, and our strength must lie in good proportions and the proper treatment of material."[9]

From 1905 to 1911 Josef Hoffmann, who was Wright's exact contemporary, was engaged in the design and furnishing of the Palais Stoclet (see Figure 20) in Brussels, to which the major members of the Werkstaette contributed objects, decorative paintings and mosaics, and furnishings. It was the unique Viennese total work of art. Although the Wiener Werkstaette had no widespread stylistic effect on American interior design until after its shop was opened in New York in 1911, the Werkstaette was continuing to build the foundations of the Modern design movement.[10]

The Ecole des Beaux-Arts

All the moral integrity of the nineteenth-century reform tradition had focused on the honest use of the machine and of natural materials, and had reinforced structural honesty in design. That last goal reflected the long tradition of rationalist design theory. The Craftsman tradition was, therefore, also in opposition to the prevailing classical revival—or academic classicism—that was promulgated by the Ecole des Beaux-Arts in Paris.

The Ecole des Beaux-Arts not only fostered a style based on historical models, but also established a working method for architectural design that remained a foundation for that profession for many decades. The Beaux-Arts method of composition focused on the importance of the plan, minimal expression of interior on exterior, the progressional aspects of passage through a series of spaces, and the *parti*—the concept that denoted the specific function and character of the building. The predominant style fostered by the Ecole des Beaux-Arts from the last third of

20. Josef Hoffmann. Dining room, Palais Stoclet. Brussels, Belgium. 1905–11. *Photograph from Karl Mang,* History of Modern Furniture *(New York: Harry N. Abrams, 1979).*

the nineteenth century—and taken up by most of its American students—consisted of axial plans, façades broken up into separate pavilion-like blocks, and a vocabulary of ornaments and of elements such as mansard roofs. Among the ornaments were carved swags, trophies, and cartouches; cove moldings around windows and doors; and other French Renaissance and later seventeenth- and eighteenth-century details that ultimately gave the style the name Beaux-Arts Baroque.

Many American architects and designers still flocked to the Ecole des Beaux-Arts for their training. Among them had been Charles Follen McKim, a partner of Stanford White in McKim, Mead & White. This Beaux-Arts classical overlay had been widely popularized in America by the World's Columbian Exposition in Chicago of 1893 with its "White City" of buildings decorated in classical ornament. Four of its pavilions had been designed by McKim, Mead & White. Their work, along with that of such architects as Carrere & Hastings (see Figure 21), can be considered a pinnacle of the Neoclassical Beaux-Arts tradition in America at that time. In twentieth-century America the Beaux-Arts influence lingered through stylistic changes—from the nineteenth century's eclectic French Second Empire to an increasingly refined expression of the classicism of the Ancients.

As the foremost practitioner of these principles in interior design in America, Elsie de Wolfe proffered a similar vein of surface ornament. From the time of the 1893 Columbian Exposition in Chicago, the Beaux-Arts approach had increasingly become the prevailing mode of American architecture and design. Of that exposition, Louis Sullivan had said that it would set back the cause of Modern, organic architecture and design in America for at least fifty years.

Organic = Integrated

The term "organic" had been invoked in early nineteenth-century German philosophy. By the time of the Crystal Palace Exhibition, it seemed to signify a return

21. Carrere & Hastings. Marble foyer, New York Public Library, New York City. 1898–1911. *Photograph © Peter Aaron/ESTO, 1984.*

in design to the principles of intrinsic growth in nature. There, that principle was manifest in leaf-covered ceramic wares and other plant-form decoration. Later, Louis Sullivan developed the term "organic" to mean that the structure of a building should be expressed on the exterior, as if structural system and exterior elevations were part of a single, growing organism. Sullivan's dictum "form follows function" is in the design-theory tradition of Rationalist structural honesty. Later, this idea was developed to mean that the form or shape of a design should follow the structural function of its construction technique, and this was to be called functionalism.

Frank Lloyd Wright's goal was to extend Sullivan's concept of the organic throughout the entire building. He used the term to mean complete consistency of design, unity of all elements from planning through construction, and ultimate integration and interrelationship of process and product, exterior and interior, large-scale elements and smallest details. He aimed for spatial continuity and an integration of plan, structure, and ornamentation.

It was from this vision of integrated design that he developed his goal of the interpenetration of interior and exterior space. For Wright, organic meant integrated and consistent. He wrote, "Integration as entity is [the] first essential."[11] In this he represented the mid- to late-nineteenth-century European quest for the "total work of art"—the *Gesamtkunstwerk*—also epitomized in the music-dramas of Richard Wagner.[12] In America Greene & Greene also held and achieved this ideal; and in Austria the founders of the Wiener Werkstaette also aspired to it. No one in his day was more successful in achieving this goal of unity—and in sustaining it over seventy years of monumental production—than Frank Lloyd Wright.

Suggested Reading

Banham, Reyner. *The Architecture of the Well-Tempered Environment.* London: The Architectural Press, 1969. Chicago: University of Chicago Press, 1969.

Behrman, S. N. *Duveen.* Boston: Little, Brown, 1972.

Brooks, H. Allen. *Contemporary Architects,* ed. Muriel Emanuel. New York: St. Martin's Press, 1980.

———, ed. *Prairie School Architecture.* New York: Van Nostrand Reinhold, 1983.

Clark, Robert Judson, ed. *The Arts and Crafts Movement in America: 1876–1916,* exhibition catalogue. Princeton: Princeton University Press, 1972.

de Wolfe, Elsie. *The House in Good Taste.* New York: The Century Co., 1913.

Fowler, John, and John Cornforth. *English Decoration in the 18th Century.* London: Barrie & Jenkins Ltd., 1983.

Giedion, Sigfried. *Mechanization Takes Command.* Oxford: Oxford University Press, 1948. New York: W. W. Norton, 1975.

Hamm, Margherita Arline. *Eminent Actors in Their Homes.* New York: James Pott & Co., 1902.

Hanks, David A. *The Decorative Designs of Frank Lloyd Wright.* New York: E. P. Dutton, 1979.

Heinz, Thomas A. *Frank Lloyd Wright.* New York: St. Martin's Press, 1982.

———. *Inside Frank Lloyd Wright: Furniture, Glass Decorative Arts.* New York: Harry N. Abrams, 1985.

Hitchcock, Henry-Russell. *In the Nature of Materials: The Buildings of Frank Lloyd Wright, 1887–1941.* New York: Da Capo Press, 1973.

———. *Architecture in the Nineteenth and Twentieth Centuries.* Baltimore: Penguin Books, 1958–82 (especially "Wright and His California Contemporaries").

———. "Frank Lloyd Wright," *Encyclopedia of Modern Architecture,* ed. Gerd Hatje. New York: Harry N. Abrams, 1964.

Hoffmann, Donald. "Frank Lloyd Wright," *Who's Who in Architecture,* ed. J. M. Richards. New York: Holt, Rinehart and Winston, 1977.

Jacobus, John M., Jr. "USA," *Encyclopedia of Modern Architecture.* ed. Gerd Hatje. New York: Harry N. Abrams, 1964.

Kaufmann, Edgar, Jr. "Interior Design: Architecture or Decoration?" *Progressive Architecture.* October 1962, pp. 141–44.

———. "Frank Lloyd Wright," *Macmillan Encyclopedia of Architects.* New York: The Free Press, a division of Macmillan Publishing Company and Collier Macmillan Publishing, 1982.

Koch, Robert. *Louis C. Tiffany: Rebel in Glass.* New York: Crown, 1964.

Lambourne, Lionel. *Utopian Craftsmen.* Salt Lake City: Peregrine Smith, 1980.

McCoy, Esther. *Five California Architects.* New York: Reinhold, 1960. (Paperback New York: Frederick A. Praeger, 1975.)

Manson, Grant C. *Frank Lloyd Wright to 1910.* New York: Reinhold, 1958.

Roth, Leland M. *McKim, Mead & White, Architects.* New York: Harper & Row, 1983.

Scully, Vincent J. *Frank Lloyd Wright.* New York: Braziller, 1960.

Smith, Jane S. *Elsie de Wolfe*. New York: Atheneum, 1982.

Smith, Mary Ann. *Gustav Stickley: The Craftsman*. Syracuse: Syracuse University Press, 1983.

Spencer, Brian A., ed. *The Prairie School radition*. New York: Whitney Library of Design, 1979.

Wharton, Edith, and Ogden Codman. *The Decoration of Houses*. New York: Charles Scribner's Sons, 1897.

Wheeler, Candace. "Interior Decoration as a Profession for a Woman," *The Outlook*. April 6 and 20, 1895, pp. 559f., 649f., respectively.

Notes

1. Margherita Arline Hamm, *Eminent Actors in Their Homes* (New York: James Pott & Co., 1902), p. 60.

2. Elsie de Wolfe, quoted from the first known history of the profession of interior design—Edgar Kaufmann, Jr., "Interior Design: Architecture or Decoration?" *Progressive Architecture* (October 1962), p. 143.

3. Quoted from Edith Wharton's autobiography, *A Backward Glance* (New York: Charles Scribner's Sons, 1933, 1964), p. 106f.

4. Candace Wheeler, "Interior Decoration as a Profession for Women," *The Outlook* (April 6 and 20, 1895), pp. 559f., 649f., respectively.

5. Edgar Kaufmann, Jr., "Frank Lloyd Wright," *Macmillan Encyclopedia of Architects* (New York: The Free Press, a division of Macmillan Publishing Company and Collier Macmillan Publishing, 1982), p. 447.

6. Frank Lloyd Wright, "In the Cause of Architecture," *Architectural Record* (March 1908); reprinted in *The Work of Frank Lloyd Wright* (New York: Horizon Press, 1965), p. 10. This is the reprint of the Wendingen edition of 1925, which was one of Wright's favorite books.

7. David A. Hanks, "Chicago and the Midwest," *The Arts and Crafts Movement in America: 1876–1916*, exhibition catalogue, ed. Robert Judson Clark (Princeton: Princeton University Press, 1972), p. 59.

8. Kaufmann, "Interior Design: Architecture or Decoration?" loc. cit.

9. Work Program of the Wiener Werkstaette, quoted from *Vienna Moderne: 1898–1918*, exhibition catalogue (University of Houston: Sarah Campbell Blaffer Gallery; New York: Cooper-Hewitt Museum, 1978), p. 87f. Reprinted there with permission from *Architecture and Design: An International Anthology of Original Articles*, ed. Timothy and Charlotte Benton, with Dennis Sharp (London: Granada Publishing, Ltd., 1975).
   Christopher Wilk points out, in a letter to C. Ray Smith dated August 1985, that the anti-machine outlook of the Wiener Werkstaette should not be overstated. He cites the first article on the Werkstaette published in the German magazine *Deutsche Kunst-und-Dekoration* (Vol. 8, No. 15, October 1904) by Joseph Lux, who wrote: "Amid the clangour of machinery the art craftsman's quieter and more inspired manual work makes its appearance here, even though machines are by no means absent. On the contrary, the Wiener Werkstaette is excellently equipped with all the technical innovations which can assist the work in hand. Here, however, the machine is not a ruler and a tyrant, but a willing servant and assistant." Many of their designs were soon made for machine production, such as furniture and perforated metal objects. Essentially, like other reformers of the day, the Werkstaette members were vehemently opposed to the "mindless imitations of old styles."

10. The influence of the Wiener Werkstaette on American design in this period seems, at this writing, not to have been widespread. But a number of designers were influenced by the group early on. Wilk points out that our view is conditioned by the fact that this period has been little researched up to now.

11. Frank Lloyd Wright, *The Natural House* (New York: Horizon Press, 1954; New York: New American Library, 1970), p. 22.

12. In recent years, a number of scholars have begun to challenge the identification of Richard Wagner with the *Gesamtkunstwerk*. See such works as *Wagnerism in European Culture and Politics*, ed. David C. Large and William Weber. (Ithaca, NY: Cornell University Press, 1984).

Chapter **3**

1910–1920: The Birth of the Modern Movement

There are two choices in most human situations, it appears—two sides to every coin, as the maxim goes. There is inside and outside, male and female, positive and negative, action and reaction, reason and emotion, intellect and heart, subjective and objective, and so on. Sometimes it seems as if the world were divided between good and bad, happy and sad. But, of course, it is not so simple—so black and white—as that. Instead, the graduated areas of gray—where two sides meet in a nonexclusive blend—make them difficult to distinguish.

The years from 1910 to 1920 offered a paradigm of this dual, polarized aspect of life. The decade was divided—ruptured—between a peaceful first half and the ravages of war in Europe. World War I completely consumed Western culture for the second half of the decade. The decade was also divided, in the art movements of Europe, between the peaceful reason of the classical intellect and the unbridled emotion of the romantic spirit. The intellectual direction led toward the pursuit of ever greater abstraction, whereas the emotional direction led to a storm and drama of expressionist movements. The second decade of the twentieth century, therefore, offered two choices to American designers: the choice between Europe and America.

Also, from the beginning of the second decade of the twentieth century, there was a new and important cross-fertilization of design ideas between Europe and America. Whereas European ideas continued to influence American designers, the influence of Frank Lloyd Wright on Europe securely put American design on an equal footing with its European counterpart. In design as well as in politics, America gave up its isolationism.

American Design: A Dichotomy

American interior design exhibited a pluralism of choices. America was a generally agrarian society in 1910, although it was changing as the cities grew rapidly. Class structure was changing with the economy, as usual. The suffragette movement to gain the vote for women was at the height of its campaigning. In the area of industrial technology, conveyor-belt assembly was begun in 1913 by Henry Ford, whose Model-T Ford had been introduced in 1908. By 1915 Ford had produced his millionth auto.

In interior technology, electricity increasingly pervaded lifestyle. New mechanical conveniences, as historian Sigfried Giedion has pioneered in explaining, included the electric refrigerator, first on the market in 1913, and electric vacuum cleaners, which were offered in mail-order catalogues in 1917 (although these large and clumsy machines were used mostly in hotels and mansions).

American interior design and architecture were, in general, more conservative at this period than were their European counterparts. The spirit of innovation, which had reached such peaks in Chicago after the fire of 1870, had given way to historical revivalism. The Neoclassical idiom promulgated by the Chicago Exposition of 1893 prevailed as the establishment style, with Elsie de Wolfe as the most prominent exemplar in the interior design field. The Arts and Crafts movement and the Prairie tradition, with Frank Lloyd Wright as the supreme proponent, was pitted against this Neoclassical Revival. By about 1915 the Arts and Crafts movement began to die out.[1]

In the interiors of the very rich, the great antiques collectors were still amassing treasures from the cathedrals, cloisters, and country houses of Europe. Funding was abundant; clients were spending freely; design factories were facile and efficient. Decorating at this time meant antiques, almost exclusively. Historical splendor and theatrical completeness were the aspirations. A client who ordered a Tudor room expected the designers to complete it with Tudor furnishings. The plunder of the periods was seemingly unconfined. Gothic and Renaissance works were the prized treasures, following the lead of art historian Bernard Berenson and art dealer Joseph Duveen. But Tudor, Jacobean, Georgian, and French periods began to supply the needs of the less rich.

The search went on in Europe to find sufficient pieces to fill a room. Architects as well as decorators joined in the search to find objects for the clubs, residences, and chapels of clients striving to create a myth of tradition. Gothic furnishings and fragments, stained-glass panels and sculptured columns, Italian and Spanish Renaissance treasures, English baronial imagery—Tudor and Jacobean furniture—as well as Hepplewhite, Queen Anne, and Chippendale pieces, and oriental carpets—all were collected with piratical greed. Interiors were rich with carved oak and ivories, cut velvet and tooled leather, Italian brocade and French marquetry. Historian Richard Pommer has noted that it looked as if the American children were dressing up in their European parents' clothing. However, during this time Americans also began collecting furnishings from their own newly rediscovered Colonial houses.

The Arts and Crafts style had been popularized for more modest homes by 1910, as *Ladies' Home Journal* indicates. Frank Lloyd Wright's message that the fireplace was the center of the home had been promulgated, and his designs for dining tables with integral candle stands or electric lighting were broadly interpreted by others. The golden oak of the Mission Style had become the popular fashion. Among the mainstream American dreams were cottages—especially the California bungalow inspired by the original work of Greene & Greene—along with their sleeping porches, which were a sign of the integrated life of art and health that the Craftsmen advocated.

22. Bernard Maybeck. Christian Science Church. Berkleley, California. 1910. *Photograph by Julius Shulman.*

But editorial and critical counsels were beginning to be offered against Mission, which had begun to be diluted with vaguely Edwardian decoration. Craftsman interiors and Mission furniture began to be elaborated as "Flanders" and "Holland Dutch" furniture. The simplicity of the Arts and Crafts movement was beginning to wane. Black oak and black walnut were offered as the substitute for golden oak. In favor of something "trimmer and better proportioned," the *Ladies' Home Journal* in 1910 advocated "simpler furniture of older times." Colonial and Queen Anne Revival in rustic Shingle-Style form seemed to be the answer, along with trimly upholstered furniture that was vaguely Cromwellian. It was apparent that the effects of the Chicago Exposition of 1893 were continuing to spread down the generations and across the country. The Arts and Crafts style had run its course by the time America entered World War I.

Academic Classicism, or the Neoclassic Revival

In contrast to Wright's pioneering effort toward Modernism, the tradition of classicism—elaborated and redeveloped in the nineteenth century and given fresh impetus in America by the Chicago Exposition of 1893—continued to grow stronger in the first two decades of the twentieth century.

In California the Arts and Crafts approach began to fade even in the work of Bernard Maybeck and Greene & Greene. Bernard Maybeck (1862–1957), who was five years older than Frank Lloyd Wright, combined the honest Arts and Crafts approach with a decorative and historical Beaux-Arts overlay. Maybeck designed his celebrated Christian Science Church in Berkeley (1910) with Gothic detailing set amid simple factory-produced elements such as cement-asbestos wall panels and metal factory-sash windows. The interior (see Figure 22) has a singularly rich romanticism despite the paradoxically straightforward construction system. But in his Palace of Fine Arts, built for San Francisco's Panama Pacific International Exposition of 1915, Maybeck adopted the increasingly popular vein of classicism.

Greene & Greene ceased to practice around 1916. In their place the buildings designed by Bertram Goodhue (1869–1924) for the San Diego World's Fair of 1915 initiated a new interest in the Spanish Colonial/Churrigueresque style at its most ornate. Instead of a regional style based in the land, Goodhue imposed a romantic imagination on the historical context of California.

Irving Gill (1870–1936) designed his Dodge House in Los Angeles in 1916. In its entry hall (see Figure 23) he forcefully demonstrated the early minimalism for which he later became celebrated. His Wilson Acton Hotel in La Jolla, California (1908), is contemporaneous with the pared-down forms of Adolf Loos in Vienna (see Figure 24). With no formal architectural training, Gill had worked for Louis Sullivan in Chicago before practicing as an architect in California. From Sullivan, perhaps, he gained his respect for the integrated whole; yet he also maintained a romantic regard for the past. In line with the Arts and Crafts movement, he admired early California missions. It was the simple adobe forms of these missions that he used as inspiration for a stripped, purified architecture and interior design.

Gill's interiors and exteriors, therefore, exhibit a mixture of historicism and Modernism, and the moving back and forth between them that was the choice of

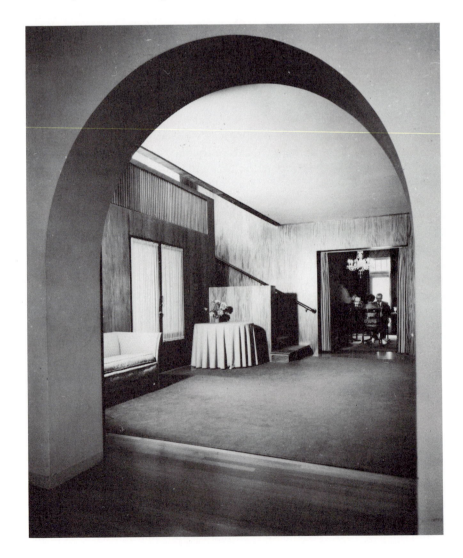

23. Irving Gill. Entry hall, Dodge House. Los Angeles, California. 1916. *Photograph by Julius Shulman.*

24. Adolf Loos, Shop for Knize. Vienna, Austria. 1898. *Photograph from Nikolaus Pevsner, Pioneers of Modern Design (New York: The Museum of Modern Art, 1949).*

the decade. His work looks like the severest kind of Modern functionalism. Yet, in terms of inspiration, the derivation of Gill's work from the California missions makes it historically oriented—if with regional validity—and puts it within the classical tradition of the day.

On the East Coast at this time, where little vanguard investigation was in progress, architects were at a peak of reinterpreting academic eclectic period styles. The Neoclassical idiom prevailed. In New York Warren & Wetmore designed their celebrated French Classical Revival Grand Central Station (1912–13). Cass Gilbert designed the Woolworth Building in Gothic style (1911–13). Perhaps the prime example of this Neoclassicism was architect Henry Bacon's 1914 design for the Lincoln Memorial in Washington, D.C. (completed 1917).

On the domestic scale of Fifth Avenue mansions, architect Horace Trumbauer designed the sumptuous foyer and reception rooms of the Louis XVI Revival Duke House in 1912. Architects Carrere & Hastings designed the classical atrium and period rooms (with the English architect-decorator Sir Charles Allom) of the house (1913–14) for the coal-and-steel millionaire Henry Clay Frick.(It is now the Frick Collection.) Both houses were recreations of late-eighteenth-century Parisian *hôtels*.

During the same period (1914–17) architect George Howe's firm, Mellor, Meigs & Howe, designed and built High Hollow for Howe himself at Chestnut Hill, Pennsylvania. It was designed as an Italian farmhouse in local stone and red brick with fifteenth-century Norman roofs. There, without borrowed ornament, but with a new sense of sculptural massing, a variation on late-nineteenth-century English "Banker's Tudor" houses came about. Howe's approach can be compared with the work of Irving Gill at this time, not only in the similarly stripped window treatments of the Dodge House and High Hollow, but also in their attempts to move beyond the customary correct historical orientation.

In this general reverence for historical models, the image of the adopted model was borrowed to bestow significance on the building or interior under question. As a determinant of the design, no consideration was given to the local context or to the regional area in which the room or building was located. Regionalism and contextualism—which aim to respect and reflect the location or site in which a building or interior is built—were not considerations of the day, much less of the Neoclassical tradition.

Furthermore, the Neoclassical tradition continued the battle of handcraft and ornamentation versus the machine and functionalism. Despite the sneering contempt—or obliviousness—of this historical tradition on the part of the growing number of modernists, the tradition continued—diminishing in numbers and in visibility perhaps, diminishing in scope and elaborateness of design, but ineradicable, it seems, from the consciousnesses and desires of designers.

The Elsie de Wolfe Tradition

As the most prominent exemplar of this Neoclassical tradition in American interior decorating, Elsie de Wolfe's position as society figure and international interior decorator continued to grow. She designed houses for the William Crockers near San Francisco, for the Ogden Armours at Lake Forest, for the Weyerhaeusers in Minneapolis, for Ethel Barrymore in New York, and for Mrs. George Beckwith in Wayzata, Minnesota, as well as a dormitory for Barnard College in New York.

It was the decade of Elsie de Wolfe's prime. She was a success as an arbiter of decorating taste and as a shrewd businesswoman. As part of her promotional performance, she turned herself into an eccentric personality—doing headstands in demonstration of her fitness and tinting her hair blue (it was said that she was the first to do so). She had defined the new profession and started it on the way toward professionalism.

In 1910 Elsie de Wolfe organized a series of lectures on art, architecture, and decoration at the Colony Club. Through such efforts more people became aware of the possibilities of taste and style—and of having designed interiors. Elsie de Wolfe also began designing a new house for Elisabeth Marbury and herself at 123 East 55th Street in Manhattan. Recreating the architectural improvements that had been made the year before to a brownstone house on East 71st Street, which she had designed as a showcase of ideas in collaboration with Ogden Codman (see Chapter 2), she elaborated on her stylistic mixture of French antiques and uphol-stered pieces, on attractive yet comfortable furnishings, on pale colors and light, on simplicity and Neoclassical proportions.

Committed as they both were to Neoclassical tradition, Codman and de Wolfe had removed the traditional nineteenth-century New York stoop and had put the entry to the showcase house at ground level through a flagstone courtyard. Codman had taken out the original stair along the party wall and had substituted a curving stair between the two parlors so as to increase the width of the rooms. Elsie de Wolfe repeated these improvements in the new Marbury–de Wolfe house. In the entry hall, checkerboard black-and-white marble flooring (see Figure 25A), a foun-tain with plants, and a copy of an eighteenth-century architect's table set the "country house" tone that was to become the essence of the de Wolfe style (see Figure 25B).

Her color scheme was again white, pale gray, and beige. (So much did she favor beige that when she first saw the Parthenon she exclaimed, "It's beige—just my color!") She used mirrors throughout the house—mirror-lined dressing rooms, mirrors inside the doors of her rose-chintz canopied Breton bed, sliding mirrored panels to close off the dining room windows, gilt-framed mirrors that were hung like paintings in the drawing room, and stair landings sheathed in squares of mirrors attached with gilt rosettes—as at Versailles.

To ensure that her influence continued to grow, Elsie de Wolfe began turning her Colony Club lectures into a series of articles. They were published in the women's magazine *The Delineator* during 1911. In the next year she reworked these articles, along with articles on her work that were published in *Ladies' Home Journal,* and in 1913 they were published in book form as *The House in Good Taste.* The book concentrated on tidying up and prettifying—unlike Catherine Beecher and Harriet Beecher Stowe's *The American Woman's Home,* which had been a main-stay of American house planning, heating, and management since it was published in 1869 (it influenced Frank Lloyd Wright's Prairie House designs). But the de Wolfe book was also unlike Wharton and Codman's *The Decoration of Houses,* in that it was clearly useful for average, as opposed to palatial, houses.

The de Wolfe book offered suggestions about painting decorations on simple furniture; about doubling the use of bedrooms as libraries/studies (and thereby recreating the eighteenth century's multiple-use spaces); about the substitution for garish colors of the pale and light palette—ivory, light gray, white, beige, rose, and pale blue. Black and white were recommended for drama, leaf green for accent. She advocated the elimination of collections of objects, including those that were treasured for their personal associations. The association with Versailles was enough for her, and reproductions were calmly admitted. Family matters did not enter Elsie de Wolfe's sphere of concern. For her, the design of houses was a matter of tidiness and order, of style and fashion.

Still, a sufficient balance or alternation was achieved in the book between middle-class economy and priceless-class patrons to make *The House in Good Taste* not only successful, but helpful. By the end of the decade it had proved popular enough to sell out several editions. Elsie de Wolfe thereby added to her successes the status of an authority/author on the subject of decorating. Despite the stylistic changes of the past half century, the tradition that Elsie de Wolfe established in

25A. Elsie de Wolfe. A typical entrance hall. New York City. Circa 1910. *Photograph from Elsie de Wolfe*, The House in Good Taste (*New York: The Century Co., 1913*).

25B. Elsie de Wolfe. Living room, own house on 55th Street. New York City. 1910. *Photograph from Elsie de Wolfe*, The House in Good Taste (*New York: The Century Co., 1913*).

both her work and her writing about it persists as the foundation of American interior decorating in the late twentieth century.

In 1913 Henry Clay Frick, who (following the death of J. P. Morgan that year) had suddenly become the most important American art collector, hired Elsie de Wolfe to design some private family rooms on the second floor of his Fifth Avenue mansion. The principal main-floor rooms were decorated by the English architect Sir Charles Allom, who had been recommended to Frick by both his art dealer Joseph Duveen and his architect Thomas Hastings. According to tradition,

Elsie de Wolfe became rich on the commission she received for counseling Mr. Frick on the purchase of fine French furniture. She had assumed the position of an international dealer in art and antiques.

The Growth of Professional Decorating

The public espousal of decorating as a factor in modern living was on the rise. The New York School of Interior Design was founded in 1916 by Sherrill Whiton. The growth of the profession of interior decorating had spread beyond the personal practice of Elsie de Wolfe. Among the other women decorators who rose to prominence in the Teens were Elsie Cobb Wilson (see Figure 26), Nancy McClelland, Ruby Ross Goodnow Wood, and Mrs. Cushing in New York; Katherine Parker in Pittsburgh; Lee Porter of Wingate & Son in Boston; Mrs. Katy Tyson in Palm Beach and New York; and Mrs. Edgar de Wolfe, who in California traded on her sister-in-law's fame.

A number of other women decorators formed the Decorators Club of New York in 1914. At the end of the decade, the Decorators Club drew up incorporation papers and the club registered about a hundred members. Prominent early members were Mrs. Mary Linton Ackerman, Miss Mary Coggeshall, Mrs. Emmott Buel, and Mrs. Gertrude Gheen Robinson (the name of her firm was "Miss Gheen"), who had been an associate of Elsie de Wolfe in London.

Elsie Cobb Wilson   Elsie Cobb Wilson began practicing in New York City before World War I and decorated many houses in Palm Beach, in New York, and on Long Island. She continued working until 1936, when her firm was reorganized as Smyth, Urquhart & Marckwald. During those years she gave Eleanor McMillen Brown (see Chapter 4) her first job.

Nancy McClelland   In 1913 Nancy McClelland established the first known decorating department in a department store. Called Au Quatrième, it was opened at Wanamaker's department store in New York and offered advice on the purchase of interior furnishings as well as antique furniture—in the Teens and 1920s "decorating" meant "antiques." Nancy McClelland went on to become one of the most respected interior designers of the next four decades. She was known for formal interiors in correct period styles. Among her favorite styles were the eighteenth-century French periods; she was soon to add English Regency, Colonial, and Duncan Phyfe (see Figure 27).

Born in Poughkeepsie, New York, Nancy Vincent McClelland (1876–1959) graduated from Vassar College in 1897. She first worked with the Philadelphia Press for four years, then joined the advertising staff of Wanamaker's in Philadelphia from 1901 to 1907. For the next six years she lived in Paris, where she took courses in art history. Then she joined Wanamaker's New York store to create and direct Au Quatrième. It was an immediate success. She was to open her own firm in the 1920s.

Ruby Ross Wood   Elsie de Wolfe's assistant on her editorial projects, actually her ghostwriter for *The House in Good Taste,* was a young journalist named Ruby Ross Goodnow. After her marriage to Chalmers Wood in the 1920s, she became celebrated as Ruby Ross Wood. She was Elsie de Wolfe's first disciple—and her major competitor.

Ruby Ross Goodnow Wood, née Pope (1880–1950), was born in Monticello, Georgia. She first worked as a reporter for a Georgia newspaper, and then edited a farm journal for William Randolph Hearst. She contributed Sunday features to other newspapers, along with personality pieces for *The Delineator,* which was

26. Elsie Cobb Wilson. Living room. Long Island, New York. Circa 1914. *Photograph from Nancy McClelland*, The Practical Book of Decorative Wall Treatments (*Philadelphia: J. B. Lippincott, 1926*).

27. Nancy McClelland. Dining room, Iselin residence. New York. Circa 1914. *Photograph from Nancy McClelland*, The Practical Book of Decorative Wall Treatments (*Philadelphia: J. B. Lippincott, 1926*).

edited by Theodore Dreiser. In 1911 Dreiser chose her to write the articles that he was to publish by Elsie de Wolfe. The next year, Ruby Ross Goodnow contracted to write a second series of articles by Elsie de Wolfe for *Ladies' Home Journal*. She answered the voluminous mail that followed these publications and quickly learned about the de Wolfe style and approach. Soon she was interested enough to go into the decorating field herself.

In 1914 she wrote her own book, *The Honest House*, in collaboration with Rayne Adams. The book is more about the planning of houses and about lifestyle than about furnishing and decoration. Its chapters include "The Quest of the Ideal House," "Good Taste and Common Sense," and "A Plea for the Hearth." They indicate the direction of the time: "Ideal" here means historical romanticism; "common sense" indicates the sensible matter-of-factness of the day; and the hearth chapter shows the influence of Frank Lloyd Wright's work. "Suitability is the first and most important law of good taste," she wrote. Among other precepts offered were "absence of unnecessary ornament"; "finer, cleaner, and more beautiful"; and "honest white paint."

Included in *The Honest House* are descriptions and photographs of the house in Forest Hills Gardens, Long Island, where Ruby Ross Goodnow and her first husband then lived. She treated the hall, living room, and dining room (see Figure 28) as a single unit. Against deep-gray walls, she set a deep-orange velvet couch,

28. Ruby Ross Goodnow Wood. Living room, Goodnow House. Forest Hills Gardens, Long Island. Circa 1913. *Photograph from Ruby Ross Goodnow and Rayne Adams,* The Honest House *(New York: The Century Co., 1914).*

large pillows in the same orange velvet, and a small black-painted table; lighting fixtures were of pewter and creamy-white pottery, with an orange-colored shade. In the dining room, oak furniture waxed warm brown rested on a red and dark-blue rug; the curtains were natural linen. The furniture, a mixture of Jacobean and Cromwellian turned pieces, demonstrated the serious consideration of historical periods.

Her upstairs sitting room featured a figured wallpaper of peacocks "perched on flowery boughs" in soft tones of dull blues and greens and gray-mauves on a dark-gray ground. The woodwork was painted the blue-green of the peacock tails, and the ceiling was silver. She also chose curtains of blue, green, and silver Japanese chintz; the daybed cover of a deep sulphur-yellow velvet; and had a rug dyed black to set it all off. For her other bedrooms, she specified cream-color woodwork and ceilings, with Japanese figured papers. Her approach was in the mainstream direction of period rooms, with the inclusion of personal preferences for color, daylight, and freshness.

In 1914 she joined the staff of Wanamaker's in Philadelphia. In 1918 she was asked to direct Au Quatrième at the New York store.

Frances Elkins   In 1918 Frances Elkins, sister of the Chicago residential architect David Adler, bought an 1824 adobe house in Monterey, California. She made the house, Casa Amesti, one of the showplaces of the state, and it began her professional career. Frances Elkins has been called one of the most creative of American decorators.

Born in Milwaukee, Wisconsin, Frances Adler Elkins (1888–1953) traveled in Europe while her brother was at the Ecole des Beaux-Arts in Paris. She studied in France, Italy, and Switzerland. By 1918 she had married socialite Felton Elkins, had bought Casa Amesti, one of the most important adobe buildings in California (now occupied by the Old Capital Club), and had had an early divorce. It was often said of these first-generation women decorators that a woman either had a happy marriage or was a decorator.

Frances Elkins's choice of an adobe house was inspired, perhaps, by the recent San Diego Exposition, which popularized Spanish Colonial architecture; certainly her choice was part of the national romanticism and search for an American tradition that occurred in the Teens. Her decorating transformed the house: She added antique English and French furniture and Chinese appointments (see Figure 29). During the decoration of Casa Amesti over the next several years, friends began asking Frances Elkins to share her decorating talents. She went on to become a prominent California traditional designer for the next two decades, and also designed interiors throughout the country.

"The ladies," as this first generation of American decorators came to be called, brought discipline and order along with style and taste to the upper-middle-class home as well as to the less rich. They continued the academic historical revival of recreating complete period rooms seriously, if somewhat inaccurately according to later scholarship and taste. In this they were passionate, if somewhat primitive. Innovation was restricted to upholstery and drapery patterns and colors, to overall color schemes, and to the discovery of interesting pieces of antique furniture.

Frank Lloyd Wright

Amid all this traditionalism the work of Frank Lloyd Wright continued to be anti-historical, innovative, and consistent. During the Teens Wright's practice expanded nationally and internationally—to California and Florida, to Canada and Japan. His commissions grew from middle-class mansions to include public and semi-

29. Frances Elkins. Casa
Amesti. Monterey, Calfornia.
1918–24. *Photograph © Fred
Lyon, 1983.*

30. Frank Lloyd Wright.
Taliesen. Spring Green, Wiscon-
sin. 1911. *Photograph © Ezra
Stoller/ESTO, 19455.*

public buildings of large size. But at home his pioneering example and his twenty-
year-old style were generally disregarded and overlooked.

In 1911 Wright began work on his own house outside Spring Green, Wisconsin. Called Taliesin, the house was designed as a residence, a studio, a farm, and
eventually as a school for his apprentices. Sited around the crest of a knoll, Taliesin

both encompasses and is dug into the rise of the land; it produces an interior courtyard and embraces the landscape. Loggias and carports help to merge the massing with the site. Floating flat roofs are intermixed with low, hovering, pyramidal gables that seem to echo the lines of the terrain. Inside, there is rusticity as well as simplicity (see Figure 30). Plain-lined built-in furnishings include drawers and bookcases, lattices and grilles, wood banding and long horizontal shelves. The latter were enriched by oriental porcelains and screens, by plants and fur throws.

Wright's house for the Francis W. Littles, at Lake Minnetonka near Wayzata, Minnesota, was designed in 1912 and begun the following year. It was not completed until after Wright's return from Japan in the early 1920s, and the design was complicated by the demands of the clients. The design is pavilion-like, constructed of traditional brick masonry, and is long, horizontal, and large. Henry-Russell Hitchcock considered the living room to be "the most spacious domestic interior Wright had ever designed"[2] up to that time. It is 49 feet 9 1/2 inches long, and symmetrically designed with 40-foot runs of windows on each side. By the time of the Little House in Wayzata, Wright had achieved the chief qualities that identify his work, as historian Edgar Kaufmann, Jr., has summarized: "the command of space as an individualized portion of a continuous whole; a rare skill in asymmetric composition; a sensitivity to materials; miscellaneous requirements of use harmonized in masterful unity in key with the environment." As an example of these qualities, Kaufmann considers the Little House living room, as it has been reconstructed in the Metropolitan Museum as "basically presentable, with a Wrightian aura, not brilliant but clear"[3] (see Figures 31A and B).

Midway Gardens In 1914 Wright completed his monumental and lavishly decorated Midway Gardens project on Chicago's South Side. Midway Gardens was conceived by the client as an open-air restaurant along the model of the beergardens in Europe. Designed as a quadrangle, with a taller wing enclosing the Winter Garden restaurant at the entry side, the open central area was flanked by raised and covered "terraces" for dining on each side; each terrace was open to and faced a covered bandshell on the far side of the table-filled quadrangle (see Figures 32A and B).

Midway Gardens did not attract the anticipated following, and subsequently declined. It succumbed to the anti-German sentiment during World War I, was eventually closed by Prohibition, and, regrettably for us today, was demolished in 1929. Of all Wright's public buildings, we may most miss this example of his artistic genius at its prime. It had an atmosphere of festivity, joyousness, and ebullience that was generally lacking in the honest, foursquare work of the Arts and Crafts movement. At Midway Gardens there was an openness that was a breath of fresh air; the architectural elements gave a sense of floating, flying wings. From the cantilevered entry marquees upward through the stepped horizontals of the ascending roof planes to the open-work rectangles—which were extended finials reaching skyward—there was an Isadora Duncan-like exultation of the healthy, happy, and full life—the life that Wright saw as integral and organic with architecture.

As Henry-Russell Hitchcock has written,

> Nowhere was interior and exterior space more elaborately interwoven and freely composed, while the ornamental effects are of endless variety and novelty. . . . Sculpture and wall paintings designed by Wright parallel the most advanced forms of European painters, barely known at this time in America through the Armory Show. And the open frames of the tower tops, a sort of linear sculpture of space, reach forward to aesthetic concepts hardly imagined abroad at this date.[4]

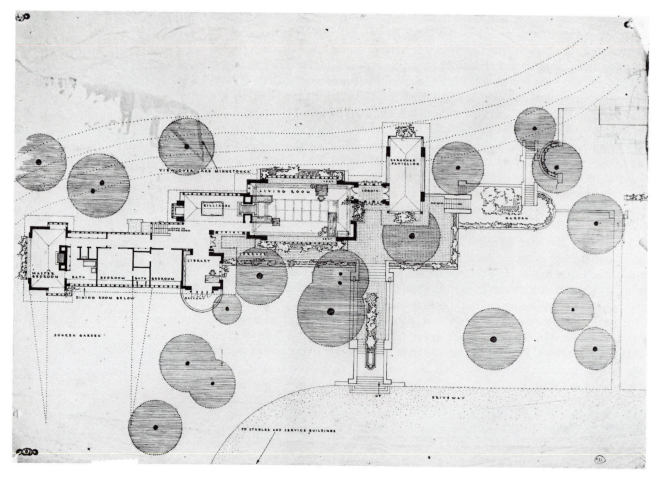

31A. Frank Lloyd Wright. Plan Francis Little House. Lake Minnetonka, Minnesota. 1913–22. *Illustration © Frank Lloyd Wright Foundation, 1942.*

31B. Frank Lloyd Wright. Living room, Francis Little House. 1913–22. As installed at the Metropolitan Museum of Art. *Photograph from The Metropolitan Museum of Art, New York City.*

32A. Frank Lloyd Wright. Midway Gardens. Chicago, Illinois. 1913. *Photograph courtesy Frank Lloyd Wright Foundation.*

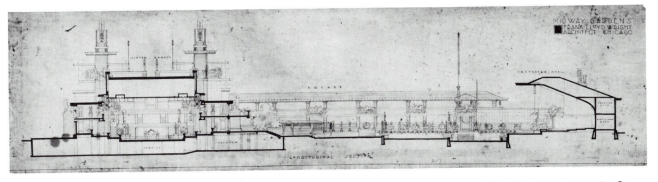

32B. Frank Lloyd Wright. Section, Midway Gardens. Chicago, Illinois. 1913. *Illustration © Frank Lloyd Wright Foundation, 1957.*

Inside the enclosed Winter Garden restaurant, balconies surrounded a tall central space (see Figure 33). In his customary manner, Wright juxtaposed the tall space with low-ceilinged spaces. Wright, himself 5 feet 8 1/2 inches tall, preferred low spaces (6 feet 4 inches to 7 feet 2 inches) and tall ones, but did not like medium-height spaces (8 feet 6 inches to 10 feet).

Wright took the opportunity to design a full range of furniture and appointments for Midway Gardens, some of which, such as the table lamps, were produced. He drew up metal-wire furniture (based on the ever-present soda-fountain wire chair); lighting; table appointments (including ceramic dinnerware); as well as murals, art glass windows, and sculptures. The sculptures were a joint effort by Wright and sculptors Alfonso Iannelli and Richard Bock.

The Imperial Hotel The decade was as divided for Frank Lloyd Wright personally as it was for the political world, with its juxtaposition of peace and war. In 1914 Wright suffered a tragedy when a houseman went berserk and killed seven

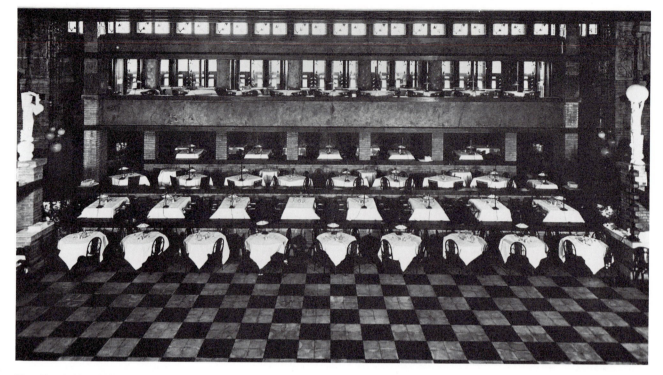

33. Frank Lloyd Wright. Winter Garden restaurant, Midway Gardens. Chicago, Illinois. 1913. *Photograph from Thomas A. Heinz.*

members of his household and burned Taliesin to the ground. So it was a godsend that his fame had already brought him the commission to design the Imperial Hotel in Tokyo. For the next six years, until the hotel was completed, Wright worked primarily in Japan.

Long interested in the art and design of Japan, Wright had first visited Japan in 1905 and was an avid collector of Japanese prints. He greatly admired the traditional Japanese house. Now he was called to take his synthesis of that simplified style back to Japan.

The Imperial Hotel scheme was an enlarged development of Midway Gardens and had lavishly scaled and lavishly ornamented public spaces (see Figure 34) and spare, simple guest rooms, which were "Zen-inspired," as Edgar Kaufmann, Jr., has written.[5] For the Imperial Hotel, Wright designed a full range of ornamental windows and sculpture and completely new furniture, lighting fixtures, carpeting, and dinnerware.

Wright's technical genius (in collaboration with Paul Mueller, who had been an engineer in Adler & Sullivan's office) devised a structural system that floated the hotel on multiple-pile foundations, and provided new plumbing and heating safeguards, as well as reflecting pools in the courtyards that additionally served as water supply for firefighting. The results brought the architect worldwide acclaim when the hotel survived the serious earthquake of 1923. (That acclaim did not rescue the hotel, however—it was demolished by the wrecker's ball in 1963.) The solidity of this earthquake-proof structure contrasted with the vast public spaces—restaurants, theater, ballroom, and private-function rooms—which were enlivened by carved and painted decorations, lighting columns, and patterned carpeting that reinforced the overall integrity. It was a total work of art.

European Design: The Case For and Against the Machine

In Europe, architecture took new impetus from Frank Lloyd Wright's work. The 1910 and 1911 Wasmuth publications of his plans and photographs and his lecture "The Art and Craft of the Machine" influenced the next generation of modern pioneers.

At the same time, several new and revolutionary art movements and design-related developments arose. They became the ultimate catalysts for the development of Modern design. The art movements focused on Cubism and Futurism in Paris. The design developments focused on the founding in Germany of the Deutscher Werkbund and the continuing development of Expressionism through groups like Die Bruecke and Der Blaue Reiter. At the end of the decade the Dutch school of De Stijl served as the catalyst to meld these directions together into the Modern idiom that was to follow. Together they led to an abstractionist architecture and design movement.

The "moral integrity" of the nineteenth-century reform movement had established the concepts of honesty of construction, honesty to materials, and simplicity. Honesty of construction meant honesty of production; in reform terms, that meant handcraft. Soon to be resolved was the case for and against the machine—versus handcraft—which continued to seesaw along with the conflict between ornamentation versus stripped functionalism. In the second decade of the twentieth century, honesty of production came to mean accepting machine production; honesty

34. Frank Lloyd Wright. Lobby, Imperial Hotel. Tokyo, Japan, 1914–22. *Photograph from Thomas A. Heinz.*

to "our own time" was adapted to mean the materials of the day—metal and glass—and no-nonsense directness.

Modern design was born in this second decade of the twentieth century. Developed first in Germany and given final synthesis by De Stijl in the Netherlands, the Modern movement was based on the final acceptance, indeed total endorsement and celebration of the machine—not only for production, but also as the aesthetic idiom and visual ideal.

Cubism and Abstraction

Around 1910, in the fine arts of painting and sculpture, a direction toward increasing abstraction was leading to Cubism, which indirectly influenced the case for the machine. That acceptance was made possible by abstraction, which was developed by the Cubists.

In 1907 Pablo Picasso and Georges Braque simultaneously yet independently began investigations that led to Cubism. They were inspired by a Paris retrospective exhibition of the work of Paul Cézanne, who had died the year before, and who had explored the breaking up of the landscape and the painterly field into rectangular segments. Cézanne had said that natural objects can be reduced to the forms of the cylinder, the sphere, and the cone. Separately, Picasso and Braque recognized that they had been similarly investigating the imposition onto nature of systems of analytically derived geometric forms. Picasso's seminal painting *Les Demoiselles d'Avignon* (1907) is considered the beginning of Cubism and therefore the first Modern painting. It demonstrates a play of flat planes and angles that depict human figures conceived in terms of African primitive art. This was one step away from natural representation and toward abstraction.

The decisive year was 1911, when Picasso painted his *Portrait of D. H. Kahnweiler* and Braque painted *Les Portugais*. In these two works the detachment from representation, through the dissolution or decomposition of the representational forms, is complete. This is the development by Cubism of semirepresentation. Later painters carried this further into totally nonrepresentational abstraction.

Abstraction, then, is the drawing out or separating of one thing from another, whether by physical or mental distillation. Abstract painting concerns itself with detaching, breaking up, and fragmenting its natural or physical subject matter into an analyzed pattern of rather more geometric shapes. Or, seen another way, it is the separating out of an analyzed or distilled geometric pattern from its basic physical subject matter. In either case, abstract artists reject the basic value of traditional representation. Natural appearances are merely the theme on which they work their variations. Their invention is concentrated on the arrangement of patterns, shapes, textures, and colors. Modern designers and architects developed this as overall surfaces and volumes composed of rectangles and squares.

From 1907 to 1914 in Paris, Cubism was developed by Picasso, Braque, and Juan Gris. By 1912 Gris was experimenting with structural grids in his paintings. These were later to become keystones of Modern design. Also in 1912 the Cubists began to experiment with collage—the tearing or cutting of pieces of paper—and, more important to Modern design, the assembly of these pre-torn (prefabricated) elements into a composition.

In sculpture the Cubists developed volumes with voids or open holes in the surface, which suggested the interpenetration of several planes and the existence of other sides and surfaces not in view. For the Cubist concept of space was an interplay between plane and depth. The Cubists therefore investigated sculptural forms that were overlapping, interlocking, and interpenetrating. At this time, physicists such as Albert Einstein were formulating new concepts of space-time and of relativity. The Cubist aesthetic correspondence—multiple focus or multiple visual viewpoints—suggested seeing from many points of view rather than entirely from a single viewpoint, in order to express the total image. This juxtaposition of fragments presented a vision, first, of discontinuity and, second, of simultaneity. These became the fundamental goals of the Modern precept of space.

There were no direct connections between the pioneer Cubist artists and the contemporaneous vanguard ideas in architecture; however, this general cultural movement toward abstraction corresponded with current developments in design and architecture. In addition, the combination of Cubism with other art movements of the day had direct influence on Modern design in the 1920s. Among those other movements were Futurism (see below) and the work of the Russian abstractionists—the Suprematism of Kasimir Malevich (1878–1935) and the Constructivism of Vladimir Tatlin (1885–1953). All these movements were coalesced by the De Stijl movement in the Netherlands (see below). Later Modern architecture incorporated into its structure the Cubists' simultaneous experience of outer and inner space.

During the early Teens Marcel Duchamp began to exhibit his "ready-made" artworks, which were prefabricated machine-made artifacts. His seminal *Coffee Mill* (1912) was followed by *Bicycle Wheel and Kitchen Stool* (1913). Both were constructed of items previously produced by machine fabrication and intended for everyday utilitarian activities. Duchamp's ready-made *Fountain* of 1915—a urinal—so scandalized people that they failed to see the aesthetic advance made by declaring that a machine-made object had aesthetic value.

The new Cubist vision, then, first presented this method of seeing the world as detached from nature, as fragmentary and geometric. Cubism thereby prepared the way for the Modern aesthetic system of prefabricated geometric elements assembled into patterns of flat planes. In so doing, Cubism also prepared the way for the acceptance of an abstraction from the human spirit, from the human hand, toward an endorsement of the anonymity and homogeneity of the machine.

Futurism

Simultaneously with Cubism, from 1909 to 1914, a movement toward Futurism in art was promulgated in Milan, Paris, London, and elsewhere in Europe by the poet and dramatist Filippo Tommaso Marinetti and others. The Milan exhibition of the "Città Nuova" (New City) by Antonio Sant'Elia and Mario Chiattone was followed by the "Manifesto dell'Architettura Futurista" (Futurist Manifesto), written by Sant'Elia, Marinetti, painter Umberto Boccioni, and others. The manifesto aimed to change the world, proclaiming that "everything must be revolutionized. Architecture is breaking loose from tradition. It is forcibly starting from scratch again." Marinetti declared that Venice should be taken down and paved over, started over.

Extreme as this wholesale acclamation of the new was, the Futurists dealt the deathblow to traditionalism and historicism in vanguard art. The Futurist manifesto acclaimed "what is light, practical, ephemeral, and swift"—ocean liners, trains, airplanes, zeppelins, and, above all, electric light. These were to be the preferences of Modern designers for the next half century. In painting, Futurist Boccioni showed a plasticity and an interpenetrating quality in his fragmentation that gave a sense of motion unforeseen by his Cubist contemporaries. In this space-time demonstration, Boccioni's paintings directly influenced Duchamp and all of Modern design.

The Futurist movement, however, was largely a verbal and pictorial activity. No Futurist buildings were built, and no interior schemes are known. But the Futurist drawings of Sant'Elia around 1912 to 1914 inspired the vision of city planners, architects, and those concerned with Modernism for the next several generations.

Americans were introduced to the new movements in European art at the 1913 Armory Show in New York City, and later in Chicago. The sensation of the show was Marcel Duchamp's *Nude Descending a Staircase*—not because it showed a nude figure, but because it was a revelation of the Cubist-Futurist depiction of motion. At this time, American interest in Modern art began.

The Deutscher Werkbund

In design, contemporaneously with these art movements, the Deutscher Werkbund was founded in 1907 at Dresden by critic and educator Hermann Muthesius, among others.[6] Most of the major German architects and designers were members, including Peter Behrens, Richard Riemerschmid, and Walter Gropius. The aims of the Werkbund, as set forth by Muthesius, were to unite creative designers and industrial production into what today we would call an industrial design society. Designers of both handcraft and machine production were brought together, and as a group they were brought to the attention of industry and commerce. In that same year Peter Behrens began his work for the electrical corporation AEG; Bruno Taut also began to work for industry; and Bruno Paul began developing a line of furniture for mass production. Richard Riemerschmid had pioneered in developing lines of furniture for mass production even earlier.[7]

Muthesius aspired to the creation of a contemporary style. In endorsing machine production he was both renouncing Art Nouveau and going beyond the contributions of the Arts and Crafts movement to unite excellence of workmanship in modern materials with the machine. Whereas the Wiener Werkstaette had hesitatingly admitted, "We . . . are aware that, under certain circumstances, an acceptable article can be made by mechanical means, provided that it bears the stamp of manufacture," they had added, "but it is not our purpose to pursue that aspect yet."[8] The Deutscher Werkbund, going further, explicitly aimed to integrate the machine style with the ideals of Arts and Crafts. It was a major step in the development of the Modern movement.

The next year, 1908, in Vienna, Adolf Loos proclaimed that "Ornament is a crime." He was reiterating what was then a sixty-year-old argument against dishonest machine ornamentation, but his slogan was taken up as a battle cry for the acceptance of the machine. Fundamental to the outlook of the German and Austrian designers of the decade was the spirit of directness, straightforwardness, or matter-of-factness *(Sachlichkeit)*, which gave birth to an art movement by that name. It has correspondence in Adolf Loos's Steiner House in Vienna (1910), with its plain and stripped garden façade, which has been so much admired by Modernists; perhaps more telling is the less-publicized arched-roof street elevation, which is a matter-of-fact solution to a zoning requirement for building height.

In 1911 and 1912 U.S. museums mounted an exhibition on the Deutscher Werkbund. It began the American public's recognition of Werkbund goals and accomplishments.

Expressionism

Many of the members of the Deutscher Werkbund were adherents of the fundamental twentieth-century design idiom based on rational, structural principles—principles derived from logical or rational construction techniques, and therefore based on the structural grid. Their forms were most often crystalline. Others of the group were more individualistic, however, aiming for what was called, at the time, "untramelled artistic creation." Their designs appeared personal and capricious, tending either to fluid, free-form, organic forms or to irregular crystalline configurations. In this latter group, known first by the self-explanatory term "The Individualists," were some of the most inventive designers of their day: Max Berg, Hans Poelzig, Bruno Taut, and others. The post–World War I work of Erich Mendelsohn was in this idiom, especially his dynamic drawings of 1914–17 and his subsequent Einstein Tower in Potsdam (1919–21). Underlying all their work was a search for a spiritual and social utopia; this search pervaded the work of the immediate World War I period.

The term Expressionism was first applied to the work of painters during this time—Emil Nolde, Oskar Kokoschka, and James Ensor—who exaggerated their forms, distorted their outlines, and applied strong colors, with the goal of expressing the moods and sensations of the mind, the imagination, and the subconscious. They were responding to Sigmund Freud's formulation of psychoanalysis and to his writings of the previous decade. Expressionist painters aimed to reveal this world of emotion, its hidden drives and mysterious motivations underlying human behavior. No such goals were contemplated by the architects and designers of interiors of the time, yet Expressionist has become the term by which the Individualist German designers are known.

Of the interiors designed in this context, Max Berg's Jahrhundertshalle in Breslau (1913)—a giant dome of reinforced concrete—was an isolated work of genius that prefigured the work of Pier Luigi Nervi in the 1950s. Hans Poelzig's Grosses Schauspielhaus in Berlin (1919) showed a Modern direction that movie house interiors could have gone.

The Birth of Modern Design

From the other school of Werkbund designers—those who followed Rationalist structural principles in composing their rectilinear designs—came what is justifiably considered the first Modern building: the Fagus Factory at Alfeld, Germany, completed in 1913 by Walter Gropius and Adolf Meyer. This was the first time a building's façade was conceived in glass, according to architecture historian Nikolaus Pevsner.[9] The south elevation is composed of glass curtain wall set between brick-faced piers, and thereby achieves the complete interpenetration of a multistory interior and exterior, the first entirely unhistorical and antitraditional use of the Modernists' materials—metal and glass—and the first use of the machine aesthetic that was to prevail for the next six decades.

The next year, 1914, at the Cologne Exhibition, Gropius and Meyer built their celebrated Werkbund Pavilion, with its glass-enclosed helical corner stair towers and wraparound glass corridor. On the other elevations the pavilion owed a great deal to the pavilion schemes and formal symmetry of Frank Lloyd Wright. But the use of glass and metal was a pioneering achievement.

Bruno Taut's Glass Industry Pavilion also opened in Cologne at the same exhibition (see Figure 35). It is a far more individualistic or expressionistic composition, having a sixteen-sided lower level, in which stairs have glass treads and risers ascending between walls of glass bricks; but the upper level is a remarkable pointed lattice or faceted dome of metal and colored-glass panels. In that year novelist Paul Scheebart's *Glasarchitektur* advocated a Futurist time when whole walls of colored glass would liberate and enhance our environments. Bruno Taut achieved that romantic image in this primary example of the emerging ideas of Expressionism. In 1917 a glass curtain-wall façade was designed by architect Willis Polk for the Halliday Building in San Francisco.

35. Bruno Taut. Glass Industry Pavilion. Cologne, Germany. 1914. *Photographs courtesy Parsons School of Design, New York City.*

With these structures the Modern style had been achieved. As a sign of the times Peter Behrens, in 1914, designed the cover of a book entitled *Arte für Alles— Art for All.* The ideological inference was inescapable: On the way was good design for everyone, art for the masses—everything for everyman. William Morris had proffered that art is valuable only "if all can share it." Mass production was the only way to make this possible; therefore machine art for the masses would be the goal from then onward. The pioneering mass production by Gutenberg had been extended to architectural design and construction. The Modern movement not only accepted the machine for the potentials of its production and distribution, but also celebrated it by adopting the machine as its visual vocabulary and idiom. So it was that the machine and factory aesthetic of the Modern movement developed.

The Impact of World War I

From the time the decade was divided by World War I (1914–18), this design progress was interrupted. Wartime depression was pervasive in most fields, with the exception of technological development. American troops entered the action in November 1917. Millions died in the trenches; flu epidemics added thousands to those numbers. In 1917 the October Revolution in Russia and the abduction of the Czar's family dramatically demonstrated the people's revolution. T. S. Eliot elegized the malaise and pervasive depression in his poem "The Love Song of J. Alfred Prufrock."

World War I was a dividing line between the old world and the new—between the old world of aristocracy and handcraft and the new world of democracy and the machine. Then the people's revolution had made a common group of humankind—a community of democracy or socialism. Whether in the emerging Modern movement or in the growing field of decorating, more and more people were to find good design available to them. Then, nineteenth-century life ended, and the modern world was irrevocably predominant.

De Stijl

Only one European country that had taken part in the development of Modern design remained neutral during World War I—the Netherlands. There, during the war, architects and designers continued to advance design and design theory. In 1917 Theo Van Doesburg began publication of the magazine *De Stijl*. Piet Mondrian, the painter, and architect-furniture designer Gerrit Rietveld were among the group endorsing Van Doesburg's ideas.

De Stijl, both the magazine and the movement, realized the ideas of the prewar years. Among them were the extreme and pure abstraction of Piet Mondrian, whose rectangular grids and primary colors provided the ultimate refinement of the model for Modernism. Gerrit Rietveld's Red and Blue Chair (1918[10]) was another De Stijl paradigm of Modernism (see Figure 36). Rietveld's Schröder House (1924) in Utrecht later provided De Stijl's major interior design (see Chapter 4). In espousing abstraction, Rational rectangular construction, and machine production, the De Stijl group coalesced all the strains that had been leading toward the Modern movement, gave them focus and refinement, and fixed the path of design for the next decade.

36. Gerrit Rietveld. Red and Blue Chair. 1918. *Photograph from The Museum of Modern Art, New York City.*

World War I ended in 1918. That year, a new design direction in favor of lightness and purism was announced: Le Corbusier and Amédée Ozenfant wrote their manifesto on Purism, "Après le Cubisme," which was given a limited circulation (see the discussion in Chapter 4). In 1919 the sculptor Constantin Brancusi created his soaring bronze *Bird in Space*, which was to become a symbol of lightness and flight in the years to come.

Also in 1919, Walter Gropius was confirmed as the director of the Bauhaus, in Weimar, where he was to establish the design school that subsequently directed the way of the Modern movement in architecture, interior, product, and graphic design. That same year, Mies van der Rohe produced his first scheme for an all-glass-and-metal curtain-wall apartment building. These end-of-decade events were to shape interiors for the next five decades.

Orientalism: The Ballet Style

Modernism was by no means pervasive or popularized in Europe during the Teens. Instead, the oriental style popularized by the Diaghilev ballet and the stage settings of Leon Bakst were the rage. In 1911 fashion designer Paul Poiret opened his decorating firm Maison Martine based on this style. Furniture became lower and smaller—deeper seating pieces, small dining chairs, low beds—and built-in cupboards came into use. The oriental style also featured textiles with elaborate patterns and vivid colors, cushions with long silk tassels, and other elements of Scheherazade imagery. This was to remain the fashionable style for interiors in France through the first half of the 1920s.

Suggested Reading

Banham, Reyner. *Theory and Design in the First Machine Age.* Cambridge: MIT Press, 1960, 1981.

Barr, Alfred H., Jr. *Cubism and Abstract Art.* New York: The Museum of Modern Art, 1936.

de Wolfe, Elsie. *The House in Good Taste.* New York: The Century Co., 1913.

Giedion, Sigfried. *Mechanization Takes Command.* Oxford: Oxford University Press, 1948. New York: W. W. Norton, 1975.

Goodnow, Ruby Ross, and Rayne Adams. *The Honest House.* New York: The Century Co., 1914.

Hanks, David A. *The Decorative Designs of Frank Lloyd Wright.* New York: E. P. Dutton, 1979.

Hitchcock, Henry-Russell. *In the Nature of Materials: The Buildings of Frank Lloyd Wright, 1887–1941.* New York: Da Capo Press, 1973.

———. *Architecture in the Nineteenth and Twentieth Centuries.* Baltimore: Penguin Books, 1958–82 (especially "Wright and His California Contemporaries").

Jaffe, Hans L. C., et al. *De Stijl: Visions of Utopia,* ed. Mildred Friedman. New York: Abbeville Press, 1982.

Jeanneret, Charles-Edouard. *Le Corbusier: 1910–65.* Zurich: Les Editions d'Architecture Zurich, 1967.

Kaufmann, Edgar, Jr. "Interior Design: Architecture or Decoration?" *Progressive Architecture.* October 1962, pp. 141–44.

McCoy, Esther. *Five California Architects.* New York: Reinhold, 1960. (Paperback New York: Frederick A. Praeger, 1975.)

Pratt, Richard. *David Adler: The Architect and His Work.* New York: M. Evans & Company, 1970.

Sharp, Dennis. *Modern Architecture and Expressionism.* New York: Braziller, 1966.

Smith, Jane S. *Elsie de Wolfe.* New York: Atheneum, 1982.

Notes

1. Although vanguard designers began to leave the Arts and Crafts movement behind by mid-decade, all across the country for the next two decades furniture and interiors continued to be designed and produced in the Arts and Crafts tradition.

2. Henry-Russell Hitchcock, *In the Nature of Materials: The Buildings of Frank Lloyd Wright, 1887–1941* (New York: Da Capo Press, 1973), caption to Figure 200.

3. Edgar Kaufmann, Jr., "Wright at the Met," *Skyline*, The Architecture and Design Review, New York (January 1983), p. 25.

4. Hitchcock, op. cit., caption to Figure 192.

5. Edgar Kaufmann, Jr., "Frank Lloyd Wright," *Macmillan Encyclopedia of Architects* (New York: The Free Press, a division of Macmillan Publishing Company and Collier Macmillan Publishing, 1982), p. 439.

6. Muthesius, although director and most prominent, was not alone in founding the Deutscher Werkbund. See Joan Campbell, *The German Werkbund: The Politics of Reform in the Applied Arts* (Princeton: Princeton University Press, 1977).

7. The 1899 chair designed by Richard Riemerschmid has become one of the pioneering classics of Modernism.

8. Work Program of the Wiener Werkstaette, quoted from *Vienna Moderne: 1898–1918*, exhibition catalogue (University of Houston: Sarah Campbell Blaffer Gallery; New York: Cooper-Hewitt Museum, 1978), p. 89. Reprinted there with permission from *Architecture and Design: An International Anthology of Original Articles*, ed. Timothy and Charlotte Benton, with Dennis Sharp (London: Granada Publishing, Ltd., 1975).

9. Nikolaus Pevsner, *Pioneers of Modern Design*. New York: The Museum of Modern Art, 1949), p. 131.

10. There is some disagreement about the date of Rietveld's Red and Blue Chair: Some say 1917–19; Wilk gives 1917–18. See Christopher Wilk, *Marcel Breuer: Furniture and Interiors* (New York: The Museum of Modern Art, 1981).

Chapter 4

1920–1930:
The First Generation

If the Teens presented a dilemma for American interior designers—a choice between America and Europe—the 1920s presented the more specific option of choosing between the design idioms of Art Deco classicism and the new Modernism of the machine. Modern design was being promulgated in Germany by the Bauhaus and in France by Le Corbusier and several of his contemporaries. Art Deco was popularly demonstrated in Paris by the Exposition Internationale des Arts Décoratifs et Industriels Modernes. In America's mainstream design, Art Deco first took the lead. For America's vanguard designers, the new Modernism was only beginning to be the revered ideal.

In the 1920s the American interior design profession began to grow in numbers of practitioners and of marketable outlets. Many of the traditional residential designers who were to become the luminaries of the profession for the next forty to fifty years arrived on the scene at this time. Later in the decade the profession of industrial design began in the United States. That is, designers for industry began to win significant commissions, and they identified themselves as an independent profession. Soon they were to develop their own style. But at the beginning of the decade, despite all these contributors to American interior design, the lead of Frank Lloyd Wright was forgotten and Europe was again the undisputed mentor.

Paris was the undisputed magnetic center of art and style to which Americans flocked for inspiration. There, during the 1920s, settled a host of expatriate artists and writers—Gertrude Stein, F. Scott Fitzgerald, Ernest Hemingway, and others. Josephine Baker's appearances at the Folies Bergère personified the popular interest in Africa and primitive art. Women of style, like Elsie de Wolfe, still sailed to Paris for their clothes.

Art Deco from France

In the summer of 1925 the Exposition Internationale des Arts Décoratifs et Indus-triels Modernes opened in Paris. It is sometimes believed by students that Art Deco was a style initiated at the 1925 Paris exhibition. But, as the analogy with anthologies previously mentioned in relation to the Great Exhibition at the Crystal Palace in 1851 clearly indicates, a style must already exist in order to be exhibited in many examples. Like other exhibitions the 1925 display was a summation of French design of the past fifteen years, allowing for the interruption of World War I. (The exhibition had, in fact, originally been planned for 1914.)

As much as the word "industry" in the title of the 1925 exposition may have signified the machine, greater prominence was given to handcrafted decorative arts. Art Deco as a style was in the French tradition of Art Nouveau, but it was less tortuous, more geometric, and in lower relief.

The sources of Art Deco included the art movements of the preceding years— Fauvism, Cubism, Futurism, and Expressionism. Art Deco adopted the wild, hot colors of the Fauve painters (dubbed "wild beasts" for their bold use of color) of 1905 and after. Following the success of Leon Bakst's designs for the Ballets Russes of Diaghilev in 1909, French style had been influenced by oriental and Russian traditions (see Figure 37).

37. Maison Martine (Paul Poiret). Bedroom. Paris, France. 1924. *Photograph from* Art et Décoration (*February 1924*).

In the 1920s Art Deco was updated. It transformed the classical vocabulary of forms and symbols derived from the classical education at the Ecole des Beaux-Arts. Art Deco motifs, therefore, were drawn from classical, or at least ancient, civilizations—sometimes combining ancient Egyptian, archaic Greek, and Mayan Mexican elements in a romantic, if anachronistic, synthesis. The tomb of Tutankhamen was opened in 1922; and its treasures were inspirational images to designers for at least the next fifteen years. From that inspiration developed the late–Art Deco classicism that combined Egyptian and Greek motifs—notably highly stylized figures in bas relief, dancing maidens holding amphoras, urns, and swags of drapery.

Other Art Deco motifs, often in gilt stucco, included conventionalized garlands and baskets of flowers—often derived from the Mackintosh rose—octagonal panels, elongated ovals, bold lines, fountains, and other Neoclassical motifs. Geometric patterns figured largely in late–Art Deco design—sunbursts, lightning bolts, electrical currents, and radio waves, which were both popularized machine-age imagery and "toned down" Cubism. It was a tentative French approach to making a modern style in the 1920s.

Metal and glass were fundamental to the Art Deco vocabulary. Exotic woods such as macassar ebony, amboyna, amaranth, rosewood, olivewood, lemonwood, and zebrawood were inlaid with ivory, amethyst, and mother-of-pearl. Furniture was elaborately lacquered or covered in snakeskin, shagreen (sharkskin), tortoiseshell, or leather. Mirror, glass, and chrome were sanded and etched in patterns. Wrought iron and aluminum were worked by highly creative metal artisans. Colors during the 1920s became lighter.

The leading interior designers of Art Deco were French. They included Emile-Jacques Ruhlmann, André Groult, Paul Iribe, Louis Sue, and André Mare, who had previously worked in the Art Nouveau idiom. Also among the highest achievements of Art Deco in France were the glass of René Lalique and Daum, the silver of Jean Puiforcat, the clothes of Paul Poiret, and the costume designs of Erté.

38. Emile-Jacques Ruhlmann. Desk, chair, and file cabinet of amboyna wood and ivory. 1918–19. *Photograph from The Metropolitan Museum of Art, New York City, Bequest of Collis P. Huntington, 1973.*

Other major French achievements of the period include the metal-and-lacquer work of Jean Dunand, the metal work of Edgar Brandt, the sculpture of Armand-Albert Rateau, and the fabrics of Sonia Delaunay. With them, but never achieving wide recognition until rediscovered in later decades, were Pierre Legrain, who was inspired by African primitive art, as the Cubists had been; and Eileen Gray, an English designer working in Paris with luxurious lacquers.

Emile-Jacques Ruhlmann

Emile-Jacques Ruhlmann (1869–1933), born in Paris, was the premier furniture designer of his day, and he also created complete interiors. His work was among the best at the 1925 exposition—a combination of refined design, luxurious and rare materials, and exquisite craftsmanship. Applied to delicately formed pieces of furniture were precious veneers inlaid with ivory, coral, shagreen, or the finest leather (see Figure 38). From 1919 to 1933 he worked only for the wealthy, because he wanted to design only the most precious and elegant furniture. His highest achievements were in the best traditions of the French cabinetmakers of the eighteenth century.

The Bauhaus: 1919–1933

In 1919 the Bauhaus school of design had opened in Weimar, Germany, under the direction of Walter Gropius (1883–1969). He had combined two previous schools—the Grand-Ducal Saxon Academy of Pictorial Art and the Grand-Ducal Saxon School of Arts and Crafts—to achieve a union and an equality of the fine and applied arts. It was a realization of the goal of the Arts and Crafts movement and of the Wiener Werkstaette.

The program of the Bauhaus in April 1919 stated: "The Bauhaus strives to bring together all creative effort into one whole, to reunify all the disciplines of practical art—sculpture, painting, handicrafts, and the crafts—as inseparable components of a new architecture. The ultimate, if distant, aim of the Bauhaus is the unified work of art—the great structure—in which there is no distinction between monumental and decorative art."[1] In this Bauhaus aim, the turn-of-the-century objective of putting the decorative arts and crafts on an equal footing with the fine arts and the ultimate goal of the *Gesamtkunstwerk*—the total, integral, consistent design—became an official educational program. Bauhaus education was to influence designers for the next sixty-five years.

However, the fundamental belief of Walter Gropius, expressed in the first sentence of the Bauhaus program, was that "The ultimate aim of all visual arts is the complete building!" Despite the statement in the same Bauhaus program that there would be no distinctions between the structural or monumental and the decorative arts, this attitude that architecture was queen over all the other arts was to persist. This hierarchy of the arts also led to the separation of the other arts from architecture and widened the rift between architectural design and interior design for almost the rest of the century. Despite the proclaimed goals of the Bauhaus, the other arts were used merely as additive applications. Ironically, this meant the ultimate banishment of decoration and ornamentation from all architecture, interior design, and furniture design—all but machine-inspired ornamentation.

Bauhaus instruction opened with a preliminary course of half a year, which was devoted to problems of form—observation of nature and materials, studies of composition, and analyses of paintings by old masters. After passing this preliminary course, students were admitted to the second part of the instructional program, which consisted of working for three years with a specific material in one of the crafts studios—stone in the sculpture workshop, wood in the carpentry workshop, metal in the metal workshop, clay in the pottery workshop, glass in the stained-glass workshop, color in the wall-painting workshop, or textiles in the weaving workshop. Each workshop was taught by two masters—a craftsman and an artist—to overcome "the disastrous secession of art from the workaday life of the people," as Gropius wrote. Johannes Itten taught the preliminary course. Over the years, the other teachers were Lyonel Feininger, Gerhard Marcks, Adolf Meyer, George Muche, Paul Klee, Oskar Schlemmer, Wassily Kandinsky, Marcel Breuer, Laszlo Moholy-Nagy, Josef and Anni Albers, and Herbert Bayer.[2]

In 1923 the first Bauhaus exhibition presented students' designs of furniture and furnishings, along with two seminal interiors. One interior was the office of the director, Walter Gropius; the other was an experimental one-family house—the Haus Am Horn—built and furnished by Bauhaus students on the grounds of the school.

Gropius's office (see Figure 39B) was arranged with a cubic volume for seating and conferences in one corner and the desk and bookshelves surrounding it on two sides (see Figure 39A). Horizontality—a major design emphasis of the Bauhaus—was expressed in the arms of the seating units as well as in the bookshelf design. To define the conference-area cube, the ceiling above was painted as a blue square. Above the desk, a light fixture of exposed incandescent tubes showed the influence

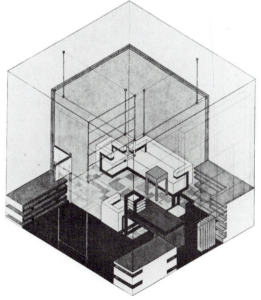

39A. Walter Gropius. Axonometric drawing, Director's office, Bauhaus. Weimar, Germany. 1923. *Illustration by Herbert Bayer.*

39B. Walter Gropius. Director's office, Bauhaus. Weimar, Germany. 1923. *Photograph courtesy The Museum of Modern Art, New York City.*

of the De Stijl Movement (see Chapter 3) and of Theo van Doesburg, who not only had taught at the Bauhaus in 1922, but had previously designed a similar fixture. Indeed, Rietveld's Schröder House, which was being constructed at this time in Utrecht, was perhaps the last flowering of the planar De Stijl style that we associate with the paintings of Piet Mondrian. On its upper floor (which was a collaboration with the client, Mrs. Truus Schröder-Schräder) sliding partitions made possible both a large open space and a series of smaller spaces. It was an example of simultaneity of time and space (see Figures 40A and B). Pursuing that imagery, wiring for the lighting in Gropius's office was carried through thin aluminum tubes, which were repeated to reinforce the linear motif.

For this same exhibition the Haus Am Horn, designed by George Muche and Adolf Meyer, had a square plan with, at the center of the main floor, a square two-story living room that was lighted by the lantern-like second story. The living room, somewhat like an atrium, was surrounded by separate and enclosed spaces (except for the study, which was open to the central space)—dining room, kitchen, bedrooms, and bath. Furnishings were designed by students, including Marcel Breuer (see Figures 41A, B, and C).

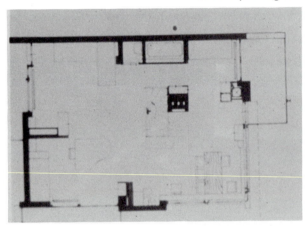 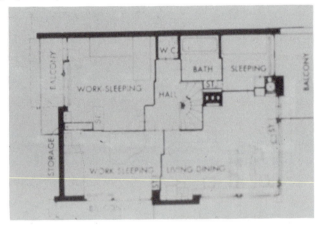

40A. Gerrit Reitveld and Mrs. Truus Schröder-Schräder. Plan of second floor with partitions open (left) and closed (right), Schröder House. Utrecht, Netherlands. 1924.

40B. Gerrit Rietveid and Mrs. Truus Schröder-Schräder. Upper level, Schröder House. Uthrecht, Netherlands. 1924. *Photograph by E. A. van Blitzen Zoon, 1925, from Gemeentelikje Archiefdienst Utrecht.*

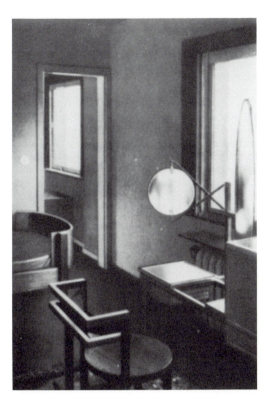

41A. Marcel Breuer. Furniture for ladies' chamber, Haus am Horn. Weimar, Germany. 1923. *Albert Langer Verlag, Munich:* Neue Arbeiten der Bauhaus Werkstaetten (*Bauhausbuecher 7*). *Photograph from Karl Mang*, History of Modern Furniture (*New York: Harry N. Abrams, 1979*).

41B. Marcel Breuer. Bed for Haus am Horn. Weimar, Germany. 1923. *Bauhaus-Archiv Berlin. Photograph from Karl Mang*, History of Modern Furniture (*New York: Harry N. Abrams, 1979*).

41C. Wilhelm Wagenfeld and Karl J. Jucker. Table Lamp, glass and chrome-plated metal, globe 17″ high, 8″ diameter. 1923–24. *Collection, The Museum of Modern Art, New York City. Gift of Philip C. Johnson.*

Gropius had stated the theme of this exhibition as "Art and Technics, a New Unity" but it was only after the Bauhaus moved to Dessau in 1925 that the school placed emphasis on the technology of the machine. The curriculum was changed at that time to reflect the fact that each teacher had become, through Bauhaus training, combination creative artist, craftsman, and industrial designer. In the Dessau studios the goal was to achieve designs that could be submitted to industry for production.[3] In due course, designs for furniture, lamps, textiles, metal, and glassware were produced by manufacturers with royalties for the student designers, as well as to the school and the teacher. Design for industry had moved to the world of education.

The new style that this approach created was efficient and functional. The matter-of-fact reduction to necessity was economical, simplified, and pure—to the point of being clinically clean. Shiny metal, richly veined stone, and nubby fabric were among the natural materials used to enrich the spare, functional designs. But structural rationalism—which posited structural logic as the basis of design—along with clarity of parts and meticulous alignment was the fundamental principle as well as the aesthetic effect of the new machine-based Modernism.

With this new emphasis, after nearly a century of debate over the machine versus handcraft and of moves for reform, the Bauhaus was able to coalesce the goals of Arts and Crafts and the Wiener Werkstaette with those of the Deutscher Werkbund and the Futurists into a modern theory of design and industry. It was a celebration of the machine, an aesthetic imagery of machine-made production. The Bauhaus, thereby, first acclaimed Machine-Age art.

It meant the coming together of the goals of Modernism—geometric simplicity, the use of machine production, the imagery of machine production, and functional (meaning structural) appropriateness. Function, materials, and the process of manufacture were the goals. Along with these came two taboos: There shall be no historicism, and there shall be no applied ornamentation.

Gropius wrote of the Bauhaus concept:

> Architecture during the last few generations has become weakly sentimental, aesthetic, and decorative. Its chief concern has been with ornamentation, with the formalistic use of motifs, ornaments, and mouldings on the exterior . . . —not as part of a living organism. . . . This kind of architecture we disown. We want to create a clear, organic architecture, whose inner logic will be radiant and naked, unencumbered by lying façades and trickeries; we want an architecture adapted to our world of machines, radios, and fast motor cars, an architecture whose function is clearly recognizable in the relation of its forms. . . . modern materials— steel, concrete, glass. . . . The old method of building is giving way to a new lightness and airiness. A new aesthetic of the Horizontal is beginning to develop . . . a new conception of equilibrium, which transmutes this dead symmetry of similar parts into an asymmetrical but rhythmical balance.[4]

These were the Futurist goals toward which the Bauhaus worked—a timely style and a ready availability through mass production by machines. Art for all—everything for everyman—had arrived.

This was the decade of the classic furniture designs of the Modern movement—those by Marcel Breuer, Mies van der Rohe, and others. As usual, technology was not as advanced as design vision. Many early Bauhaus furniture designs, like many later building systems, which were designed to be made by machine and to look as if they had been made by machine, had to be constructed by hand.

The "assembly of prefabricated and standardized parts" was the aspiration of the Bauhaus, and not to achieve it was considered a betrayal of Bauhaus principles. However, one cannot criticize technology because it is not yet advanced enough and available. Marcel Breuer's Wassily Chair (1925), designed for the house of painter and colleague Wassily Kandinsky, has a tubular metal frame inspired by bicycle production; "iron-cloth" canvas or leather bands constitute the straightforward (*sachlich*) seat, back, and armrests. But it had to be hand-welded and hand-sewn rather than machine-made. So too did Mies's cantilevered, tubular MR Chair (1927) (see Figure 42A), and the handwork required for the X-joint of the Barcelona furniture (1929) (see Figure 42B) has been much discussed by historians. But in 1928 Breuer designed the tubular metal, cantilevered Cesca Chair with seat and back pads of cane woven on wood frames, and it could be made entirely by machine production at that time. Technology was catching up.[5]

Walter Gropius

Born in Berlin, Walter Gropius (1883–1969), the first Bauhaus director, had studied architecture at the universities of Berlin and Munich and from 1908 to 1910 was chief assistant to Peter Behrens. During that time both Mies van der Rohe and Le Corbusier worked in the Behrens office. In his next years of private practice, Gropius designed the two first truly Modern buildings in collaboration with Adolph Meyer—the Fagus Factory at Alfeld (1913), and the Deutscher Werkbund Pavilion at the Cologne Exhibition of 1914 (see Chapter 3). After service in World War I, Gropius was called to Weimar to become director of the Bauhaus on the recommendation of his predecessor at the Grand-Ducal schools, the Belgian architect Henry van de Velde.

In 1925, on the move of the Bauhaus to Dessau, Gropius designed the new building occupied by the school. It is one of the most influential structures of Modern architecture. Composed of three blocks—one for classroom-studios, one for administration, and one for living quarters—Gropius's Bauhaus building in Dessau exhibits the Bauhaus design directions: horizontals—in the flat roofs, the bridge-like administration wing, and emphasis of linear windows and floor slabs;

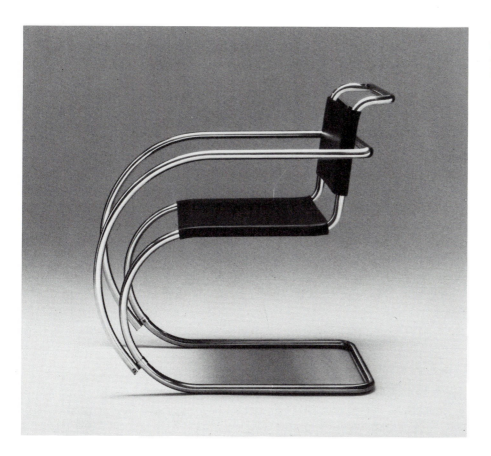

42A. Ludwig Mies van der Rohe. MR Chair. 1927. *Photograph courtesy Knoll International.*

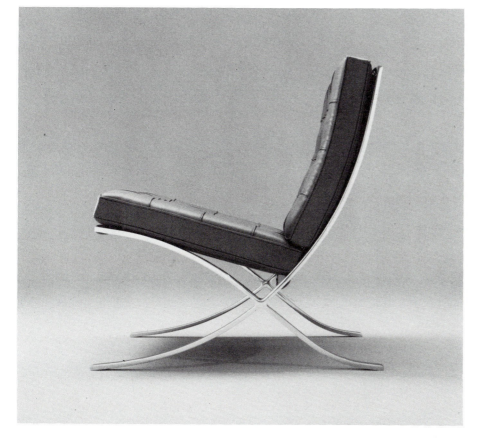

42B. Ludwig Mies van der Rohe. Barcelona Chair. 1929. *Photograph courtesy Knoll International.*

asymmetry—in the plan and vertical massing; and expression of functions—in the fenestration as well as the massing. In 1928 Gropius retired as director of the Bauhaus, and Hannes Meyer was appointed his successor.

Ludwig Mies van der Rohe

In 1930, following Hannes Meyer's resignation, the Berlin architect Ludwig Mies van der Rohe (1886–1969) was appointed director of the Bauhaus. Mies had been born in Aachen (Aix-la-Chapelle), Germany; he worked first with his father as a stonemason, and apprenticed in the offices of Bruno Paul and then Peter Behrens, while Gropius and Le Corbusier were there. His early architecture was inspired by the classicism of the nineteenth-century German architect Karl Friedrich Schinkel and by the Expressionists and the De Stijl movement. From 1921 to 1923 Mies designed his first steel-framed and glass curtain-wall tower schemes; they had expressionistic free-form plans. In 1927 he was director of the Deutscher Werkbund exposition at Stuttgart—the Weissenhof Housing Settlement or community

43A.   Ludwig Mies van der Rohe. Plan, German Pavilion. International Exposition, Barcelona, Spain. 1929. *Illustration from Philip Johnson,* Mies van der Rohe *(New York: The Museum of Modern Art, 1978).*

43B.   Ludwig Mies van der Rohe. Interior, Germany Pavilion International Exposition, Barcelona, Spain. 1929. *Photograph courtesy Mies van der Rohe Archive, The Museum of Modern Art. New York City.*

44A. Ludwig Mies van der Rohe. Study and living room, Tugendhat House. Brno, Czechoslovakia. 1930. *Reprinted by Hedrich-Blessing.*

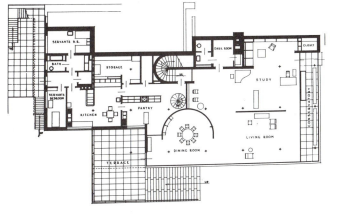

44B. Ludwig Mies van der Rohe. Plan, Tugendhat House, Brno, Czechoslovakia. 1930. *Illustration from Henry-Russell Hitchcock and Philip Johnson,* The International Style: Architecture Since 1922 *(New York: W. W. Norton, 1966).*

44C. Ludwig Mies van der Rohe. Dining room. Tugendhat House. Brno, Czechoslovakia. 1930. *Reprinted by Hedrich-Blessing.*

housing project. There he demonstrated the great social goal of early Modernism—to provide low-cost housing for everyone.

In 1929 Mies designed the German Pavilion for the International Exposition in Barcelona, Spain (see Figure 43B). The pavilion crystallized all the thinking of the first generation of modernists—machine imagery, ornamentation only through the textures of natural materials, and, most important, free-flowing space unimpeded by structural walls. Inspired by Frank Lloyd Wright, Mies developed his vision of dissolving wall planes. Mies "broke with the conception of the wall as a continuous plane surrounding the plan," wrote Hitchcock and Johnson, "and built up his composition of sections of intersecting planes."[6] The plan (see Figure 43A) clearly showed the influence of De Stijl and of Mies's own previous work in that vein. It was Mies's supreme example of reducing design to its most elemental essentials. "Less is more" was his slogan.

For the Barcelona Pavilion, Mies designed the furniture—chair, stool, and table—that became the ultimate achievements (and later the ultimate status symbols) in furniture design of this Machine Age. Revered as the Barcelona Pavilion has become, it is imperative to note that it was more of a fine-art work of architecture than an applied-art creation for a function of occupancy. It was a walk-through, unenclosed, demonstration space, not a residence or office designed to facilitate continual and habitual daily activities.

In 1930 Mies completed his Tugendhat House in Brno, Czechoslovakia (see Figures 44A, B, and C). There, in an actual house, a free-flowing interior space of monumental proportions is similarly subdivided by freestanding screens—a flat one made of Malaga onyx, which divides the study from the living room, and a semicircular partition made of macassar ebony, which surrounds the dining area. The partitions stood independent of the building structure, which was expressed as freestanding columns sheathed in cruciform-plan polished stainless steel. These were offset on a floor of white linoleum (first marketed that year in Darmstadt by Rohm & Haas). Walls were flat and untrimmed planes.

All furnishings were designed by Mies, including lighting fixtures, and located with the most meticulous care in relation to his plan and luxurious materials. Raw-silk draperies were hung at the windows, which had alternate panes that descended into the floor at the push of a button, opening the interior to the exterior without physical barrier. In the living area was a natural wool rug on which sat Mies's Tugendhat Chair, designed for the house, and the Barcelona furniture. The upholsteries were pale-green cowhide, tan glove leather, and white vellum. In the study stood a credenza of white wood and translucent dark-green glass panels; at the table-desk were MR chairs. And the dining table was surrounded by Brno chairs with tubular frames. In his interior design he was assisted by Lilly Reich.

Although he designed at every scale—from large urban-planning projects to small lighting fixtures—Mies, more than any architect since Frank Lloyd Wright, demonstrated his attention to detail. "God is in the details," he was to say later. He also showed a remarkable ability to create a total design. The decade closed, therefore, with the creation by Mies of one of the pinnacles of early Modern design—which remains one of the supreme total design works of the century—and with Mies's appointment as director of the Bauhaus. He was first vice president of the Deutscher Werkbund when he was called to the Bauhaus in 1930.

Machine-Age Furniture by Marcel Breuer

Born in Hungary, Marcel Breuer (1902–82) joined the Bauhaus as a student in 1920. He became a master or teacher in 1925 on the move from Weimar to Dessau, where he took over the carpentry workshop. Soon he was designing some of the most expressive furniture in the new machine style. In 1925 he designed the Wassily Chair for the house of his colleague Wassily Kandinsky. In that same year he designed the Laccio Table/Stool of tubular steel;[7] and in 1928 came his design of the Cesca Chair. Later in his career he became an internationally respected architect. When Gropius left the Bauhaus, Breuer also left, moving to the office he already had in Berlin.[8]

Art Moderne

Contemporaneous with the development of the Bauhaus was a new movement in France. After 1925 many French designers, perhaps already bored by Art Deco, began to turn to the new Modernism, which they had seen exhibited at the same exhibition—in Le Corbusier's Pavillon de L'Esprit Nouveau, in the Tourism Tower pavilion by Robert Mallet-Stevens, and in the Lyons-Saint-Etienne pavilion by Tony Garnier. They were also attracted to Swedish Modern design, which offered pale-toned color schemes and the look of simple provincial but graceful handcraft and machine craft. These helped to inspire a new French Modernism, which is distinguished from Art Deco by the term Art Moderne.

Stylistically, Art Deco is classical, traditional, and representational, even when geometric. Art Moderne is machine-inspired, more abstract, and more consistently rectilinear, or at least more geometrically formal. The two styles are distinguished physically, as they are verbally, by ornament and decoration versus machine-inspired abstraction. Art Moderne rejected the classicism of Art Deco and adopted, instead, the imagery of Futurism and of the machine. It proffered rectilinear forms, parallel lines, and the modern materials, such as glass, mirror, and metals. But French Modernism, except for the work of Le Corbusier, was less rigid than the purgative, ascetic approach of the Bauhaus.

The French architects and designers who led the way along this Art Moderne path were the Formalists Tony Garnier, Robert Mallet-Stevens, Djo-Bourgeois, François Jourdain, and René Herbst. Eileen Gray and Pierre Chareau, who earlier had worked in a highly refined Art Deco style, also began to work in the Moderne idiom. They were to be joined in the 1930s by Jean-Michel Frank. Le Corbusier was the supreme genius among these designers. All of them adopted Machine-Age Modernism, in varying degrees and with varied success. Also at this time, new furniture of metal and leather—some of it made by the French branch of Thonet, the makers of bentwood furniture—also began to appear in France.

From 1928 to 1932 in Paris, Chareau and the Dutch architect Bernard Bijvoet designed and built the Maison de Verre (see Figure 45), which expressed the goals of Machine-Age Moderne in its exposed steel structure and walls of lens-like glass block; it has black metal bookcases, a ladder, and industrial rubber flooring among its furnishings in the two-story living room; upholsteries on Chareau-designed sofas were tapestries by the painter Jean Lurçat.

The mechanical system in the Maison de Verre is integrated into the structural system: grilles along perimeter platforms supply ducted warm air. Electrical and telephone wiring is conveyed along the steel columns, with clustered control panels for both switches and outlets. Up lights at the upper level reflect ambiant lighting from the ceiling.

The Purism of Le Corbusier

The pioneer of this French Modernism was Charles-Edouard Jeanneret (1887–1965), the Swiss-born architect who later called himself Le Corbusier, because of his crow-like affectation of tight black suits and round black eyeglasses that emphasized his

45. Chareau & Bijvoet. Living room, Maison de Verre. Paris, France. 1929–31. *Photograph by Evelyn Hofer, New York City, 1982.*

crow-like profile. Born in La Chaux-de-Fonds, Switzerland, Le Corbusier was trained in art school in his home town. During travel to Italy and the Mediterranean he developed a lifelong admiration for vernacular white stucco structures. He then worked briefly for Josef Hoffmann; for Auguste Perret, from whom he learned about reinforced concrete; and for Peter Behrens, before setting off again for a year-long tour of Mediterranean countries—including his favorite island, Mykonos.

In 1914–15 Le Corbusier had devised his elemental structural system, le Domino, which reduced necessary building structure to a grid of freestanding columns supporting three slabs that were joined by a stair (see Figure 46). This innovative reduction of structure to its barest essentials allowed all interior walls to be located

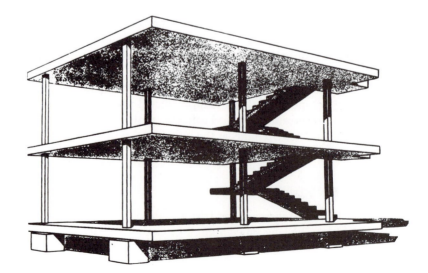

46. Le Corbusier. Drawing of le Domino. 1915. *Illustration from Charles-Edouard Jeanneret,* Le Corbusier: 1910–65 *(Zurich: Les Editions d'Architecture Zurich, 1967).*

independent of the structural grid and at random, therefore making possible the freeflowing space that became the ideal of the Modern movement. In the 1920s Le Corbusier began to demonstrate the potential of this system. It was this concept of space that Mies van der Rohe was to express so elegantly in his Barcelona Pavilion and in his Tugendhat House.

In 1918, with the painter Amédée Ozenfant, Le Corbusier published his manifesto on Purism—"Après le Cubisme." It proclaimed a new art era based on sweeping away the past, starting clean with a new slate of whitewash and with mathematically geometric pure forms of severe simplicity and economic elegance. "The purism of whitewash," it came to be called. The Purists felt that natural selection and economy through the ages had perfected the cylinder, the cube, the cone, and other such elemental forms. They felt similarly about the bottle, the classical column, and the violin. These were universal forms, impersonal and therefore heroic; they were used in both Purist paintings and architecture at the time. The doctrine was another expression of refinement and reduction with a goal of universal understanding.

Le Corbusier also eagerly endorsed the Futurist ideals of industry and the machine, of speed and lightness. The imagery of grain silos and factories, the speed of airplanes and automobiles, and the fully mechanized life aboard sleek ocean liners fascinated him. From ocean liners he drew his early Purist motif of parallel tubular railings and his interest in ladders, compartment-like tight spaces, and roofs as sports decks. He later wrote in "Vers une Architecture" that steamships manifest the virtues of discipline, harmony, and a calm vital beauty.[9] He said that they present a pure, neat, clear, clean, and healthy architecture. Except for the last adjective, these became the catchwords of later Modernism.

In 1920, by which time he had permanently settled in France, Le Corbusier began publishing the magazine *L'Esprit Nouveau*, also with Ozenfant; it lasted twenty-seven issues. His 1923 manifesto on Modern architecture, "Vers une Architecture," was first published in the magazine as "Manuel de l'Habitation." There he first stated his maxim that a house was "a machine for habitation." It expressed his espousal of the Futurist vision of the Machine Age.

From the name of the publication came the Pavillon de l'Esprit Nouveau at the 1925 Art Deco exhibition. There, he built one living unit of an apartment block that he envisioned composed of stacked multiples of that unit. It had a two-story living room overlooked by a balcony space and flowing into a dining space beyond an elevated cabinet (see Figure 47). This looked out onto a two-story terrace and garden. But it was the simple furniture, including the 1900 Thonet bentwood chairs that Le Corbusier chose—saying that there was no other good contemporary furniture to use—that further astonished exhibition-goers. Le Corbusier's manifesto-like description was, as was his custom, abrasive and eye-opening:

> The program: to reject decorative art. To affirm that architecture extends from the smallest furnishing to the house, to the street, to the city, and beyond. To show that industry creates pure objects by selection (by means of the standardized series). . . . To show that an apartment can be standardized to satisfy the needs of a "seriesman." The practical, habitable cell, comfortable and beautiful, a veritable machine for habitation. . . . A new term has replaced the word furnishing . . . the equipment of a house. . . . In replacing the innumerable furnishings of all shapes and sizes, standard cabinets are incorporated in the walls or set against the walls, so located within the apartment as to best serve its exact daily function . . . they are constructed not of wood, but of metal, in the shops where office furniture is fabricated. The cabinets constitute, in themselves, the sole furnishing for the house, thus leaving a maximum amount of available space within each room.[10]

It was the public beginning of "the poor man's style."

47. Le Corbusier. Pavillon de l'Esprit Nouveau, Paris Exhibition. Paris, France. 1925. *Photograph from Karl Mang, History of Modern Furniture (New York: Harry N. Abrams, 1979).*

For the Deutscher Werkbund exposition in Stuttgart in 1927, Le Corbusier designed two houses of the prophetic Weissenhof Housing Project. One of the houses revealed his interest in small, or rather minimal, dimensions: The size of the corridor was that of a railway compartment. Le Corbusier described it as "a house resembling a car, planned and fitted like a bus or ship's cabin. . . . A house must be thought of as a living-machine or a tool." The interior was conceived as a single large living area divided at night into compartments by means of partitions that slid into position, revealing beds that had been concealed during the day. Understanding critics agreed that this was "a new conception of living."[11]

Le Corbusier's Villa Stein at Garches (1927) clearly expresses this new doctrine and imagery. Also in 1927, with his brother Pierre Jeanneret and with his cousin Charlotte Perriand, he designed the celebrated serpentine-profile chaise longue of tubular chromium-plated steel resting on a black lacquered-steel base. Like his furniture of 1928—the Basculant/Sling Chair, the Cube Chair, also called Grand Confort (see Figure 48), and the LC5 Sofa—it was furniture for the Machine Age. When upholstered in black leather, it was similar to the furniture of Breuer and Mies at this time; but when upholstered in black-and-white pony skin, it reflected the French spirit of the 1920s.

From 1929 to 1931 Le Corbusier worked on his early-Modern masterpiece, the Villa Savoye at Poissy, outside Paris. An all-white, ship-like machine for living, the Villa Savoye demonstrates the five principles or points that Le Corbusier endorsed:

First, the concrete skeleton construction of the Domino format, which permits a structure to be raised up above the ground on columns—called *pilotis*—so that the ground is free for use by automobiles and people. Second, this cantilevered slab construction also makes "free" or independent façades possible, since the walls no longer have a load-bearing function. Third, the free façades make possible the use of ribbon windows, which ideally can be horizontal in the new Modern vision. Fourth, the Domino construction permits an open, free-form interior plan—the Modern concept of space. Fifth, the building can, and should, have a sculptural playground and garden on its flat roof.

On the ground floor of the Villa Savoye, a semicircular glass entranceway laid out between the columns instantly proclaims its independence and freedom from the grid of cylindrical concrete columns of the structural system. A long straight ramp running from ground to roof, which is adjacent to a floating spiral stair (see Figure 49A), further shows the separation of space and structure; it also expresses the interpenetration of vertical spaces.

On the main floor (see Figure 49B) the interpenetration of interior and exterior is re-emphasized by the inclusion of both the enclosed spaces and two outdoor spaces within the square plan and its perimeter wall. Most demonstrably, the ribbon windows of the living room are repeated along the open-air terrace. The cylindrical columns are straightforwardly left freestanding and unornamented in the living room. Tables are cantilevered from columns; the bathroom has a tiled chaise longue with the S-profile of the chaise longue of 1927 (see Figure 49C); but it is integrated with the adjacent bathtub, like the monolithic sculptures that were to occupy Le Corbusier later. Throughout the white Villa Savoye, occasional wall panels are painted ochre, light red, and other colors from Le Corbusier's own Purist paintings. So the decade closed in Europe with an early masterpiece by Le Corbusier, as it closed with an early masterpiece by Mies.

49A.   Le Corbusier. Plan, Villa Savoye. Poissy, France. 1929–30. *Illustration courtesy The Museum of Modern Art, New York City.*

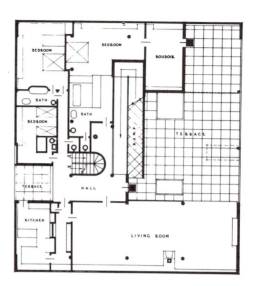

49B.   Le Corbusier. Living room and terrace, Villa Savoye. Poissy, France. 1929–30. *Photograph courtesy The Museum of Modern Art, New York City.*

49C. Le Corbusier. Bath chaise, Villa Savoye. Poissy, France. 1929–31. *Photograph courtesy Parsons School of Design, New York City*.

Design in America

Few American designers picked up on any of these European advances until after the mid-1920s. A number of immigrants, however, who had arrived during and just after World War I, began to make the new directions known.

From the beginning of the decade America was on the move and in the midst of a postwar economic boom. It produced an atmosphere of euphoria and buoyancy that earned the epithet "The Roaring Twenties." In 1920 American women were at last able to vote, and the prohibition of alcoholic drinks was introduced across the country. The ensuing days of being daringly naughty in the speakeasies were epitomized by the flapper girls and by the new dance crazes—the Charleston, the Black Bottom, and the Turkey Trot. The Argentine tango was popularized by Rudolph Valentino. The saxophone, the raccoon coat, egret feathers in headbands, and Stutz Bearcat cars were the rage. Daily radio broadcasting began in 1922, the year that Albert Einstein published *The Meaning of Relativity*. In 1926 television was invented by J. L. Baird (it was successfully transmitted in 1928, but did not become generally available until after World War II). In 1926 the first rocket-powered missiles were built. Walt Disney introduced Mickey Mouse in 1928. It was a decade of relativity and choice.

Postwar prosperity fostered a building boom and produced the second great wave of skyscraper construction. By 1920 more than half the population of the United States lived in cities. Department stores increased in number and size, as shopping became a pastime for the many women who had been liberated from household chores by technological (mainly electrical) advances. More department stores added decorating services, which still connoted the use of antique furniture. In the 1920s using antiques still implied complete and accurate—"correct"—period rooms.

The contemporary furniture industry, which had been essentially a cottage industry of artist-craftsmen and small manufacturers, began to develop large manufacturing centers such as Grand Rapids, Michigan. For buyers on the installment plan, Grand Rapids and the Southern states produced pastiches of period furniture, which was derisively called "Borax"—reportedly after the cleanser that was sometimes offered as a premium with purchase. In its watered-down way, mass-produced furniture continued the nineteenth-century tradition of revival styles.

Professional Design Education

The 1920s brought a surge of new interest and attention to design education. The National Association for Decorative Arts and Industries recognized the need for new training. Only eighteen schools offered design education. The curator of industrial art at the Metropolitan Museum of Art in New York, Richard F. Bach, led an influential campaign for better design education, which he felt should be aimed at product design directors for industry. From 1917 to 1931 he directed a series of annual exhibitions at the museum to display American industrial art. His 1932 and 1934 exhibitions had great impact. Many other exhibitions and model room displays brought new design to professional and public attention alike.

In 1923 the Finnish architect Eliel Saarinen settled in the United States and, within a decade, made the Cranbrook School of Design in Bloomfield Hills, Michigan, one of the frontrunners in American design education. During the 1930s Cranbrook was to produce many of the designers who became leaders in the 1950s and 1960s.

At the New York School of Fine and Applied Arts, Frank Alvah Parsons continued his program of interior architecture and decoration; and Grace Fakes, Hamilton Preston, and Mildred Irby taught architectural detailing. The antiques expert William Odom headed the school's summer extension program in Paris. In the mid-1920s Hope L. Foote began to teach in the interior design program of the University of Washington in Seattle. All these educators broadly influenced the traditional approach of young interior designers in the next several decades.

To recreate the tone of American design education in the 1920s, the director of New York's Museum of Modern Art Alfred H. Barr, Jr., wrote,

> Some of the younger of us had just left colleges where courses in modern art began with Rubens and ended with a few superficial and often hostile remarks about Van Gogh and Matisse; where the last word in imitation Gothic dormitories had windows with one carefully cracked pane to each picturesque casement. Others of us, in architectural schools, were beginning our courses with gigantic renderings of Doric capitals, or ending them with elaborate projects for colonial gymnasiums and Romanesque skyscrapers.[12]

American Architecture

Most architects and interior designers in America during the 1920s were still exploring the academic Beaux-Arts formula of eclectic historicism. The interiors of houses, churches, and other buildings were designed in such popular styles as Gothic, Tudor, Georgian, and Spanish. The Renaissance palazzo was still a model for many banks, such as those by York & Sawyer. Palladian-Georgian was a current mode for the thriving businesses of William Delano, David Adler, and John Russell Pope. Tudor/Gothic was the specialty of James Gamble Rogers, who had begun designing buildings in this style at Yale University in 1917 and continued throughout the 1920s.

Spanish styles became popular during the 1920s owing to the work in Santa Barbara, California, of George Washington Smith, James Osborne Craig, and William Mooser. The Spanish background of Palm Beach, Florida, was created by Addison Mizner. Mizner also acted as interior decorator on his projects, collecting and fabricating antique-style furnishings to sell to clients. Among the other fashionable residential architects of the decade with whom interior designers worked were Aymar Embury II, Harrie T. Lindeburgh, Mott B. Schmidt, and Rosario Candela.

Bertram Goodhue at this time began to work in a stripped, almost bald classical idiom that resulted in his Nebraska state capital building (1920–32). Sculpture sprouted out of the structural stonework like the faces that seem to grow integrally from Mount Rushmore. It was an early historical minimalism, of which the architect Paul Cret was perhaps the ultimate master, as demonstrated by his Folger Shakespeare Library in Washington, D.C. (1928–32).

Along with all this high-style historicism, the American public was also being treated to a popular fantasy of interiors by the movie industry. Hundreds, perhaps thousands, of movie palaces were created across the country for Warner Bros., Paramount, Fox, and Loews. The great cinema impresarios and their architects concocted a compendium of historical styles—Baghdad-Alhambra-Neuschwanstein-Versailles-Parthenon—to mesmerize a romantic and wide-eyed public. Gilded plasterwork, mythological murals, fantasy sculptures, baroque metalwork railings, and magical lighting fixtures were all created by such craftsmen as the Rambusch Studios and Caldwell Lighting in New York; Dapratto Inc. in Chicago; and D' Assenzo Studios in Philadelphia. Built in 1927, the Roxy in New York City was a 6,214-seat gilded Florentine fantasy; designed by architect Walter W. Ahlschlager, it was the most lavish of all.

Skyscrapers What most captured the aspirations of professional designers and the public alike were the skyscrapers that raced for the clouds from 1922 to 1932 in the midst of the economic boom. The most optimistic towers were blazoned across the sky at that time, showing American optimism, ingenuity, and daring. They became the great achievement of twentieth-century building, as well as the romantic icon of the decade.

In the parade of 1920s skyscrapers, we see the gradual transition from historicism toward the new Modernism. This was the second wave of skyscraper construction, following the first generation of skyscrapers that originated in Chicago in the 1870s and ended with the construction of the Woolworth Building in 1913. After the interruption of World War I, this second wave of skyscrapers was initiated by the international competition in 1922 for the design of the Chicago Tribune Tower. That competition was won by John Mead Howells and Raymond Hood with a Perpendicular Gothic–inspired scheme. Many early-1920s skyscrapers were in this historical tradition, and were ornamented with Gothic detailing, such as Raymond Hood's American Standard Building (1924). Such schemes came to be known as American Perpendicular.

By the end of the decade Hood, like other architects, had adopted Art Deco and early Streamlining motifs to the basic classical tower form. The culmination of this decade of skyscraper construction were the Art Deco–Streamline Chrysler Building (1930) by William van Alen; and the blander Art Deco Empire State Building (1930–32) by Shreve, Lamb & Harmon. Vanguard critics considered all these stylish designs either with contempt or as if they did not exist. They pejoratively called even the later 1920s skyscraper style "modernistic."

As an example of a battle of styles within a single building, the interiors of the skyscraper Waldorf Astoria Hotel in New York by Schultze & Weaver (1930) were symptomatic of the decade: The public spaces were originally Art Deco (they were Neo-Georgianized in the mid-1960s, just when the hotel owners should have known better); but the private guest rooms for the hotel's affluent clients were originally furnished with quasi-Georgian interior detailing and furnishings. The Colonial and Federal revivals were the establishment styles; Art Deco and Art Moderne were styles only for the wealthy that were depicted in movies.

Interior designers did not get to do much work inside these towers during the 1920s. But the romantic imagery of the step-topped setback skyscraper, enhanced by the soft-focus drawings of Hugh Ferriss, was soon adopted in interior design and decoration for furnishings (see Figure 50), appliances, and decorative objects.

50. Paul T. Frankl. Skyscraper Furniture. Circa 1930. *Photograph from Paul T. Frankl*, New Dimensions (*New York: Payson & Clarke, 1928*).

American Residential Interior Design

The 1920s saw a consumer buying spree. Designers continued to scour Europe for its apparently unending supply of antique furniture and old textiles—velvets, damasks, and brocades—which had been kept in the cupboards of churches and houses. Dark, heavily carved furnishings of Spanish or Italian origin were still eagerly sought after, along with heavy dark tapestries, and red velvet hangings and upholsteries. An antique church vestment was a prize in many houses. Splendor was the goal.

A number of clients began to recreate American traditions. The newly rediscovered Colonial houses of America set the aspirations of a vast segment of the population, and a Colonial Revival soon swept the nation. "Early American" became a new vogue. The open fireplace hung with antique utensils, the corner cupboard, the spinning wheel, and the cobbler's-bench coffee table were the dreams of countless homemakers.

The number of professional interior decorators increased rapidly in the 1920s. However, since the most celebrated and successful of the new women decorators had begun as society figures who decorated for their friends, they were often slightingly referred to as "the ladies." They had, to many minds, merely turned the daily pastime of shopping into a form of profit. Architects and the large decorating firms still gained most of the commissions to design interiors for major houses. However, architectural interests during the 1920s often gave short shrift to residential furnishings. Consultations with the *ensembliers* or with major art dealers, such as Duveen, Knoedler, or French & Company, were sometimes left until after the house was built. But change was in the air.

Among the new decorators to appear in America was a new wave of the old guard: Eleanor McMillen Brown of McMillen Inc.; Mrs. Truman Handy (Charlotte Chalmers) of Thedlow Inc.; Dorothy Draper; and Rose Cumming. Among those already working, Elsie de Wolfe continued her designing, her eccentric self-promotion, and her lucrative business; Elsie Cobb Wilson continued her restrained period decorating (see Figure 51) and offered a job to Eleanor McMillen Brown. Dianne Tate and Marian Hall became known for their Directoire interiors; they later redecorated Sherry's Restaurant in the former Metropolitan Opera House. Other prominent decorators in the 1920s were Mrs. Frances Lenygon, who forwarded the concept of restoration; Mrs. Polly Jessup, who continues to work in Palm Beach, Florida; Agnes Foster Wright, who was the wife of *House & Garden* editor Richardson Wright; Miss Gheen; Bertha Schaefer; Pierre Dutel; Sarah Hunter Kelly; and Dan Cooper, who was among the first to show Swedish Modern in his showroom.

Nancy McClelland   In 1922 Nancy McClelland left Wanamaker's Au Quatrième decorating department and opened her own firm, Nancy McClelland Inc., in New York. It specialized in antique furnishings, including fine French hand-painted antique wallpapers, and interior design and decorating. The interiors designed by Nancy McClelland were rather correct and formal (see Figure 52). She worked in the French periods, in Regency, and with Colonial furnishings. Among her clients were the Webbs and the Havermeyers. In 1924 she wrote an authoritative book, *Historic Wallpapers,* which was considered the first complete treatment of the subject. She followed that with *The Practical Book of Decorative Wall Treatments* (1925) and *The Young Decorator* (1927). Her writing put her in the forefront of the profession, and revealed the stylistic interests of the decade.

Ruby Ross Wood   In the 1920s, Ruby Ross Goodnow, who had married the investment banker Chalmers Wood, opened her own interior design firm, Ruby Ross Wood Inc. She designed comfortable, informal, English-style rooms. Her

motto was, "Decorating is the art of arranging beautiful things comfortably." She was a sophisticated colorist and liked fresh colors in fabrics and wallpapers. She knew the art of gracious living, and taught it to many of her clients through her designs.

In 1928 Ruby Wood was asked by Mrs. Emily Inman of Atlanta to design the interiors of Swan House, which was to be designed by the architect Philip Schultze. Ruby Wood's interiors—with black-and-white checkerboard floors in the hallway, hand-painted floral wallpaper in the dining room (see Figure 53), and comfortable antique furniture—was typical of the taste of the 1920s, but it also showed Ruby Wood's personal color sense. The house was later given intact to the Atlanta Historical Society and remains an example of decorating in the 1920s.

In 1928 the work of Ruby Ross Wood began to be published by *House & Garden*. The following year she and her husband moved into their house in Syosset, Long Island, which was designed by architect William Adams Delano. The living room was spacious, comfortable, and filled with both antique furniture and comfortable upholstered pieces all in almond greens, with a Savonnerie carpet of muted yellow-greens accented with orangey coral. In the white Adamesque dining room hung blue-and-white damask draperies with a pattern of swans—a popular motif of the 1920s. The dining table was Irish Chippendale—a style variant that was to become a tradition of Ruby Wood's design descendants. High-backed, black leather

53. Ruby Ross Wood. Dining room, Swan House. Atlanta, Georgia. 1928. *Photograph courtesy Atlanta Historical Society.*

54. Rose Cumming. Living room. New York City. Late 1920s. *Photograph courtesy Rose Cumming, Inc.*

armchairs were provided at every place. Her own bedroom had pale-green walls with panels outlined in molding; against them stood a black-painted four-poster Sheraton bed hung with oyster-white silk. Louis XV chairs, an Italian Directoire floor pattern, and shaded sconces at the chimney breast proclaimed the 1920s ideal of the refreshed English country house.

Rose Cumming   When the editor of *Vanity Fair,* Frank Crowninshield, suggested decorating as her profession, Rose Cumming said, "First tell me what it is." Her intuitive sense brought something new to it.

Born in a small village near Sydney, Australia, Rose Stuart Cumming (1887–1968) had been caught by World War I in New York on her way to England. She began decorating by working at Wanamaker's Au Quatrième boutique, briefly, then worked with Mrs. Emmet Buel. In 1921 she opened her own shop for decorating and antiques, which she ran for over forty-five years.

Her work was eclectic and eccentric, unlike the more correct period decorating of the other "ladies." It did not matter to Rose Cumming whether the period was correct, so long as the furnishings were old and beautiful, romantic and lush, exotic and original (see Figure 54). She liked good antique furniture, but she was passionate and flamboyant in her taste as well as in her behavior. It was called "flair." She wore big hats and dyed her hair violet, one-upping Elsie de Wolfe's blue tint. Once, for a customer who insisted on seeing a fabric's colors by daylight, she rolled out a bolt of chintz across Madison Avenue, then announced that there would be no sale to *that* customer.

She made a name for herself with her intuitive use of strong deep colors, such as bright pink with lavender, orchid, and deep blue. She had silks dyed and chintzes printed in her own colorations, which she sold exclusively and at exorbitant prices. Billowing draperies, sometimes puffed and gathered, hung under elaborately cut-out valances of gilt or of layered mirrors. Bedcovers were sometimes swagged up to reveal carved and gilded bed legs, creating a surprising yet lavish effect. The fabrics themselves were rich silk taffetas or Baroque-patterned damasks shimmering with silver thread. It was said that she could drape fabrics more inventively than any of her compeers, and they recognized "a glow" in her decorating.

Rose Cumming also espoused smoked mirrors, bare but highly polished parquet floors, and silver-blue foil wallpapers. Among her clients were the Potter Palmers of Chicago, Marlene Dietrich, Mary Pickford, and Norma Shearer. Among the designers who served apprenticeships with her were George Stacey, John Robert Moore, Richard Hare, Harrison Coultra, and Georgina Fairholme.

She believed that "In real decorating, there are no precedents." Rose Cumming's methodology was to "pull and drag everything back and forth, trying objects here and there, until one finds the exact place in the room where this or that piece looks best." She added, "and there it stays forever." She had been in her own house for a quarter of a century and claimed that she had "never moved one stick of furniture."[13] Her living room, therefore, was a preserved example of 1920s decorating. It was a historical eighteenth-century room with uncarpeted parquet floors on which sat Louis XV pieces, most of which were signed. The walls had early-eighteenth-century Chinese hand-painted wallpaper panels, and above hung an eighteenth-century Chinese chandelier made, unexpectedly, of papier-mâché. It was all historically possible, but the combination showed that Rose Cumming, by the end of the 1920s, was beginning to expand the boundaries of historical accuracy.

McMillen Inc. In 1924 Eleanor McMillen (she became Mrs. Archibald Brown in 1934) opened what she called "the first professional full-service interior decorating firm in America." Professional is the operative word. "When I decided to go into business, I went to business and secretarial school as well," she has said. "I thought that if I were going to do it at all, I'd better do it professionally. I wasn't one of the ladies."[14] She therefore called her firm McMillen Inc. rather than "Eleanor McMillen." Her ability as a level-headed and methodical businessperson was certainly a strong reason why McMillen Inc. continued in business as a leading decorating firm for the next fifty years. In this regard McMillen made a step forward in professionalizing the decorating field.

Born Eleanor Stockstrom in St. Louis, Missouri, Mrs. Brown (1890–) was brought up among considerable affluence. She attended finishing school in Briarcliff, New York. In 1914 she married engineer Drury McMillen and began ten years of travel related to his business. Between trips she took the three-year design course at the New York School of Fine and Applied Arts. She subsequently studied at the school's branch in Paris under William Odom's tutelage, visiting many of the great houses and museums of France and Italy. She thought so highly of this training that, for the first forty years—with one exception—McMillen Inc. hired only graduates from that school. Among McMillen's early commissions were a house for H. H. Rogers of Standard Oil and a house for Arthur Houghton of Corning Glass.

Eleanor Brown's style was based on French classicism, the prevailing taste in American society that had been established by Elsie de Wolfe twenty years before. But she added Directoire and English Regency to her repertoire and used these periods intermixed, since she cared for the background of the room—its interior architecture—and wanted it to set off the furnishings to best advantage.

Her taste was more disciplined than that of many of her contemporaries, however. She preferred to use flowered chintzes only in country houses, and then sparingly. Important rooms had painted walls within classical pilasters and niches. Always she was concerned with good scale and good proportions. She used wallpapers only in more private areas. With minor stylistic variation and with the inclusion of Art Deco–derived Modern, this was her style for the next fifty years—and it looked as fresh in 1950 and it did in 1930. In fact, the undatable quality of McMillen interiors, no matter which partner or associate was in charge, is one of the hallmarks of the firm's work.

The apartment that Mrs. Brown designed for herself in 1928, although modified slightly over the years, is an example of her work from that period. Mrs. Brown and her new associate, Grace Fakes (who taught at the New York School of Fine and Applied Arts), gave the living room (see Figure 55A) definition and symmetry by closing off one window and articulating the wall planes with white-painted pilasters and moldings. This flat and thin architectural detailing, including a pedimented door, is in the late-1920s Greek Revival or modified Directoire style. The walls were first canvas-lined then painted yellow; a black marble mantelpiece of a type advocated by William Odom had a classical revival mirror above it. On the floor was an Aubusson rug; and the furniture was a collection of Louis XVI pieces, both gilt and painted, and upholstered in yellow fabrics and leather. Two layers of tie-back draperies hung at the windows.

55A. Eleanor McMillen Brown. Living room, own apartment. New York City. 1928. *Photograph by Drix Duryea, courtesy McMillen Inc.*

55B. Eleanor McMillen Brown. Dining room, own apartment. New York City. 1928. *Photograph courtesy McMillen Inc.*

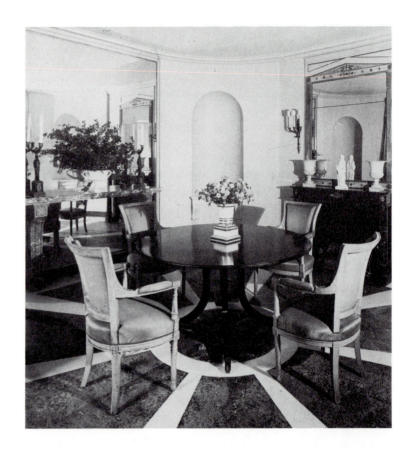

Mrs. Brown shaped the dining room (see Figure 55B) into a flattened oval with four niches, which originally remained bare. A large, framed, floor-to-ceiling mirror, which had a marble console and black-bronze Directoire candelabra on it, faced the doorway. Another pedimented mirror was above a fireplace. The floor was marbled in a sunburst pattern of green and white. At the table, a round Directoire table of dark wood, were painted Directoire chairs. Both rooms have been modified slightly in the intervening years—consoles, unifying of the furniture periods, enlarging of the mirrors into wall panels, simplification of the draperies, and, of course, changes in light levels—but the early scheme shows the late–Art Deco classical Greek decorating of the 1920s.

Thedlow Inc.   Another design firm, which maintained a major residential practice for the next forty years, was established in 1919. Thedlow Inc. was founded by the three Chalmers sisters, who formed the acronym Thedlow from letters of their first names—Theresa, Edna, and Charlotte. Charlotte Chalmers, later Mrs. Truman Handy, headed the firm. Charlotte Chalmers Handy (1892–) was born in New York, attended the Brearley School, and later was schooled in Indiana. Lyman Martin, a graduate of the New York School of Fine and Applied Arts, was to become a mainstay of the firm, which primarily designed residences for the affluent, until it closed in 1970.

Frances Elkins   Frances Elkins attracted attention in California in the early 1920s after she restored her 1824 adobe house Casa Amesti in Monterey. She soon became one of California's leading interior designers. At Casa Amesti, within the envelope of rough plaster walls, rough-planked floors, and exposed-beam ceilings, Frances Elkins placed a large English partners' desk in the center of the living room and surrounded it with several conversation groups. The seating pieces were a mixture of French, English, and Italian periods—usually pairs, but placed separately in an informal mix. She later added Chinese carpets, paintings, and porcelains. The colors were yellow, blue, and white. The room offers a rich mix of uses—both entertainment and work, both solitary and for company.

Owing to the acclaim she received for this work, in the mid-1920s Elkins began to decorate houses for friends, such as the Griffins in Pebble Beach, as well as friends in Monterey and Santa Barbara. In 1927 she opened offices in the Robert Louis Stevenson house in Monterey. At that time her work was fairly typical of 1920s period rooms. She later became known for more eclectic mixtures of periods and countries, and for juxtapositions of textures and colors—Spanish Colonial architecture with French and Italian palace furniture, the rough with the polished, the poor with the grand. Billy Baldwin was later to call her "perhaps the most creative decorator we ever had."

Syrie Maugham   One of the most prominent interior designers who practiced in the 1920s was Syrie Maugham. Born Gwendoline Maud Syrie Barnardo in London, Syrie Maugham (1879–1955) was married to author Somerset Maugham. In 1920 she had asked Elsie de Wolfe if she should open up shop as a decorator in London. Elsie de Wolfe had said no, that the field was already too crowded. Undaunted, Syrie Maugham opened her shop in 1922 and was a great success with furniture that was either pickled or decorated with painted floral designs. Her success was so immediate that, beginning in 1926, she opened shops in the United States in New York, Chicago, Los Angeles, and Palm Beach.

In her own house on the north coast of France in 1926, Syrie Maugham finished the living room entirely in tones of beige enlivened with peach silk draperies; moldings had been stripped; the concrete floor was covered in sheepskins sewn together to make a carpet; the wood furniture was stripped and pickled; and all upholstery was beige. The dining room was virtually all white: Walls were paneled in untreated waxed pine and had rock-crystal appliques around them; stripped oak chairs were covered in white leather; the dining table, also of stripped oak, was set with white porcelain-handled knives and forks, which were reproductions of early-eighteenth-century Meissen models; white silk draperies had a design in sapphire blue. Throughout, closets were papered with hand-printed Italian book endpapers.

For her London house, completed in 1927, Syrie Maugham designed a living room with white walls, white satin curtains, white-painted Louis XV bergères and wing chairs, white chair covers with flower patterns, white velvet lampshades, two large camellia bushes with white porcelain flowers, arrangements of white lilies, and mirrors (see Figure 56). An Italian bureau-bookcase was papered with engravings on a white ground and then lacquered. The dining room paneling was pickled and waxed to a honey color and offset with white brocade draperies. White-and-gold painted chairs were set at an oval table set with white porcelain. She also popularized the design of bathrooms all of mirror, and made all-white a popular vogue.

The vogue for white was not only a return to 1890s schemes of the Mackintoshes, the MacNairs, and of Elsie de Wolfe for lightening late-Victorian stuffiness. It also corresponded with the white architecture of the 1920s, and it was a direct reversal on the vogue for the black rooms that grew up early in the 1920s; and as a refinement on silver rooms, which had been papered in tea-chest paper. Both had been adopted as suitable backgrounds for lacquered furniture, which had become popular with the recalls of Egyptian, Greek, and Chinese furnishings. Syrie Maugham brought an extreme all-white lightness to these schemes.

Elsie de Wolfe   During the 1920s Elsie de Wolfe updated her style in line with the times. At her house in Versailles, called the Villa Trianon, she began to use

56. Syrie Maugham. Own living room. London, England. 1927. *Photograph from* The Studio (*February 1933*).

leopard-skin chintzes to cover eighteenth-century stools and cushions. Fur throws replaced blanker covers on beds. Silk cushions were embroidered with mottoes that were humorous, sentimental, or cute—"Never complain, never explain" was one of them. Elsie de Wolfe again offered not innovation, but the image of nightclub society as the definition of fashionable design. She seemed to reflect the giddy flapperdom of life and the surrealism of the 1920s. In 1926, at the age of sixty-one, Elsie de Wolfe married Sir Charles Mendl, British press attaché in Paris. From then on she preferred to be known as Lady Mendl.

Dorothy Draper   Dorothy Draper was the first American woman decorator to concentrate on nonresidential design. Her commissions from the 1920s through the 1950s, during which she became one of the most publicized personalities in the design world, included lobbies, hotels, clubs, restaurants, shops, and hospitals.

Born Dorothy Tuckerman in Tuxedo Park, New York, Dorothy Draper (1889–1969) attended the Brearley School in New York, and in 1912 married Dr. George Draper. After three children, they were divorced in 1930. Before that, with the backing of her family social and diplomatic connections, she opened a firm in New York called the Architectural Clearing House and began by designing apartment house lobbies. In 1925 she founded Dorothy Draper & Company, which was soon an established success.

By 1930 Dorothy Draper had designed lobbies for New York's then new Carlyle Hotel, and for the apartment house at 770 Park Avenue. Both were in the prevailing classical late–Art Deco, Greek–Egyptian idiom. The lobby of 770 Park Avenue, still virtually unchanged, has flooring of black marble with white-and-gray banding, dead-white walls, and doors in black enamel with white moldings (see Figure 57). A niche, then painted blue, features a female figure. Greek-revival sofas, then covered in terra-cotta brick red, are flanked by tables with classical motifs. The Carlyle Hotel lobbies show the same flooring scheme and classical late–Art Deco detailing, though the furnishings and colors have largely been changed. At this time, Dorothy Draper had not yet developed her Neo-Baroque style of the 1930s.

The Impact of Art Deco on America

When the Art Deco exposition of 1925 was being planned, the United States declined the invitation to exhibit its modern decorative and industrial art on the grounds that the country had no modern or industrial arts worth exhibiting. The design professions of America were galvanized by this decision: Designers were determined to sail to Paris to see what really was new and to show that America did indeed have contributions of merit in those fields.

Those who went to see the 1925 exposition, including buyers for American department stores, brought a popularizing impetus. Among the department stores, Macy's, Lord & Taylor, B. Altman, Wanamaker's, Franklin Simon, Marshall Field, and others displayed room vignettes in the new styles.

57.   Dorothy Draper. Lobby, 770 Park Avenue. New York City. 1930. *Photograph from* Architecture and Building, 1931.

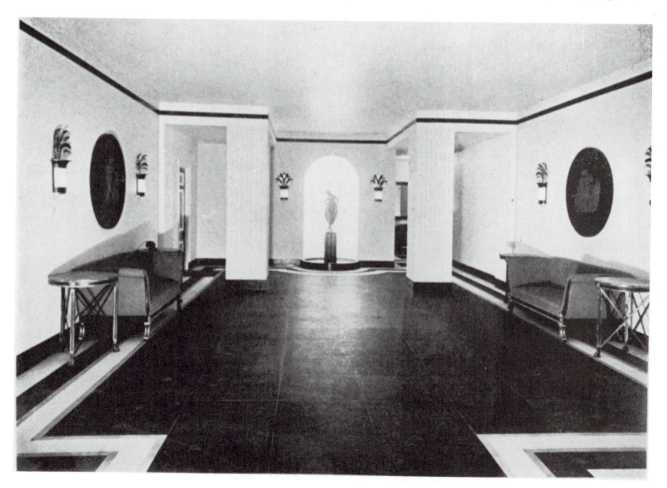

58. Joseph Urban. Own house. Yonkers, New York. Before 1926. *Photograph from Nancy McClelland*, The Practical Book of Decorative Wall Treatment (*Philadelphia: J. B. Lippincott, 1926*).

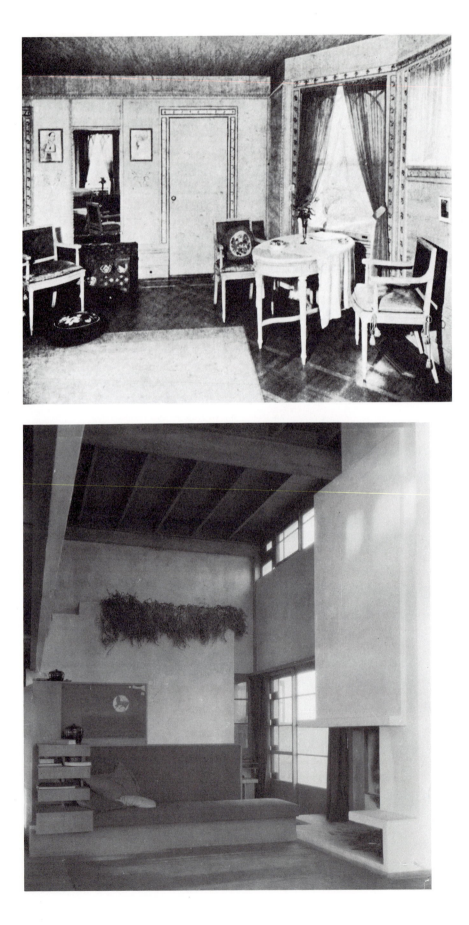

59. Rudolph M. Schindler. Living room, Lovell beach house. Newport Beach, California. 1926. *Photograph from UCSB Art Museum, University of California at Santa Barbara.*

The Spread of Modernism

The new European Modernism was first brought to the United States by a number of immigrants who began to explore new directions in America early in the 1920s. They brought the varying waves of Modernism to active production in this country.

Joseph Urban (see Figure 58) had come from Austria in 1911 to set up the Wiener Werkstaette shop in New York. He created interiors for the Ziegfeld Theater, of which he was also the architect; the Casino in the Park; the Persian Room in the Plaza Hotel; the St. Regis Roof; and the auditorium of the New School.

Rena Rosenthal opened what was considered the first contemporary shop in the United States, where the work of European designers and craftsmen was available, including the ceramics of Wally Wieselthier and Russel Wright (see below).

Paul T. Frankl emigrated from Austria in 1914. He spent the 1920s in New York, designing his attention-getting skyscraper furniture and establishing what was considered one of the first Modern furniture firms.

After the war, architects Rudolph M. Schindler and Richard Neutra came from Vienna; and, early in the 1920s, architect William Lescaze arrived from Switzerland. Rudolph Schindler designed his house on Kings Road in Hollywood (1921–22), and his beach house for the Lovells in Newport Beach, California (see Figure 59). Richard Neutra began his series of influential houses with the Lovell House in Los Angeles (1929) (see Figure 60). The latter is considered the earliest masterpiece in the International Style to be constructed in America, and the only

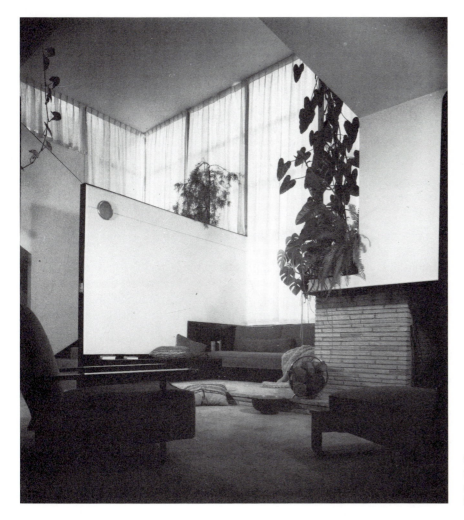

60. Richard Neutra. Living room, Lovell House. Los Angeles, California. 1929. *Photograph by Julius Shulman.*

61A. Frank Lloyd Wright. Detail, Hollyhock House. Los Angeles, California. 1920. *Photograph by Thomas A. Heinz.*

one of its period to be in the class with Le Corbusier's Villa Savoye and Mies's Tugendhat House.

During the 1920s the pioneering influence of Frank Lloyd Wright was in eclipse. His practice had dwindled while he was in Japan, but his previously designed Hollyhock House in Los Angeles for Aline Barnsdall was completed in 1920 under the supervision of his then assistant, Rudolph Schindler. The house is called the Hollyhock House because of the stylized geometric design based on the hollyhock flower that is consistently used throughout the house (see Figure 61A). The hollyhock design appears on the ornamentation of the heavy, somewhat Mayan massing of the exterior, through the interior and into the design of chairs, leaded windows, and other furnishings (see Figure 61B). Most of the original furniture, except the dining table and chairs, was designed by Schindler.

In 1923 Wright designed a house for Mrs. George Madison Millard in Pasadena, California, with textured and ornamented concrete blocks. He called them "textile blocks" because they were held together by a network of steel rods. Used inside and outside the Millard House, these textile blocks provide richly textured decoration; since some of the blocks are glass-filled, they streak the interior with pinpoints of light. Split-level in section, the house has a bedroom balcony overlooking the living room; this section produces a larger space than might be expected in the small house and, with the textile-block patterning, the house provides a rich and atmospheric setting for the Renaissance furnishings that Mrs. Millard collected and sold.

The Impact of the Bauhaus on America

"It is hard to recall when and how we in America first began to hear of the Bauhaus," the director of the Museum of Modern Art in New York, Alfred Barr, Jr., wrote in 1938.

> In the years just after World War I we thought of German art in terms of Expressionism, of Mendelsohn's streamlined Einstein tower, Toller's "Masse Mensch," Wiene's "Cabinet of Dr. Caligari." It may not have been until after the great Bauhaus exhibition of 1923 that reports reached America of a new kind of art school in Germany. . . . A little later we began to use some of the Bauhaus books, notably Schlemmer's amazing volume on the theater and Moholy-Nagy's *Malerei, Photographie, Film.* . . . A few American pilgrims had visited Dessau before Gropius left in 1928; in the five years thereafter, many went to stay as students. During this time, Bauhaus material, typography, paintings, prints, theater art, architecture, and industrial objects had been included in American exhibitions. . . .[15]

In addition, the build-up of American interest in the factory aesthetic of the Teens was seen in the paintings of Stuart Davis, Charles Sheeler, and Charles Demuth. But the direct and widespread transportation of Modern design and of Bauhaus principles and methodology to the United States had to wait until the next decade.

Industrial Design in America

Modern design from Europe strongly influenced the newly emerging designers who came to be known as industrial designers. In the decade of the 1920s, the American profession of industrial design began. It was the first American flowering of the long-brewing marriage of design and industry, and the first recognition of the potential of combining machine production with good design.

The pioneer industrial designers and their followers were to have an enormous effect on interior design through the design of furnishings, appliances, and countless other products used in houses and offices, in educational facilities and hospi-

61B. Frank Lloyd Wright.
Living room, Hollyhock House.
Los Angeles, California. 1920.
*Photograph © Ezra Stoller/
ESTO, 1954.*

tals. Soon, industrial designers took on the design of entire interiors, first for the transportation industry—ocean liners, trains, airplanes, and automobiles—and then for every other type of interior for which they could gain a commission.

Designing for industrial production was by no means an entirely new activity, of course. Witness the Deutscher Werkbund's success in the Teens. Even earlier in the Industrial Revolution, all the textiles that were woven by the new machines were designed by designers for industry. Some of these designers were architects working in their offices; others were craftsmen working at their looms. In the mid- and late eighteenth century, Jacquard and other designers of the revolutionary machinery for textile production were designers for industry. And it should be remembered that Josiah Wedgwood, of the celebrated English porcelain works, designed a number of elegant "useful" wares for the kitchen, among his designs for his industrial production. In the early and late nineteenth century also, the Shakers turned their handcraft furniture production into a machine industry. And Michael Thonet's nineteenth-century process for bending wood sparked one of the most widely recognized and popular furniture industries of the past hundred years.

In the mid-nineteenth century, as historian Edgar Kaufmann, Jr., has written:

> A few books mention that Pugin himself, the sculptor Alfred Stevens, and Henry Cole (Prince Albert's right arm in the Crystal Palace exhibition venture and thereafter) were early designers-for-industry with sizable, systematic practices. It is less clearly recognized that they had an ample following in succeeding generations. Side by side with the Arts and Crafts Movement, there were men who had no illusions about a return to the Middle Ages, who worked for machine productions, and who tried to better the prevailing standards of marketable wares. The best of them, following the lead of James A. McN. Whistler and his friend Edwin William Godwin were keenly aware of the lessons of Japanese design, first displayed to Europe's gaze at the 1862 international exhibition in London, a result of Matthew Perry's mission. Notable among these men, who became known under the tag of "the Aesthetic Movement" were Christopher Dresser, Lewis F. Day, and C. F. A. Voysey.[16]

Among the American industrial designers of the 1920s were several who had recently emigrated from Europe, where they were in the direct tradition of the Deutscher Werkbund, the Bauhaus, and the long-abuilding designers-for-industry tradition. First came Kem Weber, who was caught in America by World War I; in 1919 Raymond Loewy came from France and John Vassos came from Greece. In the mid-1920s Peter Muller-Munk came from Germany.

Some of the first Americans to call themselves industrial designers were Laurelle Guild, Egmont Arens, Ernest Elmo Calkins, and Harley Earl. The pioneer industrial designers in America who became most famous were Norman Bel Geddes, Henry Dreyfuss, Walter Dorwin Teague, Raymond Loewy, Donald Deskey, and Russel Wright. In the 1930s they created a school of industrial production and a style for their time.

Norman Bel Geddes   Norman Bel Geddes (1893–1958) began his career as a stage designer in Los Angeles and New York in 1916. Born in Michigan, he spent six months studying at the Cleveland School of Art and Chicago Art Institute before he began in the theater. He first designed settings for Max Reinhardt's production of *The Miracle*, where he turned the entire theater auditorium into a Gothic church, using wood benches as audience seating. He continued as a theater producer throughout his career.

From the 1920s onward, his reputation brought him product-design commissions. He designed automobiles for the Graham Paige Motor Company in 1927, and gas stoves for the Standard Gas Equipment Company around 1929. Bel Geddes went on to become one of the most prominent and successful of all American industrial designers. Throughout his career he was a visionary, inventing forms and techniques that would suit the futuristic spirit of the times.

Henry Dreyfuss   Another industrial design pioneer who started in the theater was Henry Dreyfuss (1904–72). Born in New York City, Dreyfuss began his design career working for Norman Bel Geddes on scenery and costumes for Max Reinhardt's *The Miracle*. He later was art director of scenery, costumes, and lighting for the Strand Theatre in New York City, where he designed over 250 weekly shows. He went on to design settings for numerous other productions, then to design theater interiors, and subsequently to design industrial products. In 1928 he opened his own office for industrial design.

In 1929 American Telegraph & Telephone Company (AT&T) asked him to do some sketches for the redesign of telephones. Dreyfuss replied that sketches were no thorough way to design such important products, and he expanded the commission to a complete design analysis and thorough solution. His continuing association with AT&T for the next fifty years produced some of his most influential industrial designs.

Dreyfuss went on to design transportation interiors, building interiors, household and consumer products, and farm and industrial products. His later independent work in cataloguing human measurements and the tolerances for human activities led to the establishment of the field of human factors engineering. It was said that Dreyfuss was dedicated to proving that people were more important than products. In the 1930s, he was to design interiors as well.

Walter Dorwin Teague   Walter Dorwin Teague (1883–1960) began his career as an illustrator and worked in advertising before opening his own advertising agency. In the mid-1920s he went to Paris to see what was happening in the new Art Moderne. On his return he designed packages, sketched a line of automobiles, and designed some grand pianos. Around 1927 he began an association with Eastman Kodak that ultimately led to his lifetime contract as design consultant to Kodak. In the 1930s he, too, began to design interiors.

Raymond Loewy   In 1919 Raymond Loewy (1893–1986) came to the United States from Paris. He started his career in New York as a fashion illustrator, advertising designer, and costume designer (for Florenz Ziegfeld). His first product design assignment was for the Gestetner Duplicator in 1929. From the 1930s through the 1960s he headed one of the largest, most successful, and best-known industrial design firms in the world. He designed offices and other commercial interiors, residences, automobiles, and numerous interior furnishings products.

Donald Deskey   Donald Deskey (1894–) worked in advertising in Chicago and New York in the early 1920s, and soon founded his own art agency. He went to Paris for a year, returned to teach in the art department at Juniata College in Pennsylvania, then went back to Paris to see the 1925 exhibition. On his second return to New York he began to produce furnishings that were sought after by architects and stage-set designers. In 1927 he was at work on a candy-vending machine. At the end of the 1920s Deskey was designing furniture and interiors for the Radio City Music Hall in Rockefeller Center (see Chapter 5).

Russel Wright   Russel Wright was one of the pioneer industrial designers; but, even more, he was an artist-craftsman devoted to the design of household objects, furnishings, and interiors. Born in Lebanon, Ohio, Russel Wright (1904–76) enrolled in art classes at the Cincinnati Academy of Art and at the Art Students' League in New York in 1920, where he studied painting and sculpture. He then went to Princeton University, where he worked with the Triangle Club, directing and designing sets. In the summers he continued to work in the theater, including a stint with Norman Bel Geddes designing for *The Miracle*. At the Maverick Festival theater in Woodstock, New York, he met and later married sculptor-designer Mary Small Einstein.

Following his theater years he began designing life-size caricature masks of celebrities. They were executed in new materials—plastic with spun glass, mirror, and marshmallows—which prefigured his inventive use of materials throughout his career. Soon miniature plaster animals were added to his designs, along with others made of aluminum and chromium-plated metal. From this investigation he moved on to produce, at the end of the 1920s, a set of spun-pewter bar accessories and then spun-aluminum table accessories and serving pieces. They were the beginning of his industrial design career in household objects—especially ceramic dinnerware, for which he became most widely known.

In this way the profession of industrial design emerged in the United States as a direct response to competition with European industry and in the direct tradition of the goals of incorporating machine production and "design for the times" into a new style for its day. The new industrial designers were to develop a new style in the 1930s.

By these means the Modern movement came to America. But in 1929, the year that the Museum of Modern Art was founded in New York, there occurred that cataclysmic event that was to affect the entire world—the Wall Street crash of October 29, 1929. Its repercussions on every field of life and design around the world lasted throughout the next decade.

Suggested Reading

Battersby, Martin. *The Decorative Twenties*. New York: Walker & Company, 1971.

Bayer, Herbert, Walter Gropius, and Ise Gropius, eds. *Bauhaus: 1919–1928*. New York: The Museum of Modern Art, 1938.

Brown, Erica. *Sixty Years of Interior Design: The World of McMillen*. New York: Viking Press, 1982.

Caplan, Ralph. *By Design*. New York: McGraw-Hill, 1984.

Fisher, Richard B. *Syrie Maugham*. London: Duckworth, 1978.

Hanks, David A. *Donald Deskey*. New York: E. P. Dutton, 1985.

Hennessey, William J. *Russel Wright*. Cambridge: MIT Press, 1983.

Hillier, Bevis. *Art Deco*. Minneapolis: Minneapolis Institute of the Arts, 1971.

Hitchcock, Henry-Russell, and Philip Johnson. *The International Style: Architecture Since 1922*. New York: W. W. Norton, 1932, 1966.

Jacobus, John M., Jr. "Architecture, American Style: 1920–45," *American Art*. New York: Prentice-Hall, Harry N. Abrams, 1979.

Jeanneret, Charles-Edouard. *Le Corbusier: 1910–65*. Zurich: Les Editions d'Architecture Zurich, 1967.

Johnson, Philip C. *Mies van der Rohe*. New York: The Museum of Modern Art, 1947, 1978.

Kaufmann, Edgar, Jr. "Interior Design: Architecture or Decoration?" *Progressive Architecture*. October 1962, pp. 141–44.

Lesieutre, Alain. *The Spirit and Splendour of Art Deco*. New York: Paddington Press Ltd., 1974.

Maxtone-Graham, John. *The Only Way to Cross*. New York: Macmillan, 1972.

McFadden, David Revere, ed. *Scandinavian Modern Design: 1880–1980*, a Cooper-Hewitt Museum exhibition. New York: Harry N. Abrams, 1982.

Meickle, Jeffrey L. *Twentieth Century Limited: Industrial Design in America, 1925–39*. Philadelphia: Temple University Press, 1979.

Pool, Mary Jane, ed. *20th Century Decorating, Architecture, and Gardens*. New York: Holt, Rinehart and Winston, 1980.

Pulos, Arthur J. *American Design Ethic: A History of Industrial Design to 1940*. Cambridge: MIT Press, 1983.

Robinson, Cervin, and Rosemarie Haag Bletter. *Skyscraper Style, Art Deco New York*. New York: Oxford University Press, 1975.

Tweed, Katharine, ed. *The Finest Rooms by America's Great Decorators*. New York: Viking Press, 1964.

Wilk, Christopher. *Marcel Breuer: Furniture and Interiors*. New York: The Museum of Modern Art, 1981.

Notes

1. Work Program of the Staatlichen Bauhauses Weimar, quoted from *Vienna Moderne: 1898–1918*, exhibition catalogue (University of Houston: Sarah Campbell Blaffer Gallery; New York: Cooper-Hewitt Museum, 1978), p. 90f. Reprinted there with permission from *Architecture and Design: An International Anthology of Original Articles*, ed. Timothy and Charlotte Benton, with Dennis Sharp (London: Granada Publishing, Ltd., 1975).

2. At the time of the 1923 exhibition, Breuer and Bayer, for example, were still students.

3. This goal was adopted as early as 1922 or 1923, but was reinforced after the move to Dessau.

4. Walter Gropius, *Idee und Aufbau des Staatlichen Bauhauses Weimar* (Munich: Bauhausverlag, 1923); translated in *Bauhaus: 1919–1928*, ed. Herbert Bayer, Walter Gropius, and Ise Gropius (New York: The Museum of Modern Art, 1938), p. 27f.

5. Christopher Wilk, *Marcel Breuer: Furniture and Interiors* (New York: The Museum of Modern Art, 1981), notes that the name "Wassily" was given to the Breuer Chair only in 1960, when it was put into production; in the 1920s and 1930s, it was known simply as "Model B3, club armchair." Also it was not made with leather until that time. Similarly, the Cesca Chair was so named (for Breuer's daughter, who was not yet born during the Bauhaus years) only in 1960.

6. Henry-Russell Hitchcock and Philip Johnson, *The International Style: Architecture Since 1922.* (New York: W. W. Norton, 1932, 1966), p. 33.

7. Wilk, op. cit., points out that Laccio was not a name of the period but was adopted when Knoll and Stendig began producing the designs. Wilk also notes that some of the pieces made under this name were not original designs, but rather adaptations of the design. The stool was original; but an extended version was not.

8. Wilk, op. cit. Breuer already had an apartment in Berlin and a furniture business, designing for Standard-Mobel.

9. Le Corbusier, *Towards a New Architecture* (London: The Architectural Press, 1949; New York: Frederick A. Praeger, 1949), p. 96.

10. Charles-Edouard Jeanneret, *Le Corbusier: 1910–65* (Zurich: Les Editions d'Architecture Zurich, 1967), p. 28.

11. Ibid., p. 50.

12. Alfred Barr, Jr., Preface to *Bauhaus: 1919–1928*, ed. Herbert Bayer, Walter Gropius, and Ise Gropius (New York: The Museum of Modern Art, 1938), p. 5.

13. Rose Cumming, quoted from *The Finest Rooms by America's Great Decorators*, ed. Katharine Tweed (New York: Viking Press, 1964), p. 51.

14. Eleanor McMillen Brown, quoted from Erica Brown, *Sixty Years of Interior Design: The World of McMillen* (New York: Viking Press, 1982), p. 15.

15. Barr, loc. cit.

16. Edgar Kaufmann, Jr., "Interior Design: Architecture or Decoration?" *Progressive Architecture* (October 1962), p. 142.

Chapter 5

1930–1940: Modernism
Comes to America

In the 1930s the Modern design movement reached the United States. It was increasingly seen in the American work of the postwar immigrants and in the work of a number of American designers who had gone to Europe in the second half of the 1920s to learn what was new.

In interior design the influential new directions were several strains from the 1920s: the Art Deco of the traditionalists that had been exhibited at the 1925 Paris exposition; the Art Moderne and Swedish Modern of the formalists that had been seen at the same exhibition; and the De Stijl–based international Modern of the functionalists that was being promulgated by the Bauhaus and by Le Corbusier (see Chapter 4). A skirmish ensued as these three new directions began to be transplanted into the home soil of Beaux-Arts academic historicism.

As a consequence, the decade of the 1930s witnessed a battle between the Futurists' look toward Tomorrow and the historicists' view of traditional American designers back to Yesterday. Designers were split into opposing camps and proclaimed rival ethics, morality, and social virtues—of historical tradition versus modern progress, of the old versus the new, of ornamentation versus purgation, and of verticality versus horizontality. Yet the use of the same modern materials by both camps, and the ability of designers to work in opposing styles at the same time, made for similarities and crossovers that make distinctions and categorization difficult, but perhaps more necessary now than ever.

In the 1930s the Modernist outlook gained a strong impetus when it became a political and economic goal as well as an artistic one. The political goal was to get the American economy and the country on the go again following the Great

Depression. The Depression that began in 1929 was an economic disaster unparalleled in modern times. More than five hundred banks failed. As the effects spread, the number of unemployed throughout the industrialized nations was estimated at 30 million in 1932; in Germany alone more than 6 million were unemployed. In the United States 9 million people were unemployed; that represented 25 percent of the work force. Unemployment spread insidiously across professions, classes, and countries until 1936 and 1937. Mortgage foreclosures and breadlines were daily concerns. The natural disaster of the Dust Bowl drought exacerbated the hopelessness of the situation.

The reach for tomorrow, therefore, was America's offer of hope; it also made the country, for the first time, a leader in the design fields. Optimism about the future was a campaign fought by President Franklin D. Roosevelt's New Deal; new jobs were created by the Works Progress Administration (WPA) from 1933 onward—including programs to support artists. Roads and transportation were improved and rural electrification spread. The Century of Progress exhibition in Chicago in 1933 was the first public design front; victory was proclaimed by the World of Tomorrow World's Fair in New York in 1939.

New Materials

A parade of new materials came before the public during the 1930s to point the way toward a cleaner, more functionally efficient, and healthier world of tomorrow. The plastics industry got its launch into major production in 1932. Celluloid had been invented in 1870 and Bakelite in 1907; but they were not adaptable to products that were durable, hygienic, colorful, and virtually unbreakable. In 1930 Plexiglas (Lucite) was invented and vinyl coating was manufactured. In 1932 a premium give-away cereal bowl for General Mills' Wheaties was made of a urea formaldehyde thermosetting plastic produced primarily by American Cyanamid; it was so popular that over 5 million were distributed. Nylon was invented in 1937. The Age of Plastics had begun.

Of other materials, glass—especially glass block—along with chromium-plated brass, Monel metal, and stainless steel, found their ways into interiors. Better linoleum, asphalt and rubber tiles, and acoustical tiles were produced. Plywood and Flexwood panels and sheets of plastic laminate spliced with chrome strips came into general use. As a poor stepchild of the Great Depression, knotty pine became the wall surfacing that bespoke the first years of the decade. In 1938 the Lumiline incandescent tube was announced by Westinghouse and General Electric. Fluorescent lighting was demonstrated widely at the New York World's Fair of 1939; and neon, introduced before 1930, became increasingly popular.

The Streamline Style

As the 1930s unfolded in America, the newly emerged profession of industrial design began to develop, or to be prominently recognized for developing, a new style for a futuristic tomorrow—Streamline Modern. Practitioners designing in this vein were pursuing a middle path between Modernism and Traditionalism, and between the Art Deco skyscraper style of the late 1920s and the Modernism and Purism of vanguard architecture. Specifically, they combined the Futurist-Expressionist interest in speed and motion into an aesthetic image. Whereas Art Moderne rejected historicism and adopted a geometric basis, Streamlining, which also rejected historicism, adopted Expressionism. But both avoided the ideological warfare over Modern versus traditional and concentrated on designing and styling. This put them at odds with design moralists on both sides.

The Streamline Decade, as those concentrating on this aspect of the 1930s have called it, based its stylistic idiom on the Futurists' love of speed and motion and on the Expressionists' sleek lines. Another inspiration was the early drawings of Erich Mendelsohn. The justification of Streamlining was speed and efficiency—including such miracles of modern technology as the pop-up toast robot in the kitchen. So Streamlining adapted aerodynamics and its most efficient form—the teardrop—which had been shown to increase speed by decreasing air resistance. Airflow designs as disparate as factory products, business equipment, household appliances, furnishings, and interiors began to come from the design offices of the new industrial designers.

Norman Bel Geddes, Henry Dreyfuss, Walter Dorwin Teague, and Raymond Loewy were the foremost of these industrial designers throughout the 1930s. Donald Deskey and Russel Wright made important contributions; Buckminster Fuller was the most visionary of these contemporaries. Most of their work was in the design of household appliances, business machines, and transportation. For this latter industry—and for museum and department store exhibitions—industrial designers got their first commissions to design interiors. Early on, industrial designers got to design some of the airplanes, ocean liners, and railroad trains that had inspired their imagistic style. Gasoline service stations, touring service centers, and other commercial interiors followed.

The airplane was the primary influence on and objective of the industrial designers. Plane exteriors developed from their angular, strut-supported, geometric wings to smooth airstream forms. Inside the first clipper seaplanes of 1931, the cabins were tubular-looking spaces lined with Flexwood and joined with wood-grained splines; decorative features such as donut life preservers recalled the sailing-yacht-like quality of seaplanes. In 1934 the Douglas DC-2 interior was designed as more stripped, functional, and mechanical-looking.

Ocean-liner interiors were a different matter because of their size and established clientele. The French *Normandie*, launched in 1932, was the last compendium of French Art Deco, with interior decorations by Jean Dunand, René Lalique, Jean Dupas, Raymond Subes, and Emile-Jacques Ruhlmann. Art Deco and Art Moderne were mixed in the interiors of the *Queen Mary*, which was designed by British designers and launched in 1934. It was called "ocean-liner modern."

No ship was produced in as visionary a Streamline style as Norman Bel Geddes's project, published in 1932 in his book *Horizons*; it was a fully enclosed water-going vessel that looked almost rocket-like. But from 1933 to 1936 Raymond Loewy designed the *Princess Anne* ferry that crossed the Chesapeake Bay from Cape Charles to Norfolk, Virginia, in as sleek a realization of this style as was achieved in ships.

From 1936 to 1938 Loewy designed the interiors of the *Panama* and other ships. Machine-art ideals and fireproof technology inspired simple industrial furnishings. Stainless-steel doors, metal tables with plastic laminate tops, metal-tube-framed chairs, and tubular lighting composed a spare, institutional, club-like atmosphere. Rounded corners and geometric motifs fixed the style as Streamline Modern. However, there were also concessions to popular taste in applied decorations, and a color scheme of coral, beige, and apple green; peach-colored mirrors, a totem of the decade, softened the scheme.

Streamline Trains

Railroad trains were the supreme realization of the Streamline ideal. The public was introduced to this new style by way of the first streamliner trains, which were exhibited by the Union Pacific and Burlington railroads at the Century of Progress Chicago World's Fair's second year, 1934. First came the Union Pacific Railroad's

City of Salina, which was made by the Pullman Car and Manufacturing Company. It had a trim interior of blue-banded walls progressing upward from dark to light blue, each band separated by an aluminum strip, and topped by a white coved or vaulted ceiling. Tubular aluminum seats were upholstered in a gold-brown tapestry.

Second of the streamliners was the Burlington *Pioneer Zephyr*, designed by architect Paul Cret with E. G. Budd and built by the Budd Manufacturing Company. It had an exterior with unpainted stainless-steel side panels that were corrugated for extra strength, but that also expressed the horizontal direction of the airstream, however much the corrugations may have impeded that stream. On the interior Cret specified bright colors accented with chrome or stainless-steel moldings. A striped linoleum floor and coved ceilings that incorporated air-conditioning and indirect strip lighting were used in the lounge and observation cars, which were furnished with tubular metal furniture and metal-based tables with plastic laminate tops. Flexwood and Masonite were also used.

62A. Henry Dreyfuss. Observation car on the *20th Century Limited*. 1938. *Penn Central Transportation Company Photograph. From Arthur J. Pulos, American Design Ethic: A History of Industrial Design to 1940 (Cambridge: MIT Press, 1983).*

The New York Central's *Mercury*, designed by Henry Dreyfuss in 1936, was conceived as a total design—integrating everything from the locomotive exterior to the table china inside. But it was Dreyfuss's design of the New York Central's *20th Century Limited* (1938) that was the high point of streamliner design.

Also a total design, the *20th Century Limited* was conceived in a kind of stately minimal vein that Dreyfuss called "cleanlining." The observation-car interior (see Figure 62A) had, at each end, a photo mural above an arc-shaped banquette and a round table; the effect was to make the interior plan bullet-nosed, like the ends of the train exterior. Sleek lozenge-plan gun-gray columns along the sides of the train car apparently supported a soffit and a shallow coved ceiling. Narrow horizontal bands atop the columns suggested capitals and continued the horizontal airflow motif of the ribbed-metal lampshades and the venetian blinds at the windows. In the *20th Century Limited* this airflow motif was more abstracted than in other train car design. Between built-in seating units upholstered in blue leather

62B. Henry Dreyfuss. Dining car on the *20th Century Limited*. 1938. *Penn Central Transportation Company Photograph. From Arthur J. Pulos*, American Design Ethic: A History of Industrial Design to 1940 *(Cambridge: MIT Press, 1983).*

were tables with integral lamps that had polished-metal shades. Gray carpeting and gray leather walls reiterated the brushed-metal finishes. The entire car had a unity that no other train car design achieved. The mirror-ended dining car (see Figure 62B) continued this theme of stripped elegance; metallic finishes in blue, gray, and rust-brown were used along with the new materials—Flexwood, cork paneling, and plastic laminates. Dreyfuss also designed the train's tableware and matchbook covers.

These early streamliners were custom-made (see Figure 63). By the end of the decade, mass production—of complete diesel locomotives by General Motors and of standard train cars by other companies—ironically signaled the end of the heyday of design innovation for streamliners.

Other Streamlined Interiors

Raymond Loewy and stage designer–author Lee Simonson created a model office and studio for an industrial designer for the Metropolitan Museum's 1934 exhi-

63. Raymond Loewy. Bar car on the *Broadway Limited*. 1938. *Raymond Loewy/William Snaith, Inc. Photograph. From Arthur J. Pulos,* American Design Ethic: A History of Industrial Design to 1940 *(Cambridge: MIT Press, 1983).*

bition Contemporary American Industrial Art (see Figure 64). The room had rounded corners of ivory plastic laminate paneling, round-ended horizontal windows, half-round metal trim, and three parallel horizontal bands—the latter a motif that became a trademark of the Streamline style. The flooring was blue linoleum; gunmetal blue metal tubular furniture had yellow leather upholstery. Desk-tables were supported on up-light verticals, suggesting a knowledge of Le Corbusier's combinations of table and column at the Villa Savoye. The up-light urn was prominent; tubular lighting was exposed. It was the epitome of the Streamline interior.

Norman Bel Geddes's House of Tomorrow (1931) combined the ideas of European Modernism with minimalist elements and Streamlining. Geddes's Elbow Room Restaurant in New York (1938), later renamed the Barberry Room, had many of the elements of Streamlining—curved walls, mirrored walls, strip lighting, horizontal emphasis—but it was an early example of the institutional style that continued in restaurants into the 1980s.

Donald Deskey   The interiors of that pinnacle of movie houses, Radio City Music Hall in Rockefeller Center (completed in 1932), are a compendium of the Deco-

64. Raymond Loewy and Lee Simonson. Model office and studio for an industrial designer. 1934. *Raymond Loewy/William Snaith, Inc. Photograph. From Arthur J. Pulos,* American Design Ethic: A History of Industrial Design to 1940 *(Cambridge: MIT Press, 1983).*

Streamline style. It was designed by an association of architects with Edward Durell Stone as project architect and with interiors and furnishings by Donald Deskey.

Deskey designed fifty rooms in the Music Hall, including furniture, lamps, fabrics, and wallpapers. The associated architects orchestrated an assembly of artworks to show the period's attention to integrating the arts into architecture and interior design. Some of those artworks include the vast lobby mural painted by Ezra Winter, sculpture by William Zorach, and sculpted bronze panels by René Chambellan depicting jazz in different countries. The main lobby (on which Deskey did not work) conjures up the ballroom of an ocean liner of the day: Oval-ended and high-ceilinged, the vast space is overlooked by balconies, sheathed in mirror, hung with vertical chandeliers, and features a monumental staircase of colossal effect (see Figure 65). Crystal spheres articulate bronze balusters. Ruth Reeves designed the geometric carpet.

In Deskey's lounges and smoking rooms (see Figure 66), metal-based furniture with black plastic laminate tops, murals based on social themes, wallpapers in harmony with those themes, and dark-toned brown, burgundy, and blue color schemes combined to make Radio City Music Hall a landmark of Deco-Streamline design.

During the decade Deskey also designed cane furniture that was produced by the Ypsilanti Reed Furniture Company and designed rooms with the most up-to-date Bauhaus imagery, using Mies van der Rohe's MR Chair.

65. Associated architects and Edward Durell Stone. Grand foyer, Radio City Music Hall. New York City. 1932. *Photograph by Anne C. Brown, © The Rockefeller Group, Inc., 1985.*

Critics of Streamlining

Functional as some airflow design was on the exterior, it was arbitrary decoration on most interior products. To Rationalists, who believed that all design should be based on structure, the exterior design of Streamlined trains and cars had little relation to inner structure or function. "Modernistic" was the pejorative appellation such designs encountered. Streamlining offered the aesthetic of industrial production in its linear, extruded elements, but more generally it offered the image of flying speed, if not the actuality of it. However, this was not unlike the early designs of the Modernists that offered the image of the machine without the actuality of it. But the Modernists ultimately attained their goal of structural honesty; Streamlining did not.

Styling such as Streamlining also offered the manufacturers of industrial products the newly acclaimed advantage of obsolescence, based on changing styles. In the early days of the Depression this apparent guarantee of future sales seemed like a lifesaver. If products could be restyled with new advances, greater efficiency, and more up-to-date appearances, sales would increase. If sales increased, not only would the financial status of individual manufacturers improve, but the national economy would get a boost. The nation got behind this idea; Streamlining was adopted as a political and economic goal. To the Streamline designers, this was a means of forwarding their version of Modernism. To crusading Modernists, who believed that theirs was a style without change, for all times and all peoples, the

66.   Donald Deskey. Ladies' lounge, Radio City Music Hall. New York City. 1933. *Photograph by Anne C. Brown, © The Rockefeller Group, Inc., 1985.*

concept of purposely built-in and designed-in obsolescence was anathema—second only to historicism and ornamentation, of course.

Beyond Streamlining: Interior and Industrial Design

Russel Wright and Buckminster Fuller are notable among those designers who did not go in the direction of Streamlining. Although they worked in disparate styles, both would have an impact on American design.

Russel Wright   Russel Wright was less concerned with Streamlining, and was perhaps more influential than other industrial designers on interior design during the 1930s. He displayed a dedication to American nationalism and the American way of life in the household objects and interiors that he specialized in designing.

Early in the decade he and his wife Mary developed a line of spun-aluminum serving pieces that accommodated the new servantless, and therefore less formal, way of dining and entertaining that came with the decade. Wright invented the concept of "stove-to-table ware." He went on to expand his aluminum line, to design modestly priced flatware and chromium-plated table accessories, and furniture.

His designs were derived both from Streamlining and from the Bauhaus, yet had their own distinctive look that was associated with modern informal living. The chair he designed in 1932 for his own use (see Figure 67) was somewhere between late–Art Deco–archaic and the Peasant style. Constructed of primavera wood, it had a leather sling back and a pony-skin seat.

In 1934 Wright designed a sixty-piece line of coordinated furniture for the Heywood-Wakefield Company. The line introduced a new concept—the sectional sofa, which was to become a staple of furniture designers. One copper standing up light in particular was something of a classic.

In 1935 he designed his widely successful Modern Living line of furniture for the Conant Ball Company. Reminiscent of Swedish Modern in its bentwood arm construction, the furniture was available in a reddish maple tone and in blonde wood. The latter was especially appealing to 1930s taste. Constructed of native woods, the Modern Living line offered an American flavor with something of a Craftsman recall. It was the first total design room furnishing to be made available as mass-market home furnishing. The association of his name with the furniture in advertising made Russel Wright known nationwide.

In 1937 Wright designed his ceramic American Modern Dinnerware, which was first produced in Steubenville, Ohio, in 1939. It was his biggest commercial and artistic success. Its forms were reminiscent of the undulating lines of Hans Arp and the amoeboid motif (see Figure 91). The dinnerware was produced in plain muted colors—Seafoam Blue, Granite Grey, Chartreuse Curry, and Bean Brown. It was the first dinnerware intended to be used in mixed rather than matched sets.

Among their residential interiors, Russel and Mary Wright's own duplex on Park Avenue (1938) was lined, beneath the balcony, with large squares of flat wood paneling, which were rotated to emphasize the decorative qualities of the grain. The ceiling was covered with a pattern of squares and lattices. Draperies at the large-gridded windows hung from the high ceiling to the floor.

Although Russel Wright belonged to the first generation of American industrial designers, he always was more of a craftsman-designer than a businessman-consultant. As idealistic as his American nationalism was, it was not universally admired in a decade that still looked to Paris as the art center of the world.

Buckminster Fuller   As independently original an inventor-engineer-architect as Richard Buckminster Fuller (1895–1983) was, his commitment to production by industry links his first proposals with industrial design. His circular metal-

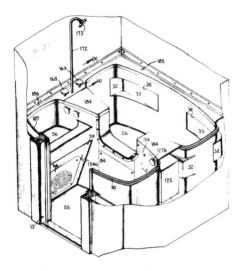

68. Buckminster Fuller. Dymaxion bath. 1927. *Illustration from Donald J. Bush,* The Streamlined Decade *(New York: Braziller, 1975).*

67. Russel Wright. Armchair with pony-skin seat. 1932. *Photograph from George Arents Research Library for Special Collections, Syracuse University.*

skinned Dymaxion House concept (1927) had adapted airplane construction techniques to the housing industry. His Dymaxion bathroom designed in 1927—produced as a prototype in 1930, of which about two dozen were produced in 1936, and the design patented in 1938 (see Figure 68)—was of sheet metal composing two compartments. One was the tub-shower compartment; the other was the sink-toilet compartment. The idea had to wait until the 1960s before production in plastic made such bathrooms commonly available.

Industrial Design Education

Educational programs in industrial design were slow to be established. The first degree-granting program in industrial design was offered in 1935 at the Carnegie Institute of Technology (now Carnegie-Mellon) in Pittsburgh. Other programs were at Pratt Institute in Brooklyn, at New York University, and at Columbia University. In 1935 the WPA provided a grant to establish the Design Laboratory school in New York, with Gilbert Rohde as director; but it was underfunded and short-lived.

Professional organizations for industrial designers began in 1938 with the American Designers Institute, founded in Chicago. Although its original members were mostly concerned with home furnishings, the organization was the precursor of the Industrial Designers Institute.

The Spread of Modernism in America

California had already welcomed the first architectural examples of European Modernism produced in this country. They were two houses: one by Schindler and the other by Neutra.

69. Joseph Urban. Apartment for Katherine Brush. New York City. 1932. *Photograph from Martin Battersby,* The Decorative Thirties *(New York: Walker & Company, 1971).*

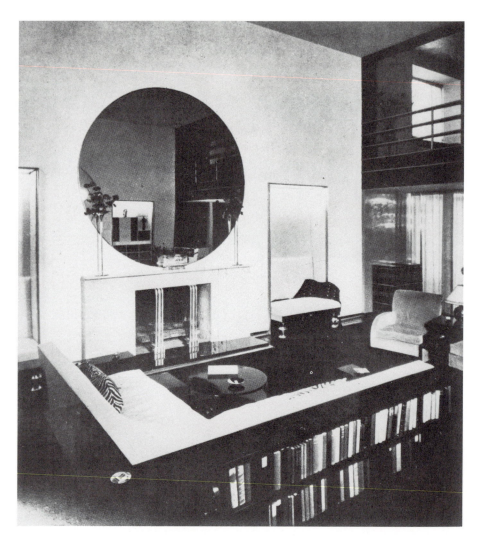

The Viennese architect Rudolph Schindler (1887–1953), who had worked as Frank Lloyd Wright's assistant during the Imperial Hotel days, designed the earliest American masterpiece in the new international Modern style—the Lovell House at Newport Beach (1925–26). It hovers over the beach on an exposed, open, and plug-in concrete structural frame; one end of the two-story living room has a floor-to-ceiling glass wall with detailing that we would associate with Wright's work at that time; at the other end is a surprisingly spare tall-backed banquette adjacent to a frameless two-sided fireplace. The combination is European–American Modern.

In 1929 another Viennese architect, Richard Neutra (1892–1970), built the Lovells' Los Angeles house, which is recognized as the only American design that can be considered to approach the quality of the Tugendhat House and the Villa Savoye of the same period. This design is a multilevel steel-frame house built on a hillside, with an exterior that reflects the combined Futurist-factory aesthetic in its large grids of glass and horizontal bands of white wall. The interior began to set the pattern for Neutra's later light and open metal-and-glass houses in California in the 1930s and 1940s.

Paul T. Frankl continued to design in the Modern idiom, getting more and more spartan after his skyscraper furniture of 1930. Joseph Urban (1872–1933), the Viennese architect and theater designer, also decorated in the Art Moderne style. Just before he died Urban designed an apartment in New York for Katherine Brush (see Figure 69). He used sleek-lined mantelpieces, banquette sofas with built-in bookcases along the backs, white leather upholstery, zebra-skin cushions, round mirrors, and Wiener Werkstaette appointments by Josef Hoffmann and Dagobert Peche. The color scheme was a bold white, black, and red.

Two Banking Halls: Irving Trust and PSFS

No better example of the rise of Modernism over lingering Art Deco can be found than two banking halls in two skyscrapers of 1932: the banking/reception hall of the Wall Street headquarters of the Irving Trust Company, designed by architect Ralph Walker of Voorhees, Gmelin & Walker (1932); and the Philadelphia Saving Fund Society.

In the tall, lozenge-shaped space of Irving Trust (see Figure 70), flaming

70. Ralph Walker. Banking hall, Irving Trust Company. New York City. 1932. *Photograph by Nyholm Lincoln, courtesy Haines Lundberg Waehler, Architects/Engineers/Planners, the successor firm to Voorhees, Gmelin & Walker.*

mosaics—graduated from red to orange—created a brilliant room. It represented the last effects of Art Deco in America.

The banking hall of the Philadelphia Saving Fund Society (PSFS) (1931–32), by George Howe and the Swiss architect William Lescaze, was a rugged and dynamic combination of De Stijl, Constructivist, and Expressionist directions (see Figure 71A). The PSFS exterior was the first International Style skyscraper produced in America, and it remained the most progressively Modern skyscraper until Mies's work after 1951.

In the main banking room (see Figure 71B), which was elevated on the second floor to permit the ground level to be occupied by street-enhancing shops, the tall

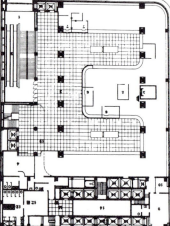

71A. Howe & Lescaze. Plan, banking hall, PSFS. Philadelphia, Pennsylvania. 1931–32. *Illustration from Henry-Russell Hitchcock and Philip Johnson,* The International Style: Architecture Since 1922 *(New York: W. W. Norton, 1966).*

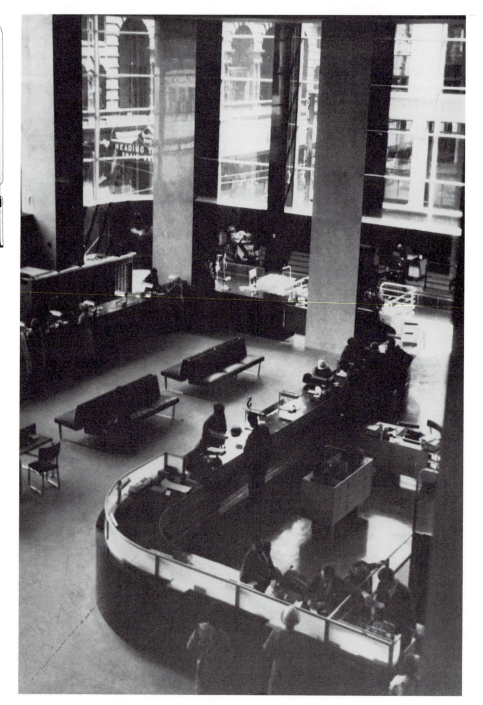

71B. Howe & Lescaze. Banking hall. PSFS. Philadelphia, Pennsylvania. 1931–32. *Photograph by Richard T. Dooner.*

freestanding columns and broad expanses of window wall were in deep contrast with the classicized Beaux-Arts buildings visible across the street. The radius-corner plan of the central tellers' counters and of the corner mezzanines reflected the rounded exterior corner of the base of the building. Black, gray, and white marble were used to finish the columns, floor, and counter fronts. Chromium-plated metal furniture upholstered in blue leather was designed by the architects to complete this first-generation Modern interior in America.

Elsewhere in the PSFS building, sleek, glossy, linoleum floors and lacquered columns were lighted by strips of fluorescent tubes to compose interiors of sparkling severity. Howe had decided his interiors would be based on "the elimination of meaningless mouldings."[1] More attention was given to such technological innovations as air-conditioning (PSFS was the second completely air-conditioned American skyscraper, following the 1928 Milam Building in San Antonio); acoustical ceiling tiles on a metal spline system were another innovation. In the executive offices on the 32nd floor, luxurious wood partitions were exploded by natural light effects both above the partitions and in the free-flowing spaces beyond.

The interior design of general offices in skyscrapers, except in rare instances, was still largely the purview of the client's office manager. This was a situation that did not change materially until the 1950s. Rare, then, were the Larkin Building of 1904 and, in the 1930s, PSFS and Frank Lloyd Wright's S. C. Johnson & Son Administration Building (see below).

The Cranbrook Academy of Art

Modern design education in America also received a new impetus at this time from the Cranbrook Academy of Art, which opened in 1932 in Bloomfield Hills, Michigan, outside Detroit. It was sponsored by the philanthropist George G. Booth and designed and directed by the Finnish architect Eliel Saarinen, who designed the campus buildings and their interiors (see Figure 72).

Many of the major designers and craftsmen of the next decade were associated with Cranbrook—either as family, faculty, or students. They included Eliel Saarinen, sculptor Carl Milles, ceramic designer Maja Grotell, and textile designer Marianne Strengell. Many of the designers who became the design leaders of the next decade studied at Cranbrook: Charles Eames, his wife Ray Kaiser Eames, Harry Bertoia, Benjamin Baldwin, Harry Weese, Edmund Bacon, Jack Lenor Larsen, Ralph Rapson, Pipsan Saarinen Swanson, and David Rowland. Florence Schust Knoll, who attended Cranbrook's Kingswood School for Girls, was a protégée of the Saarinen family. After terms as graduate students, many of these students went on to teach on the Cranbrook faculty. Cranbrook students in the 1940s included Don Knorr, David Rowland, and Niels Diffrient, all of whom became leading designers of furniture and other products.

Cranbrook Academy did not hold regular classes. Modeled on the American Academy in Rome, it offered graduate studio work in consultation with faculty artists-in-residence. The academy proposed no specific style or approach; its goal was the studio process rather than the designed product. Its influence was seminal.

The Promulgation of the International Style

In the first half of the decade the Modern movement as defined by the Bauhaus was spread to the American public. Alfred Barr of New York's Museum of Modern Art recalled that by 1930 there had been "a few pilgrims, a few students, and a few exhibited pieces, plus several books." Then, at the 1930 Paris exhibition of the Salon des Artistes Décorateurs, "the whole German section was arranged under

72. Eliel Saarinen. Dining room, President's House, Cranbrook Academy. Bloomfield Hills, Michigan. 1928–30. *Photograph from The Metropolitan Museum of Art, courtesy Cranbrook Archives.*

the direction of Gropius. Consistent in program, brilliant in installation, it stood like an island of integrity, in a mélange of chaotic modernistic caprice, demonstrating (what was not generally recognized at that time) that German industrial design, thanks largely to the Bauhaus, was years ahead of the rest of the world."[2] Next, Bauhaus lighting fixtures and chairs began to be imported into America privately, and American students at the Bauhaus began to return. Meanwhile, progressive architects in America were creating works in the idiom—Neutra, Schindler, Howe & Lescaze, and a few others.

The most widespread promulgator of the Bauhaus in the 1930s was undoubtedly the new Museum of Modern Art, which opened in New York in 1931. Its exhibitions of art, design, and furnishings were to influence the public for the next forty years. In 1930 Philip C. Johnson, then the twenty-three-year-old director of the department of architecture at the Museum of Modern Art, produced his first exhibition of Modern furniture and decorative arts.

In 1932 Henry-Russell Hitchcock and Philip Johnson organized their celebrated International Exhibition of Modern Architecture. It traveled for twenty months to eleven cities and was followed by a more portable version that traveled for six years. At the same time, Hitchcock and Johnson produced their seminal book, *The International Style: Architecture Since 1922,* which explained and defended the style, detailed its principles and taboos, and suggested how it might be adapted for American use.

The exhibition and book did not announce anything previously unheard of to the leading edge of the design professionals in America who were already working in the idiom; still, the book and exhibition together produced another of those anthologies or compendium expositions that further spurred on that vanguard of the profession to newer things. The exhibition and the book summed up the European achievement, gave it a name, and spearheaded the establishment of the Modern style in the minds of the public—and future clients— in the United States. The term International Style became a symbol of the American crusade for Modernism throughout the next quarter of a century (see Figure 73).

International-Style Principles

Hitchcock and Johnson defined the canon of the International Style:

> There is, first, a new conception of architecture as volume rather than as mass. Secondly, regularity rather than axial symmetry serves as the chief means of ordering design. These two principles, with the third proscribing arbitrary applied decoration, mark the productions of the international style.[3]

The authors did not list articulation of structure as a principle, nor clarity and alignment, which became essential in later International-Style work in America. And in their effort to distinguish a new art-historical style and give it historical credence, they proclaimed its formalist virtues over any functionalist aspirations.

This division had already created a rift among practitioners in Europe. It had caused Alfred Barr to name the new style "Post-Functionalism." In addition, in an effort to remove all political overtones of Marxist communism, the authors negated the social goals of the European movement, which had aimed to create good design for everyman. "This architecture will actively raise the general standard of living," the Russian Constructivist El Lissitizky had written in his mani-

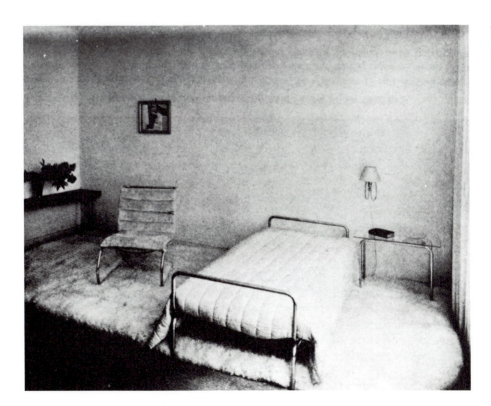

73. Lilly Reich. Bedroom, Berlin Building Exposition. Berlin, Germany. 1931. *Photograph from Henry-Russell Hitchcock and Philip Johnson,* The International Style: Architecture Since 1922 *(New York: W. W. Norton, 1932).*

festo of 1929. In so doing, Hitchcock and Johnson would later be accused of making Modernism into an aesthetic system without a social calling.

In *The International Style* Hitchcock and Johnson distinguished three concepts of interior space:

> first, the inside of the volume of the building, consisting of the entire content of the building or of a considerable part of it; second, interiors which open up into one another without definite circumscribing partitions; and finally, the ordinary enclosed room. . . .
>
> The second sort of interiors is the particular invention of the international style. In contrast to the completely enclosed rooms of the past [the International-Style designers] stress the unity and continuity of the whole volume inside a building. The independence of the dividing screens and their variation in size and placing contrast with the regularity of the [independently] isolated [structural] supports. The flow of function and the relation of one function to another can be clearly expressed. The different screens serving different purposes may well be of different materials provided always their thinness and freedom from structural duty is stressed. While the visible supports give an underlying rhythm, the variety of the screens produce, as it were, a melody which may be restrained or lyric as the architect wishes.
>
> The development of free planning, particularly with the use of curved and oblique screens, has been carried furthest in constructions of definitely architectural character. It gives to modern interiors a new kind of abstract space design unknown in the architecture of the past. But it is one of the elements of modern architecture which is easily abused, both practically and aesthetically. . . .
>
> Enclosed rooms of ordinary size, the third sort of interior, seldom have definite architectural character. They depend for their interest on their proportions and on their contents.[4]

Two years later, in 1934, the Museum of Modern Art produced its Machine Art Exhibition under the direction of Philip Johnson. It was a celebration of the goals and achievements of the Bauhaus in this regard, but it also reached out to include some of the work of American industrial designers, which was being exhibited simultaneously by the Metropolitan Museum of Art's Richard F. Bach. The basic tenets of machine art were defined at the time as geometry (the square, the circle, and the triangle—or, more accurately, despite Gropius's assertion—the cube, the cylinder, and the cone); precision; simplicity; and economy. The machine-art philosophy was shared by both the International Style and the Streamlining of the industrial designers. Similarly shared were the use of slick machine surfaces, chromium, and primary colors.

As Edgar Kaufmann, Jr., has written, "The Bauhaus believed architecture was the governess of the arts and acknowledged its ancestor-worship of the Arts and Crafts. . . . Nothing did more to confirm the architect's belief in his supremacy as universal designer and in his art as the ruling authority for design."[5] So the split in the professions was continued.

But in 1933, when Hitler had become Chancellor of Germany and the persecution of Jews began, the National Socialist (Nazi) government had closed the Bauhaus—as if Modern furniture, flat-roofed architecture, and abstract painting were degenerate and an attack on the state. The best designers of Germany and Austria began to be scattered around the world.

Finally, as a contributor to the promulgation of the Modern movement in America, the settings of Hollywood movies had, from 1930 onward, begun to feature International-Style design (see Figure 74). Those settings were surely as convincing—and probably more immediate and wide-reaching—in etching an image of Modern design into the minds of the general American public. All these factors contributed to the promulgation of the International Style in America.

74. Cedric Gibbons. Movie set for MGM's *The Easiest Way.* 1931. *Photograph from The Museum of Modern Art/Film Stills Archive, New York City.*

The Resurgence of Frank Lloyd Wright

During this period Frank Lloyd Wright, long considered passé and already in his sixties, completely rejuvenated himself and his style of work. He designed two masterpieces in the 1930s that place him among the most daring of American designers for all of this century—Fallingwater, and the S. C. Johnson & Son Administration Building.

Fallingwater

Fallingwater (see color plate 2) at Bear Run, Pennsylvania, near Pittsburgh, was designed in 1934 and completed in 1936. It was a luxurious weekend house for Edgar Kaufmann, the Pittsburgh department-store owner. His son, Edgar Kaufmann, Jr., who later became a brilliant architecture and design curator, an influential critic, historian, and teacher, had been a fellow at Taliesin and it was he who recommended Frank Lloyd Wright to his parents. At Fallingwater Wright eschewed all regional or historical recalls—of Roman villas, as in the Prairie houses, and of Mayan Mexico, as in his California houses of the 1920s. Instead, he combined his vision of organic architecture—expressed as natural fieldstone masonry growing out of the rugged, rocky site—with daring cantilevers of concrete over the water-fall. The cantilevers proclaimed the horizontal "white architecture" of the 1920s more dramatically and with more clarity than even Le Corbusier or Mies had done in Europe—despite Wright's vehement denunciations of European Modernism; and the combination with the indigenous rocky site showed his continuing dedication to the organic continuity of architecture and nature.

Inside (see Figure 75A), the main floor of Fallingwater consists almost entirely of a single space spreading out into subordinate spaces—including the terraces, which are connected to the water below by a seemingly suspended staircase. The entry side, where the masonry of the house is anchored to counterbalance the cantilevers, is solid and enclosed; the water side is open through walls of glass and red-painted metal to the views of the wooded landscape and to the sounds and rainbows of the waterfall. The structural achievement is of unparalleled daring and virtuosity for its time. Upstairs were family bedrooms, each of which opened onto one of the cantilevered terraces.

In the living room (Figure 75B), the fireplace is sited just behind the rock on which the family used to have picnic outings before the house was built; and that rock is left exposed, rising gently out of the concrete floor as the central origin and heart of the house. The rock masonry walls inside are more rugged and rough than the rectangular masonry forms of the exterior. Banquettes and wardrobes are built-in throughout the house to reinforce the rectangular slab motif on which the concept is based, and even the design of the freestanding furniture reiterates the cantilever motif.

North Carolina walnut and walnut veneer are used throughout the house, with the graining run horizontally instead of the more typical vertical runs; the intent was to reduce warping from the moisture of the waterfall, but, clearly, it had to do with contemporary design thinking as well. The heating system is run through built-in seating, tables, and bookshelves, which were made by the Gillen Wood-working Company of Milwaukee with some of the craftsmen who had made furniture for the earlier Prairie houses. The lighting in the upstairs bedrooms is incorporated into the wardrobes as indirect fluorescent up lights. The warm wood tones meld with the rock and the sand-color concrete so that the red window framing seems the only color in the house. Yet nature provides its tapestries beyond.

Justifiably published in every major book on Modern building design, Fallingwater is Wright's quintessential realization of organic integration: of site and natural materials with building; of natural and handcraft imagery with the industrial and Modern aesthetic of the twentieth century. It is a total work of art at its most complex juxtaposition of two seemingly disparate elements—handcraft and nature along with the machine. Now open to the public, Fallingwater is a milestone for all designers.

The S. C. Johnson & Son Administration Building

At the S. C. Johnson & Son Administration Building in Racine, Wisconsin (1936–39), Wright showed that he could also work in the Streamline style yet broaden its impact to achieve a kind of timelessness and innovative genius that far surpassed others working in that vein (see color plate 3). In the large (128 feet by 228 feet by 20 feet high) main bullpen office space which updated the Larkin Building's skylighted and clerestoried atrium, tall slim lily-pad-topped columns are a structural tour de force; the enclosed, air-conditioned, indirectly lighted environment is the stuff of Futurists' dreams; and the furniture—of wood on metal tubing in a rich rust color to blend with the brick of the building—was the world of tomorrow (see Figure 76).

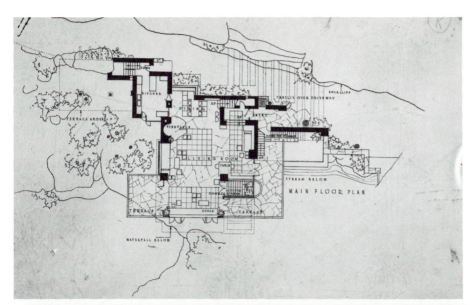

75A. Frank Lloyd Wright. Plan, Fallingwater. Bear Run, Pennsylvania. 1934–36. *Illustration © Frank Lloyd Wright Foundation, 1942.*

75B. Frank Lloyd Wright. Living room, Fallingwater. Bear Run, Pennsylvania. 1934–36. *Photograph © Ezra Stoller/ ESTO, 1963.*

76. Frank Lloyd Wright. Metal office furniture, S. C. Johnson & Son Administration Building. Racine, Wisconsin. 1936–39. *Photograph courtesy Johnson Wax Company.*

The furniture again showed Wright's devotion to the smallest detail of every project—and to the concept of total design. Composed of the circular motifs used throughout the building, the vocabulary of the furniture reveals how significantly Wright had rejuvenated himself since his work on the more rigidly rectangular Larkin Building. Desks were constructed by Steelcase Inc. of tubular steel with triple-decked walnut tops that have round ends. Tubular steel composes the sides of the desks, reiterating the tubular glass and other horizontal motifs throughout the building; drawers are semicircular in plan and swing in on pivots to be closer to the desk user. The semicircular desk-top ends are cantilevered beyond the ends of the vertical supports. An integral wastebasket is hung up on the ladder support to facilitate floor cleaning. Chairs, both executive and secretarial, are designed on the same tubular ladder principle, but with semicircular ladders. The backs tilt on pivots with changing seating positions. Secretarial chairs were designed with only three legs. The concept was futuristic and innovative, but the good posture demanded of the user—keeping both feet on the floor for balance—was not universally attainable, and many of the chairs have been converted to four legs.

Partitions, clerestory windows, and interior domes are constructed of Pyrex glass tubing, again showing Wright's futuristic use of glass. On the exterior, the virtuosic use of glass tubing laid up as bands between brick masonry creates the most continuous horizontal windows imaginable. And the lighting effect on the outside at night brilliantly demonstrates Wright's design imagination. In the next decade he was to add a tower to this complex that was an even more extraordinary feat of cantilevering and of innovative glass-wall design.

At this same time, also, in his Wingspread House for Herbert F. Johnson north of Racine, Wisconsin (1937), and in his Sunbelt studio Taliesin West in Scottsdale, Arizona (1938), Wright continued to show his inventiveness and daringly visionary interiors and furnishings. He was over seventy at the end of the decade—and he had twenty years more of productive work to go.

Design in France

A refined and reductive style appeared in Paris in the 1930s. It was somewhere between the work of traditional decorators working in the late–Art Deco vein—such as Jules Leleu, André Groult, and Emile-Jacques Ruhlmann—and the work of the Formalists, who were contributing to the development of Art Moderne—such as Pierre Chareau, François Jourdain, Eileen Gray, and Le Corbusier. The leading French designer in this direction was Jean-Michel Frank. His influence on American interior designers was enormous.

Jean-Michel Frank

Born in Paris and educated in law, Jean-Michel Frank (1895–1941) had traveled extensively before he became interested in eighteenth-century styles around 1927; in 1929 he began to work with decorator Adolphe Chanaux on an apartment for himself. A darling of society, his work attracted the attention of clients and patrons, including the Vicomte and Vicomtesse de Noailles, fashion designers Elsa Schiaparelli and Lucien Lelong, as well as Nelson Rockefeller in New York and Templeton Crocker in San Francisco. For these and many others he designed interiors.

In 1932 Frank and Chanaux opened a shop in Paris for the sale of their furniture designs and as headquarters for their interior decorating. From the first year of operation, their furnishings were eagerly bought by designers such as Elsie de Wolfe, Syrie Maugham, Frances Elkins, and Eleanor Brown for use in American interiors. Chanaux had studied at the Ecole des Beaux-Arts and had worked with decorator André Groult and with Ruhlmann before beginning his association with Jean-Michel Frank.

Rare among decorators, Jean-Michel Frank designed complete and "total" interiors—room architecture as well as furniture and appointments. Also, in the tradition of the *ensembliers*, Frank and Chanaux assembled a collaborative of other artists and designers with whose decorative arts they could furnish their interior design concepts; these included stage designer Christian Berard, architect-decorator-furniture designer Emilio Terry, and Swiss sculptor Alberto Giacometti and his brother Diego. Frank worked with the Giacometti brothers on sculptures and on sculpted furnishings beginning in 1934—notably a series of bronze lamps and white plaster lamps, sconces, and sculptural up-light urns. Carpets were designed by Christian Berard, or after his drawings. The assemblage by so many different designers was in the direct tradition of the eighteenth century, if now reminiscent of some newly personalized Wiener Werkstaette creation.

The Frank Style   The style of Frank and Chanaux was based on refined simplicity and chaste purity, on proportion and balance, and on sensitivity to textures and materials. Frank's concepts depended on form and line, and on juxtapositions and contrasts of fullness with emptiness. He avoided superfluous objects and ornamentation. Moldings and valances were stripped away. Rooms were left bare and box-like. The lines of furniture were straight and unornamented—simplified to a functional minimum. He preferred not to hang pictures in his interiors, only to exhibit sculpture. The beige-white palette of the 1930s was his arena. Still, since Frank's designs were not based on the machine aesthetic, they were neither clinical enough nor vanguard enough to be accepted by the Modernists from the Bauhaus or Purism.

The Jean-Michel Frank style was reductive rather than additive and elaborate; it was abstracted, refined, stripped, and minimal. It was also rather classical, in that it made references to simplified Louis XVI and primitive art and to archaic

Greece and ancient Egypt. The tomb of Tutankhamen, opened in 1922, was still an inspirational image of late–Art Deco classicism.

Frank's fundamental belief was that an apartment could be furnished by unfurnishing it.[6] Sometimes he called his finished rooms "unfurnished" because they were so comparatively bare. Some rooms were "empty" except for a solitary piece of furniture, a Grecian bust, or an Egyptian fragment. An oft-repeated joke was that in an apartment by Jean-Michel Frank you had to go through three bare foyers before finding the lady of the house seated at a plain table on which was only the nose of a statue. "Ah, but the nose was from Alexandria," went the joke. Jean Cocteau said, on seeing one of Jean-Michel Frank's interiors, "Pity the burglars got everything."[7]

Frank's Materials   What Frank eliminated from the forms of his interiors was made up for by sumptuous materials. The materials used by Frank and Chanaux were among the most recherché, rare, and luxurious that they could imagine: Walls were covered in rare woods, varnished straw marquetry, sanded white lacquer, or parchment (also called vellum or sheepskin). Frank's rare woods included macassar ebony, Brazilian rosewood, okoume from Gabon, adze-finished oak, black pearwood, as well as sand-jetted woods. Furniture finishes included bleached split-straw marquetry, veneers of glittering gypsum mica, white shagreen marquetry, gilded wood, and white lacquer. Some furniture was inlaid with ivory, embossed with bronze or silver. White plaster lamps or lamps with quartz crystal or bronze bases had vellum lampshades. Upholsteries were cowhide, lambskin or golden lambskin, lambswool or saddle-sewn leather, fawn leather, champagne-colored satin, and white leather. Among Jean-Michel Frank's combinations of wood and upholstery were sycamore wood with golden lambskin; varnished oak with white leather; ebonized pearwood with wool tweed; sycamore wood and champagne satin; oak and wicker, ebonized beech and tweed.

With his rare and unusual materials, Frank made unexpected contrasts: He had Louis XVI armchairs stripped and recovered them in cowhide or men's suiting cloth. He offset his elaborately sheathed furniture with the simplest canvas-covered director's chair—albeit a hand-carved director's chair. He also used straw, cane, and plain white plaster. In his work, he seemed to combine the monumental and the palatial with the simple Peasant style.

Some of Jean-Michel Frank's interiors were like small jewel boxes. In the drawing room of his own apartment, the walls were covered in straw marquetry, chairs and a low screen were upholstered in white leather, and low occasional tables were finished in mica squares. The library had walls upholstered in natural leather, chairs and sofa upholstered in pale-colored leather, a mantelpiece of travertine, low tables of sanded oak, and nesting tables covered in parchment. In the bedroom the bed was a thin mattress atop a wide low platform. At the same time his partner Adolphe Chanaux designed a similar platform bedroom that was all sparse primitiveness.

In the townhouse mansion of Vicomte and Vicomtesse Charles and Marie-Laure de Noailles, Frank created the two most important rooms of his career, beginning in 1932. In the grand salon, or main drawing room (see Figure 77), he lined the walls with squares of tawny parchment, which made the rooms look as if they were constructed of blocks of stone; he hung draperies of heavy beige silk; he laid *parquet de Versailles* on the floor, over which was a *tête-de-nègre* carpet. He offset this pale envelope with monumental double doors of burnished bronze. A mantelpiece was finished in small squares of glistening mica.

Rounded puffy sofas and chairs were upholstered in white leather (in 1936 the upholstered furniture was replaced by a more boxy, rectilinear group, again in white). Small screens at the end of the sofa as well as a small two-door cabinet and

77. Jean-Michel Frank. Living room, townhouse of Vicomte and Vicomtesse de Noailles. Paris, France. 1932. *Photograph from Leopold Diego Sanchez and Andree Putman,* Jean-Michel Frank *(Paris: Editions du Regard, 1980).*

a library table were finished in fan-patterned straw marquetry. Other low tables were finished in shagreen or bronze, and on them sat lamps with bases of crystal or ivory and with silk shades. One lamp was shaded by sheaves of thick split ivory set into a bronze base. Other materials were beige velvet, pale-beige leather, oyster-white plush. The effect was of timeless, ethereal monumentality. This interior was as grand and imposing, as monumental and rich as some pharaoh's treasure-laden tomb. But the Noailleses hung their important collection of paintings in this room against Frank's wishes, and that created a rift between client and designer.

Less typical was Jean-Michel Frank's work in New York in the apartment of Nelson Rockefeller (1937). There (see color plate 4) he provided the furniture, carpets, and lighting fixtures in a living room designed by architect Wallace K. Harrison. The walls were sheathed in polished oak from floor to ceiling, with a minimal molding making the connection/transition. Windows and valances as well as the surround of the fireplaces at each end of the room were framed by undulating, semi-Rococo, semi–Art Nouveau lines, and in one fireplace surround was a mural executed by Henri Matisse; Fernand Léger painted a fresco surrounding the other fireplace.

Seating pieces were all overstuffed units with the same lines, and stubby legs of Louis XV inspiration. Flanking the Matisse fireplace were gilt armchairs adapted from Louis XVIII models. Tables included straight-lined pieces as well as gilded consoles, lamps, and firedogs by the Giacometti brothers. The console was a semi-circular, gilded wood piece with surrealistic legs. An Aubusson carpet of leaves floating on a solid ground was designed by Christian Berard. Paintings by Picasso from the family collection hung on the walls. The room and furnishings were to be recast in the 1980s (see Chapter 10).

Jean-Michel Frank's work in South America at the end of the decade, and in San Francisco for Templeton Crocker, was also less sparse than the work in France for which he is most admired; but it was rich in imagination. The Templeton

Crocker apartment had a dining room and a breakfast room entirely in lacquer by Dunand, a black marble and crystal fountain from St. Gobain in the party room, and two splendid bathrooms. One was in black Belgian marble and hammered glass; the other was in Swedish green marble and etched glass. The living room was somewhere between ocean-liner Modern and a prefiguring of 1950s Modernism. The bedroom had one of Frank's platform beds that prefigured 1970s Minimalism.

Perhaps more than any other French designer of the 1930s, Jean-Michel Frank influenced American residential design—due largely to his influence and exposure to American interior designers at the Paris program of the New York School of Fine and Applied Arts, where he served as a critic. Much of his idiom has been carried down to our own day by the older, established American decorating firms—who espoused his French Modern as their model. It is from his designs that the later, popular Parsons table was derived.

Surrealism

Surrealism began to have a recognizable influence on interior design in the late 1920s in Europe. In 1924 André Breton had issued the First Surrealist Manifesto, "Surrealism," which applied Freud's theories to art and took imagery off (literally) to another world, a dreamworld. Sigmund Freud's turn-of-the-century theories had begun to have general currency beyond Vienna; his influence had become pervasive. Carl Jung had published *Psychological Types* in 1920; psychology had become the new twentieth-century science. Apparently inconsistent with reality, Surrealism was above and beyond reality. It was in the cyclic twentieth-century tradition that, along with Abstraction and musical Dissonance, has been called Irrationalism.

Surrealism espoused weightless inversions, random influences and content; all devised to change perception, and ultimately to change the world. Surrealism was thought of as revolution, a system of radical change. It quickly confused these political goals with artistic goals. Among the Surrealists, who passed through several stylistic periods, were Hans Arp, Paul Klee, Pablo Picasso, Man Ray, and Joan Miró; Max Ernst stayed with Surrealism for the longest run; Salvador Dali and René Magritte mocked the merely functional from the 1930s through the 1950s. But the strongest impact of Surrealism on interior design was to be seen in the 1930s.

Surrealism was the new spirit of the decade—a mannered inversion of the expected, paradoxical, ironic, sardonic, perverse, and whimsical. It was popularized as that brand of humor called "camp." Surrealism was manifest in the work of Jean-Michel Frank and his collaborators, as well as in the work of other French and English designers. Soon, Surrealism became an influence on American design and display.

Dada and Surrealism had been investigated by the painters Salvador Dali, René Magritte, Giorgio de Chirico, and Man Ray, and by filmmaker Luis Buñuel since before the 1930s. Buñuel's film *Le Chien Andalou*, sponsored by Charles de Noailles, had been privately shown in 1929 and 1930. Salvador Dali's painting *The Persistence of Memory* dates from 1931. Meret Oppenheim's *Object (Déjeuner en fourrure)*—the fur-lined teacup—was done in 1936. It was artists' interpretation of Freud's interpretation of dreams, which began to be more popularly known in the 1920s and 1930s. In interior design this Surrealism was demonstrated by a kind of discontinuous, dissociated, manic humor, by dreamlike fantasy, the baroquely bizarre and perverse.

In Jean-Michel Frank's work the Surrealist element was displayed as a combination of human forms and foliage inspired by Matisse and Picasso, but inter-

78. Jean-Michel Frank. Cinema-ballroom for Baron Roland de l'Espée; with sofa by Salvador Dali inspired by Mae West's lips. Paris, France. Circa 1936. *Photograph from Leopold Diego Sanchez and Andree Putman, Jean-Michel Frank (Paris: Editions du Regard, 1980).*

jected into functional furnishings such as tables and lamps, vases and sconces. Draperies of molded plaster of Paris, or of real fabric oddly draped over windows and stair rails, appeared in the fashion salons of Lucien Lelong and of Elsa Schiaparelli. A cinema-ballroom for Baron Roland de l'Espée (see Figure 78), which showed the influence of Jean Cocteau and of Salvador Dali, had each wall a different color—pink, pale blue, sea-green, and straw-yellow—a carpet of Pompeian red, and stage-set theater boxes in the corners draped in purple velvet. Between the boxes was a lip-shaped red satin sofa modeled on Dali's lips of Mae West. Frank also designed interiors for Guerlain perfumes with stage-set trompe l'oeil by Christian Berard; the influence of ballet, theater, and Picasso's harlequins was rampant.

Elsewhere, Surrealist tables and stools were designed with human legs and feet as table legs and feet; life-size hands held sconces or vases; feet and legs made other appearances in furniture of the period. Frank also used the tables designed by Emilio Terry with white plaster bases of large-scale palm leaves, scallop shells, and other neo-Baroque and neo-Rococo imagery, such as the white plaster palm-tree torchères that figured largely in this period and later.

Le Corbusier also became involved with the Surrealist theme in the mid-1930s. The Surrealist influence on his architecture has since been analyzed, though he would not have admitted or perhaps recognized it. For the Paris apartment of the Mexican art patron Carlos de Bestigui, Le Corbusier created a Futurist "machine for entertaining" in 1931. The spaces he designed for de Bestigui were stark, austere, high-ceilinged white boxes with large expanses of floor-to-ceiling sliding glass. At the touch of buttons, walls disappeared or reappeared, windows slid into walls, and chandeliers moved along recessed tracks in the ceiling to permit movies to be projected without interference.

But the furnishings were a different theme altogether: By the time the architecture of the apartment was finished, de Bestigui had become interested in Surrealism, and the furnishings were designed in that idiom by de Bestigui or—one

79A. Le Corbusier and de Bestigui. Living room, de Bestigui apartment. Paris, France. Circa 1936. *Photograph from Martin Battersby,* The Decorative Thirties *(New York: Walker & Company, 1971).*

is tempted to suspect—by Emilio Terry. Terry, the architect-decorator who designed the white neo-Baroque scrollwork furnishings for Jean-Michel Frank, was the Paris-born scion of a wealthy Cuban family. In the living room (see Figure 79A) the fireplace was jammed uncomfortably in a corner and appointed with a nineteenth-century gilt-framed mirror and prismed girandoles. An ornate Venetian chandelier hung in the middle of the room over an opulent, puffy ottoman with a scalloped base and fringe. Overstuffed sofas and chairs in a Victorian mode had the same upholstered treatment. Hung at the windows were ice-blue velvet floor-to-ceiling draperies bordered with a Second Empire design. A life-size blackamoor figure in porcelain was a blown-up version of eighteenth-century figurines; the blackamoor became a component of many interior schemes by different designers in these years. Here, the scale and the sense of period were bizarre. Electricity may have moved walls in this apartment, but the nighttime lighting was solely from candles. Such was Surrealistic fantasy.

In the movie room (see Figure 79B) heavy gold-and-white Second Empire furniture, looking only slightly better than merry-go-round appointments, surrounded a carpet with a coat-of-arms medallion surrounded by fleurs-de-lys. Le Corbusier's spiral ribbon-balustraded stair looked unclimbable. The movie projectors were concealed behind gilt-framed mirrors that had ormolu candle brackets superimposed on them—the dismembered-hand motif of Surrealism.

The outdoor terrace joined in this Surrealistic exercise by becoming an outdoor room—literally (see Figure 79C). Carpeted with grass and daisies, the sky-blue walled space with its sky-ceiling was furnished with a marble Baroque commode sporting a birdcage and mechanical bird; the space also had a Baroque marble fireplace appointed with clock and candlesticks. Above the mantelpiece a circular frame offered a view to the Arc de Triomphe and Paris rooftops. Hedges in boxes slid away electrically to reveal other views. Le Corbusier may have created the spaces for this apartment, but Carlos de Bestigui clearly directed the bizarre Surrealist decor.[8]

79B. Le Corbusier and de Bestigui. Movie room, de Bestigui apartment. Paris, France. Circa 1936. *Photograph from Martin Battersby,* The Decorative Thirties *(New York: Walker & Company, 1971).*

79C. Le Corbusier and de Bestigui. Terrace, de Bestigui apartment. Paris, France. Circa 1936. *Photograph from Martin Battersby,* The Decorative Thirties *(New York: Walker & Company, 1971).*

The Peasant Vernacular

More typical of Le Corbusier's interiors at this time was vernacular, provincial architecture and peasant-style furniture. Spare and minimal, rustic and simple, this primitive style suggests the influence of Picasso's studio and of modern Primitivism. Beginning with the Errazuris House in Chile (1930) and the de Mandrot

80. Le Corbusier. Own bedroom. Paris, France. Before 1935. *Photograph from Martin Battersby,* The Decorative Thirties *(New York: Walker & Company, 1971).*

House (1931), he used local stone walls along with the stucco and glass of International Style. In the de Mandrot House, the ceiling was of natural plywood and the floor of local tiles. Simple wood furniture accompanied metal tubular furniture designed by René Herbst and Hélène de Mandrot.

Similar was Le Corbusier's design for a weekend house outside Paris. Le Corbusier explained that because the house was to be as little visible as possible, its "height was reduced to 8 ft."[9] That was a notable statement. The roof was flat, but the interior ceilings were reinforced barrel vaults, giving the interior a cosiness and richness as well as more height than expected. Some of the interior walls were of local stone; glass blocks constituted other walls. Flooring was of white ceramic tile, fireplace and mantel of exposed brick. The furnishings were, again, a mixture of rustic, provincial pieces. Le Corbusier was already moving beyond the Machine-Age Modern of the 1920s and working also in a more poetic, simple regional idiom.

Most of Le Corbusier's work of this decade, however, was directed toward urban-planning projects of a large nature, and his publications did not emphasize interior design. From 1936 to 1945 he designed the Ministry of Education Building for Rio de Janeiro in Brazil with Oscar Niemeyer, Lucio Costa, and other Brazilian architects on the team. The sunscreens surrounding the building provided a new word in architecture—*brises-soleils*—and a lesson about the need to shield glass curtain walls from the sun that was not well heeded by later architects. This slab-like building, which was the impetus for the United Nations Secretariat building in New York, became the model for numerous other office buildings for the next thirty years.

Design in England

One of the more prominent English decorators of the 1930s, Sibyl Colefax, started her business in 1933. She specialized in Regency schemes and was later joined by

John Fowler, a restoration specialist who had great knowledge about the history of draperies and also was gifted with a special color sense. Other prominent English designers of interiors and furnishings in the 1930s included decorator and fabrics designer Arundell Clarke; architect Raymond McGrath; Oswald P. Milne; Oliver Hill; Humphrey Deane; Ronald Fleming; and Oliver Bernard, who designed the glass, mirror, and lightning-streaked interiors of the Strand Hotel in London. Ambrose Heal and Gordon Russell were the major English furniture designers at the time. Photographer Cecil Beaton and stage designer Oliver Messel also began influencing and designing interiors at this time.

Unlike the American traditional decorators who were generally concerned with correct period rooms through the 1920s, those in England were more casual about their historicism. This surprised American designers who visited England; it also reinforced the early American concern for proper period restoration of American interiors.

The English continuation of romantic historicism was accompanied by fancifully decorative painted panels and murals—shepherdesses and harlequins, pastoral and aerial scenes, along with trompe l'oeil. English artists who became popular in this work included Rex Whistler, Duncan Grant, Etienne Drian, Allan Walton, and Eugene Berman.

Syrie Maugham   Although the Depression forced the closing of her shops in America, Syrie Maugham continued to decorate in Europe and America throughout the 1930s. She worked in the pale-toned color range, but white became her trademark and on it she made her reputation. She specified white for mirror frames, rugs, and satin draperies; she had furniture painted, often white; she used white china figurines of birds, white bamboo, white plaster palm-tree table bases. Many of her white pieces of furniture came from the shop of Frank and Chanaux in Paris. These latter designs were attributed to both Serge Roche and Emilio Terry (see Figure 81). Syrie Maugham also used Giacometti's white plaster urn up lights.

81. Syrie Maugham. Dining room, own country house, The Pavilion. Weddesdon, Bucks., England. 1935. *Photograph by Millar & Harris, London.*

White camellias and white lilies were her trademarks, and calla lilies became a symbol of the time.

Syrie Maugham extended the white motif by using mirrors and glass—for table pedestals, lamp bases, and folding screens. It all seemed the ultimate blizzard of white. But white was not her only approach. Although fairly casual about historical elements, as most of her English contemporaries were, she sometimes left original woodwork and lightened rooms with her mirrors, white, and fresh pale colors.

One of her most influential interiors was a bedroom in Mrs. Tobin Clark's David Adler–designed house in San Mateo, California (1930). All the furnishings were white, including wood tables, upholstered chairs, draperies and venetian blinds, a four-poster bed, and a zigzag-sculpted white carpet by Marian Dorn. The Swedish white linen walls had an overall scroll pattern in two tones of green that created a fresh trellis around the room. Syrie Maugham's design for Mrs. Clark's bedroom (see Figure 82) was much imitated and recreated during the next several decades.

American Decorating

During the Great Depression much of the design world had to turn inward to behind-the-creative-scenes activities that continued to support the field—and to federal arts projects. Professional interior design societies in America were consol-

82. Syrie Maugham. Bedroom for Mrs. Tobin Clark. San Mateo, California. 1930. *Photograph courtesy Jerome Zerbe.*

idated by the founding in 1931 of the American Institute of Interior Decorators (now the American Society of Interior Designers). New York already had its Decorators Club for women only, and a Society of Interior Decorators for men only; Chicago had sponsored the Woman Decorators' Association; and there was an Interior Decorators Club of Philadelphia.

The American Institute of Interior Decorators, organized in Grand Rapids, Michigan, was to provide a focus and a podium for all of the young profession as well as a meeting ground with the furniture industry with which it was so closely associated. The first president was Chicago decorator William R. Moore. In 1936 the headquarters of the new professional organization was moved to New York and its name and initials changed to American Institute of Decorators (AID). It was to be renamed the American Society of Interior Designers (ASID) in the 1970s.

Grand Rapids and Southern furniture plants continued to produce cheap furniture. "Early American Maple" furniture poorly pretended to recreate the image of the Colonial revival of the 1920s, which was given popular impetus by the opening of Colonial Williamsburg in 1932. The search for new historical periods led to the rediscovery of mid-nineteenth-century balloon-back Louix XV Revival chairs and loveseats, which came to be labeled "Victorian furniture"; and there was some degree of interest shown in Art Deco styling by the use of blue mirrors and rose-beige mirrors. But a new sense of the importance of historical accuracy and a new knowledge of antique furniture was growing in Grand Rapids. It was to be seen in the furniture designs of Gilbert Rohde and Edward Wormley (see below). That conscience also included an awareness of the rich clients of interior decorators.

At this time, too, new professional magazines appeared to spark communication (and advertising) in the field. *Home Furnishings Daily* had begun publication in 1929. In 1932 *The Decorator's Digest* was founded; it was renamed *Interior Design and Decoration* in 1937 and, by the early 1950s became simply *Interior Design*. In 1934 *The Upholsterer*, which had been published since 1888, was renamed *The Interior Decorator*; it became *Interiors* in 1940. These publications assumed that the profession had a broadening base, that the model set by the "great collectors" of the previous decades was gradually shifting to include more of the population. The new young profession was coming of age.

While in architectural interiors the battle raged on between "warm" handcraft and the "cold" machine, between romantic historicism and vanguard Modernism, in residential decorating it was a much more one-sided approach. Many more decorators continued to practice in the tradition of Elsie de Wolfe's "good taste." This was not surprising in view of the educational commitment to French historicism, but it is ironic in view of the potential exposure to concurrent French modernism on the part of students in Paris.

Still, American residential designers did demonstrate a few definite moves in the direction of simplification and Modernism. Among them were the essays in Art Moderne and in the late–Art Deco idiom that combined simplified classical motifs from both Egypt and Greece. After the Depression American decorating began to express the spirit of Parisian Surrealism in small yet notable areas. The mannered twists of Surrealism were somewhat responsible for the loosening up of correct period styles. Designers looked for new themes, such as all-white rooms or outdoor rooms that were inside, and vice versa. Relieved from the Depression, inspired by the new wave of synthetic materials, American designers were riding high on a wave of daring and inventiveness. It led to a new American eclecticism that began in the 1930s.

Among the prominent American designers of the 1930s was the first generation of women decorators—Elsie de Wolfe, Ruby Ross Wood, Rose Cumming, and Nancy McClelland—along with the second generation—McMillen Inc., Thedlow Inc., Dorothy Draper Inc., Smyth Urquhart & Marckwald, and in Chicago Mabel Schamberg, Lorraine Yerkes, and Irene Sidley. In California, Frances Elkins was at the peak of her career. Among the designers who began their practices in this decade were Mrs. Henry Parish II and Melanie Kahane, as well as a new generation of male designers including William Pahlmann, Edward Wormley, George Stacey, Pierre Dutel, T. H. Robsjohn-Gibbings, and Billy Baldwin. In Chicago Samuel Marx decorated the Pump Room. Joseph B. Platt brought his interior design influence to bear on the public with his settings for the movies, among them *Dinner at Eight*, *Rebecca*, and *Gone With the Wind*.

McMillen Inc.

As the Depression hit McMillen, the early years of the 1930s were spent designing and making miniature rooms for benefits and for exhibitions, such as Chicago's 1933 Century of Progress World's Fair. When things picked up after the Depression, McMillen showed that American designers could work in the latest Art Moderne style. The entry foyer of the Cosmopolitan Club in New York (1933) stressed classical balance and a black, white, and gray-banded flooring pattern along with Deco-Moderne detailing of the stair railing. In 1934 McMillen designed a store for Steuben Glass on Fifth Avenue that also revealed classicized Art Moderne design and simplicity, as well as glass furniture (appropriate for the client). Glass spheres supported the upper tier of a metal, mirror, and glass display table.

As head of McMillen, Mrs. Brown constantly sought out new artists, and her eagerness to accept new art forms within the traditional context kept the work of the firm fresh and continually evolving. The list of McMillen's residential clients in the next years reads like a Social Register: Cravath, Lorillard, Porter, Rogers, Bliss, Choate, Busch, Goelet, Mosely, Lambert, Smith, Paley, Duke, Post, Ford, Guest, Kress, Field, Chase, Hennessey, Vanderbilt, Winthrop, Topping, Stevenson, Mellon, Burden, Hutton, Cowles, Houghton, and so on.

Ruby Ross Wood

From behind her pink-tinted round tortoiseshell glasses, Ruby Ross Wood was working in her casual, comfortable English style. She used English and French eighteenth-century furniture, as well as Directoire furniture, but always with comfortable overstuffed seating pieces.

In the mid-1930s Ruby Wood explored the all-white, no-color direction of the decade. For her own New York living room she used white-lacquered floors, brown-and-white Moroccan rugs, a white-painted table 12 feet long that was piled with magazines and personal photographs, and large dark-blue porcelain lamps with white paper shades. These latter, as opposed to the then fashionable silk lampshade, came to be a tradition of high-style decorating. In this room Ruby Ross Wood also used blue-and-white-striped bed ticking for all upholstery and drapery. Many designers later claimed credit for the first use of ticking as a decorative fabric. This uncommon use of a common material was, perhaps, in the general spirit of the Peasant style (see page 143f.) as well as in the spirit of the mannered twists of style that recurred throughout the decade.

In 1936 Ruby Wood designed the interiors of the Palm Beach, Florida, house of the Woolcott Blairs, whose architect was David Adler. The living room had walls of pale buff with white trim and floors of parchment-colored Cuban marble, which was bordered in bleached oak. In the center of the room she placed a Louis XV frame table with a honey-brown leather slipcover-top, scalloped on the edge and banded in white carpet tape. Such tape also became a tradition. Chairs were covered in matching fabrics; sofa covers and curtains were of a beige cotton from Sweden; and occasional chairs were covered in Elsie de Wolfe's trademark leopard chintz.

1. Frank Lloyd Wright. Unity Temple. Oak Park, Illinois. 1906. *Photograph by Thomas A. Heinz.*

8. Philip Johnson Associates. The Four Seasons Restaurant. New York City. 1959. *Photograph © Ezra Stoller/ESTO, 1960.*

9. McMillen Inc. Residence for Gregory B. Smith. New York City. 1962. *Photograph courtesy McMillen Inc.*

10. Billy Baldwin. Own apartment. New York City. 1963. *Photograph by Horst.*

11. Alexander Girard. Corporate program for Braniff International. 1965. *Photograph by Louis Reens.*

12. Moore, Lyndon, Turnbull, Whitaker, with Lawrence Halprin and Barbara Stauffacher. Supergraphic stripes and mailboxes as lockers, Athletic Club Number One. Sea Ranch, California. 1967. *Photograph by Morley Baer.*

13. Moore, Lyndon, Turnbull, Whitaker. Faculty Club. University of California at Santa Barbara. 1967–68. *Photograph by Morley Baer.*

Included were a pair of Adam cabinets of pale, stripped pine and carved wood palm-tree-shaped torchères. This interior, also, was in the no-color and white tradition of the 1930s.

Ruby Ross Wood gained a new influence in 1935, when she hired Billy Baldwin as her assistant. He was to work with her until she died in 1950. She also contributed to *Vogue* as a columnist on decoration from the late 1930s into the 1940s.

Nancy McClelland

Nancy McClelland continued to operate her 57th Street shop for the sale of fine wallpapers and as the headquarters of her decorating business. During the 1930s her writings indicated the decade's changing interests in stylistic periods: *Furnishing the Colonial and Federal House* (1936) and *Duncan Phyfe and the English Regency* (1939).

Her great interest became the restoration of interiors in historic American buildings. She worked on museum restorations such as Shelburne Village and Williamsburg, and did interior restoration work on Blair House in Washington, D.C.; on the Jumel Mansion in New York; on George Washington's home, Mount Vernon; on General Lee's headquarters in Fredericksburg, Virginia; and on the Henry Wadsworth Longfellow House in Portland, Maine. Mary Dunn, Inez Croom, and Michael Greer came to serve their apprenticeships with Nancy McClelland Inc. (Nancy McClelland and Mary Dunn subsequently became presidents of the American Institute of Interior Designers; McClelland's term was from 1941 to 1943.)

Rose Cumming

During the 1930s Rose Cumming continued to design residences and operate her shop for antiques and colorful chintzes. In this decade she extended her flamboyant, daring, and eclectic approach. Like Elsie de Wolfe, who capitalized on her own flamboyant personality, Rose Cumming wore big hats, and fastened swatches of fabric samples as jewelry on her black dress; with her hair dyed violet, she made an imposing impression. When there was no work, she unhesitatingly added cut fresh flowers (and a waterfall) to her shop's wares. She also demonstrated her taste for Chinese monkeys, frogs, mice, and snakes. These were all combined into occasionally Venetian fantasies of taffeta-swagged beds, and Chinese silver-and-flowered wallpaper fiestas.

One of her interior designs in the 1930s had soft yellow antique Chinese wallpaper with flame-colored taffeta draperies. Another had honey-colored walls and draperies trimmed in apple green. One bedroom she designed had walls gleaming with blue-mauve metallic foil paper, an eighteenth-century Chinese carpet "of the 1,000 vases" on the parquet floor, and an iron sixteenth-century Portuguese bed hung with silver-and-blue lamé. At the windows was cloth of silver sari silk hung under elaborately patterned mirror valances. Around the bed were silver-plated Moorish tables and stools believed to have belonged to Catherine the Great. An eighteenth-century Persian child's bed served as a low table; a gilt wood and tôle (painted tin) chandelier was seventeenth-century Italian; one Louis XV chair had a pink silk upholstered seat. It was a fantasy of imagination.

Dorothy Draper

In the 1930s Dorothy Draper increased her influence on the design of hotels, restaurants, and offices by ridding them of stuffiness and by introducing strong, overscaled elements and vivid colors. Large, bold, and strong were her catchwords.

83. Rose Cumming. Bedroom for her mother. New York City. Circa 1934. *Photograph by Harold Haliday Costain, courtesy Rose Cumming Inc.*

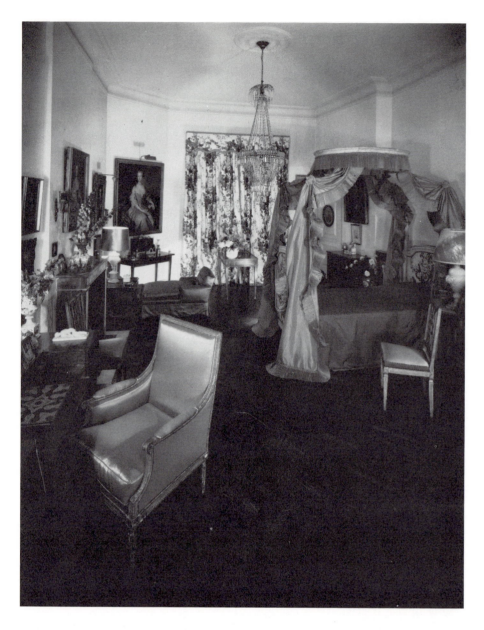

Her favorite periods during this decade, as Lester Grundy joined the firm, became Italian and English Baroque, but she was not concerned with historical accuracy. Instead, she adapted the designs of William Kent and Grinling Gibbons to late Art Deco. She became known for bold white plaster appliques—and consoles, frames, and accessories—with overscaled scroll motifs of leaves, feathers, and cockleshells. She used these plaster-white elements strikingly against dark-green or dark-burgundy walls.

Draper made most of her decorative elements overscaled. She doubled the proportions of the traditional checkerboard floor pattern. She also used wallpaper with wide pink-and-white stripes; wall coverings with glossy black patent leather finishes; elaborately swagged drapery; puffy chenille upholstery; and chintzes with large-scale clusters of cabbage roses in bold lipstick reds and emerald greens. These became her trademarks, and soon became the basis of widespread neo-Baroque in the 1930s. Though Dorothy Draper might not have understood the analogy, her designs also showed the influence of Surrealism.

In the early 1930s Dorothy Draper designed the interiors of the River Club in New York and of the Gideon Putnam Hotel in Saratoga Springs, New York. Her work also extended to real estate consulting: She styled the exteriors of New York's Sutton Place row of brownstones—the façades were painted black with white trim, each front door was painted a different color, and the fire escapes were dressed with scrollwork.

In the mid-1930s Dorothy Draper designed a formal octagonal entrance hall in the style of her 1920s work, but with new materials and with her new large-scale elements. The foyer had a flooring pattern of black with a white border, but the material was the new linoleum. The walls were gray, the ceiling white; but to lower the ceiling, she had a black band painted at the ceiling cove and divided the wainscoting into two bands, one of black and one of white. In this severe scheme, which had a large-scale white plaster clock above the fireplace, the chimney breast was painted a clear yellow.

In 1935 she designed the interiors of the Arrowhead Springs Hotel in Southern California. It had all her trademarks: overscaled lamps, overscaled sofas, overscaled chenille upholstery, and overscaled neo-Baroque white plaster appliques. At Arrowhead, also, she used geometric carpets, cabbage-rose chintz, and white-painted furniture against dark walls.

In 1937 Dorothy Draper completed one of her largest commissions, the thirty-seven-story Hampshire House apartment-hotel on Central Park South in New York (see Figure 84). There she designed everything from the interior architecture and

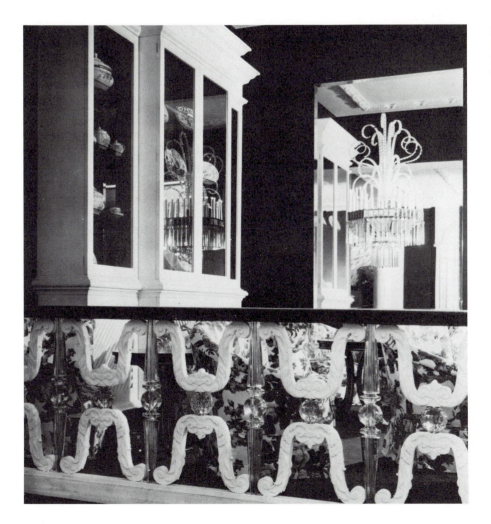

84. Dorothy Draper. Hampshire House. New York City. 1937. *Photograph by Hans van Nes, courtesy Carleton Varney.*

furniture down to the buttons on the bellboys' liveries, the toothpicks, and the stationery. Her goal was to design rooms that would have an English country-house atmosphere rather than the customary hotel look. In the lobbies, her customary black-and-white marble floors took shape as bold-scaled checkerboards; doors were mahogany with egg-and-dart carvings and bolection moldings of mirror. These were flanked by metal trees in espaliered form.

The lobby to the second-floor banquet and function rooms was designed as an outdoor space—garden furniture stood outside a bow-windowed Georgian building exterior. Called The Cottage, it became one of the most popular rooms in New York for deb parties in the next years. The dining room was designed as two spaces in one, separated only by columns. One half was a patio garden, with bold checkerboard flooring, wire-like wrought-iron chairs with cockleshell-shaped backs, and ceiling-height metal-leafed trees. The other half was a formal interior dining room with a wood-burning fireplace, high-back chairs covered in red velvet (they were slipcovered in rose chintz for summer), and a vast crystal chandelier in the shape of a wedding cake. This space looked out through a paneled glass wall to a real garden decked with urns, with flowers and plantings, and with a vast neo-Baroque, scrollwork-and-fishscale-patterned fountain. It all showed the mannered inversions for the sake of theatricality that Surrealism inspired. There, in Hampshire House, Dorothy Draper lived—with a contract for maintaining the hotel—and there she finished her first book, *Decorating Is Fun!*

Frances Elkins

During the 1930s Frances Elkins's practice spread nationwide as she began to collaborate with her Chicago-based architect-brother David Adler. From 1931 to 1935 she designed the interiors of four houses designed by him that are indicative of her 1930s approach, and she also designed the interiors of the Cypress Point Club in Pebble Beach.

For the house of Mrs. Evelyn Marshall Field, in Syosset, Long Island, George I paneling was installed in the library. There Frances Elkins assembled Queen Anne and Georgian pieces along with comfortable upholstered furniture. The living room had floral-patterned chintz upholstery, Georgian wood furniture, and a Chinese screen.

For the house of Mrs. Kersey Coates Reed, in Lake Forest, Illinois, also in 1931, Frances Elkins created a silver-and-white guest bedroom that had silver foil walls, a four-poster bed with ivory posts ornamented with silver; a japanned Queen Anne *secrétaire* and a bombé chest of drawers complemented the otherwise pale scheme. The same house had a mirrored powder room with silver-leaf moldings and fireplace surround all enriched with wainscoting that was lacquered yellow. Here, Frances Elkins installed Georgian seating pieces with elaborate scalloped aprons.

Also indicative of 1930s interior design, Frances Elkins's interiors for Mrs. J. Ogden Armor, in Lake Forest, Illinois (1934–35), had Georgian furniture with a Chinese carpet in the living room, shieldback Hepplewhite chairs and a Sheraton sideboard in the dining room.

But, that same year, a new influence was to be seen. Frances Elkins had begun to import furnishings from the Paris shop of Jean-Michel Frank in 1932, and she used his lamps for many clients, whose interiors began to reveal a Paris-inspired sensibility.

In the house of Mr. and Mrs. Leslie Wheeler, also in Lake Forest, Illinois, the paneled library (see Figure 85) with round-pedimented bookstacks had zebra-skin rugs on the floor, and the living room sported a carpet in a bold Chinese key design. In the dining room, Queen Anne chairs—all side chairs at the breakfast table bay; all armchairs at the main dining table—flanked pedestal tables in the

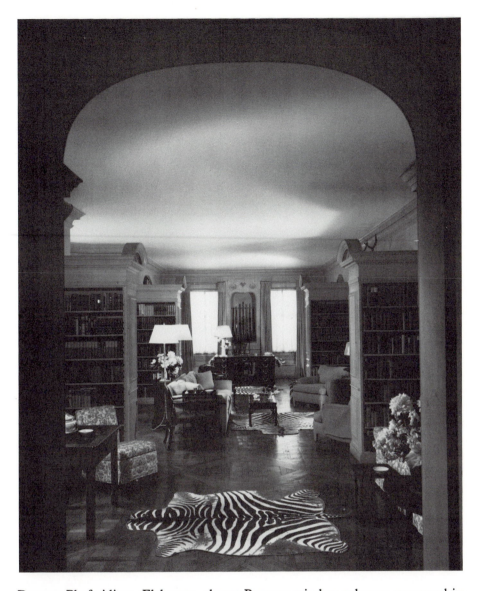

85. Frances Elkins with David Adler. Library for Mr. and Mrs. J. Leslie Wheeler. Lake Forest, Illinois. 1934–35. *Photograph © Ezra Stoller/ESTO, 1966.*

Duncan Phyfe idiom. Elaborate, almost Baroque window valances were used in both living and dining rooms.

The bar and cardroom she designed in 1938 for the Zellerbach residence (see Figure 86) in San Francisco not only showed the influence of this new Parisian outlook, but also revealed the complete formation of her own eclectic American style. In that project Elkins mixed her modification of Portuguese Chippendale–inspired banquette and chairs with a Jean-Michel Frank metal cocktail table and wall sconces, and a Hollywood-looking mirror-framed mirror. It was her own brand of international eclecticism, and it was in the vanguard of the special American eclecticism of the 1930s. By the end of the decade she was producing neo-Baroque interiors in public buildings as well—including the interiors of the Royal Hawaiian Hotel in Honolulu, the Santa Anita Turf Club, and the interiors of the Pebble Beach Club and the Women's Pavilion at the San Francisco World's Fair of 1938.

Mrs. Henry Parish II

In 1933 Mrs. Henry Parish II began her interior design practice in Far Hills, New Jersey. She continued to work prominently for the next fifty years and was one of

86. Frances Elkins. Hallway, Zellerbach residence. San Francisco, California. 1938–39. *Photograph © Fred Lyon, 1983.*

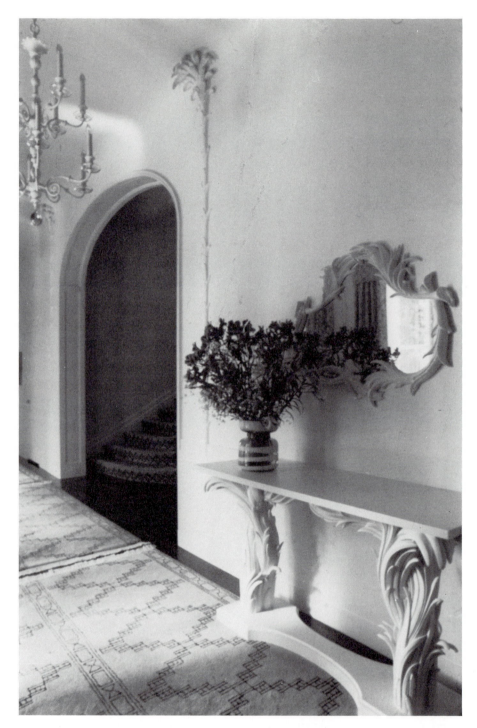

the most celebrated residential designers from the 1960s to 1980s. She became known for her casual, comfortable "undecorated" English country-house look.

Born in Morristown, New Jersey, Dorothy May Kinnicut (1910–)—called "Sister" by her family and friends—had no formal training in design, but she had traveled extensively, had visited great houses, and to that experience she attributes her educated eye. To the lack of such experience she also attributes the uneducated eyes of others. Her association with the decorating world began when she married: Her mother asked Eleanor McMillen to decorate and furnish the new bride's Gracie Square house in New York. At the low point of the Depression, Mrs. Parish began decorating for friends and soon built up a residential clientele.

T. H. Robsjohn-Gibbings

Close in spirit to the work of Jean-Michel Frank was the work of T. H. Robsjohn-Gibbings, who came to New York from London. In 1936 the thirty-year decorating career of Robsjohn-Gibbings began when he opened a showroom on Madison Avenue.

Born in England, Terence Harold Robsjohn-Gibbings (1909–73) studied architecture at the University of Liverpool and then worked as a designer in London and as art director for British International Pictures at Elstree before being brought to the United States by Charles Duveen, the antique-furniture dealer and brother of art dealer Sir Joseph Duveen. After the Depression "Gibby," as he was nicknamed, opened his own firm.

The showroom carried the late–Art Deco idiom of archaic classicism farther by recreating ancient Greece (see Figures 87A and B). It had broad expanses of

87A. T. H. Robsjohn-Gibbings. Own showroom with Klismos Chair. New York City. 1936. *Photograph by Richard Garrison.*

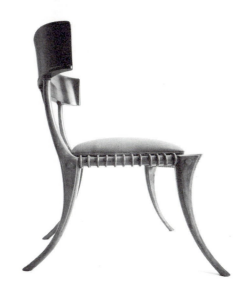

87B. T. H. Robsjohn-Gibbings. Klismos Chair. Circa 1936. *Photograph © Ezra Stoller/ESTO, 1963.*

plain wall with a double-banded baseboard and a textured cornice; a mosaic of Greek dancing maidens formed the floor; and Klismos chairs, which Robsjohn-Gibbings had recreated from originals in Greece, sat serenely like thrones among other Greek-modeled furnishings.

His clients in the next years were Mrs. Otto Khan, Mrs. Myron C. Taylor, Elizabeth Arden, Antoine, the hat designers John Fredericks and Lily Daché, Thelma Chrysler Foy, Doris Duke, Conrad Hilton, Neiman-Marcus, and the River Club.

Robsjohn-Gibbings designed furniture in a refined, minimalist vein, notably a simple table desk (1937) with solid side panels as supports that had its drawer space not hung beneath the apron, but elevated above it like a writing desk. His most popular chair design—so popular that it became known as "The Robsjohn-Gibbings Chair"—was a simple pale walnut armchair (1938) with linen-upholstered, buttoned cushions that were supported on leather strapping. The influence of Swedish Modern was apparent.

In 1939, for the California showroom of jeweler Paul Flato, Robsjohn-Gibbings designed a set of paneled doors of birch that were paneled with superimposed tiers of flat squares mitered to look pyramidal. The simplicity and monumentality of the concept were much emulated. Furnished with chairs of strapped leather, reminiscent of Alvar Aalto's slightly earlier designs, the effect was so refined that it seemed as if, within traditional decorating, a move toward reductiveness, simplicity, and purification had begun to reflect the tendencies of Modern design. This similarity to academic Modernism was curious, especially since Robsjohn-Gibbings wrote so vehemently, in the next decade, against Bauhaus design.

Edward Wormley

Among the influential American interior designers who started their careers in the 1930s, Edward Wormley sustained the longest continuity as a furniture designer. From 1931 until 1968, a period of thirty-seven years, he designed 150 pieces of furniture a year for the Dunbar Furniture Company of Berne, Indiana. It was a model of sustained productivity, infused inspiration, and professional perseverance.

Born in Oswego, Illinois, Edward Wormley (1907–) attended art school at the Art Institute of Chicago for a year when he was nineteen, then joined the design department of Marshall Field in Chicago from 1927 to 1930. There he designed residences for the department store's customers, advised on furnishings, and in the last year he was there began designing a line of furniture that was to be produced for the store by the Berkey & Gay Company. That project led to a brief employment with Berkey & Gay, after which he went to Dunbar.

Early production samples of Wormley's designs for Dunbar were immediately bought by the newly opened Mechandise Mart in Chicago—and immediately sold. The Merchandise Mart's showrooms and semi-annual markets for the trade were to become a basic influence on mainstream taste in succeeding decades. Soon, market reaction convinced Dunbar to put Wormley's sample designs into production. Each year, he produced a traditional line and a contemporary line (see Figure 88). His sources of inspiration became wide-reaching over cultures and eras. Combinations of Hitchcock benches as seen through Japanese simplicity were highpoints of his refined eye. Wormley's work, therefore, became a new resource of contemporary American-made furniture for the interior design field.

William Pahlmann

Acclaimed in the mid-1930s for his showstopping displays and model rooms at Lord & Taylor in New York, William Pahlmann was influential in loosening the

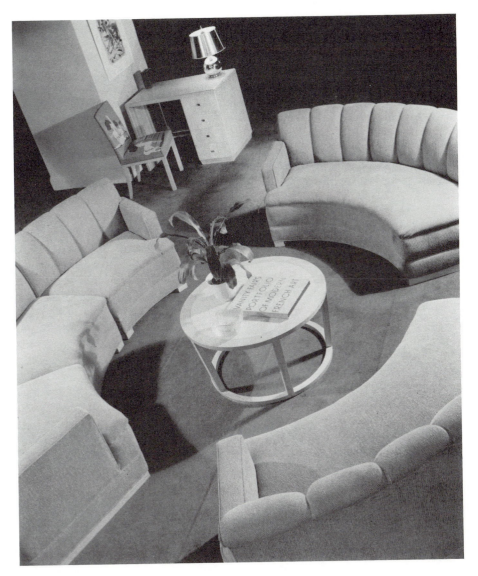

88. Edward Wormley. Sectional furniture for Dunbar. 1935. *Photograph by Frank Willming, courtesy Edward Wormley.*

grip of correct period rooms on the work of American interior designers and in fostering the new interior design eclecticism of the 1930s. His eye was good enough to combine and mix centuries, cultures, and contrasts in a daredevil manner, yet make them seem to work. In the 1940s and 1950s he went on to become one of the most successful interior designers of the century.

Born in Pleasant Mound, Illinois, William Carroll Pahlmann (1900–) moved with his parents to San Antonio, Texas, at the age of nine, and went to school there. As he grew to 6 feet 1 inch tall, he took on the Texan image with its large, expansive, and outgoing manner. After a series of construction and traveling salesman jobs, he took a correspondence course with *Arts and Decoration* magazine; and in his mid-twenties he determined to be a designer. In 1927 he enrolled in the New York School of Fine and Applied Arts, where he drew well and put himself through school as a song-and-dance man in Broadway musicals. Pahlmann continued in the school's Paris program, and got the grand tour of Europe, where he met his first important clients.

Back in America in 1931, he designed residences for them—the Seton Henrys at Pen Ryn, Delaware; then for Mrs. William Paley on Beekman Place in New

York; and for Mrs. Pauline Rogers at Southampton, Long Island. He also worked briefly for the B. Altman department store.

In 1936 Pahlmann joined Lord & Taylor to do interior display in the home furnishings division. His merchandise displays attracted great crowds, gained much publicity, and brought him immediate professional recognition. What was unique about his model rooms was his theatrical sense and eclectic style. The Lord & Taylor displays always had a theme that related to store merchandise (see Figure 89A) or to the merchandise and crafts of specific countries, such as Swedish Modern (see Figure 89B). His displays, which included a Swedish dining room with painted furniture and a family room with a rug of irregular stripes, established his color sense. The most celebrated of these promotions was "Pahlmann Peruvian" (see Figure 113) for which he brought back Peruvian handcrafted fabrics, fringes, and objects, as well as paintings, silver, and Inca treasures. Crowds were estimated at between 20,000 and 30,000 per month. It was the beginning of the prominence of theatrical model rooms in the merchandising campaigns of American department stores.

In those room displays, Pahlmann was acclaimed for his color schemes, and some of those combinations became associated with him at the time. He lists some of them in his 1955 book, *The Pahlmann Book of Interior Decorating:* in 1938— "cinnamon, tan, and sage green"; also "pistachio green, grape, and white"; and also "sky blue, elephant gray, and pink." This latter became widely popular in the next several years. In 1939 he combined "black, white, cerulean, and orange." In 1940 he presented "Harlem pink, Regency green, and white"; "sulphur yellow, olive green, and rosy red"; and "brick, bottle green, rawhide, and bleached cypress." Pahlmann Peruvian in 1941 featured "Cuzco blue, lime, fuschia, deep blue, and whitewash"; another of his Peruvian combinations was "avocado, lime, plum, tan, orange, and white." Pahlmann's color schemes demonstrated the American eclecticism of the 1930s.

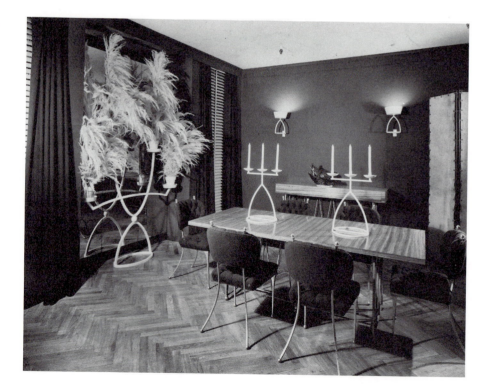

89A.   William Pahlmann. Model room for Lord & Taylor's "Dramatic Rooms" promotion. New York City. 1938. *Photograph by Van Nes–De Vos, courtesy William Pahlmann.*

89B. William Pahlmann. Model room for Lord & Taylor's "Swedish Modern" promotion. New York City. 1938. *Photograph courtesy William Pahlmann.*

89C. William Pahlmann. Model room for Lord & Taylor's "Excitement in Summer Decor" promotion. New York City. 1939. *Photograph courtesy William Pahlmann.*

Billy Baldwin

In 1935 Billy Baldwin became an assistant in Ruby Ross Wood's firm and began to make a name for himself. Born in Roland Park, Maryland, William Baldwin (1903–84) studied for two years at Princeton University and by the end of the 1920s had built up a decorating clientele in the Baltimore area. He met Ruby Ross Wood in 1930 and moved to New York to work for her five years later. His design of his own office at Mrs. Wood's established what became one of his trademarks— the glossy dark-brown wall, which he used for the next four decades.

For Ruby Ross Wood, in 1935, he worked on the interiors of the Woolcott Blair House in Palm Beach, Florida, and in 1938 designed the interiors of a house in Montego Bay, Jamaica. There the influence of Surrealism was to be seen. The scheme that he and Mrs. Wood decided upon was to be "in the spirit of a ballet, whimsical, light, and sketchy."[10] In the living room, the sofa was upholstered in bright yellow, the chairs in white with yellow-stenciled orchids. Two metal commodes were painted with trompe l'oeil drapery by Joseph B. Platt. A dining area had wire-like wrought-iron chairs painted the color of bougainvillea, a wire-based table with an apron of large-scale white fringe, and a cantilevered console-sideboard with the same fringe decoration. The theatrical whimsy of it all was indicative of the new eclectic, perhaps Surrealist spirit of 1930s design.

Europe and America: The Threat of War

In 1934 Hitler was appointed Chancellor of Germany. Only two years later Mussolini annexed Abyssinia as part of Italy. Then, too, began the Spanish Civil War; Picasso's mural *Guernica* shrieked in anguish at this event in 1937. In 1938 Germany mobilized its armed forces, and the Anschluss of Austria began; it was soon followed by the fall of Czechoslovakia and France and by the London blitz.

After the Bauhaus was closed in 1933, the first of the Bauhaus faculty to flee from this onslaught and come to the United States were Anni and Josef Albers; in 1933 they began teaching at Black Mountain College in North Carolina. Walter Gropius and Marcel Breuer came in 1937, after interim sojourns in London. Gropius came to head the Graduate School of Design at Harvard University, where he remained until 1953, and Breuer came to teach in Gropius's program. Walter Baermann settled at the California Institute of Technology. Also in 1937, Laszlo Moholy-Nagy, who had gone to England when Gropius did, came to Chicago to head the New Bauhaus, which was renamed the School of Design in the following year.

In 1937, too, Mies van der Rohe made his first trip to the United States. In 1938 Mies settled in Chicago, where from 1938 to 1958 he was Director of Architecture at Armour Institute (renamed the Illinois Institute of Technology in 1940); and where, from 1938 to 1969, he maintained an architecture practice. Bauhaus faculty member Herbert Bayer came to the United States in 1938 to work with Walter and Ise Gropius on the Museum of Modern Art's retrospective exhibition "Bauhaus, 1919–1928." The influence of these immigrants from the Bauhaus, however indirect their connections were with American industry, was to become the foundation of American design education for the next two decades.

The World of Tomorrow

The New York World's Fair of 1938–39, like the simultaneous World's Fair in San Francisco, was politically both the victory celebration over the end of the Depression and a futile hope that what was happening in Europe would not come to a showdown. For industrial designers and architects, the New York World's

Fair was as close to a realization of tomorrow's world of Streamlining as they were to get.

Norman Bel Geddes and architect Albert Kahn created the pavilion for General Motors, with its popular "Futurama"—a scale model of the future American city and countryside as viewed from a moving train of two-person wingchairs with audio speakers in the wings. The city and the countryside were seen in daylight and by night, in fair weather and in foul. The recreation of this stratospheric inspection tour of Sant'Elia's Futurist metropolis was eye-opening and magical. Henry Dreyfuss's "Democracity" presentation inside the Perisphere seemed anticlimactic by comparison.

Walter Dorwin Teague created the Ford Motor Company Pavilion, with its rooftop speedway test-drive or ride in a new bright-colored Ford. Inside the Ford Pavilion Teague also designed a lounge that was free of the stylistic motifs of either Deco's radiowaves of Streamlining's airstreams. A chandelier of vertically run, indirectly reflected fluorescent tubes hung over a sofa-and-endtable group that was designed as a single unit (see Figure 90). Lamps with cylindrical brass shades were built into the endtables. The overall group was tied together visually by a white stripe, like large-scale welting. It prefigured the furnishings in the railroad observation cars of the next decade.

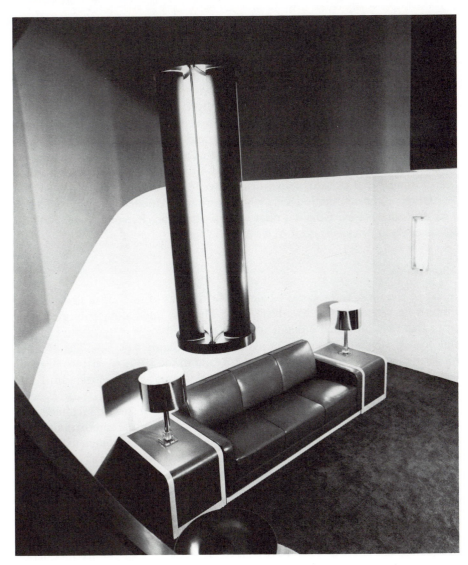

90. Walter Dorwin Teague. Lounge, Ford Pavilion. New York World's Fair. 1939. *Photograph courtesy Walter Dorwin Teague Associates, Inc.*

91. Russel Wright. American Modern dinnerware. Designed 1937, produced 1939–59. *Photograph by Courtney Frisse, courtesy The Smithsonian Institution.*

Russel Wright (see Figure 91) also designed exhibitions at the fair, the largest of which was for Focal Foods; it was similar to his showroom for the International Handkerchief Company of the same year. At the Focal Foods display, visitors walked through dimly lit halls subdivided by large geometric and biomorphic sculptural units. Amoeboid show windows revealed symbolic and realistic elements of food; dioramas depicted food production and distribution. For these Wright designed Surrealistic displays—a field that smiled, a group of flying lobsters. It was at this time that Salvador Dali designed his jewelry group in which a garnet heart thumped and pulsated. Surrealism pervaded.

Other architects and designers whose work was exhibited at this World's Fair were Donald Deskey, Gilbert Rohde, Morris Lapidus, Egmont Arens, William Lescaze, Oscar Niemeyer, and Alvar Aalto.

Alvar Aalto

A star of the New York World's Fair show, in terms of interior design, was the Finnish Pavilion designed by Alvar Aalto. The vast undulating ceiling of wood strips that Aalto designed brought attention to that Modern master from Finland, and created curiosity about his other works (see Figure 92). The Scandinavian Modern idiom had been popular since 1925, and in the 1930s Americans began to have access to the furniture designs of Bruno Mathsson, Borge Mogenson, Kaare Klint, and Magnus Stephensen.

Born in Kuortane, Finland, Alvar Aalto (1898–1976) studied architecture at the Technical University of Helsinki. He was first recognized internationally for his design of the Tuberculosis Sanatorium at Paimio, Finland, completed in 1933. His major early interiors had included the Viipuri Library, completed in 1935, with its undulating wood lecture room ceiling (see Figure 93), which was determined by acoustical considerations, and its daylighting domes over the two-level reading room. Aalto's concern for lighting and acoustics inspired new considerations for the Modern movement.

In the Paimio and Viipuri buildings Aalto used chairs, stools (shown in Figure 93), tables, and children's furniture that he had designed for factory production

92.   Alvar Aalto. Finnish Pavil-
ion, New York World's Fair. 1939.
*Photograph © Ezra Stoller/
ESTO, 1940.*

93.   Alvar Aalto. Lecture hall in
the library. Viipuri, Finland.
1930–35. *Photograph by Artek
Oy AB, Helsinki. From Karl
Mang, History of Modern Furniture (New York: Harry N.
Abrams, 1979).*

94. Alvar Aalto. Villa Mairea. Noormarkku, Finland. 1937–39. *Photograph © Ezra Stoller/ ESTO, 1960.*

using new techniques of laminating and bending birch plywood; this furniture had been put into production by Artek of Finland during 1932–33. It had the lightness and simplicity that imbued all his work, and it soon became internationally known after being exhibited in the Paris Exhibition of 1937 and the New York World's Fair of 1939. Besides, in expressing the cantilevered chair forms of other Modern designers in fresh, pale, light wood, instead of in shiny, machine-made tubular metal, Aalto provided another alternative as well as opposition to the (equally) machine-made imagery of the German school of Modernism.

From 1938 to 1939 Aalto had worked on his Villa Mairea, in Noormarkku, Finland, for his lifelong patron Maire Gullichsen, with its sensitive integration of an L-shaped plan into the landscape and with its plan and section influenced by De Stijl—especially Rietveld's Schröder House of 1924. Inside, Aalto displayed his delicate if perplexingly ambiguous manipulation of the Modern concept of free-flowing space. The Villa Mairea interior offered multiple levels and multiple vistas (see Figure 94); it had double-functioning elements such as the undulating entry wall that both separated the foyer from the dining room and also inflected or directed circulation into the house. Within this sophisticatedly complex envelope, simple though elegant provincial-idiom wood furnishings were combined with crisp Machine-Age objects such as lighting fixtures. In his interior designs Aalto was assisted by his wife, Aino Marsio Aalto, who was an architect as well as his partner. She died in 1949.

By the time of the 1939 World's Fair, Aalto had clearly established his position as one of the principal masters of International Style. He was unique among them in bringing an atmosphere of warmth and sensitivity, thoughtfulness, grace, and charm to the stark, Machine-Age, structurally oriented style. And his furniture, which was widely imported for use in American interiors during the 1930s, had established his reputation here as a designer before his influence as an architect was seen.

The New York and the San Francisco World's Fairs of 1939 were the last creative steps forward for Streamlining, and they were also the last bubble of the effervescent, perhaps desperate, optimism of the 1930s. It was a victory short-lived. For Americans, it was a blind optimism that corresponded to the manic Surrealism of the Europeans. World War II lasted from 1939 to 1945. During that time 35 million died in warfare and 10 million more died in Nazi concentration camps. During the winter of 1939–40, among those fleeing the holocaust, Jean-Michel Frank left France for South America and soon came to the United States on the invitation of several former clients, including Templeton Crocker, and at the urging of former students and friends of his from the Paris program of the New York School of Fine and Applied Arts, including Eleanor McMillen Brown. Frank's depression over the war, however, led to his suicide in 1941, when he jumped out of a New York building. For interior designers, too, the war had hit home.

Suggested Reading

Albrecht, Donald. *Designing Dreams: Modern Architecture in the Movies*. New York: Harper & Row, 1985.

Alvar Aalto. New York: Rizzoli, 1978.

Baldwin, Billy. *Billy Baldwin Remembers*. New York: Harcourt Brace Jovanovich, 1974.

Battersby, Martin. *The Decorative Thirties*. New York: Walker & Company, 1969, 1971.

Bayer, Herbert, Walter Gropius, and Ise Gropius, eds. *Bauhaus: 1919–1928*. New York: The Museum of Modern Art, 1938.

Brown, Erica. *Sixty Years of Interior Design: The World of McMillen*. New York: Viking Press, 1982.

Bush, Donald J. *The Streamlined Decade*. New York: Braziller, 1975.

Design in America: The Cranbrook Vision, 1925–1950. New York: Harry N. Abrams, 1983.

Draper, Dorothy. *Decorating Is Fun!* New York: Art & Decoration Book Society, 1939.

Fisher, Richard B. *Syrie Maugham*. London: Duckworth, 1978.

Frankl, Paul T. *New Dimensions*. New York: Payson & Clarke, 1928.

———. *Form and Re-Form*. New York: Harper & Row, 1930.

Giedion, Sigfried, ed. *A Decade of Contemporary Architecture*. New York: Wittenborn, 1954.

Hanks, David A. *The Decorative Designs of Frank Lloyd Wright*. New York: E. P. Dutton, 1979.

———. *Donald Deskey*. New York: E. P. Dutton, 1985.

Hennessey, William J. *Russel Wright*. Cambridge: MIT Press, 1983.

Hitchcock, Henry-Russell, and Philip Johnson. *The International Style: Architecture Since 1922*. New York: W. W. Norton, 1932, 1966.

Jacobus, John M., Jr. "Architecture, American Style: 1920–45," *American Art*. New York: Prentice-Hall, Harry N. Abrams, 1979.

Jeanneret, Charles-Edouard. *Le Corbusier: 1910–65*. Zurich: Les Editions d'Architecture Zurich, 1967.

Johnson, Philip C. *Mies van der Rohe*. New York: The Museum of Modern Art, 1947, 1978.

Kaufmann, Edgar, Jr. "Interior Design: Architecture or Decoration?" *Progressive Architecture*. October 1962, pp. 141–44.

McCallum, Ian. *Architecture USA*. New York: Reinhold, 1959.

McCoy, Esther. *Five California Architects*. New York: Reinhold, 1960. (Paperback New York: Frederick A. Praeger, 1975.)

————. *The Second Generation*. Layton, Utah: Gibbs M. Smith, 1984.

Meickle, Jeffrey L. *Twentieth Century Limited: Industrial Design in America, 1925–39*. Philadelphia: Temple University Press, 1979.

Pahlmann, William. *The Pahlmann Book of Interior Decorating*. New York: Thomas Y. Crowell, 1955.

Pool, Mary Jane, ed. *20th Century Decorating, Architecture, and Gardens*. New York: Holt, Rinehart and Winston, 1980.

Pratt, Richard. *David Adler: The Architect and His Work*. New York: M. Evans & Company, 1970.

Progressive Architecture. February 1982. Special issue on International Style commemorating the fiftieth anniversary of the Museum of Modern Art Exhibition.

Pulos, Arthur J. *American Design Ethic: A History of Industrial Design to 1940*. Cambridge: MIT Press, 1983.

Sanchez, Leopold Diego, and Andree Putman. *Jean-Michel Frank*. Paris: Editions du Regard, 1980.

Stern, Robert A. M. *George Howe*. New Haven: Yale University Press, 1975.

Tweed, Katharine, ed. *The Finest Rooms by America's Great Decorators*. New York: Viking Press, 1964.

Notes

1. Robert A. M. Stern, *George Howe* (New Haven: Yale University Press, 1975), p. 62.

2. Alfred Barr, Jr., Preface to *Bauhaus: 1919–1928*, ed. Herbert Bayer, Walter Gropius, and Ise Gropius (New York: The Museum of Modern Art, 1938), p. 5.

3. Henry-Russell Hitchcock and Philip Johnson, *The International Style: Architecture Since 1922* (New York: W. W. Norton, 1932, 1966), p. 20.

4. Ibid., pp. 86ff.

5. Edgar Kaufmann, Jr., "Interior Design: Architecture or Decoration?" *Progressive Architecture* (October 1962), p. 144.

6. Leopold Diego Sanchez and Andree Putman, *Jean-Michel Frank* (Paris: Editions du Regard, 1980), p. 14.

7. Ibid.

8. Christopher Hemphill believes, after interviewing the nephew of Carlos de Bestigui (sometimes spelled Bestiguy) and the nephew of Emilio Terry, when neither made claims or suggestions regarding the involvement of Terry in the design of the furnishings for this apartment, that it was de Bestigui and not Terry who directed the decoration.

9. Charles-Edouard Jeanneret, *Le Corbusier: 1910–65* (Zurich: Les Editions d'Architecture Zurich, 1967), p. 67.

10. Billy Baldwin, *Billy Baldwin Remembers* (New York: Harcourt Brace Jovanovich, 1974), p. 70.

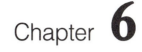

Chapter 6

1940–1950:
The Second Generation

Once again a decade was divided by war into an active and an inactive period for designers of interiors. But the order of those periods was reversed in the 1940s— the war and inactivity came first, and the reactions that followed were markedly different.

When the 1940s began, World War II had been in progress in Europe for a year, devastating the populations, resources, treasures, and emotions of Western Europe and North Africa. But the United States was not yet actively fighting. Here, wartime efforts were directed toward whatever technological inventions might bring the war to quick conclusion.

For civilians, installing blackout curtains and drilling for blackouts and air raids were the order of the day, along with rationing food and gasoline and salvaging aluminum and other metals for reuse. Progress in interior design was curtailed while many interior design professionals made their contributions to the armed forces, notably in camouflage work. But none of those precautions and deprivations prepared Americans for the Sunday morning surprise attack on Pearl Harbor on December 7, 1941.

The shortage of materials led to wartime make-do: The old elegant materials that Modernists had relied on to provide natural texture and ornamentation were not available; the new materials were common materials that were used in uncommon ways. Exaggeratedly rough natural textures had been used by German architects, including Mies and Breuer, during the 1930s and were more widely seen as used by the Slavs and Balts at the 1938 Paris Exhibition; wartime shortages made them a necessity in the 1940s. Burlap and jute fabrics were lauded as wall coverings and drapery materials; sisal carpeting provided pattern and texture; interwoven strips of webbing were hung like hammocks within chair frames to supplant uphol-stery. Cardboard egg crates were used to texturize some ceilings. This was the first mass adoption of the Dada-Surreal concept of found objects.

Stylistically, the motif of the early 1940s was the bulbous curve and the amoeba form with its undulating, biomorphic outline. It was derived both from camouflage shapes and from the work of painters Pablo Picasso and Joan Miró and sculptors Hans Arp and Alexander Calder. It was a free-form shape like a painter's palette. Americans had been introduced to this undulation as an interior motif by Alvar Aalto's glass vase (1936–37), by his Finnish Pavilion at the New York World's Fair (1939) (see Figure 92), and also by the Brazilian Pavilion at that same fair. In Brazil the parabola forms of Oscar Niemeyer and others presented a conga line of undulation. In New York biomorphic furniture was designed by Frederick Kiesler in 1938 and was exhibited at Peggy Guggenheim's Art of This Century Gallery beginning in 1942.

Among interior furnishings the Hardoy or Butterfly Chair (1938) (see Figure 95), designed by Antonio Bonet, Juan Kurchan, and Jorge Ferrari-Hardoy, was

95. Antonio Bonet, Juan Kur-chan, and Jorge Ferrari-Hardoy. Butterfly Chair, metal rod and leather, 35″ high. *Collection, The Museum of Modern Art, New York City, Edgar Kaufmann, Jr., Fund.*

96. Isamu Noguchi. Free-form coffee table for Herman Miller Inc. 1944. *Photograph courtesy Herman Miller Inc.*

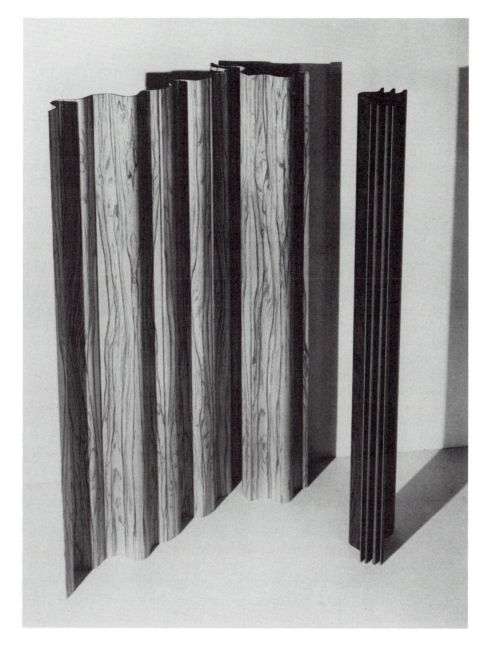

97. Charles Eames and Ray Eames. Folding, undulating molded plywood screen. 1946. *Photograph courtesy Herman Miller Inc.*

the popular epitome of this form. Isamu Noguchi's free-form coffee table for Herman Miller Inc. is another evocation (see Figure 96). The undulations of Charles Eames's folding screen (1946) reiterated the motif (see Figure 97). The cutleaf philodendron, the indoor plant that most approximated the amoeba form, was adopted as the plant of the decade. The use of plants was canonized both as the principal means of providing decorative sculpture and as the means of bringing nature indoors. The use of indoor plants sought to create the interpenetration of inside and outside that Frank Lloyd Wright had been proclaiming since 1900. In the 1940s this shape became a mass fashion in interior design; by the 1950s it resulted in the kidney-shaped swimming pool.

In the fine arts the spare, gaunt wartime realism of Edward Hopper and others would be displaced by Abstract Expressionism in 1947 and 1948. Other motifs that found their way from the fine arts to interior design in the 1940s were the "cheese holes" of sculptors Jean Lurçat, Henry Moore, and Barbara Hepworth. Notably, these holes were adapted to the design of seatbacks.

Alexander Girard

One American designer who began to make a name for himself toward the end of the war was Alexander Girard, who designed houses and commercial interiors in the Detroit area. Although an architect, he has devoted his career to the design of interiors, exhibitions, and textiles.

Born in New York City, Alexander H. Girard (1907–) was raised in Florence, Italy, studied at the Royal Institute of British Architects in London, at the Royal School of Architecture in Rome, and at New York University. He worked in architects' offices in Florence, Rome, London, and Paris, before opening his own practice in New York in 1932. In 1937 Girard moved to Detroit, where he designed interiors for the Ford Motor Company (1943) and Lincoln Motors (1946). He designed several houses, as well as the influential exhibition "Design for Living" for the Detroit Institute of Arts in 1949. Girard and his wife Susan began collecting folk art and primitive art around 1939; it was to influence much of his later work. Girard later became renowned for exhibition design as well as interior and fabric design.

In 1943 Girard designed a cafeteria to seat 1,400 employees of the International Detrola Corporation in Detroit. It was a preview of the restaurant designs he was to become acclaimed for in the 1950s. The space was a long rectangular industrial-loft space with a grid of structural columns that Girard made efforts to disguise rather than express (see Figure 98). He introduced an entry foyer, with a bulbous curving plan, and established a diagonal orientation to the cafeteria with a bulb-ended, free-form serving and kitchen area. He furred out the interior columns as canted or rotated rectangles and ellipses, and furred out the perimeter columns to reinforce the diagonal orientation. This inflection was the keynote of the circulation plan. He located three executive dining rooms behind the serving-kitchen area and turned one of the central columns into a large circular divider that incorporated storage and a stage for company presentations and speeches. The cafeteria tables were also rotated along the diagonal axis, even at the perimeter. All of this was topped by a suspended ceiling with recessed lighting troffers. It was one of the early suspended ceilings.

He used simple materials, typical of the availabilities of the day: Natural woods—mostly white pine and red cedar siding—were used for wall surfaces; asphalt tile surfaced the floor, part of it in a striped pattern; columns were faced with bent plywood strips. Window recesses were filled with undraped venetian

98. Alexander Girard. Plan, employee cafeteria, Detrola Corporation. Detroit, Michigan. 943. *Illustration from Architectural Forum (October 1944).*

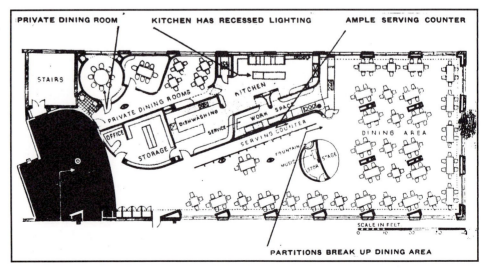

blinds. Tables had metal column bases; chairs were molded plywood from Artek of Finland. The color scheme was gray-green, beige, and red.

During 1946–47 Girard designed an office-showroom in Detroit for his practice—in an old hamburger stand. This and other renovations were early examples of the recycling that was to become a major direction of future decades. Girard's search for new textures was typical of the decade: vertically striated plywood in its natural pale yellow-tan color was used for wall surfacing; asbestos cement was painted gray-blue; natural jute and burlap fabrics were used on the walls; the fiberboard ceilings were painted black; and tan carpeting was used on the floors. A glass partition separated one room from another; lighting was from exposed spotlights and ellipsoidal can lights. Most telling of the 1940s search for natural textures was the large-scale stainless-steel mesh covering of the front door.

Shortly thereafter, Girard moved his office and showroom to Grosse Pointe, Michigan, where he painted the interior structural and mechanical elements in a gray and off-white scheme: Exposed steel beams were painted dull black, steel columns painted blue-white, ducts were enameled white; and exposed nuts and bolts were painted orange-vermilion. This textured color-coding was indicative of the 1940s and its respect for natural materials. Split-bamboo screen, natural plywood, and hung cabinets, along with a vertically striated divider and shelves hung on vertical wall-attached strips, demonstrated the end-of-the-decade interest in the linear string-and-wire motif.

In 1948 Girard designed a new, modest, board-and-batten house for himself and his family. Planned as blocks of rectangles, the interior boxes were broken up by inflected diagonals and corner doorways (see Figure 99A). The 20- by 30-foot living room was subdivided—into areas for entryway, study, and three different seating groups—by room dividers. One divider was a freestanding fireplace; the other was a boomerang-plan banquette and screen (see Figure 99B). On the living room side of the screen, which was made of plywood painted gray, hung a display of the Girards' collection of paintings, masks, and folk art. On the work-study side of the screen were pin-up boards as well as shelf on shelf of repeated jars, crocks, bottles, cups, and boxes for equipment, along with toys and other objects.

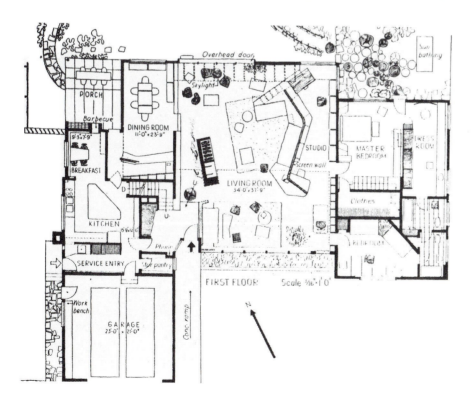

99A. Alexander Girard. Plan, own house. Grosse Pointe, Michigan. 1948. *Illustration from* Architectural Review *(April 1950).*

99B. Alexander Girard. Own house. Grosse Pointe, Michigan. 1948. *Photograph © Ezra Stoller/ESTO, 1952.*

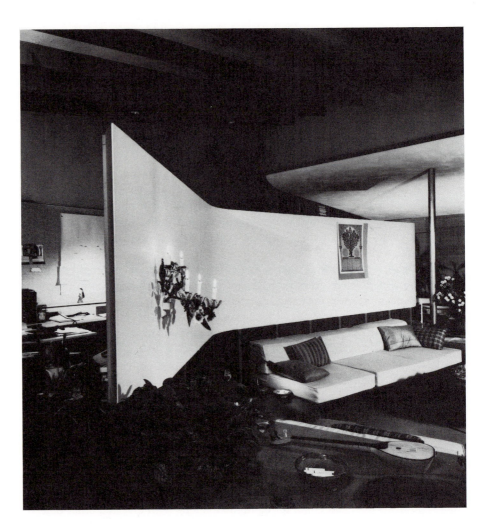

In the dining room of this same house was a boomerang-plan serving bar that hovered on attenuated pipe legs. In the kitchen a triangular island counter with chamfered corners separated the L-plan cooking area from the family dining table. The bedrooms established Girard's minimized bedroom concept, which set a model for hotel bedrooms for the next two decades. Throughout the house indirect cove lighting and spotlighting were used, as well as new materials and furniture such as black plastic laminate tabletops and countertops, natural fir plywood, wire-based chairs, and chairs by Saarinen and Eames as well as the popular Butterfly Chair. Colors used in the house were orange, yellow, magenta, blue, and purple. Throughout the house were Peruvian rugs, collections of Mexican figurines, Chinese paper kites, nativity scenes, birdcages, and other folk art. The Girards' collection of folk art from South America and of Victorian artifacts had already been started. In this house Alexander Girard began to show the flair for assembly and display technique he would refine and elaborate in the coming years. That technique was to make him one of the most respected exhibition designers of the next two decades.

The Scandinavian Influence

Throughout the decade the influence of Scandinavian design on American interiors was prevalent. It had been introduced in the 1930s as Swedish Modern, and continued to make the 1940s known, logically, as the Scandinavian Decade in America. The foremost Swedish furniture designer in the United States during the 1940s was Bruno Mathsson (1907–), whose pale, cool designs included a trend-setting armchair of bent plywood and fiber webbing in 1940; it had followed a reclining chair with a similar bent-plywood frame designed in 1935. Mathsson's work had become a mainstay of Swedish Modern in the mid-1930s, when he developed his split-top leg for tables and beds.

In 1941 the Danish designer Jens Risom, who had designed furniture for the Knoll Furniture Company, opened his own firm in New York, devoted mainly to furniture design, and helped to popularize Danish Modern during the decade. By the end of the 1940s Danish and Finnish designs were somewhat more popular in the United States than the Swedish Modern idiom. In 1949 the Dane Hans Wegner (1914–) designed his classic chair with its exposed sculptured frame of oak or teak, and with a cane seat and cane-wrapped back. It became so popular that it was known for the next decade simply as "The Chair" (see Figure 100). Many people felt that The Chair was reminiscent of ancient Chinese tradition. The sinuous furniture designed by Finn Juhl (1912–) was introduced to the States in the same year. Other popular Danish designers were Borge Mogenson (1914–72); Magnus Stephensen (1903–); and Mogens Koch, whose classic folding chair (1938) was among the earliest popular Danish designs.

Among the Finns Paavo Tynell's pinpoint-pierced brass lamps with their snowflake-like umbrellas of flower petals charmed Americans after 1947; and Ilmari Tapiovaara (1914–) pioneered in knock-down furniture designs. In 1947 Alvar Aalto designed his acclaimed coffee table of birch and glass, and from 1947 to 1949 he worked on the design of Baker House, a dormitory for the Massachusetts Insti-

100. Hans Wegner. The Chair. 1949. *Photograph courtesy Knoll International.*

tute of Technology in Cambridge, Massachusetts, with an undulating plan, which was his first architectural work in the States since the Finnish Pavilion at the 1939 New York World's Fair. The Scandinavian designers offered a pale palette of natural woods that was acceptable to several segments of the population: those accustomed to 1930s colors; those who preferred a homey, easy, somewhat provincial style, such as those nostalgic for Arts and Crafts simplicity and those who admired the Peasant style of Picasso; those young people whose budgets permitted only the simplest of good design; and, in addition, the confirmed Modernists, who were dedicated to the texture and honesty of natural materials.

After World War II

The impact of postwar economic and social changes in America was enormous. Postwar victoriousness and optimism brought about prosperity and a widespread and freewheeling building boom that was forwarded by wartime technological advances. Technological innovation was the aspiration of the day. The return of the armed forces brought both a baby boom and manageable FHA home mortgages for veterans. The annual number of new-home construction starts grew from 200,000 in 1945 to 1,154,000 in 1950.

This contributed to the building boom and began the suburbanization of America. It was the beginning of the end of servants; no servants at home meant do-it-yourself for everyman. At this time, too, television and the family room became regular components of American interiors. The number of television sets produced in America mushroomed from zero in 1945 to 7.5 million by 1950.[1] They produced a new spider's web of antennas over the cities of the land. For interior designers, what had been a comfortable practice for a few mushroomed into big businesses for a great many. Not only residential and club interiors were their commissions, but transportation and many more commercial projects were on the horizon.

The epochal explosion of the atomic bomb at Hiroshima and Nagasaki in 1945 had opened the Atomic Age. The horror and awesomeness of the event, however, were of less concern to the general American population than the potential of atomic fission. The concept caught the imaginations of designers. A popular inspiration and motif were atomic and molecular shapes made of metal rods with small disks or spheres attached at the tips (see Figure 101). This atomic-molecular motif was often expressed with wire or string, especially in the cat's-cradle structures of tables and chairs, and, architecturally, of staircases, which were aimed at dematerialization. It was a symbol of the new exposure to atomic power as well as the feeling of discontinuity that the revelation of atomic fission produced.

An Expanded Availability of Furnishings

New materials, new furnishings, new technologies, and new availabilities were abundant. Among the newly available technologies was plastics, which began to influence design in the 1940s. Americans had begun to get used to the quickening of travel and communications before the war. Air travel had begun to increase in frequency and distance. Long-distance telephoning and radio reception became expected components of living.

Americans began to travel widely, and a new generation discovered Europe. Americans were liberated and began to take a new look. The desire for everything from everywhere and the availability of imports and inspirations from all countries and all periods began to be expected as well. Hawaiian and Brazilian motifs—large tropical leaves and bamboo, as well as Carmen Miranda—were incorporated into North American imagery. Eclecticism was rampant. It brought with it broad-

101. George Nelson. Wall clock for Howard Miller Clock Company. 1949. *Photograph by Michael Norgart, courtesy Fifty–50 Gallery, New York City.*

reaching romanticism, exuberance and excitement, and flamboyance. It also brought incompatibilities of forms, lines, colors, textures, periods, and cultures.

As Edgar Kaufmann, Jr., wrote of the 1940s,

> America assumed a new position as a source of design creativity. Her product designers had overcome their original brashness, had looked long and intelligently at the ideals upheld by their critics, had absorbed a second generation of practitioners, and were maturing successfully. American architects, who had enjoyed something of a world reputation for several generations, also moved ahead, incorporating many influences and emerging with a new commercial style that swept across the metropolitan centers of the world. Architectural firms had no hesitation in adding [interior design] departments for the purpose. Some of the freest modern furnishings found their best utilization through such intermediaries.[2]

Postwar Designers

New industrial designers, such as Gilbert Rohde and Edward J Wormley, filled the gap in demand for new interior furnishings along with the established industrial designers from the 1930s. Among the new furniture designers was a group who had studied at the Cranbrook Academy in Michigan. Others included Paul Frankl and Paul Laszlo in California; the sculptor Isamu Noguchi; furniture designers Wharton Esherick and George Nakashima; and a host of others. The California design team of Van Keppel and Green began at this time also. Paul McCobb designed furniture—both chairs and case pieces—and, later on, furniture systems for Modernage, Raymor, and his own firm. Among the best new fabrics designers were Dorothy Liebes, Boris Kroll, Vera Neumann, and Arundell Clark, who had moved here from London, as had carpet designer Marian Dorn. The V'Soske family also experimented with carpet textures and designs, and the introduction of brilliantly colored silks from Thailand was made at this time by Jim Thompson's firm, Thaibok.

Dorothy Liebes Most influential among the new fabric designers was Dorothy Liebes. Born in California, Dorothy Wright Liebes (1899–1972) studied at the

University of California at Berkeley and Columbia University in New York City. She had operated a studio in San Francisco specializing in custom-handwoven work for architects and decorators since 1930. Her handweaving was notable for its bright colors in unusual combinations—orange and sage, fuschia and chartreuse—and for its unconventional yarns and other materials.

She first became involved in larger-scale production in 1940, when she was engaged by Goodall Fabrics in Sanford, Maine. In 1948 she moved her design studio to New York City. She was to go on, in the next decade, to initiate a revolution in machine-weaving techniques based on her handweaving, and to become a leader in the color revolution.

Cranbrook Academy Among the new furniture designers of the 1940s was the group that had studied and taught at the Cranbrook Academy in the 1930s (see Chapter 5). They included Charles Eames, Eero Saarinen, Florence Schust Knoll, Benjamin Baldwin, Harry Bertoia, Harry Weese, and Ralph Rapson. These designers and architects were to become leaders of the second generation of Modern design.

For the Cranbrook designers of the 1930s, the decade began with the award to Charles Eames and Eero Saarinen of two first prizes in New York's Museum of Modern Art's "Organic Design in Home Furnishings" competition of 1938–41, which was directed by Eliot Noyes, then a recent graduate of Walter Gropius's program at Harvard. Their award-winning designs were a chair of molded sheet plywood with a sculpted outline, and a series of gangable cabinets, drawer units, and coffee tables.

The technical innovation of the chair was that its plywood components were bent in two directions, making it more complex than either the bentwood furniture of Belter or Thonet or the plywood chairs of Aalto and Breuer. That chair was revolutionary; it became the inspiration for chair designs after the war by Eames and Saarinen separately—Eames for the Herman Miller furniture company and Saarinen for Knoll Associates, both in 1946. It then became the inspiration for the world of interior and furniture designers.

Eero Saarinen The son of Cranbrook's president, the Finnish architect Eliel Saarinen, and his weaver wife Loja, Eero Saarinen (1910–61) was born in Kirkkonummi, Finland, and was brought by his family to the United States when he was thirteen. He first intended to be a sculptor, but decided to become an architect and studied at Yale University.

After travel in Europe Eero Saarinen joined his father's architecture office from 1936 to 1941. It was in that period that he worked with Charles Eames on the "Organic Design" competition (see Figure 102). During the war he worked in Washington for the Office of Strategic Studies from 1942 to 1945, then returned to practice with his father until the latter's death in 1950. In 1948 Eero Saarinen gained international recognition for his competition-winning design for the Gateway Arch in St. Louis, Missouri. From that point on he became, for the next decade, the most promising American architect.

Charles Eames Charles Eames was one of the major interior and furniture design innovators of the twentieth century. His award-winning furniture designs with Eero Saarinen pioneered a new approach that changed the course of twentieth-century furniture.

Born in St. Louis, Missouri, Charles Eames (1907–78) studied architecture at Washington University in St. Louis, and began to practice architecture in 1930. After studying at Cranbrook on a fellowship offered him by Eliel Saarinen in 1938, he headed the Department of Experimental Design at Cranbrook Academy, where

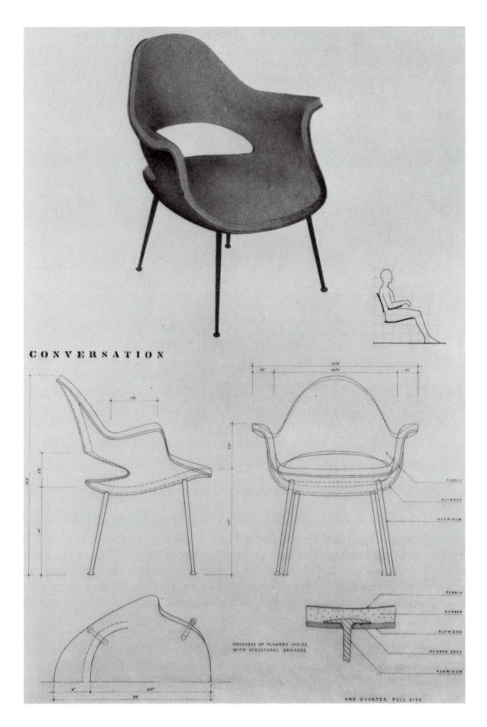

102. Charles Eames and Eero Saarinen. Conversation Chair, competition drawing, colored pencil, wood veneer, and paper cutouts on white poster board, 20″ × 30″. Organic Design competition winner. 1940. *Collection, The Museum of Modern Art, New York City.*

he met his future wife and partner, Ray Kaiser Eames. In 1942, when the Eameses had moved to California, they were commissioned by the Navy Department to develop splints, stretchers, and glider shells out of molded plywood. Their technical findings advanced the design of their subsequent plywood furniture.

Eames began to design furniture for the Herman Miller company in 1946 (see Figure 103). His chairs of molded plywood were cut from plywood sheeting, which had been made since the early 1930s, but had only recently become available for uses other than doors, drawer bottoms, and automobile running boards. The chairs, which won immediate acclaim both for their structural ingenuity and for their

103. Charles Eames and Ray Eames. Molded plywood chair. 1946. *Photograph courtesy Herman Miller Inc.*

sculptural affinity with the amoeba-form of Hans Arp, were sometimes dubbed "potato-chip chairs."

To the serious direction in Modern design, Eames brought a touch of whimsy and sculptural lightness with these forms; but his design was backed up by meticulous analysis, technological invention, and innovative genius. Eames has been called the most original American furniture designer since Duncan Phyfe, and the designer of three major chairs of the twentieth century.[3] He and Ray Eames went on to design other furniture, furniture systems, exhibitions, and buildings, and to make major advances in movie production for the next thirty years.

Florence Schust Knoll Another Cranbrook affiliate, Florence Schust Knoll (1917–) also began to leave a mark on the interior design world in the 1940s. Born in Michigan, she studied at Cranbrook's Kingswood School for Girls and became a protégée of Eliel Saarinen and his family. She continued her education at the Architectural Association in London, and graduated from Mies van der Rohe's architecture program at Armour Institute (now the Illinois Institute of Technology). She worked briefly as an architect for Breuer, Gropius, and Herbert Bayer before becoming involved with the new Modern furniture of the 1940s—specifically, the Knoll Furniture Company (see below).

The New Modern Furniture Manufacturers

The availability of Modern, practical, and durable new furniture expanded greatly during the 1940s, owing to the founding of two major new furniture firms—the Herman Miller company and the Knoll Furniture Company.

Knoll Furniture Company

Knoll Furniture was founded by Hans Knoll (1914–55), who had come from Germany and established the Hans G. Knoll Furniture Company in 1938. Emigrés from the Bauhaus had found a receptive ground for their buildings, but appropriate furniture was not available in the United States. Other Modernists who searched for suitable furniture were Florence Schust, recently from Cranbrook. She met Hans Knoll, formed a business with him in 1943, and in 1946 they founded the Knoll Planning Unit for the design of interiors—offices, residences, and college dormitories. In 1946, the year they were married, the name of their firm was changed to Knoll Associates. Hans Knoll was killed in an auto accident in 1955; but in slightly more than a decade he and Florence Knoll had initiated some of the significant second-generation Modern furniture designs and had established what became known as the "Knoll look."

Among the first furniture they produced were designs by Eero Saarinen, whose first designs for Knoll in 1943 were chairs of cut-out laminated wood frames with seats and backs of woven canvas strips. Other early designers of furniture for Knoll were Pierre Jeanneret from France; Jens Risom from Denmark; Ralph Rapson, who had been at Cranbrook; and George Nakashima, who had recently forsaken architecture for furniture crafting (see below). In 1948 Knoll produced Saarinen's Womb Chair design, making it the first known molded fiberglass-reinforced plastic shell to be mass produced. It was the precursor of a series of office chairs that Saarinen designed that came to be known as "the chair with the hole in the back" (see Figure 104).

104. Eero Saarinen. Womb Chair (left); chair with hole in back (right). 1948. *Photograph courtesy Knoll International.*

In 1948 Knoll Associates began producing Mies's Barcelona chairs and stools and Mies's Tugendhat coffee table. The act made them seem promulgators of the Bauhaus ideal.[4] The same year Knoll began producing textiles designed by Marianne Strengell, who had headed the weaving studio at Cranbrook. Knoll was among the principal creators of Modern interiors of the succeeding decades.

Herman Miller Inc.

The Herman Miller company of Zeeland, Michigan, was another of the Modern furniture firms that came to prominence in the 1940s. From the mid-1930s the Herman Miller company, headed by D. J. DePree, had been producing Modern furniture designed by the industrial designer Gilbert Rohde. Other early furniture designers whose works were produced by Herman Miller in the 1940s were Paul Laszlo and the sculptor Isamu Noguchi.

Born in 1904 in Los Angeles and trained in Japan, Noguchi studied sculpture with Constantin Brancusi and later, in addition to his sculpture, also designed furniture for both Herman Miller and Knoll. In 1944 he introduced a palette-shaped or free-form table for Herman Miller that became a symbol of organic furniture for the decade. His paper lanterns for Knoll (1948) reinterpreted the traditional Japanese concept in a new guise.

George Nelson

After Gilbert Rohde died in 1944, D. J. De Pree turned to George Nelson as his new design consultant. Nelson, with Henry Wright, had become known for the Storagewall concept, introduced in 1945, which was developed into a prefabricated closet-like piece of case goods with flexible shelving that could also be used as a room divider. It was the first of Nelson's series of provocative and innovative concepts for the furniture industry.

Born in Hartford, Connecticut, George Nelson (1908–86) graduated from Yale College and, in 1931, from the Yale School of Fine Arts. He went on to study architecture at Catholic University in Washington, D.C., winning a Prix de Rome that allowed him two years of travel and study in Europe.

Back in Depression-ridden New York in 1934, he first worked as an editor of *Architectural Forum* magazine, eventually becoming its co-managing editor with Henry Wright. During this time he worked both as architect and author, collaborating with Henry Wright on the book *Tomorrow's House* (1945). There, they put forward the concept of Storagewall, which provided storage space in increased wall depth. The next year Nelson began to design furniture for Herman Miller, and soon became the firm's director of design.

In 1947 he left magazine work and established George Nelson & Company, industrial designers. He designed furniture, graphics, promotion, and showrooms for the firm. Under his auspices Herman Miller was guided to a position as one of the two foremost producers of Modern furnishings in the United States. In the late 1940s George Nelson persuaded Herman Miller to produce Charles Eames's furniture designs, and he negotiated the firm's association with Alexander Girard in the early 1950s. By the 1960s Herman Miller had become the design laboratory for the American furniture industry.

Among Nelson's design innovations were the slat bench (1948), the headboard with adjustable backrests (1948), and the L-shaped desk (1949) (see Figure 105). He continued to invent for the furniture industry for the next three decades. George Nelson has demonstrated the extraordinary talent of conceptualizing environments with a freewheeling and unfettered vision that sees past traditions, customs, and barriers to arrive at innovations of virtually poetic imagination.

105. George Nelson. The L-shaped desk from Executive Office Group. 1949–50. *Photograph courtesy Herman Miller Inc.*

His concepts more than his formal detailing make him one of the geniuses of twentieth-century design, which he considers to be principally a matter of clear thinking and hard work.

The Eames Chairs

In 1946 the Herman Miller company introduced the first of Charles Eames's chair designs. For Eames, the century-long goal of industrial mass production—and mass distribution—was immediately realized.

The chair, a version of the earlier potato-chip chair, was made in two heights— for dining and for lounging—with steel rods (5/8-inch-diameter legs, 7/8-inch back stile) forming the frame. Molded plywood panels (5-ply, 5/16-inch thick) are attached to the steel-rod frame with rubber shock mounts. Leg pads were originally rubber, later nylon. The overall composition has both technical innovation and the look of technology, a light and delicate air despite structural strength and durability, and it captured something of the sculptural imagery of Alexander Calder's mobiles of that decade. It became one of the classic chairs of the twentieth century. The earlier version of the Eames Chair had bent plywood legs, making it perhaps more 1940s in appearance and more integral in materials. But the steel-framed chair was the progenitor for the 1950s.

Eames continued to experiment with molded plywood until 1948. During that time he produced his folding, molded, undulating plywood screen, and a series of other pieces that were produced by Herman Miller.

Harvard under Gropius

The 1940s were the prime years of Walter Gropius's influence in bringing the Bauhaus educational program to America as director of the Harvard Graduate

School of Design (1937–53). From 1937 to 1946, Marcel Breuer also taught there. Their exposition of Bauhaus teaching, which proclaimed an ideal faith in social betterment, was revered at the time in architecture and education circles across the country. From that program came a dozen of the foremost architects, who were also designers of major interiors in the next decades: Edward Larrabee Barnes; John Johansen; Philip Johnson; I. M. Pei, and his partners Henry N. Cobb and Araldo Cossutta; Paul Rudolph; Ulrich Franzen; and Victor Lundy. They were to become leaders of the second generation of Modern design.

Gropius's program emphasized functional planning and expression, clarity and simplicity, and visual interest and texture. Walter and Ise Gropius's own house of 1938 in Lincoln, Massachusetts, indicated the kind of simplicity intended. Its living space was dividable by sliding fabric partitions; its hallway was sheathed in vertically scored siding to reflect the regionalism of New England clapboard construction; and its exterior was textured by horizontal windows, glass block, and a slat-trellised terrace. This more relaxed International-Style house along with other similar houses by Marcel Breuer, which had local fieldstone fireplaces or bases, was proclaimed as the idiom of the new American everyman. It was a non-style for all time, and it continued to affect American interior design for the next three or four decades.

The Spread of the Miesian Idiom

Philip Johnson

Philip Johnson was the most prominent advocate of the work of Mies van der Rohe, and he was also the most active disciple in demonstrating the potential of the Miesian idiom.

Born in Cleveland, Ohio, Philip Cortelyou Johnson (1906–) graduated from Harvard University in 1930, where he studied philosophy and the classics. From 1932 to 1934 he was director of the department of architecture at the Museum of Modern Art in New York, and in 1932, at the age of twenty-five, he mounted the exhibition "The International Style: Architecture 1922–1932" and co-authored with Henry-Russell Hitchcock the catalog of that exhibition (see Chapter 5).

In 1940 he returned to Harvard to study architecture under Gropius and Breuer, graduating in 1943. In 1942, while he was an architecture student, Johnson designed a house for himself in Cambridge, Massachusetts, that was modeled on the courtyard-house concepts of Mies in the 1930s. Johnson finished these Miesian interiors with the furniture by Mies that he had acquired in the 1930s.

Johnson resumed his position at the Museum of Modern Art in 1946, and in 1949 directed the construction in the museum garden of a modern house by Marcel Breuer. In 1955 he established his own design office. During that time he designed another house for himself in the Miesian idiom. That Glass House in New Canaan, Connecticut, made him—and that idiom—famous to a general public.

Glass Houses

Mies's glass-and-steel house for Dr. Edith Farnsworth in Plano, Illinois (near Fox River, Illinois), had been initiated as a design in 1946; but was not completed until 1951. During this time Johnson had completed his own celebrated Glass House. The Farnsworth House and the Glass House (as well as the Irwin Miller House by Saarinen and Girard discussed on page 220) raised consciousness for the potential of Modern glass architecture in creating timeless elegance and classic simplicity. These glass houses were unabashedly honest about structure; they were models of clarity and alignment, and models of the use of sumptuous natural materials. Their Machine-Age directness achieved unparalleled Modern richness through the juxtaposition of the purest Machine-Age refinement against the rich variety and color of the living natural landscape.

Mies's Farnsworth House   The Farnsworth House (see Figure 106A) of white-painted, wide-flange steel columns and all-glass walls elevates a single space floored in travertine above a terrace entry—and, in fact, above the ground, over which it hovers. In a new way appropriate to its age, the Farnsworth House makes architecture one and the same with interior design. The interior space, 54 by 28 feet, has no divisions except for a core of utilities running along one of the long sides in the form of a rectangle with projecting fins at the outer corners (see Figure 106B). That core incorporates all the mechanical and service systems for the house: At the center are the furnace, heating ducts, and water heater; a bathroom is at each end of the core; on the back side of the core is a galley kitchen—two refrigerators and two ranges are beneath the single counter, which also contains dishwasher and sink; on the other side of the core are a fireplace and a paneled storagewall overhang that shelter the firewood and create the semblance of an inglenook.

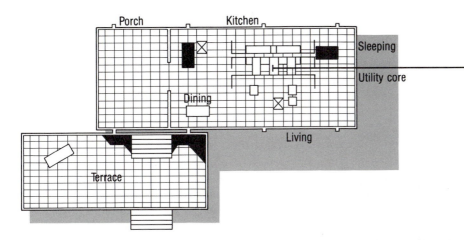

106A.   Ludwig Mies van der Rohe. Plan, Farnsworth House. Plano, Illinois. 1946–51. *Illustration from Mary Jane Pool, ed., 20th Century Decorating. Architecture, and Gardens (New York: Holt, Rinehart and Winston, 1980).*

106B.   Ludwig Mies van der Rohe. Entry. Farnsworth House. Plano, Illinois. 1946–51. *Photograph by Bill Hedrich, Hedrich-Blessing.*

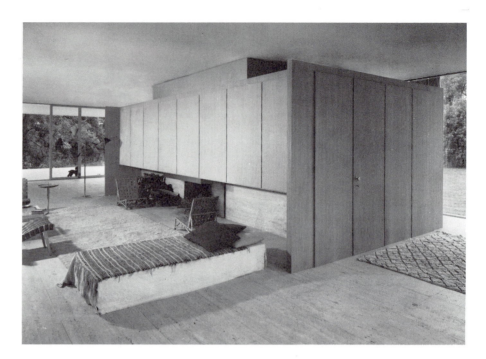

Dr. Farnsworth's furnishings (see Figure 106C) were Scandinavian Modern instead of Mies's own designs, and for that reason the house was not widely published as an epitome of the Machine-Age idiom. But as a minimal, atticless, basementless, suspended industrial object—an object that is ineffably serene, precisely conceived, and meticulous in detail—the house is an archetypal image of the plug-in unit that spurred the design imaginations of the next two decades. "Architecture is the will of an epoch translated into space," Mies wrote.[5]

Johnson's Glass House   In 1949 Philip Johnson completed his Glass House in New Canaan, Connecticut (see Figure 107B). Designed for his own use in 1947, the Glass House was widely publicized immediately and brought an eye-opening new image of lightness, transparency, freedom, and the end of the Victorian era of hideaway window draperies.

Not only are interior and architecture of the Glass House one and the same, but the exterior landscape became the wall decoration of historical tradition. Set

107A. Philip Johnson. Plan, Glass House. New Canaan, Connecticut. 1949. *Illustration from* Selected Writings of Philip Johnson *(Japan: ADA Edita Tokyo, 1979).*

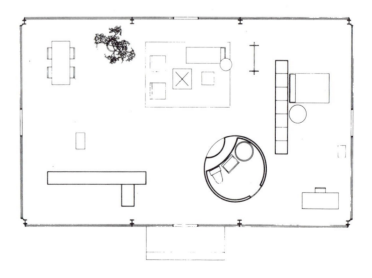

107B. Philip Johnson. Living room, Glass House. New Canaan, Connecticut. 1949. *Photograph courtesy Philip Johnson, Architect.*

off by its machine-image black-steel structural frame, this transparency seemed the ultimate realization of the glass-architecture aesthetic as well as of Frank Lloyd Wright's early interpenetration of interior and exterior.

Inside, the single space—56 by 32 by 10 feet 6 inches high, which is set on a concrete slab on grade—contains living and dining areas, kitchen, and bedroom; each is set off from the other by walnut storage-cabinet dividers. The "room divider" became a motif of the next several years. Only the bath is separate and enclosed, being incorporated into a brick cylinder along with a fireplace. Heating is provided by radiant electrical heating in both the floor and the ceiling.

The original furnishings (see Figure 107B) were a compendium of the classic designs of Mies and Breuer from the 1920s—Barcelona and Brno chairs in natural pigskin, and the Mies couch and bolster in black nylon, which Johnson had acquired in 1930, sitting on a white-wool carpeted island on the highly waxed dark brick floor itself. The glass walls were shielded, when required, by sliding panels of fabric, which were hung in flat sections of natural-color pandanus cloth reminiscent of Japanese shoji screens. To enrich these furnishings, Johnson displayed a sculpture of two female figures by Elie Nadelman and a painting attributed to Poussin. A tall wrought-iron candelabrum, designed by Johnson, originally stood near the fireplace cylinder to add a further touch of the patina that was so much desired during the late 1940s.

In the bedroom area the bed was covered in a quilt of bottle-green raw silk; the desk top was covered in black leather; the tubular Brno Chair in natural calfskin; and Breuer's Laccio Stool in black leather. Johnson spoke much of the historical background of the house, and these historical overtones contributed to a large part of what were seen as the timelessness and accessibility of the house for non-Modernists.

Mies's Lakeshore Drive Apartments   From 1949 to 1951 Mies was working on his first pair of curtain-wall apartment towers in Chicago on Lakeshore Drive. These were the first realizations of his high-rise curtain-wall schemes of 1921–22, and they were, essentially, stacked versions of the Farnsworth House in different configurations. Except for the planning of the apartments and the finishing of the lobby spaces, those apartment interiors were little known compared with his exterior architecture, until the 1970s, when apartments began to be recreated faithfully to the Miesian idiom. Meanwhile, other disciples were reinterpreting Miesian architecture for corporate towers.

Skidmore, Owings & Merrill

The architectural firm of Skidmore, Owings & Merrill (SOM), which had been initiated in 1936, began to develop its design department in 1945 for the interiors of Cincinnati's Terrace Plaza Hotel. It was the beginning of new interior design departments in large architectural offices; this development was brought about by the desire to have an integrated approach—total design—in the Modern idiom.

The Benjamin Baldwin was in charge of the hotel's interior design; with him were Natalie DeBlois and Davis Allen, who later directed interior design in SOM's New York office. The department designed everything that went into the hotel—furniture, fabrics, china, match folders, and uniforms. The hotel was Modern—though not yet in the full Miesian idiom that SOM was to develop in the 1950s.

The Terrace Plaza Hotel was also one of the first public buildings in America to follow the Bauhaus aim of incorporating the work of fine artists as well as interior craftsmen. The design included murals by Joan Miró and Saul Steinberg, a mobile sculpture by Alexander Calder, as well as furniture by Benjamin Baldwin and Davis Allen, fabrics by Cranbrook's Marianne Strengell, and metal lighting fixtures by Ward Bennett. The subsequent work of SOM was to make the Miesian idiom prominent throughout the world—both for its handling of exterior planning, massing, and structural elements, and for its interior design and finishing.

The Eames House

One other house of the late 1940s confirmed the machine imagery of the Modern idiom. The Eames House (1949) in Pacific Palisades, California, by Charles and his wife Ray Eames, was another metal-and-glass house; but it incorporated aspects of California informality and found objects in the Dada-Surrealism vein (see Figure 108).

The Eameses constructed their house of standard items from manufacturers' catalogues—steel columns, open-web metal joists, windows, and metal siding, as well as transparent and translucent glass. They assembled these components into a Mondrianesque image of differently colored and textured rectangles that had straightforward sophistication and a light gridded rhythm reminiscent of traditional Japanese houses. The Eames house design was a rare example of architects making architecture and interiors out of specified rather than designed components—selecting and arranging, rather than redesigning every element. It was a model for future architecture, but it was not the principal model that architects of the day elected to emulate.

The interior of the Eames house was furnished with their own plywood chair and case-piece designs. The shelving units manipulated the spidery-wire aesthetic of the late 1940s by exploiting the tensile qualities of lightweight steel wire as bracing. Filled with plants and collections of objects (some of them South Amer-

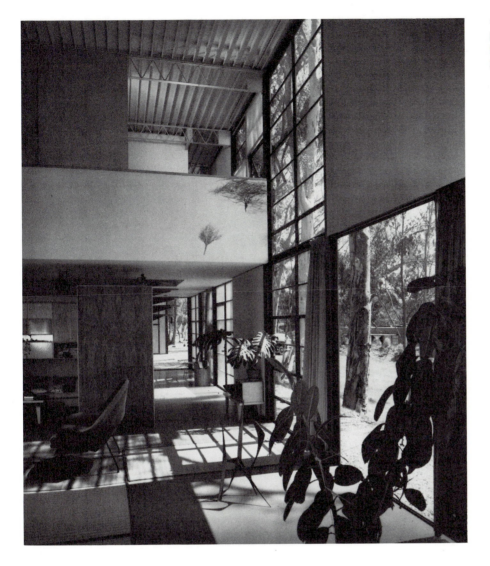

108. Charles Eames and Ray Eames. Eames House. Pacific Palisades, California. 1949. *Photograph by Julius Shulman.*

ican), Eames's furniture, and Noguchi's paper-lantern lighting, the Eames House interior became another prototypical image of Miesian design. Along with the Case Study house for John Etenza by Eames and Saarinen, it was a less rigid and formal image than that of Mies or Johnson.

The Bay Region Style

In California at this time there also emerged a local idiom based on the earlier houses of Bernard Maybeck and Greene & Greene (see Chapter 3) called the Bay Region style. It vied with the formalism of International Modern by offering informal living and patios. The houses of architects William B. Wurster, Harwell Hamilton Harris, Gregory Ain, J. R. Davidson, and Rafael Soriano made them leaders of this movement, which featured relaxed planning and natural wood textures that were a West Coast equivalent to the contemporaneous houses of Gropius and Breuer. Richard Neutra and Rudolph Schindler (see Chapters 4 and 5) continued their more structurally crisp California houses, finishing their interiors in exposed plywood sheeting, built-in storage units, and the new 1940s furniture.

Paul T. Frankl, from Vienna, and Paul Laszlo, who had come from Hungary in the 1930s, also worked in this California Modern idiom. Boxy square furnishings

109. Paul T. Frankl. Residence in California. 1940s. *Photograph by Julius Shulman.*

of reeded or dowel-paneled wood reiterated the bamboo motif in Modern terms (see Figure 109). The California industrial designer Kem Weber also designed reeded walls and modernistic furnishings, such as for the Bismarck Hotel (1944). Some of the forms of these designs had the lingering air of Streamlining, but the aim was to follow the Modern tenet of accepting, as the only ornamentation, the textures of natural materials.

Concurrently, two furniture makers on the East Coast formed a link with this Bay Region style through their continuation of the California Arts and Crafts tradition of the earlier part of the century. George Nakashima and Wharton Esherick made furniture by hand; both worked in a sculptural, somewhat rustic aesthetic that recalled their own native regions and backgrounds.

Wharton Esherick (1887–1974) was born in Philadelphia and studied at the School of Industrial Art there and at the Pennsylvania Academy of Fine Art. From the 1920s onward he continued the Arts and Crafts tradition, operating a crafts shop at Paoli, Pennsylvania. His work suggested a combination of Windsor, William Morris, and Early American spindleback chairs. Esherick developed a sinuous, sublimely refined line that gained him the reputation of "dean of twentieth-century American woodworkers."

George Nakashima (1905–), born in Spokane, Washington, studied architecture at the University of Washington and at the Massachusetts Institute of Technology. He first worked in the architecture firm of Antonin Raymond in Tokyo and India. From the mid-1940s he designed chairs and other furniture in New Hope, Pennsylvania, working in an idiom that suggested an Early American heritage as well as traditional Japanese forms. He also designed furniture for Herman Miller Inc.

The furniture of both designers was eagerly sought-after as an alternative to clinical machine-imagery Modern furniture. Their delicate lines and graceful intensification of the graining of natural woods enhanced interiors for the next several decades.

"Traditional" versus "Contemporary"

World War II affected American decorating along with the rest of life. Many of the new generation of male decorators went off to serve in the armed forces. William Pahlmann directed a camouflage school for the Air Force; also in attendance were theater designers Jo Mielziner, Donald Oenslager, and display designer Tom Lee, who would later become a prominent designer of hotel interiors and exhibitions. The effect of theater, display, and camouflage on American interior design has not yet been adequately explored.

At home, during the war, Mrs. Henry Parish II moved into an apartment in New York City and, with several colleagues, formed the Budget Decorators. Eleanor McMillen Brown organized exhibitions of antique furniture; after the war she exhibited contemporary French furniture.

The prominent American decorators of the decade were George Stacey, McMillen Inc., Mrs. Henry Parish II, William Pahlmann, Edward Wormley, Valerian Rybar, Bertha Schaefer, Eleanor LeMaire, Elizabeth Draper, Sarah Hunter Kelly, Joseph B. Platt, Joseph Mullen, and Billy Baldwin. Mabel Schamberg practiced in Chicago; and in California, Frances Elkins worked toward a California regionalism. Other prominent interior designers in the 1940s were Paul Laszlo, Paul T. Frankl, Robsjohn-Gibbings, and James Amster.

The spread of Modernism in the United States did not bring the end of historicism. Decorators working in the historical and period-room tradition continued to explore different periods and combinations to renew their direction. Diane Tate and Marian Hall recreated rooms in the Robert Adam idiom and also designed ship interiors. McMillen Inc. explored earlier eighteenth-century English decoration furnished with Sheraton and Hepplewhite pieces.

The beginning of a Regency revival was apparent. A Victorian revival was also witnessed, perhaps inspired by the film version of *Gone With the Wind*—the settings of which had been furnished by Joseph B. Platt, who also wielded influence as decoration consultant to *House & Garden*.

Rooms with dark-green walls—forest green—became a popular scheme during the 1940s. Green walls were a trademark of Elsie de Wolfe, who also continued her use of leopard-patterned chintz and a white chintz with green fern fronds. Among many others who adopted deep greens were Thedlow, Dorothy Draper, and Billy Baldwin.

A rich new array of fabrics, wallpapers, and furniture became available. Colonel Roger and Mrs. Zelina Brunschwig became mainstays of interior designers. The search for the new meant not espousing the Modern idiom, but trying the untried—previously not-revived historical periods, innovative directions, uncommon color combinations, and different textures. Surrealism enjoyed another wave of popularity after the war: disembodied hands went public as sconces; the disembodied eye was taken up by the vanguard, Dali included. Billy Baldwin wrote of the second half of the 1940s, "Decorating in America was just about as emotional an art as it ever has been."[6]

Design Education

A new educational influence on interior designers came about with Hope Foote, who was appointed chairman of the department of interior design at the University of Washington. She brought a new vitality to the Pacific Northwest, which had not been prominent in interior design circles before.

In 1940 the New York School of Applied and Fine Arts was renamed the Parsons School of Design, after its past president, Frank Alvah Parsons. Van Day Truex was appointed president of Parsons, bringing a new fame to the school that had been the principal educator of New York traditional decorators since the early part of the century. Truex had been a painter and knew the art world. As a teacher and editor of taste, he brought the life of creative people to his students and directed them to travel, look, feel, and try the new. He emphasized historical accuracy, drawing, and experimentation, and set the direction for a whole generation of designers.

During those years, shop window design became a major activity—some of the windows were considered art-form tableaux. They greatly influenced other designers as well as the public. Among the windows that people flocked to see every time they were changed were those at the shops of Rose Cumming, Greeff Fabrics, James Pendleton, Roslyn Rosier, and Jarvis House. Henry Callahan continued the tradition at Lord & Taylor. It was almost a necessary opening-night activity to see these new ideas.

Influential Designers

Dorothy Draper

At the height of her career in the 1940s, Dorothy Draper was in the tradition of "lady decorators," but her work was primarily in commercial buildings, especially stores and hotels. Her design of the public rooms Camellia House for the Drake Hotel in Chicago (1940–41) demonstrated her flamboyant neo-Baroque trademarks: large-scale, deeply sculpted, white plaster ornaments—volutes and scroll moldings, cartouches, and borders composed of such motifs as leaves, feathers, and shells.

Her restaurants often featured these overscaled decorations—including mirrors, chandeliers, and borders for doors and windows—against dark-green or burgundy walls. Here was English–French Baroque decoration blown up to an even larger scale, remaining ungilded and all white, like some Surrealist negative (though she would not have thought so), yet somehow immediately accessible to the public as well as to designers. It was a distinctive innovation.

Dorothy Draper's influence was popularized through her position as design consultant for the *Good Housekeeping* magazine studio from 1939 to 1946. John B. Wisner was her assistant from 1941 to 1946. During that time (1943–44) she designed the 46th Street Theater in New York and the Mayflower Hotel in Washington, D.C. In planning the guest rooms for the Mayflower Hotel, Dorothy Draper's goal—as it had been with slightly earlier hotel projects of hers—was to change the appearance of the conventional twin-bedded room of the day. Instead, she made them look more like sitting rooms.

To achieve the sitting-room effect, Draper placed standard twin beds away from the walls, like conventional facing sofas. Boxsprings and mattresses were fitted with a backrest, one armrest, and bolsters; the entire unit was covered in upholstery fabric rather than customary bedspread material. Sometimes these upholstered beds were hinged at the front edge of the armrest so that they could be swung out to facilitate making up of the beds. Lacquered cabinets served as end tables and also provided for pillow storage. These were among the early convertible sofa-beds. The innovation became standard in hotel design during World War II, when the shortage of hotel rooms for meetings and business appointments made the use of guest rooms as meeting rooms necessary.

Almost all of Dorothy Draper's innovative ideas were related to her belief that decoration was an important factor in the promotion of the hotel or property under consideration. That was perhaps what made her work so well suited to public spaces. At one hotel she convinced the management to put the unusually high cost of maintaining elaborate muslin casement curtains into the advertising budget.

110. Dorothy Draper. Quitandinha Hotel. Petropolis, Brazil, 1946. *Photograph by Studio Rembrandt, courtesy John B. Wisner.*

Dorothy Draper also began to use wall stencils to increase the potential of her overscaled decorative elements. These were developed to match her large plaster elements, since no large-patterned wallpapers were then available. Floral patterns, connecting ribbons or scrolls, or overall damask-like patterns were stenciled on canvas-covered walls that had been painted white. In this way she influenced the market style and marketing.

Her interiors for the Quitandinha Hotel in Petropolis, outside Rio, Brazil (1946), continued this tradition (see Figure 110) with what seemed like even larger-scale checkerboard marble floors; heavy white moldings on black doors; bold white consoles, sconces, and chandeliers; cabbage-rose chintz; and red and green combinations. When people said the latter looked like Christmas, Draper replied that she wanted rooms to look bright and happy. In 1947, when the Greenbrier resort hotel in White Sulphur Springs, West Virginia, was reclaimed from its wartime use as a government hospital, Draper redecorated it with her trademark motifs, in an overall scheme of white and green. It seemed at the time like the springtime after the war. For this project Glenn Boyles, teacher and illustrator, was her chief designer.

Frances Elkins

In California, mostly for houses in Pebble Beach and San Francisco, Frances Elkins continued to develop a mixture of unlikely and wide-ranging periods and furnishings. In her own adobe house in Monterey, with its ceiling of rough white-painted boards, Frances Elkins, in 1945, had her brother, David Adler, install a Georgian fireplace and cornice. She added these to her Louis XIII chairs, Sheraton consoles, Regency stools, contemporary sofas, Chinese carpets, and Venetian prints.

In the bedroom, French provincial furniture was covered with red and white *toile de Jouy*. Biedermeier pieces were used in the foyer; Directoire wallpaper by Zuber was used in the upstairs hallway; and elsewhere, sculpted white-plaster shell-like forms were used as up lights. Prominent colors were yellow with turquoise; and white with pink, red, and gray. Her sophisticated and international mix of periods brought freshness, originality, and flamboyance to the historical correctness of previous decades.

During the 1940s Frances Elkins worked with California craftspeople to develop an appropriate style for Northern California. Leaning toward Mexico for inspiration, she used Marian Dorn's heavy handwoven rugs, hand-tooled leather, and pottery instead of porcelain. She worked with Dorothy Liebes on coarse-woven fabrics shot with shimmering metal threads to texturize her spaces. She commissioned Tony Duquette to design his first console of antlers. She had chairs carved in Queen Anne style, but finished in bleached oak. She had terrazzo-topped coffee tables made. And she played with pattern-on-pattern (see Figure 111), which may have inspired Billy Baldwin's admiration. It was another approach toward regionalism, corresponding to the West Coast's Bay Region style.

111. Frances Elkins. Winslow residence. Pebble Beach, California. 1949—50. *Photograph by Julius Shulman.*

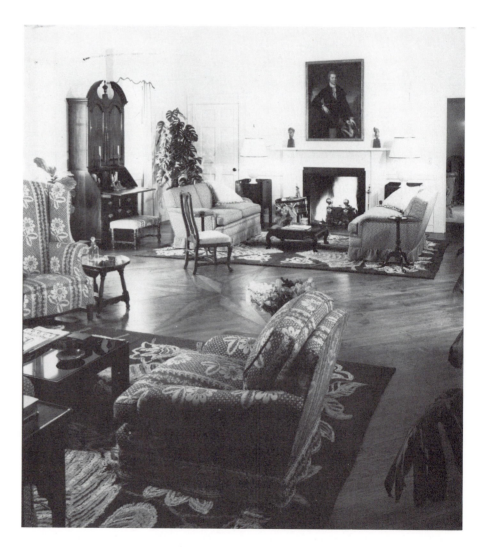

Hers was a personal anthology of periods that was freer than the strict historical recreations of many of her contemporaries. This eclecticism became the mainstream direction of decorating in the next decade.

Ruby Ross Wood

The living room that Ruby Ross Wood designed for herself and her husband in the 1940s was "an entirely red room," as Billy Baldwin described it. Floors were "carpeted wall to wall in a dark damson color"; walls were strié, the color of "rich red currant"; curtains were "ruby-red satin"; tufted Victorian furniture was upholstered in "the color of a Harvard-red carnation"; and objects "ran the whole spectrum of red, with bright punctuations of scarlet."[7] It was not the first red room, but its pervasive color scheme established a tradition in many designers' minds for the next several decades.

Billy Baldwin

Just after World War II the first published credits for "William Baldwin of Ruby Ross Wood" began to appear. Billy Baldwin had become an assistant in Ruby Ross Wood's decorating firm in 1935. In the early 1940s he served in the U.S. Army. When he returned to Ruby Ross Wood, he began his series of residential interiors for the theater producer Gilbert Miller and his wife Kitty Bache Miller. The design of his own apartment (see Figure 112) in 1946 featured dark, glossy green walls—

112. Billy Baldwin. Own living room. New York City. 1946. *Photograph by Danny Wann, courtesy Condé-Nast Publications Inc.*

the color of a wet gardenia leaf, he wrote—with curtains of emerald-green silk, and furniture slipcovered in darker-green textured silk.

Billy Baldwin was also associated with the combination of dark-brown walls and furniture, enlivened by large black-and-white drawings on the walls and green accents—occasional tables and lamp bases. Another of his combinations featured pink walls, white woodwork, and a bold black-and-white runner on a black floor.

"Transitional Modern" and "Contemporary"

In the 1940s the decorating field began to veer toward Modern design without full commitment or espousal of the purgative, machine-based idiom. It produced an interest in a wider range and mixture of historical periods, broadening the more strict adherence of older decorators to single periods or styles for each room. It also admitted the value of Scandinavian Modern and, later in the decade, of Italian Modern to soften the German-French Machine-Age idiom.

This leaning also produced some new American furniture designs with more varied eclecticism, both somewhat pared down and calling on period styles beyond the eighteenth-century canon. This furniture was a compromise to make the Modern idiom acceptable to a broader public, and it came to be called Contemporary. Among the designers whose work was in this middle ground were William Pahlmann, Edward Wormley, T. H. Robsjohn-Gibbings, and Russel Wright.

William Pahlmann

For the first two years of the decade William Pahlmann continued his series of flamboyant display rooms at Lord & Taylor in New York (see Figure 113). After serving in the U.S. Air Force from 1942 to 1946 as director of a camouflage school, Pahlmann opened his own design firm in New York. He went on to design department stores and boutiques, restaurants and nightclubs, country clubs and hotels,

113. William Pahlmann. Model room for Lord & Taylor's "Pahlmann Peruvian" promotion. New York City. 1942. *Photograph courtesy William Pahlmann.*

showrooms and offices, hospitals and apartment-house lobbies, as well as residential projects. Bonwit Teller's president, Walter Hoving, was a regular client, for whom he designed six or seven stores.

Pahlmann's expressed aims were to blend modern living with tradition. He designed a house for himself that combined a 200-year-old Chinese table, a recent Charles Eames chair, a brass Moorish brazier, and a Louis XVI armchair upholstered in sky-blue leather. He was extravagant, sometimes outrageous in this eclecticism, but he was influential in opening the doors and relaxing the rules of preceding decades. It was typical of the expansion of influences in the 1940s.

During the 1940s William Pahlmann continued to gain attention for his use of color. He was influenced by the colors of Dorothy Liebes and was credited with using the first of her window blinds in New York. He especially used a blue-green that came to be called "Pahlmann blue"; he was always opposed to dead-white and used off-white instead. In 1940 he presented Harlem pink, Regency green, and white; sulphur yellow, olive green, and rosy red; and brick, bottle green, rawhide, and bleached cypress. Pahlmann Peruvian in 1941 featured Cuzco blue, lime, fuschia, deep blue, and whitewash; another of his Peruvian combinations was avocado, lime, plum, tan orange, and white. Such color names led to the term "decorator colors." After the war he was associated with medium cerulean, lime, magenta pink, and white, as well as deep sage, ripe persimmon, and French blue. Each of these color combinations was for a single room. Together, they indicate both the Pahlmann palette and the progression of the decade. Pahlmann served as president of the New York chapter of AID from 1948 to 1950.

Edward Wormley

Another prominent transitional designer—the term is his—was Edward Wormley. He continued to design interiors—ranging from residences to showrooms and

114. Edward Wormley. Own office. New York City. 1945. The Klismos Chair is Dunbar's reproduction in 1939 of Jean-Michel Frank's reconstruction of a chair measured from a bas relief at the Acropolis. *Photograph by F. M. Demarest, courtesy Edward Wormley.*

offices (see Figure 114)—but made his major contribution designing furniture for Dunbar.

During the war he headed the Furniture Unit of the Office of Price Administration in Washington, and in 1944 he opened his own firm in New York City. There he continued to design furniture for Dunbar and Drexel and lighting for Lightolier. His showroom for Lightolier at the end of the decade had a mahogany wall that was detailed as masonry-like blocks that decreased in size as they rose to the ceiling. This forced perspective was designed to inflect the viewer's attention to the ceiling-hung fixtures on display; it was a device that presaged the interior techniques of the 1970s.

Wormley aimed to combine traditional forms with Modern ones, especially with Scandinavian Modern, and produced what became known as Contemporary furniture designed to appeal to a widely divergent buying public. He called this "transitional design." His designs were directed to mass-production techniques and changing markets. He was notable for producing line after line of new pieces year after year—for thirty-seven years. Few other designers of the period demonstrated this kind of professional perseverance, endurance, and productivity.

T. H. Robsjohn-Gibbings

During the war the individualist designer T. H. Robsjohn-Gibbings participated in camouflage experiments at Columbia University, and was vehement in expressing his views on design: *Goodbye, Mr. Chippendale* and *Mona Lisa's Mustache* (see Suggested Reading) were among his best-selling books. He could not easily be categorized as a decorator in the American tradition of historicism, because his work was so vanguard.

115. T. H. Robsjohn-Gibbings. Chest with clapboard-like drawer pulls. 1941. *Photograph from* Interior Design *(May 1961).*

In 1941 he designed store interiors for Neiman-Marcus. In 1942 he designed a living room with shadow-blue walls against which sat a dark-gray upholstered sofa with fuschia cushions; these were flanked by Louis XV chairs covered in violet fabric. That color scheme was to influence designers for a decade. A coffee table he designed in 1942 had a free-form glass top in the then typical mode—standing on three legs with their stretcher running along the floor. It was another of the amoeboid designs that epitomized the early part of the decade. A living room he designed in 1944 with a stripped and molding-less envelope had bare floors and red-lacquered bamboo-framed furniture covered in a printed fabric with a large-scale tropical leaf design. The Hawaii-Rio motif was thereby established.

Robsjohn-Gibbings designed his first mass-produced furniture for the Widdicomb Furniture Company in 1946. His designs included bleached-oak desks and chairs. The desks had glass tops; the chairs were slung with ash-gray leather. Other pieces were of pale walnut; some case pieces had flush doors; others had handleless drawers designed like overlapping clapboards for the drawer pulls (see Figure 115). His coffee-table designs were of comparatively distended length. There was always a strength of severity and elegance about his work.

Russel Wright

Another individualist designer, Russel Wright, could not be easily categorized as either an industrial designer, decorator, or Modernist. He worked to bring Modern design to the American public. Exempted from armed service in the 1940s because of age and poor eyesight, Russel Wright, with his designer-wife Mary, continued to design interiors, furnishings, and industrial products.

In the spirit of Modernism's goal of social improvement, though stylistically opposed to the Bauhaus, Wright conceived a complete line of home furnishings designed and produced by a cooperative of sixty-five artists, craftsmen, and manufacturers, and accessible to middle-income families. It was called the American Way. It never attained either high quality of design or, despite considerable press coverage, popular success. The war killed it.

Among the Wrights' interiors in the 1940s were a redesigned floor for Saks' 34th Street store, their own house in New York, and their country house, Dragon Rock. They designed kitchen appliances, glassware, table linens, aluminum and pewter serving pieces for the dinner table, plastic trays and colanders, and a line of free-form "art" ceramics. In addition, they designed a line of stainless flatware with plastic handles, four lines of furniture, numerous lighting fixtures, and ceramic dinnerware. Their stackable Iroquois Casual China of 1946 was produced in colors that were typical of the decade—ice blue, forest green, avocado, and lemon yellow; it was strongly resistant to breakage and became widely popular until 1959.

At the end of the 1940s Russel Wright's Meladur melamine plastic dinnerware was put into production. It was a popular American symbol throughout the decade, showing the importance of new materials and the importance of industrial designers.

The Low-Cost Furniture Competition

In 1948, because of the continuing need for less expensive, well-designed, and well-made furnishings after the war, the Museum of Modern Art in New York exhibited the results of the "International Competition for Low-Cost Furniture Design," directed by Edgar Kaufmann, Jr. First prize went to Don R. Knorr of San Francisco and Georg Leowald of Berlin-Frohnau. Knorr's chair, made by Knoll Associates, was a truncated cone of sheet metal on wire legs. Leowald's seating design had a molded plastic back sliding in metal grooves. Charles Eames shared second prize for a molded fiberglass chair, made by Herman Miller; it was

116. Charles Eames and Ray Eames. Molded plastic armchair for Herman Miller Inc. 1949. *Photograph courtesy The Metropolitan Museum of Art, New York City. Lent by I. Wistar Morris, III.*

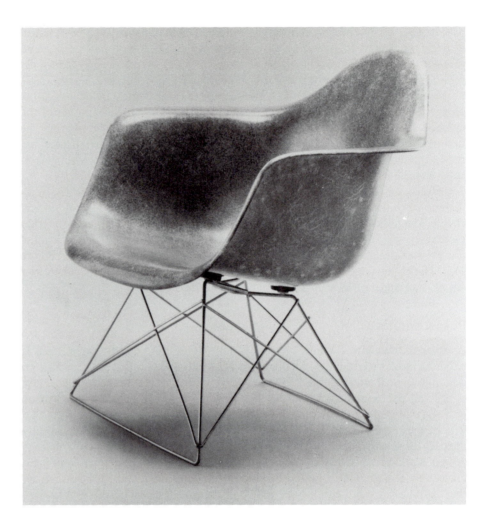

a development of the 1940 competition winner with Saarinen (see Figure 116). British designers Robin Day, Clive Latimer, and Ernest Race also won awards and mentions.

The Italian Influence

At the end of the decade a new wave of interior design and furnishings began to come from Italy. Those designs had a spare, sculptural quality that was soon to force out the heavy square look of the early part of the decade. This furniture, along with other Italian industrial designs and a new vogue of filmmaking, brought glamor and admiration back to Italy once again, making Italy a deeply ingrained influence on the design world for the next four decades.[8]

Italian craftsmanship was revived by a number of collective studios of artisans in Milan and Rome, aided by a cooperation among big business, small workshops, and progressive designers and spread by triennial exhibitions in Milan. The design of Olivetti typewriters by Marcello Nizzoli (1948–49) was an inspiration for designers of furnishings. Modern furnishings were based on craftsmanship with wood in natural finishes and with sometimes sinuous, spidery, and relaxed lines. Structural elements of steel exploited the potential thinness and distendedness.

This new Italian design approach indicated a clear formal logic, yet it had a sculptural freedom that was spontaneous-looking, playfully witty, and light-hearted.

Wire-hung stairs and bookcases by Franco Albini, and wire-like bases for tables and desks made of slim metal rods or bars, expressed the discontinuity and the atomic-molecular idiom of the decade. Sculptural reflector lighting was often attached to poles in a manner that was more reminiscent of display and exhibition techniques than of traditional interior design. Paintings and drawings, too, were hung or mounted this way in residential and commercial interiors in Italy.

Most influential on Americans was the use of Modern furnishings alongside Baroque sculptures with antique patina, or the combination of handcraft with machine-craft; even Renaissance and Baroque paintings were supported on exposed metal standards, some with construction-like scale and texture. In this latter direction, the poetic juxtapositions of Carlo Scarpa (1902–78) in restoring museums and in museum installation design became the supreme inspiration. Prominent Italian designers at this time also included Gio Ponti and the firm of BBPR (Banfi, Belgiojoso, Peressutti, Rogers)—all of whom were architects. Furniture by other Italian designers, such as Tempestini, Parisi, Peretti, and Carlo Mollino, whose furniture designs aimed to be fantastic, captured the attention of American interior designers. Italian sculptors of this period, such as Agenore Fabbri, also influenced American interior designers. Italian design could not be ignored for the next three decades.

The End of an Era and a New Beginning

The Last of "The Ladies"

The year 1950 saw the death of three influential designers: Sybil Colefax, Ruby Ross Wood, and Lady Mendl—Elsie de Wolfe. Sir Charles and Lady Mendl had moved to Los Angeles during World War II. There she pursued her Louis XV and Louis XVI adaptations, often in collaboration with Los Angeles artist Tony Duquette, adding such personal touches as a drapery-framed mirror over a fireplace, along with contemporary fabrics and carpets. Their house in Beverly Hills had one room tented with green-and-white-striped awnings, another room with a lattice-work ceiling; and she used black floors, wrought-iron furniture painted white, and leopard-skin chintz upholstery. In 1950, at the age of eighty-five, Elsie de Wolfe died.

Frances Elkins would die in 1953. Syrie Maugham continued her exploitation of white, but enriched it with antique wallpapers and furniture of high quality, adding tufted Victorian loveseats and chairs to her trademarks; she was to die in 1955. Nancy McClelland died in 1959. It was the end of the first generation of "lady decorators."

The Arrival of Air Conditioning

A new technological age was about to dawn. General use of air conditioning was to begin around 1950 with the designs in New York for the United Nations headquarters and Lever House, the headquarters office building of Lever Brothers. Residential use became widespread at this same time, after the development of a sufficiently small air-conditioning unit.

Air conditioning had been developing since the turn of the century. The inventor of air conditioning, Willis Havilland Carrier, patented "dew-point control" in 1906. This permitted the control of atmospheric humidity by raising or lowering temperature. Carrier devised his method by observing fog. First developed to provide fresh air in factory and industrial environments, some form of air conditioning had been installed in Frank Lloyd Wright's Larkin Building (1904) and in the New York Stock Exchange (1904). Shortly thereafter, air-conditioning systems were developed for hotel dining rooms and ballrooms, and, in the 1920s, Pullman cars and theaters began to be air-conditioned. Graumann's Metropolitan Theater in Los Angeles was air-conditioned in 1922 by Willis Havilland Carrier. So it was the movies that first introduced the public to air conditioning for comfort, as opposed to industrial efficiency.

The first office buildings to be air-conditioned were the Milam Building (1928) in San Antonio, Texas, by architect George Willis and engineer M. D. Diver; and the PSFS building in Philadelphia (1932–34) by Howe & Lescaze (see Chapter 5). At that time Radio City Music Hall was also air-conditioned. By 1936 lounge, dining, and sleeping cars on major long-distance trains had already been air-conditioned; and by the end of the 1930s department stores and shops across the country began to be air-cooled. The availability of fluorescent lighting at the end of the 1930s made lower heat loads possible, and therefore lowered the cost of air conditioning. So all was ready for the development of general air conditioning by the end of the 1940s.

Residential interiors also had to wait until around 1950 for a compact air-conditioning unit to be developed. Experiments with residential air conditioning had been going on since 1929, when General Electric installed a room cooler in Carrier's own house. Other isolated experiments in residential air conditioning were made in the Chicago area in the early 1930s. In 1932 Carrier's Atmospheric Cabinet was marketed, but it was cumbersome and expensive and designed to be installed in the cellar. It took until 1946 to 1948 for smaller through-wall air-conditioning units to be developed by the McQuay Company and General Electric. Air conditioning did not reach New York office buildings until 1947.

By the 1950s, air conditioning was readily available for all interiors. A new kind of interior comfort had arrived for the rest of the twentieth century—and also another technological and design challenge for the designers of interiors. When the next decade opened, the full range of the Modern dream—Futurist, Expressionist, and Bauhaus—was available to Modern American designers of interiors.

Suggested Reading

Baldwin, Billy. *Billy Baldwin Remembers.* New York: Harcourt Brace Jovanovich, 1974.

Banham, Reyner. *The Architecture of the Well-Tempered Environment.* London: The Architectural Press, 1969. Chicago: University of Chicago Press, 1969.

Darling, Sharon. *Chicago Furniture: Art, Craft, and Industry 1833–1983.* New York: W. W. Norton, 1983.

Design in America: The Cranbrook Vision, 1925–1950. New York: Harry N. Abrams, 1983.

Design Quarterly. "Nelson/Eames/Girard/Propst, The Design Process at Herman Miller." Minneapolis: Walker Art Center, 1975.

Drexler, Arthur. *Charles Eames.* New York: The Museum of Modern Art, 1973.

Emery, Sherman, ed. 50th Anniversary Issue, *Interior Design,* April 1982.

Gueft, Olga. "Two Decades of Interiors: 1940–1960," *Interiors.* November 1960.

Hennessey, William J. *Russel Wright.* Cambridge: MIT Press, 1983.

Herdeg, Klaus. *The Decorated Diagram: Harvard Architecture and the Failure of the Bauhaus Legacy.* Cambridge: MIT Press, 1983.

Hiesinger, Kathryn B., and George H. Marcus, eds. *Design Since 1945.* Philadelphia: The Philadelphia Museum of Art, 1983.

Hillier, Bevis. *The Decorative Arts of the Forties and Fifties Austerity Binge.* New York: Clarkson N. Potter, 1975.

Jacobus, John M., Jr. "Architecture, American Style, 1920–45," *American Art.* New York: Prentice-Hall, Harry N. Abrams, 1979.

———. "Postwar Architecture, 1945–60," loc. cit.

Kaufmann, Edgar, Jr., "Interior Design: Architecture or Decoration?" *Progressive Architecture.* October 1962, pp. 141–44.

Mang, Karl. *History of Modern Furniture.* New York: Harry N. Abrams, 1979.

McCoy, Esther. *The Second Generation.* Layton, Utah: Gibbs M. Smith, 1984.

Meadmore, Clement. *The Modern Chair.* New York: Van Nostrand Reinhold, 1975.

Rae, Christine. *Knoll au Louvre.* New York: Knoll International, 1971.

Robsjohn-Gibbings, T. H. *Goodbye, Mr. Chippendale.* New York: Alfred A. Knopf, 1944.

———. *Mona Lisa's Mustache: A Dissection of Modern Art.* New York: Alfred A. Knopf, 1947.

The Architecture of Skidmore, Owings & Merrill, 1950–1962. New York: Frederick A. Praeger, 1963.

Notes

1. Arthur J. Pulos, *American Design Ethic: A History of Industrial Design to 1940* (Cambridge: MIT Press, 1983), p. 422. In the prewar period, hundreds of RCA television kits had been produced as early as 1928. The war halted production.

2. Edgar Kaufmann, Jr., "Interior Design: Architecture or Decoration?" *Progressive Architecture* (October 1962), p. 144.

3. Arthur Drexler, of the Museum of Modern Art in New York, made this statement without considering such late-nineteenth-century furniture designers as Henry Belter, George Hunzinger, or other inventors of ingenious multipurpose furniture.

4. Knoll's production of furniture designs from the Bauhaus period was of the most expensive custom variety. As such, it had nothing to do with the Bauhaus ideal of producing furniture for everyman at prices everyman could afford. The Barcelona furniture, of course, had nothing to do with the Bauhaus, except that Mies was to become its director shortly after the designs were completed.

5. Ludwig Mies van der Rohe, *Aphorisms on Architecture and Form* (1923); quoted in Philip Johnson, *Mies van der Rohe* (New York: The Museum of Modern Art, 1978), p. 188.

6. Billy Baldwin, quoted in *20th Century Decorating, Architecture, and Gardens,* ed. Mary Jane Pool (New York: Holt, Rinehart and Winston, 1980), p. 10.

7. Billy Baldwin, *Billy Baldwin Remembers* (New York: Harcourt Brace Jovanovich, 1974), p. 39f.

8. The first opportunity for most Americans to see the new Italian design was at a traveling exhibition titled "Italy at Work," which began its American tour at the Brooklyn Museum.

Chapter 7

1950–1960: The Triumph of Modernism in America

For American designers of interiors, confident of America's design leadership at last, it was, as the press said, "the fabulous fifties." The capital of the art world had shifted from Paris to New York. In politics the Iron Curtain had fallen across postwar Europe, creating a threatening and edgy coexistence; nevertheless, it was a decade of comparative peace. Economically—for Americans, at least—it was a decade of enormous prosperity. That prosperity fostered the largest building boom in American history—one that was to last twenty years. Together, these factors produced an ebullient optimism.

The boom was upward and outward. More Americans attended college than ever before, owing to the G.I. Bill of Rights; more Americans traveled to Europe than ever before, owing to new jet air travel that began in 1952. And more Americans built houses—the suburbanization of America continued uncontrolled. The baby boom that began in the late 1940s produced the coming need for more high schools; by the end of the 1950s schools could not be built fast enough.

In that building boom, at the beginning of the 1950s, the dreams of the first-generation Modernists came to fruition in the new wave of International-Style skyscrapers. In 1951 Mies at last built his thirty-year-old vision of a structural frame sheathed with a glass curtain wall in his 860 Lake Shore Drive Apartments in Chicago. Its lobbies were furnished with his Barcelona furniture of the late 1920s, which Knoll Associates had reintroduced in 1948.

Le Corbusier had built the first of the slab-like towers that had been fundamental to his garden-city vision: the Ministry of Education in Rio de Janeiro (1945). His second slab tower was the United Nations Secretariat, completed in 1950 in

New York, designed by a committee of international architects—including Sweden's Sven Markelius and Brazil's Oscar Niemeyer—with Le Corbusier as its recognized design progenitor, and Wallace K. Harrison as its director of planning and design committee chairman. By 1952 Le Corbusier had also realized his concrete apartment slab, the Unité d'Habitation in Marseilles, in which the apartment interiors reflected his 1920s admiration for ocean-liner compartments. It was in the 1950s that interior designers—rather than office managers, as had previously been the case—became involved in office interiors in skyscrapers.

Technological Advances in Interior Design

The technological advances resulting from the war set the nation on a dedicated technological path. Among the technical advances that most influenced interior design were the public availability of television, the further development and widespread use of synthetic materials, and the development of the suspended ceiling.

Plastics

By the mid-1950s synthetic fibers and permanent forming or shaping had brought a whole new world of manmade materials. Among them were plastic sheeting and panels, vinyl upholsteries and drapery fabrics, new artificial leathers and other coated textiles, and synthetic carpets by the mile. Plastics were used more and more broadly for chair frames, tables, and other furniture, and for every conceivable household equipment, utensil, furnishing, bibelot, and toy.

The situation raised a serious question that the plastics industry fumbled for a long time to answer: What was the inherent nature of plastic? Manufacturers seemed unable to accept the solid-colored, untextured nature of natural plastic, saying it had "no intrinsic nature." Instead, they used the new artificial material, largely, in imitation of natural materials—vinyl wood, vinyl stone or ceramic tile, vinyl tortoiseshell and suede, and so on.

For those brought up on the philosophy of honesty of materials, it was a painful time. Seemingly, only when plastic was used to approximate glass did the two approaches come together. Otherwise, there was imitation—or, what began to seem worse, the ubiquitous use of flecked, spotted, spattered, and otherwise patterned plastic panels and sheeting. In the popular sector flecked and speckled freeform patterns—amoebas, snowflakes, and boomerangs—appeared in plastics, fabrics, and objects. Plastic of all patterns had gold and silver flecks blown into it, as if it were mica. With the alleged purpose of "not showing dirt," these patterns were designed for those who could not bear the visual vacuum of plain blank walls in the International Style.

The 1950s became known as the Plastic Decade, a decade of exuberance to the point of silliness. It was an age that appreciated cuteness in objects and design, objects that were considered kitsch by many. Disneyland opened in California in 1955; and during the decade the excessive hotel designs in Miami Beach, such as the Fontainebleau by architect Morris Lapidus, were opened. Two-tone cars, clothes, and houses appeared. All these, however, were designed to appeal to the status symbolism of the popular market. The "Good Design" shows at New York's Museum of Modern Art, which were planned to counteract this unrefined vision, represented the attitudes of the decade's vanguard and its mania for modernity.

The Suspended Ceiling

Another widely influential innovation in interior design during the 1950s was the development of the suspended ceiling, which aided the building boom materially.

The suspended ceiling—now an accepted part of our vocabulary for commercial and institutional buildings—permitted the integration, for the first time, of mechanical systems and lighting systems into a finished ceiling surface. Like other developments, the suspended ceiling had not come about entirely without precedent. It derived from isolated attempts at concealing air-conditioning ducts on the one hand, and at concealing lighting fixtures on the other.

Early examples of concealed air conditioning began with the installation in the Kuhn Loeb Bank in New York (1906), where air-conditioning was concealed behind a glass-skylight-like ceiling. When Willis and Diver's Milam Building went up in San Antonio in 1928, with its air-conditioning ducts running in furred-down spaces above the corridors and conditioned air supplied through louvers over the office doors, something like a prototypal suspended ceiling had been achieved. But lighting was not yet a part of these schemes.

The concealment of lighting fixtures in ceilings and wall units had also been seen since the first decade of the century. Recessed lighting had been pioneered by Frank Lloyd Wright as early as the Robie House (1909). Drawing on this tradition in the mid-1920s, Rudolf Schindler's beach house for the Lovells (1926) incorporated lighting into vertical fin-like structures with alternating rectangles of light and opaque panels that historian Reyner Banham called "light-towers" and "light-ladders." Richard Neutra's Lovell House in Los Angeles of 1927 had a long, rectangular lighting unit suspended from the ceiling on thin cables; but its form, as a linear fixture running nearly 50 feet over bookcases and reading locations, also put it into the new tradition of lighting troffers.

During 1927–28 the Arizona Biltmore Hotel by Albert Chase McArthur, with Frank Lloyd Wright's influence and consultation, offered integrated and recessed lighting in glass-block-like units, similar to Wright's work and to Schindler's Lovell House light-towers. From 1924 to 1927 Erich Mendelsohn had designed indirect lighting concealed in open, linear coves along ceilings and walls; sometimes the coves were repeated continuously to achieve a linear, parallel-lined effect like Streamlining. In 1936 Frank Lloyd Wright used indirect lighting on the backlit, glass-tubed ceiling of the main office space of the S. C. Johnson & Son Administration Building.

None of these installations of air-conditioning or lighting, however, were yet integrated together into ceilings. The next development came in that still underacclaimed pioneer among Modern skyscrapers—Howe & Lescaze's PSFS building in Philadelphia (1932). There, in the lobby areas, air-conditioning ducts were run in furred-down spaces in the ceilings, and conditioned air was supplied through ring-diffusers surrounding recessed lighting fixtures. It was the first step in combining air-conditioning outlets and lighting fixtures that became standard in the developed suspended ceiling.

Still one further element in the development of the suspended ceiling was the design of the ceiling surface itself. First came several systems of using the space between floor slab and bottom of open-web steel joists—either running ductwork and electrical lines through the space, or using the overall space as a plenum, in which the entire open area, without being ducted, is used to distribute conditioned air. By 1936 there were ceiling systems of perforated tiles to form the ceiling surface as a continuous diffusing outlet. These were the first suspended ceiling surfaces that permitted the integration of all these mechanical elements. Meanwhile, the black-painted ceiling with exposed but painted-out mechanical systems was the standard during the 1940s. In 1947 came the louvered or egg-crate suspended ceiling.

Around 1950 several versions of the fully integrated suspended ceiling appeared. The General Motors (GM) Technical Center by Saarinen, Saarinen & Associates opened in Warren, Michigan, in 1950, when Willis Carrier finished air-conditioning the United Nations Secretariat building in New York. Both buildings have overall suspended ceilings in the fully developed manner that became the standard for the next several decades. The GM Technical Center ceiling offers a highly flexible overall grid, the squares sometimes filled entirely by lighting louvers, sometimes by rectangular troffer-like lighting fixtures and opaque ceiling panels. At the United Nations Secretariat building, rectangular lighting troffers are set between square air-conditioning diffusers, both of which are recessed in a plain, white-tile ceiling surface. The variations and the refinements occupied designers of interiors for decades.

The development of the suspended ceiling led to increasingly comfortable year-round environments. It also led to a new design concentration for interior designers. Integrated suspended ceilings opened the door to the design of systems of partitions and furniture that were integrated with that ceiling and with the rest of the building. Such systems were to become the whetstone of the late-Miesian idiom. Based on clarity and articulation of individual parts and on alignment of each element with the overall building, partitioning systems became the new wheel— to be reinvented by the designers of architectural interiors for the next two decades. The goals of clarity and alignment, and the imagery of the grid, were, thenceforward, to be served as never before.

Formalism versus Functionalism   Here, in the development of the suspended ceiling, we see once again the battle between formalism and functionalism, which had divided the Bauhaus thirty years before. The honest functionalist exposure of mechanical systems, such as was demonstrated at the United Nations General Assembly building in its lobby (see Figure 117) and in its Trusteeship Council Chamber by Finn Juhl (1952–53), was in contradistinction to the concealment of all these functions behind a suspended ceiling, as in the United Nations Secretariat building. To the formalists these ceilings increased the possibility of a "clean"— the byword of the decade—aligned, and consistent interior. No other development at this time more clearly illustrates the different potentials of formalism versus functionalism. Again, for designers, there was a choice to be made between the two directions. In America in the 1950s, the formalists won out.

Functionalism was given lip service by the adoption of a single, universal formal system developed by Mies. "Form follows function" was the commandment of the decade. But it was variously interpreted—not only as "form should be derived from function," but also as "form merely comes after function." And the discussion lasted more than a decade. In fact, the forms and formalism of Mies, under the banner of functionalism, were adopted as the mainstream of mid-century Modernism. Formalism, which had been rejected, in principle, by the mainstream of early Modernism, came to be, in actuality, the first cause and crusade of the second generation of Modern designers.

The International Style: Triumph of the Modern Crusade

In the 1950s in America, the International Style was finally accepted by a wide spectrum of the population, becoming the adopted style of commerce and proclaiming the victory of Modernism over historicism/traditionalism. This mid-century Modernism focused on function, technology, and economy, with innovation and refinement in design as the means of improving the quality of people's lives. The pristine, purgative clean-lined Miesian aesthetic formed the mainstream of the decade. That idiom relied on overall, pervasive structure as the keystone, emphasizing clarity, regularity, and alignment more than the earlier International Style's irregular and dynamic features. The repetition of the square module was the standard form of both unification and visual pattern.

117. Le Corbusier, Wallace K. Harrison, Sven Markelius, and Oscar Niemeyer. Lobby, United Nations General Assembly building. New York City. 1952. *Photograph courtesy UNATIONS.*

The International Style of the 1950s varied, however, especially in its social goals, from the goals of the 1920s and 1930s. Earlier Internationalism had aimed to provide mass housing and better work environments for everyman. Mid-century American Internationalism was seen as creating palaces for the giants of commerce; and in the 1960s and 1970s this was considered a debasement of first-generation Modernism—despite the fact that better work environments had been provided for an entire generation. But the differences were also stylistic. The change had been evident immediately at the GM Technical Center, where a brighter range of colors and of ornamental detail was apparent.

In the office-building boom of the 1950s, which created the third generation of American skyscrapers, the new patrons were the rich giants of corporate enterprise. The building boom meant that new headquarters offices sprang up everywhere, creating a great demand for interior design services. Surprisingly, despite the example of Frank Lloyd Wright's Larkin Building and his S. C. Johnson & Son Administration Building, the design of general offices had been, through the 1940s, primarily the province of office managers. From the 1950s onward, as Edgar Kaufmann, Jr., wrote, "the day of the *retardataire* client was past, even among corporations. . . . Eventually industry and business became the most courageous of all commission-givers."[1]

Saarinen's General Motors Technical Center

Among the first of these new corporate structures was Eero Saarinen's complex of buildings for the GM Technical Center at Warren, Michigan (1946–50). The rural location was evidence of the flight to the suburbs that was taking place by businesses as well as by home owners.

The planning and furnishing were in the forefront of the decade's updated International Style. The center was planned on a pervasive 5-foot module, but colors and textures were richer than earlier Miesian work, especially colored exterior panels. The suspended ceilings in the lobby of the Research Administration Building were square wood panels molded with a circular motif that was alternately cut out to receive down lights. Trim rectilinear Saarinen-designed furnishings, a variation on Le Corbusier's Grand Confort furniture, reiterated the modular approach. In this lobby, also, the decade's theme of discontinuity or alienation was reflected in a lightweight wire-tensioned spiral stair (see Figure 118), which became a symbol of dematerialization for the next two decades; its design is attributed to Kevin Roche. Furnishings in the luxurious executive offices and elsewhere in the complex were drawn mainly from those produced by Knoll Associates. The No. 71 and 72 Chair—the chair "with the hole in the back," as it became known—was first used at the GM Technical Center.

118. Saarinen. Saarinen and Associates. Lobby staircase, General Motors Technical Center. Warren, Michigan. 1950. *Photograph © Ezra Stoller/ ESTO, 1955.*

Skidmore, Owings & Merrill

The most prominent of the new large Modern design firms was the architecture firm of Skidmore, Owings & Merrill (SOM). SOM became almost synonymous with the building boom of the 1950s and with corporate design, and did perhaps more than any other design firm to establish the Miesian idiom as the mainstream of Modern architecture.

Begun in 1936 in New York (see Chapter 5), SOM later operated offices simultaneously in Chicago and San Francisco, and in Portland, Oregon (after 1955). In the next two decades the firm expanded further. SOM developed a team or group practice, a method of organizing separate teams to provide comprehensive design services for each project. Their work included planning, architecture, engineering, and interior design for large and small projects—commercial, industrial, and educational buildings; hotels, hospitals, airports; recreational, religious, and residential facilities.

The teams were also responsible for urban planning projects and central business district redevelopment. Among SOM's works are some of the best major office towers and rural office headquarters buildings in this country.

Gordon Bunshaft   The chief of design in the New York office of SOM was partner Gordon Bunshaft, who was a major influence on office interiors from the 1950s to the 1970s. Born in Buffalo, New York, Gordon Bunshaft (1909–) studied architecture at the Massachusetts Institute of Technology (MIT), and first worked for architect Edward Durell Stone and for industrial designer Raymond Loewy. He joined SOM in 1937, spent the war years from 1942 to 1946 in the Army Corps of Engineers, and returned to SOM in 1946, first in Chicago, then in New York. He was made a partner of the firm in 1949, and from that time on was the formidably outspoken chief design partner of the New York office, designing or overseeing virtually everything that was designed there.

With Mies as the model, SOM produced several dozen buildings that made good architecture seem like explications of the Miesian gospel. Although this culminated in the Seagram Building (1954–58) in New York by Mies van der Rohe and Philip Johnson, it was largely because of SOM and Gordon Bunshaft that the Miesian idiom became pervasive as the mainstream idiom and technology at mid-century.

Among Bunshaft's works was the early masterpiece Lever House in New York (1952), which followed closely on the completion of the United Nations Secretariat building. Lever House set the new archetypal model for the third generation of skyscrapers, including SOM's other New York landmarks: the Pepsi Cola Building (1960), the Chase Manhattan Bank headquarters (1961), and the Union Carbide Building (1961).

For the interiors of Lever House, Bunshaft developed a suspended ceiling system wherein the lighting troffers were recessed into an acoustical-tile surface with square air-conditioning diffusers between the troffers rather than at their long ends. The partitioning system at Lever House was comprised of wood-veneered panels between thin metal posts. The glass curtain walls were screened by a new mesh fabric called a casement, which was designed by Jack Lenor Larsen (his first major commission). Here was the beginning, not only of a new phase of skyscraper construction, but of a new look for open offices—long lines of rectangular desks cleanly placed in relation to the building, to sources of light, and to circulation corridors—a strength through repetition.

Another work by SOM in which Bunshaft influenced interior design was the Manufacturers Hanover Trust Company branch bank (1954) at Fifth Avenue and 43rd Street in New York. There, Bunshaft applied Miesian idiom to banking, completely transforming the former idiom of granite-and-bronze temple-fortress into one of pristine, crystalline, unprotected glass.

Behind the glass on the street level, Bunshaft located the vault, with its huge door of burnished stainless steel designed by Henry Dreyfuss. He placed the main banking floor on the second level, drawing customers all the way across the first floor, which was for quick-stop customer service, and up an escalator. The main banking floor was entirely consistent with the exterior—all clarity and alignment. A grid of suspended ceiling—luminous panels between unequal strips of metal, the wider of which incorporated air conditioning and down lights—and a grid of terrazzo were aligned with the columns and the tellers' counters, which were stripped of their traditional grille-work cages. "Open" was the keynote of mid-century Modernism. Behind one leg of the tellers' counter stood a 70-foot-long screen of bronze panels created by Harry Bertoia. For this interior SOM consulted with the firm of Eleanor Le Maire on the selection of furniture and fabrics.

SOM and the Knoll Planning Unit   From 1954 to 1957 SOM and Bunshaft designed the rural headquarters for Connecticut General Life Insurance Company in Bloomfield, Connecticut, five miles from the insurance city of Hartford. The interiors were designed in consultation with the Knoll Planning Unit headed by Florence Schust Knoll (see below). It was in this project that the American International Style interior reached its first peak. Florence Knoll's Planning Unit pioneered in studies to determine how work procedures affect office layouts and furniture.[2] Clean, crisp, serene, efficient, and businesslike, interiors by SOM and the Knoll Planning Unit were the models for Modern designers for the next ten years.

At Connecticut General the 6-foot module of the building was reiterated throughout the interior as well as the exterior. Terrazzo flooring was divided into 6-foot squares. The suspended ceiling was composed of 2- by 3-foot modules, which were rectangles of interlocking fins of perforated sheet metal with exposed fluorescent tubes within them. The depth of the fins prevented the bare-bulb effect in perspective. The partitioning system (see Figure 119) at Connecticut General

119. Skidmore, Owings & Merrill and the Knoll Planning Unit. Office module, Connecticut General Life Insurance Company. Bloomfield, Connecticut. 1957. *Photograph © Ezra Stoller/ESTO, 1957.*

120. Skidmore, Owings & Merrill. Inland Steel Company Building. Chicago, Illinois. 1958. *Photograph © Ezra Stoller.*

was designed to be movable, and was composed of metal posts that plugged into the ceiling grid and held 6-foot-square panels of glass or solid clear colors. It was at Connecticut General that the full integration of interior and exterior design based on a modular dimension began to take over the profession's focus on rectilinear total design.

Davis Allen   Davis Allen headed SOM's interior design department for thirty years. Born in Ames, Iowa, Davis Allen (1916–) was raised in Chicago and attended Brown University and the Yale School of Architecture. He first worked in the early Knoll Planning Unit with Florence Knoll. After this he spent nearly two years with Harrison & Abramovitz, Architects, doing design work on the United Nations General Assembly building interiors; he then worked six months with Raymond Loewy. Allen joined SOM in 1950 and worked on the Istanbul Hilton Hotel, the Inland Steel building in Chicago, and on the Crown Zellerbach building in San Francisco.

The Chicago office of SOM designed the headquarters of Inland Steel Company in Chicago (1956–58). In its interior the building was based on a 5-foot-2-inch module so as to integrate a ceiling system that used an exposed 60-inch fluorescent tube as well as sound, heat, and air conditioning. With offices of 10-foot squares, smaller desks than the then standard 72-inch desk had to be designed (see Figure 120). Davis Allen, as senior interior designer at SOM Chicago at the time, designed a new 60-by-30-inch desk for the Inland Steel interiors that later was put on the general market by Steelcase and the G. F. Furniture Company.

Davis Allen moved to the SOM New York office to design the interiors for the Chase Manhattan Bank headquarters (1958–61). Allen also supervised SOM's furniture designs. Ward Bennett was engaged by Chase Manhattan as a consultant to provide small artworks, antiques, and objects to accessorize the interior. This

121.   Skidmore, Owings & Merrill. Union Carbide Building. New York City. 1960. *Photograph © Ezra Stoller/ESTO. 1960.*

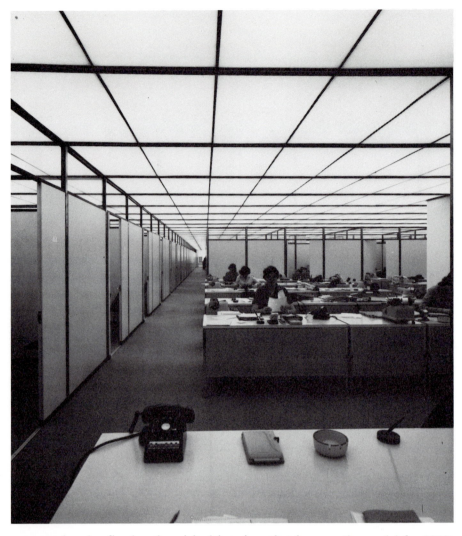

team produced refined and enriched interiors that became the model for 1960s Modernism.

Throughout the next three decades SOM, with Bunshaft as chief of design and with Davis Allen as head of the interior design department, worked a series of variations and refinements on all these interior elements—for the Reynolds Metal Company in Richmond, Virginia, in 1958; for Pepsi Cola in New York City in 1960; and for Union Carbide (see Figure 121) in New York in 1961. The Chicago office of SOM, at this same time, varied and refined interior systems and furnishings for the U.S. Air Force Academy in Colorado (1954–62) and the Harris Trust and Savings Bank in Chicago (1957–60).

Also notable among SOM's interiors in the 1950s were the Crown Zellerbach building in San Francisco (1957–59), on which Davis Allen worked; the First City National Bank in Houston (1959–61); and the Upjohn Company building in Kalamazoo, Michigan (1959–61). These developments are a monument to the flowering of the Miesian idiom at mid-century—and they are SOM's monumental achievement in modular regularity, integration, innovation, and total design.

The Knoll Planning Unit

For two decades following the mid-1940s the Knoll Planning Unit was the leading independent modern interior design firm in America. Under the direction of Florence Knoll as interior designer, the Knoll Planning Unit designed interiors for offices, banks, hotels, embassies, universities, and hospitals.

In 1951 the Knoll Planning Unit designed a new showroom for Knoll, at 575 Madison Avenue in New York City, that demonstrated what came to be called "the Knoll look" (see Figure 122). The showroom featured a black metal grid that hid the building's architectural irregularities with infill panels of primary colors in the De Stijl manner. The showroom was adopted as a model of the new wave of International Style planar, rectilinear interiors.

The San Francisco showroom that Knoll Planning Unit designed in 1957 took advantage of the high loft space to include two levels set off by a white-painted structure and ceiling of closely spaced fins. This was offset by brightly colored panels of an even clearer and stronger palette, which Knoll offered as its contribution to the new rich colors at the end of the decade (see below).

The Planning Unit's corporate office designs—for CBS (beginning in 1954); for the H. J. Heinz Company in Pittsburgh (1958); and for Cowles Magazines (completed in 1961)—were among the most sumptuous and refined in America. Florence Knoll's work demonstrated an impeccable sense of clean detail, a deft manipulation of domestic scale for institutional spaces, a precise juxtaposition of pure forms, and a crisp yet rich orchestration of textures. She truly believed that the world could become a better place through Good Design.

122. Florence Knoll. Knoll showroom. New York City. 1951. *Photograph courtesy Knoll International.*

The "Good Design" Shows

Continuing to spread the gospel of Modernism, the Museum of Modern Art, from 1949 to 1955, mounted a series of annual "Good Design" exhibitions directed by Edgar Kaufmann, Jr. They showed how meticulous discrimination could fill every interior with clean and sparkling machine beauty, readily available in the market-place. Kaufmann, who later wrote that Elsie de Wolfe had added the "good" to the all-too-prevalent taste of her day, similarly added the "good" to the too widely expanding design activity of the 1950s. "Good design" became a widely adopted concept in America at this time, through the exhibitions by museums and marketing centers. A design center was opened in London in 1956. Industry, business, and governments seemed to be convinced at last that good design was at least good public relations.

The first Good Design show, mounted in New York in 1949, traveled, like successive others, to the Merchandise Mart in Chicago six months later.[3] Designed by Charles and Ray Eames, the first of these exhibitions included Russel Wright's American Modern Dinnerware and folding chair for Samsonite, as well as nine designs by Edward Wormley for Dunbar. The 1950 show was designed by Finn Juhl; the 1952 exhibition was designed by the young architect Paul Rudolph; and the 1953 and 1954 exhibitions were designed by Alexander Girard. For these five years every major American and European designer was represented in these Good Design shows, the influence of which was enormous.

In its continuing promulgation of Modernism, the Museum of Modern Art built complete Modern houses for exhibition in its garden. Marcel Breuer had designed one in 1949; California's Gregory Ain designed another in 1950. Thousands of people toured these houses, and many gained their first views of what Modern architecture and Modern design could be.

The New Space Planners

With the construction of offices booming in major American cities, a number of urban interior designers seized this opportunity and applied themselves almost exclusively to the area of office design. They proclaimed a new wing of the profession under the name "space planners," although planning spaces had always been a major concern of both architects and residential decorators.

In the 1950s virtually all designers of interiors were still called "decorators." But, by mid-decade, designers of nonresidential spaces were moving toward use of the term "interior designer." The founding of the National Society of Interior Designers in 1957 helped to forward the use of this term. Still, few architect-trained graduates were interested in working for an interior design firm.

So polarized had the distinction between interior design and interior decorating become that they did not think of interior design as a wing of architecture, but as being of lesser interest. The majority of architecture firms involved in designing the big new buildings had become so specialized that their design procedures codified the division. Architects were accused of not giving adequate attention to the details of planning and finishing interiors. Design education, in addition, reinforced this separation. Architecture students were not taught much about the design of interiors, and interior design students were not taught much about architectural directions. Nor were there yet any degree programs in interior design. This situation would change at the end of the decade; but it had created the opening for the new space planners.

The situation also revealed the need for step-by-step analysis of human functions and activities. Average human measurements, dimensional tables, and graphic standards were drawn up, notably those by Henry Dreyfuss in his *Designing for*

People and *The Measure of Man*. Thereby the new discipline of "human factors" was established, and it put the design of commercial, institutional, and educational spaces on a considerably more scientific basis.

Among the new space planning or office design firms were Designs for Business with Gerald Luss as chief designer; Saphier-Lerner-Schindler; the Space Design Group; and ISD. Others were Maria Bergson Associates and Eleanor LeMaire Associates. Designs for Business won considerable acclaim for a more woodsy style of modular and movable partitioning systems and furnishings. Among the selling points of Designs for Business were analysis and flexible systems that would permit rearrangement, expansion, and relocation of offices without massive construction procedures or costs. Their major commissions included offices for Tower Fabrics in 1954, offices for C. J. La Roche & Company in 1958, and fourteen floors of offices for Time-Life Inc. in New York City, in 1959.

Industrial designers also figured in the new space planning and design of offices and other interiors. Henry Dreyfuss, besides continuing to design products and ocean liners, such as the *Independence* (finished in 1951), also designed offices. Raymond Loewy worked on products, packaging, kitchen equipment and cabinets, and offered space planning for offices, stores, and virtually any other type of interior. Loewy was at the peak of his career, both as a designer and as a celebrity. His "design factory" was one of the largest and provided apprenticeship for countless young designers and architects.

Walter Dorwin Teague did space planning for the offices of Reichold Chemicals and many other companies. Space planning for office interiors was also offered by the firms of Donald Deskey, Lippincott & Margolies, and other industrial designers. It was at this time that the new efficiency experts called "systems analysts" began to affect the profession of office design. Industrial design had become pervasive throughout the furnishings industry, but it had acquired a sleek, sometimes glib overlay that made it unrelated to the honest functionalism of Modern design.

European Influences

Italian Modern

In the 1950s the attenuated look that exploited the tensile qualities of steel was further explored by Italian designers. They created wire bases and frames for tables and chairs; spindly, spidery lighting fixtures—among the most prominent of which was the three-branch swivel standing fixture with conical shades (1949), designed by Barbieri and manufactured by Arteluce of Milan. This "wire look" was a continuation of "le Style Atomique," as the French had called it.

In 1952 Gio Ponti designed his version of the Chiavari chair; it became a staple of inexpensive elegance. In addition, furniture by Carlo Mollino and Parisi continued their sculptural vein with gazelle-like animal forms. Painted screens and ceramic dinnerware by Arnoldo Fornasetti—some of it with a Surrealist motif of disengaged eyes—became popular at this time. Highly original were the designs for furniture and interiors by the Castiglioni brothers.

Danish Modern

New in the 1950s was the ascendancy of Danish Modern over other Scandinavian expressions. Although Finland's Alvar Aalto put forward his fan-shaped joint between legs and tops of stools and tables in 1954, Danish Modern offered a sensuous expressiveness that was based in handcraft rather than the machine, and therefore produced an atmosphere of a softer elegance. "Warm" was the common praise of the decade, in opposition to the "coldness" of machine-image Modern.

The Danish designer Finn Juhl created the Trusteeship Council Chamber of the United Nations headquarters in New York (1952) with its walls of undulating battens, derived from Alvar Aalto's vocabulary. Hans Wegner continued to produce sculptural wood chairs with richly exposed graining and gracefully refined forms. Poul Kjaerholm began to be recognized for furniture with combinations of brushed stainless steel and pale ash butcher-block-like wood construction. Kjaerholm's armless chair (1956) had a brushed stainless-steel frame covered in raffia.

The fabrics of Unika-Vaev splashed onto the market with geometric patterns and vibrant colors. The sublimely sinuous silver serving dishes of Henning Koeppel seemed to typify the decade, and were among its peaks of achievement. At the end of the decade Vernor Panton's chair—a single piece of plastic cantilevered for base, seat, and back (1959–60)—achieved what Rietveld had set out to do with his Zigzag Chair (1934) and Eero Saarinen had aimed for with his Pedestal Chair— to unite structure and seat with a continuous seamless material.

The Growth of American Modern Furniture

More Modern furniture began to be produced by the U.S. furniture industry in the 1950s. The leaders in this activity were Knoll Associates and Herman Miller Inc.

Knoll Associates

At Knoll the designs of Finn Juhl, Jens Risom, and Mies were joined by the designs of Franco Albini, Pierre Jeanneret, Ralph Rapson, and Marcel Breuer. In 1952 Harry Bertoia designed his series of wire chairs, culminating in the Diamond Chair, which was produced by Knoll in two sizes (see Figure 123A). Saarinen's Pedestal Furniture (1955–56) was intended to reduce the number of furniture legs in a room

123A. Harry Bertoia. Diamond Chairs. 1952. *Photograph courtesy Knoll International.*

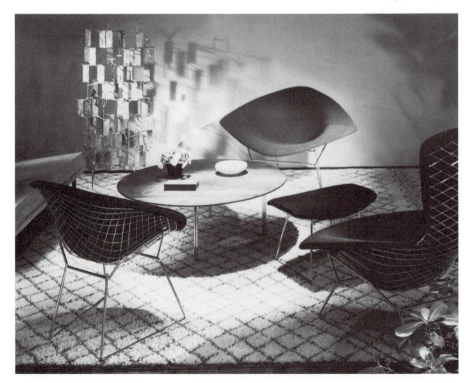

(see Figure 123B). Anni Albers, who had taught fabric design at the Bauhaus, began to design fabrics for Knoll in 1959.

Florence Knoll also contributed designs to the firm's line. They were usually what she called "fill-in pieces" that were not otherwise available: seating units—chairs and sofas—and case pieces that were based on a modular, square concept, furthering the idiom of De Stijl and the popularity of Mondrian (see Figure 123C). Her furniture looked more serenely classic with each design. Florence Knoll's furniture designs proffered Miesian steel bases and luxurious and luscious marbles, which were sometimes white as cakes of snow glistening in the spotlights. Florence

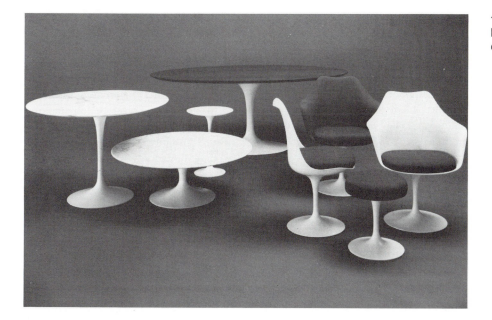

123B. Eero Saarinen. Pedestal Furniture. 1955–56. *Photograph courtesy Knoll International.*

123C. Florence Knoll. Lounge chairs, table, sofa. 1950s, 1960s. *Photograph courtesy The Metropolitan Museum of Art, New York City, Collection CBS, Inc.*

Knoll said they looked like "sugar cubes." She also conceived the boat-shaped conference table that made narrower conference spaces negotiable. Planned originally for office use, the Knoll furniture was soon adopted for residential use as well.

In 1958, when she was among the most influential designers of both furniture and interiors, Florence Knoll married Harry Hood Bassett. She sold her interest in Knoll to Art Metal in 1959 and retired from the presidency the following year, remaining as a consultant. In 1965 she withdrew from all connections with Knoll to work as an independent designer.

Herman Miller Inc.

Herman Miller continued in the 1950s to produce innovative and straightforward furniture by Charles and Ray Eames and by George Nelson. Nelson also negotiated the association of Alexander Girard with the firm in 1952 to design textiles.

Plastic shell chairs were designed by the Eameses in 1950 on spidery metal-rod legs. Their all-wire chairs were produced in 1951; their plastic-shell stacking chairs in 1954. The large bent-plywood leather-cushioned chair and ottoman were produced in 1956 (see Figure 124A). Aluminum-framed pieces began to appear from their design boards in 1958; the first had pre-molded vinyl upholstery slings. It was a corpus of work that established Eames as the most innovative designer of the decade and changed the look of interiors throughout the country.

George Nelson also continued to produce innovations in furniture design in astonishing numbers. During the 1950s his designs included the first metal case pieces hung within a structural frame (1954) in the manner of architectural construction. These pieces had recessed tracks in the drawers, which slid on the horizontal members of the frames.

124A. Charles Eames and Ray Eames. Chair and ottoman. 1956. *Photograph courtesy Herman Miller Inc.*

124B. George Nelson. Marsh-mallow Sofa. 1956. *Photograph courtesy Herman Miller Inc.*

At that time, Nelson designed his pole-and-shelf bookcase systems that reversed the customary wall-mounted support systems. In preceding designs metal runners mounted on the wall served as tracks for cantilevered brackets that supported shelves. In Nelson's version the Comprehensive Storage System poles (1956) were freestanding out from the wall, and the brackets were cantilevered toward the wall so that the shelves stood between the poles and the wall. The system was therefore independent of built-in construction. Designed concurrently with, but independently of, related shelf systems for store display, Nelson's Comprehensive Storage System prefigured architectural developments that placed structural supports outside the curtain wall.

An example of the dematerialization or discontinuity of the decade was George Nelson's Marshmallow Sofa (1956) (see Figure 124B). The sofa derived, conceptually, from the idea of using self-skinning foam plastic—as in automobile armrests—instead of stitched upholstery. In execution, however, each cushion had to be upholstered separately.

One other chair was widely acclaimed and popular in this decade—the three-legged chair, designed in 1952 by Katavolos-Littell-Kelley and produced by Laverne Inc., with a leather sling supported by a T-shaped back member. The Lavernes also produced a mammoth-scale wall covering that was a reinterpretation of endpapers for books.

Residential and Technical Advances

Lighting

The contribution of artificial lighting to interior design continued to become more crucial in the 1950s, and it received both greater attention and greater sensitivity.

Lighting designer Richard Kelly began to demonstrate the need and value of the lighting consultant. Most apparent was the effect of the new suspended ceiling on interior lighting, as well as on the urban scene at night. Especially striking was the emphasized image of horizontality—that goal of the early International Style—which lighted suspended ceilings brought to the black-and-white striping of buildings. Kelly's all-over illuminated ceiling at the Seagram Building was the most eye-opening of all these demonstrations.

Throughout the decade the lamp—conceived of as a shaded candle—was anathema to Modernists. Instead, geometric cans, which pointed unidirectional light, or pull-down shaded lighting fixtures became the accepted models. Folded paper shades from Denmark made by Le Klint, along with the pinpoint-pierced brass shades of Finland's Paavo Tynell and lamps from Italy, gave a more playful facet to the bullet- and cone-shaped reflectors of the 1940s.

Isamu Noguchi's Akari lamps—paper bubbles and assemblages of other geometric forms made of paper, in the construction technique of traditional Japanese lanterns—were introduced by the Bonniers shop, which had been designed by Warner-Leeds. (One partner, Harold Leeds, went on to become the chairman of Pratt Institute's department of interior design.)

George Nelson lighted three showrooms for Herman Miller with adjustable lamps clipped onto Bulldog Trol-E-Ducts that were attached to a grid of white-metal pipes as an open suspended ceiling. Greta von Nessen continued the Bauhaus tradition of lighting inherited from her husband. Paul Laszlo and others took up the leaning wire standard-lamp concept, perhaps derived from the firm Stilnovo in Italy. And the luminous, varicolored glass shades of Italy's Paolo Venini became social symbols of equal prominence with the copper-shingled "artichoke" chandelier of Denmark's Poul Henningsen.

New Products

Drywall construction—using gypsum-board panels instead of troweled, wet plaster—began after the war in the suburban housing boom, owing to rising costs of plaster work caused by the declining plaster trade. Drywall was to move into office design in the 1960s, and to make the plaster trade almost obsolete in the 1970s.

Television and high-fidelity sound systems became widely available around 1950. Antennas could be seen sprouting from virtually every roof. The 1953 coronation of Great Britain's Queen Elizabeth II was the first internationally televised event that captured a wide audience. From then onward the TV set became the twentieth-century fireplace—sometimes it was even designed to look like a fireplace. It was hidden inside cabinets, set into small-screen units, and then wide-screen sets on splayed-legged units appeared. Decorators continued to hide them for decades, continuing the battle between functionalism and formalism.

Alexander Girard

The J. Irwin Miller House

Eero Saarinen's and Alexander Girard's house for J. Irwin Miller, in Columbus, Indiana (1952), was among the significant residential designs of the decade. It was a model of the forthcoming reinterpretation of or move beyond the Miesian idiom.

Inside a 100-foot-long and 80-foot-wide rectangular pavilion that had wide expanses of glass shaded by a wide overhanging flat roof, the interior featured a skylighted living room with the first sofa-deep square conversation pit (see Figure 125). The pit was fully carpeted and upholstered, entered down padauk-wood

125. Eero Saarinen and Alexander Girard. J. Irwin Miller House, Columbus, Indiana. 1952. *Photograph © Ezra Stoller/ESTO, 1958.*

rubber-laminated steps, and lined with multipatterned and multicolored pillows in fabrics designed by Girard and fabrics found by him in Morocco, Tunisia, Indonesia, and India.

Along one 50-foot-long wall of the living area was a floor-to-ceiling-height wall of book and display cases, storage cases, and a patchwork quilt of objects from around the world that expressed both the decade's "one world" and "global village" awareness as well as Alexander Girard's singular new vision of display. Among the objects were a Chinese birdcage and a Peruvian figure-pageant; antique Italian, Greek, and Chinese objects; an English antique brass box; a Victorian flower montage; a French Provincial clock; Hopi Indian figures; Latin American religious figures; Venetian glass birds; an Early American toy; an eighteenth-century Austrian chest; East Indian gouaches and bronzes; a Balinese carving; a New Mexican crucifix; Mexican candelabra; an oriental lute; and a William Blake engraving. Interspersed were books, decorative backings of fabric and paper, and storage for camera equipment and television.

Among the innovations in this interior was the exploration of the vertical dimension of space in this room and the interplay of heights. The floor was pierced, recessed as a conversation pit; above, at the standard height, was a grand piano; the display-storage wall rose from floor to ceiling; and in between, suspended in air, were both a ceiling-hung cylindrical fireplace screened by a bead-chain firescreen and a Kashmir shawl hung as a flat panel at the main entrance. The stretching up and down for space; the reaching across the world and across time for texture, pattern, color, culture, and inspiration; and the combination within a serene pavilion seemed, at the time, like the ultimate enrichment of the Machine-Age idiom—and without the representational motifs of previous decades.

Girard's Santa Fe House

In 1953, after he established his association with the Herman Miller company as fabrics designer (see below), Girard and his family moved to Santa Fe, New Mexico, to live and work in an old adobe house that he remodeled (see Figure 126A). Adopting the culture of the old Southwest, the Girards designed not a temple to Modernism but, with tradition-shattering innovation, established a link between Modernism and the old tradition of interior design *ensembliers* (see Chapter 2).

Somehow, he managed to appease both traditions. The adobe, some of it 200 years old, was refurbished or build anew and painted white, like the bare rafters (see Figure 126B). Doorways were left frameless and doorless; other square and rectangular openings were cut from room to room to serve as picture frames. An adobe support for cushions constituted a sofa—prefiguring the work of the Minimalists two decades later; an adobe table and stool, an adobe chaise and display platforms also stood in the living room. Floors were a dark reddish stone, laid fairly unevenly; and this was offered as the rationale for suspending the pine-board dining table on stainless-steel cables tensioned from ceiling to floor. Reported as stable, but admittedly wiggly at times, the table was nevertheless in the tradition of the atomic-molecular style and the wire idiom of the late 1940s. Perhaps as a contrast, a French butcher's table of metal rods and brass mounts stood prominently silhouetted in the hallway. The few other movable pieces of furniture were chairs by Eames and Saarinen, and bubble lighting by Nelson.

One living room wall displayed the Girards' steadily increasing collection of folk art and other handcrafted objects: kachina figures by the Hopi of Arizona, a Tibetan devil trap, East Indian puppets, Peruvian ceramics, Mexican painted chests, and other paintings from South America. Behind a serving-and-display shelf in the dining room was an irregularly striped mural painted by Girard in pinks, reds, and blues. Among the objects displayed against that mural were Guatemalan chests, a Sicilian cart, and Bohemian glass candle sconces. There was a brass Moroccan coffee table, an Indian spread, and objects from other places and times.

It was a house of delicate, intricate things to be examined at close range. Like Alexander Girard's other work, it had the pattern, texture, and color that the purgative Modern movement had caused people to starve for. His house and his work were warm and human. And Girard offered all that with the sensitivity of a

126A. Alexander Girard. Plan, own house. Santa Fe, New Mexico. 1953. *Illustration courtesy of the architect.*

126B. Alexander Girard Own house. Santa Fe, New Mexico. 1953. *Photograph by Julius Shulman.*

fresh and original mind, with spareness and elegance. He brought the joy of collecting folk art and internationalism to the sober monumentality of Modernism.

Girard's Other Commissions

Girard was approaching the peak of his career in the 1950s. He designed residences as well as showrooms for Herman Miller; served as consultant to I. M. Pei on the interiors of the Denver Hotel; designed an apartment in Los Angeles for movie director Billy Wilder; and designed offices for Irwin Miller in Columbus, Indiana. In the Miller offices, Girard's interpretation of a doorstop as a recessed hemisphere to receive the doorknob showed the sublime wit that—at rare intervals—elevates interior design to an art form. The socket in the wall seemed so natural that one wondered why it was not used before. Of this kind of vision, Dr. Samuel Johnson in the eighteenth century had written, "The first effect is sudden astonishment, and the second rational admiration."

For Herman Miller's 1958 San Francisco showroom, which was in a 1907 music hall (a notable early example of the recycling of buildings that was to become widespread in the 1960s), Girard emphasized the existing decor to produce an updated multicolored carnival midway of the Gay Nineties. To him we owe the subsequent wide use of lines of marquee-like lightbulbs in interior work. Fabrics were displayed as flat or folded panels on wire-hung brass poles to subdivide the space. Mirrors, beading, and brilliant colors added to the carnival midway effect.

Girard also continued his series of spectacular exhibition designs. Among them were two Good Design shows for the Museum of Modern Art (1953 and 1954), and "Textiles and Ornamental Arts of India" (1955), also for the Museum of Modern Art. That Indian exhibition remains one of the most dazzling displays within living memory. Throughout his work Alexander Girard brought a new canon of decoration in a witty and whimsical idiom, with spontaneity, and with pure sensual pleasure and joy.

Individualist Designers

Several others who designed interiors in the 1950s demonstrated similarly icono-
clastic and individualistic approaches—moving beyond the Miesian doctrine that
was, at that very time, becoming publicly accepted. Among them were Bruce Goff
and Russel Wright.

Bruce Goff

Architect Bruce Goff, who worked out of Oklahoma, made a strong statement about
interior design in the 1950s. Viewed by doctrinaire Modernists as eccentric and
irrelevant, Goff's designs presented such a multitude of approaches, influences,
techniques, and materials that his work defied categorization—other than to call
him individualistic, expressionistic, and pluralistic.

An exact contemporary of Russel Wright, Bruce Alonzo Goff (1904–82) was
born in Alton, Kansas, and was educated in public school in Tulsa. Apprenticed
to the architecture firm of Rush, Endacott & Rush at the age of twelve (he worked
there from 1916 to 1930), Goff had designed major buildings before he left high
school and at the age of twenty-two designed a church in Tulsa that brought him
international attention. In the 1930s he worked for the industrial products design
firm of Alfonso Iannelli in Chicago, was in private practice as an architect, and
became director of design for the VitroLite Division of Libbey-Owens-Ford Glass
Company. He served in the U.S. Navy Construction Batallion from 1942 to 1945,
and settled to teach at, and later to head, the school of architecture at the University
of Oklahoma from 1948 to 1955. He was in private practice in Oklahoma, Kansas
City, and Texas from then until his death in 1982 at the age of seventy-eight.

Two of Goff's house designs alone qualify him for a place in the history of
twentieth-century interior design: the Bavinger House in Norman, Oklahoma (1950),
and the Price House in Bartlesville, Oklahoma (1956). The Bavinger House has a
spiral plan of saucer-like spaces suspended by tension cables from a steel mast
centered within a fieldstone wall that spirals inward like a nautilus shell. This was
Goff's first full realization of free-flowing space that had been pioneered in the
Teens and 1920s and that he himself had explored since the 1940s. Inside, suspended from the steel mast, are five living areas in the form of carpeted saucers,
each stepped up 3 feet above the preceding one, each one with a cylindrical satellite
closet sheathed in copper, and separable from the overall space only by fishnets or
by opaque draperies. The wire-suspended stair that gives access to these spaces
rises over a pool, a conversation pit, and a plant-filled, skylighted, conservatory-
like world in which the flying saucers float.

The Price House, which immediately reveals the influence of Frank Lloyd
Wright, contains Goff's most innovative and refined interior. Based on a triangular
3-foot module in both plan and section, the house was planned as a large triangle
with its sides extended beyond the angles. Outside, the sloping walls and roof are
covered with gold-anodized aluminum; hard coal and large chunks of rough blue
glass are used for the masonry walls.

Inside the triangulated space (see Figure 127) the walls slope outward to
become a backrest for reclining. The living room has a hexagonal conversation pit
with a mosaic-topped cocktail table. Thick white nylon carpet covers the floor,
banquettes, and lower part of walls; part of the floor is surfaced in white vinyl
sheeting to provide a dance floor.

Goff's furnishings and finishes display an array of "found" or "ad hoc" materials—anthracite coal, sequins, mosaics, chunks of colored glass; they offer fantasy
with abandon. Part of the ceiling above the conversation pit is covered with goose
down. Gold-colored plastic rain—the plastic tinsel used by display studios—hangs

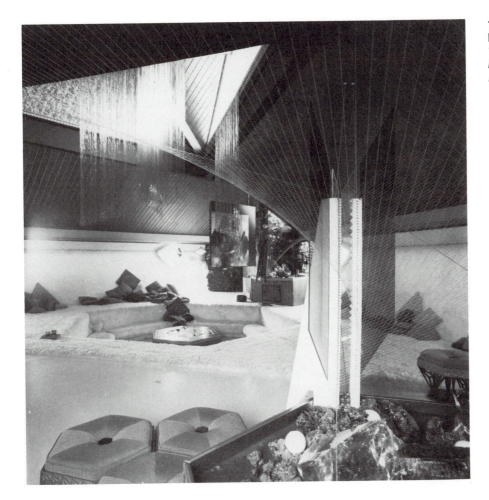

127. Bruce Goff. Joe D. Price House. Bartlesville, Oklahoma. 1956. *Photograph by Joe D. Price, courtesy Bruce Goff Archive.*

as a chandelier above the conversation pit; light-reflecting and air-mobilized, the plastic rain is a startling reinterpretation of the traditional beaded curtain. Lighting is provided from indirect coves that are of stamped gold-anodized aluminum, and from behind the blue glass chunks. Critic Jeffrey Cook has written of Goff's work that it "simultaneously epitomizes the vagaries of the century and some of its most creative variants."[4] The 1950s were called "funky" as well as "fabulous," and any number of critics made an analogy between 1950s design and the concurrent Theater of the Absurd.

Russel Wright

During the 1950s Russel Wright was at the peak of his recognition and productivity. He continued his search for an appropriate expression of American living in the post–World War II era. His province was the middle America that was becoming more design conscious, of necessity tending toward a more casual, servantless lifestyle than was previously known. His concepts were "easier living," "informal hospitality," and "stove-to-table ware." As evidence of his recognition, Russel Wright's designs were included in numerous exhibitions, including the "Good Design" shows at the Museum of Modern Art. In 1952 he was elected president of the American Society of Industrial Designers.

Among his 1950s design commissions for table and household objects were appliances for dining room and kitchen, American Modern glassware, aluminum and pewter table pieces and cutlery, American Modern flatware, and ceramic dinnerware. He continued to design the Melamine plastic dinnerware, for which he became celebrated—Meladur (1949), Residential (1953), and Flair (1959). He also designed plastic tablecloths and mats, other table linens, and paper plates and cups.

Russel Wright's designs for interior furnishings in the 1950s included carpets, drapery fabrics, upholstery fabrics, vinyl upholstery colors, floor tiles, and lamps. He also designed folding metal "patio" chairs and tables for Samsonite in 1950; his colors were aqua, coral, chartreuse, and green. That same year he also designed a group of fifty pieces for Stratton Furniture Company's Easier Living line; it was sold exclusively by Modernage, New York, a prominent popularizer of postwar Modern furniture.

The Easier Living line was a model of inventive ideas for functional use: One side panel of the lounge chair folded up to provide a writing surface; the other side folded out to produce a magazine rack; a coffee-table top slid open to expose a water- and alcohol-proof porcelain tray; bed headboards tilted to expose storage space and to provide comfortable backs for reading in bed. A nightstand had pullout shelves to hold books or trays. Slipcovers snapped on and off. It was as homey American in concept as the American ideals of Frank Lloyd Wright (they were not related). Like him, Russel Wright's personal style was soon rejected in favor of the European import—Machine-Age Modern—which more crisply, glitteringly, and soon richly outshone his soft curves and muddy pastels.

In 1955 Russel Wright designed a line of school furniture for Samsonite in steel tubing with plywood and plastic writing surfaces. To the burgeoning school-design field, Russel Wright brought a new line of brighter colors—brighter than the gunmetal gray and "eye-ease green" that had preceded, but not so vibrant as the colors of Dorothy Liebes or Alexander Girard. Wright's colors were yellow-ochre, light red, gray-blue, and gray-green. Even in his color sense, Russel Wright was a transitional "Contemporary" designer. But by 1953, he felt, "contemporary began to be defeated."[5]

Among his interior designs in the 1950s were a showroom for Stratton Furniture Company and a house in Croton-on-Hudson, New York. But it was his own house—Dragon Rock, in Garrison, New York—that was his interior design preoccupation, and to which he increasingly withdrew as the stylistic winds blew in a direction different from his own. His house, now called Manitoga, was completed between 1956 and 1961. Perched above a water-filled quarry, Dragon Rock was divided into public and private wings, each with views of the romantic "improved" natural landscape.

In the interior Russel Wright aimed to find a harmony between the natural and the manmade, a harmony of both continuity and contrast. One bathtub had its own rocky waterfall. He mixed real and natural materials with synthetic and artificial ones. Styrofoam insulation was exposed between natural wood beams of the living-room ceiling (see Figure 128); kitchen and bathroom partitions, like the transparent Melamine dinnerware, were of plastic in which real wild flowers from the surrounding woods were cast.

He used materials that were beyond the consideration of most serious designers. Textures and colors of draperies, upholsteries, rugs, and accessories—even cabinet doors on double hinges—were varied with the seasons. With his fascination for labor-saving devices, a counterbalanced kitchen storage shelf could be raised to the ceiling; drawers for silver opened into both the kitchen and the dining area. It was, perhaps, a final step to integrate the world of industry with the world of the artist and nature, and it was a tentative, faltering step toward the coexistence of the natural and the manmade that was to be proclaimed in the next decade.

Russel Wright, as William J. Hennessey has written, "ranks with this nation's most original, inventive, and influential designers. . . . His . . . work opened the

128. Russel Wright. Dragon Rock. Garrison, New York. 1956–61. *Photograph by Louis Reens.*

eyes of millions of ordinary Americans to the aesthetic possibilities of everyday life."[6] He was to create one additional masterwork in the 1960s (see Chapter 8) before his career came to an end.

Other Influential Designers

Paul Rudolph

During this decade the work in Florida of the young architect Paul Rudolph came to attention for its delicate textural effects—using filigree screens, fishnet casement draperies, string-tied hammocks, fabric throws, and lacy tree ferns—which offset dramatic structural expressions. Born in Elkton, Kentucky, Rudolph (1918–) studied architecture at Alabama Polytechnic Institute (now Auburn University) and at Harvard's Graduate School of Design under Gropius. The war interrupted his studies and he spent three years in the Navy in ship construction at the Brooklyn Navy Yard.

After returning to Harvard to complete his master's degree, he joined Ralph Twitchell in an architectural partnership—Twitchell & Rudolph—in Sarasota, Florida. There, he began to make a name for himself for small houses that utilized relatively unconventional structural systems and elements for residential buildings. Furnishings for these houses were spare, square, and largely built-in. Movable pieces were usually slim-legged metal pieces with something of the wire look— Eames and Bertoia wire chairs, string-strung chairs, and the like—along with wood-framed seating pieces and platform sofas that were upholstered in white. Rust-colored cushions and natural leather reiterated the wood tones of the furniture frames. They were simple furnishings, selected to meet the criteria of Modernism from the few available designs.

Benjamin Baldwin

Benjamin Baldwin, who became a leader of Minimal interior design in the mid-1960s and 1970s, and a prominent designer of furniture later in his career, began to become a prominent designer in the 1950s. Born in Montgomery, Alabama, Benjamin James Baldwin (1913–) studied painting with Hans Hofmann and architecture under Jean Labatut at Princeton (he received his M.F.A. in 1938) and under Eliel Saarinen at Cranbrook Academy (1938–39). He subsequently worked in Eliel and Eero Saarinen's architecture office (1939–40).

Just before the war (1940–41) Baldwin was in architectural partnership in Chicago with Harry Weese, who later became his brother-in-law. Together they entered designs and won top prize for outdoor furniture and honorable mentions for living room furniture, bedroom furniture, and lighting in the Museum of Modern Art's 1940–41 "Organic Design Competition."

Baldwin served in the Navy during the war and afterward worked with Skidmore, Owings & Merrill in New York (1945–47), helping to establish the firm's interior design function. During that time he was in charge of interior design for

129. Benjamin Baldwin. Own house from dining room to living room. Chicago, Illinois. 1957–58. *Photograph by Idaka.*

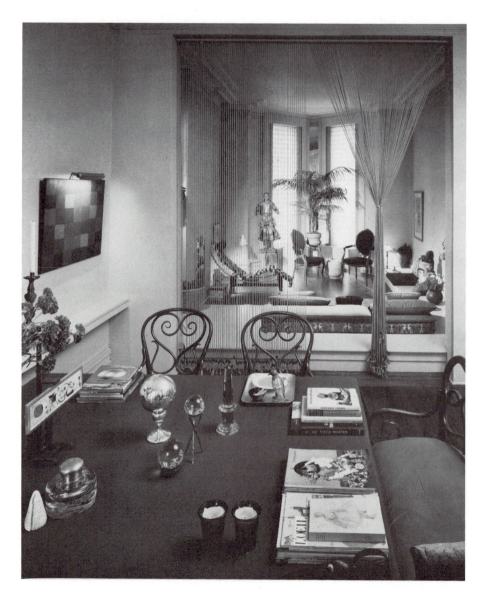

the Terrace Plaza Hotel in Cincinnati. He then established his own practice in New York and later formed a partnership with William Machado for the design of interiors and textiles, first in New York, then in Montgomery, Alabama (1948–55), and later in Chicago (1956–63). It was there that he began to receive significant commissions for the design of furniture, textiles, industrial design, and residential and office interiors, including offices for the Solo Cup Company in 1958.

Baldwin's own Chicago house (1957–58) showed the spare-rich approach with which he later became associated. In a late-nineteenth-century townhouse with adjacent living room and dining room open to each other, Benjamin Baldwin elevated part of the living area on an L-shaped platform; floors and windows were bare; cushion seating was on the platform. In addition, there was a collection of chairs and objects that, though few, reached out across all centuries and cultures— Venetian Louis XV chairs, a Le Corbusier chaise in zebra skin, a gilt Baroque figure, and Modern, oriental, and ancient artworks and objects.

The dining room (see Figure 129), separated by an open curtain of heavy jute packing cord weighted by plumber's washers, had a glass-fronted fireplace that was elevated to the height of the large dining-reading-work table; dado-height narrow shelves held artworks and objects; the chairs were curlicue-bentwood by Thonet. The house was spare and clearly in a Modern sensibility, but it was also reaching out beyond Miesian purity to encompass the rich historical traditions, textures, and colors of our cultural heritage.

From 1963 to 1973 Benjamin Baldwin practiced in New York. He then moved his independent practice to East Hampton, Long Island, and Sarasota, Florida, between which locations he divides the year.

Ward Bennett

Another designer of interiors who was to become a major influence in the next several decades was Ward Bennett, who began to turn to the design of interiors and furnishings in the 1950s. Born in New York City, Ward Bennett (1917–) first worked in display and design for fashion designer Hattie Carnegie, and helped Carnegie on a house she was having refurnished by Syrie Maugham in Redbank, New Jersey. Bennett also worked in theater design on Broadway. He studied painting with Hans Hofmann and came under the influence of sculptor Constantin Brancusi. He began working on sculpture and jewelry, sharing a studio with Louise Nevelson.

In the 1940s he had begun to design furnishings, including the lighting he worked on for SOM's Terrace Plaza Hotel in Cincinnati at the invitation of Benjamin Baldwin.

In the 1950s he began designing interiors and was thrust into international prominence by his appointment, at the end of the decade, as design consultant to David Rockefeller on the interior furnishings and art collection for the headquarters of the Chase Manhattan Bank, the interiors of which were being designed by Davis Allen of SOM. For that project Bennett acquired, selected, and placed small artworks, antiques, and appointments throughout the building. Many of his furniture designs, which were being produced by Lehigh Furniture Company at that time, were used by SOM for the Chase project.

In the late 1950s Ward Bennett designed a living room around that device of the decade: a conversation pit with fireplace.[7] It was a room based on platforms, an idea that gained considerable popularity in the next two decades. Wide, low platforms were built around the perimeter of the room, leaving a rectangular conversation pit, which was lighted from beneath the platforms. Tufted and quilted mattress-like pads were used as the seating; one had bolster-cushions as the backrest, the other was a version of Mies's sofa with cylindrical bolster. In one corner was a lighting fixture composed of an up light that was reflected from a shallow, conical metal disk hung from the ceiling on wire. It was a discontinuous lighting fixture.

As the decade came to a close, Ward Bennett and Benjamin Baldwin led in a search for the ultimate purity of the International Style. With them and a few others, that style reached its final refinement as the Minimal style or Minimalism. They developed a sparse elemental look, a museum-like placement of objects in space, and a visual richness within that rarefied atmosphere.

Luis Barragan

The influence for this new Minimalism, in addition to the development at this same time of Minimal sculpture, was the work in Mexico of Luis Barragan. A poet of solitude and of meditative space, Luis Barragan (1902–) was born near Maza-mitla in the state of Jalisco, Mexico. In the 1920s he moved to Mexico City, was trained as an engineer, and traveled to Europe, where—in Spain—he became fascinated by the terraces, patios, and water gardens of Moslem architecture.

From 1927 to 1936 he worked as an architect in Guadalajara, designing houses and a park playground that prefigured his later landscapes. His work in that period combined the Moslem architecture he had seen in Spain with the indigenous architecture of Mexico.

From 1936, he designed houses and an apartment building in Mexico City in the idiom of the "white architecture" of the early International Style; and in 1945 he began planning the subdivision El Pedregal; there, on a landscape filled with volcanic boulders, he juxtaposed crisp, spare, white houses and phosphorescent red metal entry gates and car turnarounds. After a visit to North Africa in 1951, his work began to achieve the sublime, poetic, sculptural abstraction that made him increasingly influential.

Barragan's own house in Mexico City, designed in 1947, became the touchstone of the early Minimal movement in interior design in the 1950s (see Figures 130A and B).[9] Focused on interior, on garden and patio, and on roof terrace, the house is elemental in its use of planes and materials, making it like a primal myth of a house. It echoes the continuity of uninterrupted Vernacular tradition. Planar walls intersect strongly and starkly and are occasionally finished with the joyous decoration of sumptuous and vibrant colors, sometimes on the exterior as well— pink, lemon, magenta, fuschia, and coral. In this regard, Barragan's work has given a new life to the planar idiom of De Stijl.

The view from the library toward the garden looks over a series of interior partitions of varying heights and through the reception room to a window with cruciform mullions. It is both a three-dimensional homage to the square, like Josef Albers's paintings, and a religious confirmation. The stair of seemingly folded wood cantilevered from the wall of the library rises to a wood door that is, so the legend goes, always closed (see Figure 130B). It is a stair steeped in the surreal, as is the roof terrace, which has been increasingly enclosed by Barragan over the years, more colorful, and abstract, with only the Mexican sky for its changing ceiling. Here, at the boundary between architecture and nature, Barragan has created his most magical and mystical spaces.

Luis Barragan's chapel (see color plate 6) and garden at Tlalpan for the Capuchinas Sacramentarias del Purismo Corazon de Maria (1952–55) was his other masterwork interior in this decade. The chapel is set back behind a garden and was planned with a patio between it and the convent (see Figure 131). In the chapel Barragan employed rough-textured concrete in flat unbordered planes, but it is painted a glowing yellow. A triptych reredos designed by the sculptor Mathias

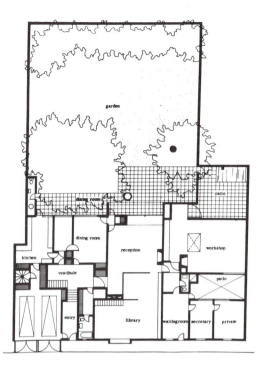

130A. Luis Barragan. Plan, own house. Mexico City, Mexico. 1947. *Illustration from Emilio Ambasz,* The Architecture of Luis Barragan *(New York: The Museum of Modern Art, 1976).*

130B. Luis Barragan. Library and stair, own house. Mexico City, Mexico. 1947. *Photograph © René Burri, Magnum.*

131. Luis Barragan. Plan. Chapel at Tlalpan. Tlalpan, Mexico. 1952–55. *Illustration from Emilio Ambasz,* The Architecture of Luis Barragan *(New York: The Museum of Modern Art, 1976).*

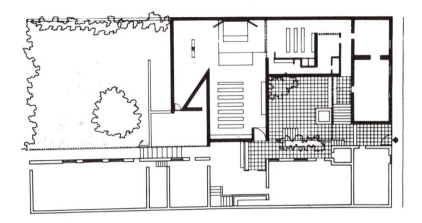

Goeritz is plain and unornamented except by its gridwork pattern of gold leaf. Both the simple and unadorned standing cross, which is lighted by a gold glass window also designed by Mathias Goeritz, and the simple wood benches recall those at Le Corbusier's Chapel at Ronchamp (see below).

Between the chapel and an adjacent smaller chapel, which is for confession and meditation, Barragan designed a lattice screen of wood that is lighted from above to produce a semi-wall of mystical lightness. Outside in the patio is another lattice screen, this one of concrete that is painted pale yellow on the outside and brighter yellow on the inside.

At Tlalpan there is throughout an atmosphere of golden mystery, an ineffable serenity that is also somewhat surreal—not the bizarre, desperate Surrealism of 1930s interiors, but that of de Chirico's empty outdoor spaces. Barragan's Surrealism evokes the eternal peace of religious meditation. The chapel at Tlalpan became a pivotal icon for designers.

The Resistance to Modernism

It would be completely misleading to suggest that the triumph of Modernism in the 1950s was an unresisted coup. Many professional designers and the general public alike were vehement in their opposition to the spread of the European import. Anti-Modernism was an entrenched camp from 1913 to 1960, and certainly afterward. Historical revivalists dug in their heels. Understandably, those trained in one style or generation cannot change overnight to another craft or approach. The triumph of Modernism was more dependent on the growth of the new, young generation than it was dependent on a change of sympathies. However, in their search for the new, which appealed to both designers and their clients, the well of historical styles had begun to run rather dry, and the compromise of the Transitional-Contemporary style was something of a mediator.

Traditionalism and Historicism

The scope of interior work for traditional designers expanded in the 1950s beyond the work for the affluent that had been their mainstay since the beginning of the century—houses and country clubs, yachts and executive offices. Now there were not only more of those projects, but also work for a greater number of private clients with smaller incomes. Countless semiprofessional and amateur decorators appeared to help out. In addition, there was now a great deal more corporate work for traditionalists as well as for Modernists—executive offices, suites, and floors of offices; hotel suites; and entire hotels.

Now too there were more commissions from industry, including airplanes and products for interior design use. The goal of the Deutscher Werkbund and of the Bauhaus to unite artist/designers with industry had been achieved. Only the criterion of quality remained to be raised.

Because of the increase in interior design work, it was more important than ever to distinguish works of quality and innovation from mere rehashes with better-produced (but still Borax) furnishings. The French eighteenth-century styles were now produced in all degrees of quality and accuracy.

Still, there was a yearning for the new—patterns and materials, shapes and other cultures—to the point of excess: trompe l'oeil and marbleizing (especially in imitation of malachite and lapis lazuli) were the rage. Country-house decorating fostered interiors that were essentially theatrical stage settings with little relationship to either function or contemporary life. Fantasy and romantic association or aspiration seemed to lead both designers and clients of these creations. The bywords of these sentiments were "comfortable" and "warm." In the search for patina, as large parts of our environmental heritage were being swept away by the building boom and urban renewal, antique or reproduction antique furniture and objects prevailed in this sector of the profession.

French Provincial   Unpainted French Provincial pieces, which were sometimes distressed—beaten, battered, and chained—and aged in an effort to antique them, were a romantic symbol of the decade. Was it, in fact, a revival, a rediscovery, or a new invention? Even more suspect in provenance was the "Mediterranean" furniture that became popular with the middle market during the 1950s. It was based on an arch detail in walnut and other dark-toned woods, which were given a rough finish. To vanguard designers it was the Borax of the day.

Victorian Revival   The revival of interest in Victorian art and design gained new impetus during the 1950s, sparked no doubt by the hundredth anniversary of the Crystal Palace Exhibition. In England, scholarly studies about the Victorian age appeared, including Henry-Russell Hitchcock's *Early Victorian Architecture* in 1954.[9] In America, the Brooklyn Museum opened its corridor of Victorian period rooms in 1953. They were widely published and drew great crowds. And in 1960 the Brooklyn Museum held the first major exhibition of Victorian decorative arts in this country; it was called "Victoriana."

The Residential Designers

Among the established decorating firms that were at the peak of their popularity with the affluent were McMillen Inc., Thedlow Inc., and Mrs. Henry Parish II, in New York; and 1930s revivalist Michael Taylor, the idiosyncratic John Dickinson, and the Neoclassicist Anthony Hail in San Francisco.

Always concerned with new art forms, Mrs. Archibald McMillen Brown felt that there were so many new ideas coming from France that, in 1952, she exhibited French Modern furniture, pictures, and art objects by twenty-six Parisian artists, designers, and craftsmen in the rooms of McMillen's brownstone offices. For McMillen's efforts in promoting French contemporary design, Mrs. Brown was awarded the Légion d'Honneur. French Contemporary/Moderne was, thereafter, a staple of the firm's designs.

Mrs. Henry Parish II (see Figure 132), by the end of the decade, had worked for then Senator and Mrs. John F. Kennedy, as well as for the Vincent Astors at Rhinebeck, New York, and for the Charles Engelhards in South Africa.

Michael Greer, who had first worked with Nancy McClelland, became interested in Napoleonic steel furniture and in Directoire style. It had made him something of an authority, and he created a number of stylish and truly refined if precious interiors in that style. Among them were his own apartment of 1954 and the restaurant Le Directoire in New York City.

French decorating firms also began to establish a secure clientele among this new international traveler set. They included Stephane Boudin of Jansen, the firm of Alavoine, and designers Jean Royere and Pierre Scapulla, the latter of whom created some of the most acclaimed historical restorations of the decade. The young American designer Charles E. Sevigny stayed in Paris after his education at the Parsons program there and designed interiors for the U.S. Foreign Buildings Operation. For them he showed a way to combine the new American International-Style furnishings with French antiques.

English designers also began to make an impact on American interior design, especially the recently prominent David Hicks, who was to bring a new look to floors with his checked and gridded carpet designs and his bathrooms with tubs centered in the room. Stage designers Oliver Messel and Cecil Beaton continued to design interiors and printed fabrics.

Dorothy Draper continued her practice in commercial interiors, including renovations of San Francisco's Fairmont Hotel and Mark Hopkins Hotel; New York's Park Lane Hotel and Barclay Hotel; and hospitals, retail stores, and automobile interiors for Detroit. She also wrote a newspaper column, beginning in 1959, that was syndicated to seventy papers. It made her one of the most popular names in interior design. Dorothy Draper was gradually to stop working in the next decade, when her firm was acquired by Carleton Varney. Although Mrs. Draper died in 1969, the firm bearing her name continues to design commercial interiors to this day.

132. Mrs. Henry Parish II. Own living room. New York City. Circa 1955. *Photograph from Katharine Tweed, ed.,* The Finest Rooms by America's Great Decorators *(New York: Viking Press, 1964).*

Among other designers doing commercial work were Maria Bergson & Associates, Emily Malino, Melanie Kahane, Elizabeth Draper, and Ellen Lehmann McCluskey, as well as the new group that called themselves space planners.

T. H. Robsjohn-Gibbings

T. H. Robsjohn-Gibbings continued in his spare, classically derived idiom based on natural materials such as marble, on solid colors, and on squares as in overscaled ottomans, square lampshades, and frameless fireplaces. In 1951 he designed a bathroom for *Look* magazine with wall-to-wall and floor-to-ceiling heavily veined white marble and with walnut furniture that had all the sleekness of later Minimalism—without moldings or reveals.

He designed a display living room for the National Homefurnishings Show the next year with the same floor and wall surfacing; with exaggeratedly long and low fireplace, mantelpiece, and furniture; and with a leopard-skin rug. A walnut chair carved in simulated bamboo was a Robsjohn-Gibbings design of 1954, and screens with varying patterns ornamented his interiors for the rest of the decade.

Among the most extravagant of his interior designs was a dining room in the Graf House in Dallas by Edward Durell Stone in which the dining group floated

133. Edward Durell Stone and T. H. Robsjohn-Gibbings. Dining room, Bruno K. Graf House. Dallas, Texas. 1958. *Photograph © Ezra Stoller/ESTO, 1958.*

on a circular island in a pool flanked by one of Stone's pierced screens (see Figure 133). Robsjohn-Gibbings's table was a truncated fluted column of walnut.

His furniture designs of this decade, many produced by the Widdicomb Furniture Company of Grand Rapids, also included an amoeba-shaped cocktail table with two additional tiers of smaller amoebas, and case pieces that dispensed with visible drawer pulls by using clapboard-like overlapping drawers. His continuing interest in classicism also offered round arched panels and fluted columns.

Billy Baldwin

Following the death of Ruby Ross Wood in 1950, Billy Baldwin reorganized the firm with Edward Martin in 1952 and continued designing as Baldwin & Martin. He adapted the square, cane-wrapped side chair that Jean-Michel Frank had designed in the 1930s. He began to work with pattern-on-pattern, which became one of his trademarks, and often hung all the walls of a room with printed fabrics shirred on poles (see Figure 134). He liked simple, inexpensive furnishings—Indian prints

134. Billy Baldwin. Fabric-draped living room. New York City. Circa 1955. *Photograph by Horst.*

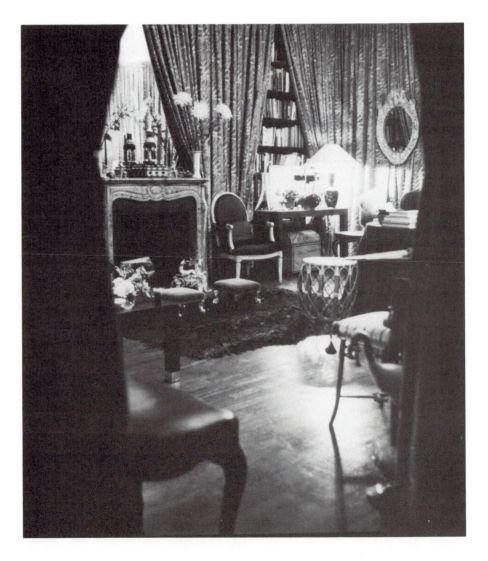

and rush matting—but used them with surprising elegance. He liked fabric-draped tables, wicker furniture, and chintz slipcovers. An admirer of Matisse, he filled his rooms splashily with fresh bright blues, pinks, and greens, with flower patterns, and white furniture. It was an Americanized country-house look.

Early in the decade Billy Baldwin transformed his own living room from its dark-green scheme (see Chapter 6) to one of white-painted walls with yellow silk curtains, for which he used imported Thaibok dress material for the first time, and vivid yellow satin upholsteries.

In 1955 Baldwin refinished his living room again. Without changing the furniture plan, he recovered walls, sofa, and windows with a white-on-white French linen-and-rayon brocade; with it he added apricot cut-velvet upholstery, brown-and-cream basketweave-patterned cut-velvet, and brown satin on a draped table. The transformations revealed how he stayed ahead of his time. In the same year he designed an apartment for Cole Porter in New York. The walls were covered in tortoiseshell vinyl, against which he designed tubular brass bookcases. He filled the rooms with a mixture of Cole Porter's French antiques and contemporary pieces.

During the decade he designed stage settings for producer Gilbert Miller, as well as a dining room for the Gilbert Millers' residence that had walls the color of strawberry sherbet and a Bessarabian carpet with a black background and medallions of pink and red flowers. He covered one floor with saddle-leather pieces studded with brass, an idea that was to be widely imitated.

As the 1950s continued, Baldwin & Martin decorated a house on Long Island by painting the principal rooms white glossy enamel—including the floor of one sitting room—and using a single brightly multicolored, boldly patterned floral chintz on the large upholstered pieces in each room. Most other furniture was also finished in white—lacquer tables, upholstered furniture, a white rug in one sitting room, and white-lacquered carved Victorian Louis XV Revival armchairs. (The concept has been credited to Edward Martin.)

Billy Baldwin's spare, meticulously chosen appointments and table vignettes completed his trademark. Those vignettes were composed assemblies of objects—two Japanese lacquer bowls, two turtle backs, one brass turtle from Morocco; or he combined bamboo, brass bamboo, a plant in a cloisonné jardiniere, a silver cigarette box, and a small oil painting; he also used watercolors, bronzes, cachepots, porcelains, pre-Columbian sculptures mounted on Plexiglas, and a wide range of small, textured, folk art and museum-like objects, and unusual objects from around the world. The vignettes were composed as carefully as still-life paintings, and showed Billy Baldwin's eye for texture, scale, juxtaposition, and detail.

Michael Taylor

In the 1950s the designs of Michael Taylor came to national prominence. Born in Modesto, California, Michael Taylor (1927–86) grew up in Santa Rosa and began his career at Jackson's furniture store and with the decorator Mrs. Kasper in San Francisco. In 1952 he formed a partnership with Frances Mihailoff and began to design his off-white rooms with tall doors and other large-scale pieces. He formed his independent practice in San Francisco in 1957.

Taylor liked to use color, but not many colors in a single space, feeling that "a good room should be predominantly one color." He also liked to use a single pattern throughout a room. He used semitropical plants extravagantly, since it was possible to maintain them well in the California climate. "Plants have a way of preventing a room from appearing overdecorated; they also soften the light," he said.[10] Michael Taylor's style is a special unorthodoxy that at its best is alive with freshness.

Taylor was strongly influenced by Syrie Maugham. When Frances Elkins died, he bought much of her business property, including lamp molds and other furniture designs that Mrs. Elkins had acquired from Syrie Maugham.

Taylor then began to revive and reinterpret the all-white room schemes of Syrie Maugham. In one California bedroom (1957), Taylor reinterpreted Syrie Maugham's celebrated bedroom for Mrs. Tobin Clark in San Mateo, California (see Chapter 5). In Taylor's reinterpretation all the walls, ceiling, carpet, and furniture were white, including an English chinoiserie four-poster bed (he did another bedroom in this scheme with two four-posters), benches, and lamps. He draped the beds and side tables in white patterned brocade. Mantelpiece, andirons, occasional tables, and accessories were also white. Two small armchairs copied from the Syrie Maugham collection, as were the beds and benches, were uphol-stered in white but accented with green tufting buttons and green ribbons; the bench pads were covered in green, in a patterned fabric like the bed drapery. Tree ferns and other green plants brought the crisp fresh scheme to life, while a tall ornate Venetian mirror of fine quality and one multicolor painting gave the room sparkle and accent.

John Dickinson

In California, John Dickinson began to come to attention. Born in Redlands, California, John Dickinson (1920–82) studied at the Parsons School of Design in the 1940s and returned to Redlands to do his apprenticeship in a furniture store. He later moved to San Francisco to begin his career with E. Coleman Dick, and soon began to be recognized for his idiosyncratic approach. His style matured in the next several decades, which were cut short after too-few completed projects in the 1970s (see Chapter 9).

Albert Hadley

Among the new designers of the decade was Albert Hadley, teacher and residential designer who was to become one of the leading residential designers of the next three decades. Born in Nashville, Tennessee, Hadley (1920–) began his design career by working for A. Herbert Rogers in Nashville. But with his eyes set on New York, he went in 1946 determined to meet Eleanor McMillen Brown, Billy Baldwin, George Stacey, William Pahlmann, and other important designers of the time.

After Mrs. Brown asked if he had been to Parsons, he learned that she hired only Parsons graduates. He enrolled in the Parsons six-week summer course and was awarded the Elsie de Wolfe scholarship to study in Paris. He graduated from Parsons in 1949.

He next worked for Roslyn Rosier, one of the most inventive antique dealers in New York, and then was asked by Van Day Truex to teach at Parsons in New York and Europe. Among his students in the next five years were Joseph Braswell, David Whitcomb, Carrie Donovan, Jay Hyde Crawford, Thomas Morrow, A. T. Hammet, and Albino Cimonetti.

After that five-year teaching period, Hadley was in independent practice for a period and in 1956 joined McMillen Inc. as a staff decorator. Among his first acclaimed interiors was a bedroom in New York for theater director Joshua Logan, who wanted the room to complement his paintings. Hadley's design was conceived to be like a Vuillard painting—all pattern on pattern, in the new wave of the decade—and something of what the designer considered "a fantasy." His own apartment, always in transformation, featured carved wood white palm-tree tor-chères that had been acquired from Elsie de Wolfe and are believed to have been

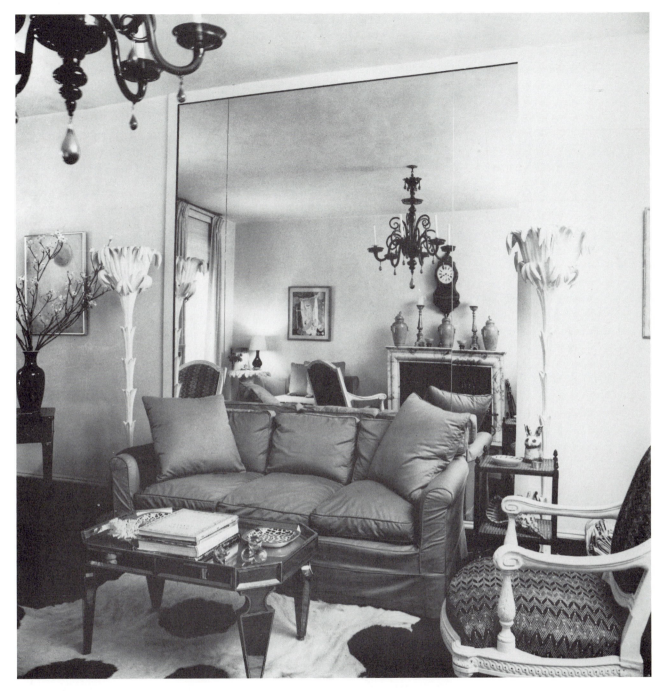

designed by Emilio Terry (see Figure 135). They started a revival. From then on Albert Hadley began to be known for his fresh imagination and thorough historical background. He was to join Mrs. Henry Parish II in 1961.

135. Albert Hadley. Own apartment. New York City. Late 1950s. *Photograph by Richard Jeffery.*

Other Residential Designers

Other prominent residential designers in the 1950s were James Amster, Yale R. Burge, David Whitcomb, and Braswell-Cook. The firm of Tom Lee Ltd., which combined traditional and Modern design for exhibition and hotel spaces, also came to the forefront of interior design at this time. The model rooms designed by Barbara D'Arcy for Bloomingdale's began to attract crowds and publicity from

1957 on. As much as any other designer, Barbara D'Arcy made the public aware of the varieties of style that the decade offered—both historicism and Modernism, as well as eclectic and imaginative mixtures of substyles and periods. That leavening helped the public to understand Modernism's honesty and discretion in design.

The Transitional–Contemporary Designers

William Pahlmann

In the 1950s William Pahlmann was at the height of his career, designing hotels and offices, residences and apartment lobbies, exhibitions and showrooms, department stores and shops, as well as interior design products. Among his clients were Henry Morgan & Company, John Wanamaker and Bonwit Teller stores, and hotels in Miami, Atlanta, and Atlantic City. In 1950 he served as president of the New York chapter of the American Institute of Decorators. He wrote *The Pahlmann Book of Interior Design* in 1955. He also wrote a syndicated newspaper column called "A Matter of Taste."

Pahlmann and his associates—who included Daren Pierce, George Thiel, James Hendrix, and Jack Conner—designed rooms as striped tents, and mixed antiques and contemporary pieces. Throughout the 1950s William Pahlmann Associates also designed fabrics, wallpapers and other wall coverings, carpets and floor tiles, lighting and lighting fixtures. In 1952 the firm designed a line of furniture with oversize castors—chairs, tables, and even a credenza that had twin beds in it. The castors made the pieces more easily mobile to swing around to face the television; it was called the Momentum Line (see Figure 136). They used that line along with wall-hung exposed bookshelves, Moroccan carpets, and antiques covered in glossy tortoiseshell leather. It was a highly patterned and textured decade.

136. William Pahlmann. "Momentum" Furniture. 1952. *Photograph courtesy William Pahlmann.*

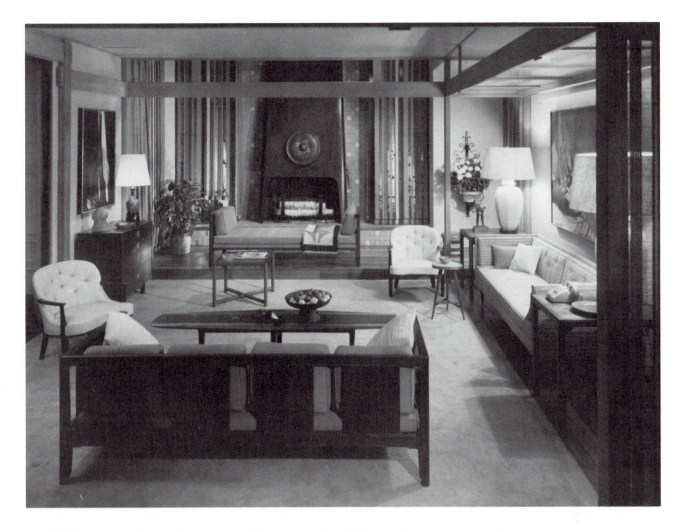

137. Edward Wormley. Model living room for Dunbar's Janus Collection. Chicago, Illinois. 1957. *Photograph courtesy Edward Wormley.*

Pahlmann was also in the forefront of the new color richness that swept the end of the decade (see below). Among the color combinations he was proud of introducing were *tête de nègre*, green, orange, and deep cerulean blue for the lounge of the Columbus Hotel in Miami (1953); driftwood, lime, orange, and white (1954); Siamese pink, sandalwood, ivory, and pink (1955); and Venetian red, Florentine green, Carrara white, and vulcan brown (1956).

During the decade he was design consultant to Restaurant Associates, for whom he designed The Forum of the Twelve Caesars, The Brasserie, La Trattoria, Charlie Brown's, and the Zum-Zum chain. He also served as consultant to Restaurant Associates on Philip Johnson's Four Seasons Restaurant (see Chapter 8).

Edward Wormley

Throughout the decade Edward Wormley continued to produce line after line of furniture designs—150 pieces a year for the Dunbar Furniture Company. Nine of his designs were chosen for the Museum of Modern Art's Good Design show of 1951. His A Chair of 1959 with its wood frame of compass-shaped rear legs and caned back was among the most popular. Dunbar's advertising campaign of furniture photographed outdoors—on the plains of the Midwest or Africa—captured public attention.

Wormley also produced numerous showrooms (see Figure 137) and interiors. Among them was his own apartment design in Manhattan, which was a laboratory of his ideas. One of his designs with Bertha Schaefer in 1955 was for an L-shaped living room in which the L was used as a bedroom with a three-cushion sofa; walls and ceiling were covered in a blue strié paper; blue-gray taffeta draperies were hung at the windows; the carpet was of blue chenille; furnishings were Wormley's designs for Dunbar.

Other American Furniture Designers

Swelling the ranks of designers to meet the demand for interior furnishings were Tommi Parzinger, who continued to produce lacquer and brass furniture in the lingering Wiener Werkstaette idiom, and who opened a showroom in 1954; Paul McCobb, who designed rational Machine-Age pieces and storage walls; and Harvey Probber, Paul Laszlo, and Hoffman & Hedrich.

Professional Organizations

In 1957 the National Society of Interior Designers (NSID) was founded, making two rival, competitive, and redundant professional organizations. It was a situation that lasted until 1975. But the very name of the new organization furthered the move away from the term "decorator." It was not without some resistance that this happened—Billy Baldwin, for example, refused to be called an interior designer—and to this day many of the traditionalists prefer to call themselves decorators. In 1961 the American Institute of Decorators changed its name, but not its acronym (AID), to American Institute of Interior Designers. The new twentieth-century profession was at last mature.

Renewal versus Heritage

The Federal Urban Renewal program was passed by Congress as part of the Housing Act of 1954. Since the 1930s the "elimination of slums" had been a goal. In the 1950s a "slum" seemed to mean any building over thirty years old. At this time the federal highway program began to cut swathes around and through American cities. These highways usually were planned to run through slum areas, stripping them away. Stripped away along with the "slums" were superb old buildings, treasuries of our culture, architecture and interiors of all descriptions. It was all in the goal of stripping away that taboo of Modernism—history. It was also with the aim of creating the city beautiful, the *ville radieuse* concept of Le Corbusier, the city filled with gardens and sunshine—the triumph of Modern urban planning. In this decade construction of cultural centers and performing arts centers was initiated, and many much-needed new housing developments were created. But often, to make them, the continuity of cities was shattered.

This fitted in with the decade's viewpoint on quality: If a thing was good enough in isolation, then it could stand next to anything else also good. It was the attitude of Good Design. But it disregarded stylistic and other incompatibilities, disregarded context and continuity. So it was that isolated towers—detached on podiums or plazas, devoid of commercial shops with urban vitality, and discontinuous with pedestrian traffic—gradually replaced what was old in our downtowns.

The Search for Texture and Patina

At the same time a counterdirection showed an innate human need for salvaging the old, for the patina of centuries. Bereft of ornament and decoration due to the International Style's taboo against historicism and applied decoration, designers wriggled in desperation to find some substitute for this culturally established need.

Objects such as carriage lights, balancing scales, and old equipment and tools—optimally of brass or bronze—were sought after and collected by the score as decorative pieces that offset the new, crisp Modern interiors. Even in the realm of architecture the newly developed steel COR-10—which weathers to develop its own rusted finish as a protective surface—was adopted. The balance of two directions and textural effects was continued.

A New Free-Form Expressionism

Even within the Modern movement after the middle of the 1950s, former disciples of Mies and Gropius began to invert their theories—or to expand their theories in order to enrich the idiom. The impetus of this was not only their own search to enrich the Modern idiom as the second generation of Modernists, but also the example of Le Corbusier, who completely rejuvenated his own work—as well as that of all other designers from then on—with the design of his Chapel at Ronchamp.

The Chapel at Ronchamp

The culmination of this search for something beyond the machine-image rectilinear Modernism of Mies was Le Corbusier's masterpiece of architectural sculpture, the Chapelle Notre-Dame-du-Haut (see color plate 5) at Ronchamp in the south of France (1950–54). A free-form sculpture unparalleled among all previous buildings, Ronchamp was initially considered both expressionistic and irrational, on the one hand, and a compendium of religious symbolism on the other. Its symbolism was hauntingly evocative, if mannered and elusive. Le Corbusier called it "ineffable space."

In terms of form-giving, Ronchamp was the apotheosis of free-form. It was epochal in the design of architecture and interiors, and brilliantly if disturbingly presented a new alternative of organic plasticity. It changed the potential of architecture and interiors at mid-century by offering this totally new option. Its free-form vocabulary was emphasized by being contrasted with rectilinear elements to create both tension and balance.

At Ronchamp Le Corbusier inscribed a center axis in the flooring, and rectangular window and door openings, along with rectangular furniture and altar elements to reinforce the contrast. But the plan and section were a free and unprecedented assemblage of undulating curvilinear forms (see Figure 138A).

The interior (see Figure 138B) is essentially a single major space with ancillary spaces formed by the apparent folding or curving of concrete wall surfaces to enclose three chapels. Rough-textured walls of white-painted concrete, which was sprayed over masonry, are sloping—both toward the top and progressively thicker in plan. The floor slopes down to the altar on the natural grade. The curving, up-turned gray ceiling floats above the walls on pins and on a spacer, which is sometimes translucent. Benches are grouped into a trapezoidal block. Windows, rectangular and square, are of varied sizes and in random pattern, with glass that is both clear and colored, but always transparent; they create truly mystical pinpoints of light away from the outerworld.

The chapels, one of which is painted an intense red, are lighted by half-domes with glass on one side. The wall leading to the sacristy is painted violet. This nebulous, flowing world is mysterious and mystical, supremely evocative of religious atmosphere—though personally, willfully, and iconoclastically so, in view of traditional ecclesiastical architecture. For both religious interiors and for form-making, Ronchamp was epochal.

Le Corbusier showed at Ronchamp—as he had showed at the Unité d'Habitation apartment house in Marseilles (1947–52) and at his later Jaoul houses at

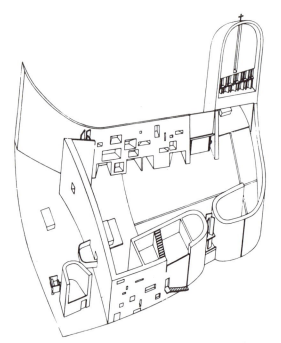

138A. Le Corbusier. Perspective axonometric diagram, for Chapel at Ronchamp. Ronchamp, France. 1950–54. *Illustration from Duane and Sarah Preble,* Artforms *(New York: Harper & Row, 1985).*

138B. Le Corbusier. Notre-Dame-du-Haut. Ronchamp, France. 1950–54. *Photograph © Ezra Stoller/ESTO, 1955.*

Neuilly-sur-Seine (1955–57) and at the Convent of La Tourette near Lyons (1957–60)—how rough strength could be as powerful an achievement as refined sophistication. The free-form plasticity achieved at Ronchamp opened a new avenue for the world of design.

Due largely to Le Corbusier's work at this time, concrete came to be thought of almost as a superscale modeling clay; by analogy, it took the clay of the potter's wheel and threw it now at the scale of buildings. No one could make a claim that the history of concrete—or indeed the production and use of it—was directly descended from the production or use of ceramics. Yet the mixture of earth and water, of molds and forms, and of curing processes seemed—after Ronchamp provided its leap of vision—sufficiently similar to make the analogy with the larger-scale, and thereafter ever more pliable and potentially sculptural, building industry.

European Parallels

Ronchamp was the beginning of a new era in design. There had been a few precedents—in the work of the German Expressionists, in the work of Erich Mendelsohn, and elsewhere. Another forerunner of Ronchamp's sculptural quality was Frederick Kiesler's Endless House project, which had been frequently revised from 1923 to 1960. The Endless House was an egg-shaped sculptural dwelling with continuously curvilinear walls and no distinctions between floors, walls, and ceilings. Never built, it was widely influential through publications.

In Europe the search for such texture and sculptural character was expressed by England's New Brutalism, which gave rugged functionalism the lead over smooth formalism. It was epitomized in the work of Peter and Alison Smithson and in the work of James Stirling. In addition, Alvar Aalto's Town Hall at Saynatsalo, Finland (1951), along with his church at Vuoksenniska, Imatra (1957–59), continued his personal free-form Expressionism. More sculpturally expressionistic was the Opera House for Sydney, Australia, designed by Denmark's Bjorn Utzon (1958–68), with its roof of sail-like structures at the edge of the Sydney harbor.

This direction was strongly reflected in interior work by Arne Jacobsen's new kind of Expressionism in his SAS Royal Hotel in Copenhagen, where the Egg and Swan chairs that Jacobsen had designed in 1959 gave sculptural life to the International Style surroundings.

The Decade of the Parabola

In South America the work of Oscar Niemeyer at the new capital city of Brasilia reiterated these sculptural directions. Neo-Baroque parabolas and inverted parabolas were to be seen on Oscar Niemeyer's new buildings in Brasilia—the Presidential Palace (1958) and the government parliamentary buildings, which were completed the next year.

From the United States came some elaborately convoluted sculpturing—all under the name of concrete technology. These structural gymnastics aimed to proclaim an independence from the Miesian rectangle. Other structural gymnastics, such pyramidal forms called hyperbolic-paraboloids, were added to this search to go beyond the square and the rectangle. This direction gained the epithet "the new sensualism."

It was all part of the search by the second generation of Modernists to go beyond the tenets of their predecessors and teachers. They aimed not to imitate the teaching of Mies or Gropius, but, as Paul Rudolph said, to bounce off those satellites to aim at a new direction. The new generation began to explore plasticity, classicizing elements, decorative and historical motifs, and vernacular and contextual approaches. They based their thinking on the functional diagram, but aimed to enrich it with visual interest. That plastic direction included Minoru Yamasaki's vaulted St. Louis Airport (1956), Philip Johnson's open-air church in New Harmony, Indiana (1960), and Saarinen's TWA Terminal (see Chapter 8). This search for new form also led to Saarinen's Pedestal Furniture (1955) and to the new rich colors in fabric design (see below).

In this vein, in the mid-1950s, Eero Saarinen's chapel for the Massachusetts Institute of Technology (MIT) in 1955 had a mystical interior, intended to be daylighted by reflections from a moat through floor-height arched windows, and a glittering reredos of gilt-bronze confetti-like screen by Harry Bertoia. Saarinen's John Deere Building in Moline, Illinois (1958–62), which was the first to use the new weathering COR-10 steel, had offices of especial elegance and richness beyond the work of his contemporaries.

At its most common, the automobile tail fins introduced by Detroit in 1956 reiterated this new sculptural direction of the decade. Stylistically, it was the age of the two-tone design—cars, jackets, and upholstery. And between the freest freeform sculpture of Ronchamp and the sleekness of rectilinear machine-image International Style, the polished bronze sculpture of Constantin Brancusi's *Bird in Flight* became a mediating symbol.

The Interiors of Louis Kahn

After the early 1950s the work of Louis Kahn began to influence architecture and interior design with another approach to sculptural effects. Following the opening of his Yale Art Gallery (1951–53), Kahn was on his way to becoming the reigning American architect, as he certainly was after the death of Eero Saarinen in 1961.

Born on the Island of Saarama, Estonia (now USSR), Louis I. Kahn (1901–74) was brought to Philadelphia by his parents in 1905. He studied art at the Pennsylvania Academy of Fine Arts in Philadelphia; he studied architecture at the University of Pennsylvania till 1924. He worked for other architects through the Depression and for the WPA, and formed partnerships with George Howe and Oscar Stonorov primarily designing housing until the late 1940s. Then he began to teach at Yale. It was not until after his Yale Art Gallery building was in progress, when he was over fifty, that he began to become known beyond Philadelphia.

Louis Kahn's Yale Art Gallery spaces offered universal loft space with a degree of flexibility for changing exhibitions owing to some demountable, though heavy, partitions. But it was the clarity of his design and the ornamental quality of his tetrahedral concrete ceiling that showed the way to the new richness in architecture and interiors.

Louis Kahn's interiors, following on the raw concrete work Le Corbusier planned for the Indian capital of Chandigarh, added a superscale dimension of similar motifs along with the grace and refinement of concrete and brickwork that made him a poet of materials. His Richards Medical Center in Philadelphia proclaimed him the most influential architect of his day when the drawings were shown in the late 1950s (see Chapter 8). Kahn's First Unitarian Church in Rochester, New York (1959–67), was an interior of major significance. Its monumental skylit monitors or lanterns admitted ever-changing light onto the sanctuary and onto its Jack Lenor Larsen–designed tapestry hanging.

The Filigree Screen

Among the ornamental devices that architects and designers adopted in the 1950s were openwork, patterned screens. They were a 1950s device to provide texture as well as ornament for the new Modernism that forbade other than integral ornamentation. Even then, it was only under the guise of a sunscreening device or some other lighting or privacy function that such screens could be accepted. Louis Kahn's Art Gallery ceiling was prototypical in this direction of patterning to counteract the ubiquitous planar surfaces of Modern design (though it was closer to the space-frames of Buckminster Fuller than to other openwork screens, and by no means a direct influence on interior designers).

At the same time the young architect Paul Rudolph designed a curve-plan screen made of folded cardboard between wood strips for his entry to the Museum of Modern Art's Good Design show of 1952. The California architects Campbell & Wong installed cut-and-pierced lattice Japanese screens in several interiors they designed. But it was the work of Edward Durell Stone, who devised an openwork structural concrete block that when stacked formed a filigree screen, that brought this concept to popularity and ultimate overuse. Stone's American Embassy in New Delhi (completed in 1954)—along with his U.S. Pavilion for the Brussels World's Fair (1958), his house for Mr. and Mrs. Bruno K. Graf in Dallas (1958), and his own townhouse on Manhattan's East 64th Street (1959)—catapulted both the architect and the filigree screen into international prominence.

In this same vein, though usually constructed of aluminum, were the large-scale screens used to shield the sun—as well as to provide integral ornamentation to buildings—by Minoru Yamasaki. His McGregor Conference Center for Wayne State University in Detroit (1958) and his Reynolds Metal Office Building in Southfield, Michigan (1959), were immediate popularizers of this new Decorated Modern style, which his theme arches for the Seattle World's Fair (1962) capitalized.

In interiors, then, it was the decade of filigree screens. They offered layering and semitransparency as well as pattern and texture. Moroccan panels and mesh casements were other variations on this concept. Harry Bertoia's sculptural metal screens were a vanguard of this direction. One of the most popular versions was the sinuous interweaving openwork screen designed by Erwin Hauer. Some called this the reaction against and rejection of Modernism; others called it the search for pattern, texture, and decoration to fill the gap that Modernism had created with its taboos against these fundamental elements of design.

The New Color Richness

Midway in the 1950s, Bauhaus principles were enriched by the sensuous colors of the color-field school of Abstract Expressionism. In the art world Abstract Expressionism was making New York the new art capital. The color-field painters aimed to make statements with abstract fields of large colored areas. The romantic colors of the color-field painters—Bernard Newman, Mark Rothko, Robert Motherwell, Adolph Gottlieb, Clyfford Still, and Ad Reinhardt—though sometimes dark and somber, were far more sensuous than the primary colors that had been the staple of De Stijl–Bauhaus ideology. They opened a new color freedom in the design world of the 1950s.

In fabrics the romantic colors—sometimes deep and mysterious, sometimes vibrant and pulsating—of Dorothy Liebes, Alexander Girard, Jack Lenor Larsen (see color plate 7), Jim Thompson, and Boris Kroll—revolutionized the color sense of the 1950s and helped to make more palatable to more people the spare designs derived from Miesian principles. The rich Siamese silks imported by Jim Thompson's firm Thaibok and the fabrics produced by Franco Scalamandre and Greeff Fabrics also continued this direction, which *House Beautiful* deemed "the return to elegance."

Dorothy Liebes

Dorothy Liebes (see Chapter 6) was the pioneer in this new color richness in fabrics for the general public (see color plate 7) as her commissions for large-scale work came from du Pont in 1955 and Bigelow-Sanford in 1957. For them she adapted the unusual materials and color combinations of her handweaving to machine-weaving techniques. Among her combinations were leather, rayon, silk, and metal thread; or bamboo splits, wood dowels, rayon, cotton, chenille, and metallics such as Lurex. She also used plastics, sequins, grass, and ticker tape in her weaving. Typical placemats and, later, roll-up window blinds might have flat bamboo strips, matchstick bamboo dowels, and ribbons of narrow purple grosgrain and wide purple satin.

Boris Kroll

During the 1950s weaver-designer Boris Kroll established the colors and textures that became his signature. Born in Buffalo, New York, Kroll (1913–) began working in his brother's Modern furniture factory in New York at the age of seventeen and recognized that there were only a few good traditional weaves available. He has spent the rest of his life remedying that situation.

He opened his first showroom in 1934, and in 1936 established his first collection of handwoven imported fabrics. At this time he also taught himself to weave, and became dedicated to the jacquard loom. During the 1930s he provided fabrics for Robsjohn-Gibbings's Weber House, for Raymond Loewy's exhibition room at the Metropolitan Museum of Art, for the Neiman-Marcus and J. L. Hudson department stores, and for several ocean liners. At the end of the 1930s he switched from handweaving to power production. He spent the war in armed service stationed in the Pacific, and in 1946 began to open his string of showrooms across the country.

In the 1950s his signature weaves and colors were hot and vibrant. His Caribbean collection of 1952, Mediterranean collection of 1955, and Etruscan collection of 1956 established him as a colorist and were major contributions to "the return to elegance." In 1953 he won thirteen awards in the Museum of Modern Art's Good Design show.

Jack Lenor Larsen

Fresh in the world of fabric design (see color plate 7), Jack Lenor Larsen made his debut with the fabrics commissioned for Lever House in 1952 (see above) and continued as one of the most imaginative designers of textiles for the next three decades. Born in Seattle, Washington, to Danish-Canadian parents, Larsen (1927–) studied architecture at the University of Washington in Seattle, then studied furniture design, but settled on weaving. He attended Cranbrook Academy from 1950 to 1951, and opened his New York studio later that year. At that time he demonstrated the direction for which he has become recognized—weaving on power looms with handspun yarns and random repeats to create a handwoven look.

Larsen has concentrated on the structure of fabrics more than on printed applied patterns, although he was first to introduce printed velvet upholstery in 1959, the first stretch upholstery in 1961, and the development of warp-knit casements such as the Saran monofilament Interplay (1960). Among his commissions have been fabrics for Pan Am and Braniff; large-scale theater curtains for Wolf Trap Farm Park performing arts center in Virginia and for the Phoenix Civic Plaza concert hall; quilted silk banners for the Sears bank in Chicago's Sears Tower (1974); and numerous other commissions and collections of fabrics.

Alexander Girard

In the Modern movement's concentration on structure, only one designer triumphed in the realm of printed pattern—Alexander Girard. He was color consultant to the GM Research Center from 1951 to 1952, and in 1951 began to design fabrics for Herman Miller.

Girard's fabrics (see color plate 7) reclaimed the province of two-dimensional applied pattern that was initiated by the fabric designs of C. F. A. Voysey at the end of the nineteenth century, and they were also part of this color revolution. He acclaimed "simple geometric patterns and brilliant primary color ranges."[11] His fabrics were riots of color—one design of 1/4-inch stripes alternates purple, green, orange, blue, and magenta to produce a spontaneous, fun-filled revelation. Dismissing representational pattern because of the distortions created when draped and folded, Girard adopted stripes and checks, and repeated geometric forms such as circles and hexagons.

Simplicity and a planar effect are fundamental to his designs. "His endless variations on related stripes, checks, and solids primarily within the confines of one weave, one yarn, and one density prove his innovative prowess," Jack Lenor Larsen has written.[12] Girard continued to design fabrics for the next two decades.

A New Elegance in Furniture

In the area of furniture design Eero Saarinen's Pedestal Furniture of 1955, produced by Knoll, signaled not only the arrival of the plastic chair in an elegant form, but also its adoption for use in living rooms and board rooms. In 1958, therefore, when Saarinen's Expressionistic TWA Terminal design was beginning to capture people's fancies, the Museum of Contemporary Crafts in New York mounted an exhibition of the glass and metal work of Louis Comfort Tiffany. The design world was prepared to accept whiplash curves and sensuous colors as a bold new direction.

Frank Lloyd Wright

The H. C. Price Company Tower

In the early 1950s Frank Lloyd Wright also built his first, and only, freestanding skyscraper—the H. C. Price Company Tower (1953–56) in Bartlesville, Oklahoma. He had added a tower to the S. C. Johnson & Son Administration Building, but the smaller Price Tower was his only freestanding high-rise project.

Based on a 1929 proposal, the Price Tower is a residential and studio complex with double height and mezzanine spaces based on an interlocking plan of triangles and trapezoids and sheathed in copper panels, copper louvers, and glass. In the 1940s Wright had begun to investigate designing buildings as single geometric forms, such as triangle and arc; subsequently, he composed projects from repeated modular units such as triangle, hexagon, and circle. Price Tower was in this vein.

The furniture Wright designed for these spaces—in line with his goal of consistent, integrated, total design—was of cast aluminum in forms that reiterated the elements of the plan. The design of this furniture seemed at the time rather bizarre and unrealistically futuristic; yet it was to prefigure or, perhaps, serve as the basis for countless movies and television productions about outer-space travel twenty and thirty years later. His designs for other furniture, fabrics, and wallpapers were mass-marketed during the 1950s, but it was an homage rather than a financial venture.

The Guggenheim Museum

The decade closed with the death of Frank Lloyd Wright in April 1959, two months before his ninety-second birthday. His Guggenheim Museum (1943–60) was in construction and nearly finished, giving New York City a major building by Wright. A total design based on the circle inside and out, the poured-in-place concrete Guggenheim Museum has a breathtaking interior space (see Figure 139) that is one of the masterpieces of twentieth-century design—Philip Johnson called it one of the greatest rooms of the twentieth century.

The museum interior combines formalism and functionalism in its expanding spiral ramp, which is a single, continuous circular route along which artworks are displayed on the perimeter wall. Regardless of the controversial nature of the ramp as a way of seeing paintings and sculptures—and there are vehement opinions on both sides—the ramp is dynamic enough a line for the space to require no further ornamentation. A skylight-dome 92 feet above ground level relates the space to

139. Frank Lloyd Wright. Guggenheim Museum. New York City. 1943–60. *Photograph by Julius Shulman.*

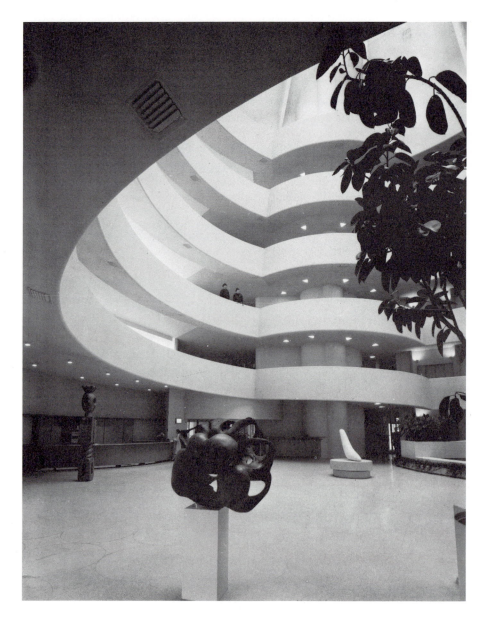

outdoor nature and light; though one can regret the pattern of the supporting ribs that the building code dictated, instead of Wright's proposed design of glass tubes, like those at the S. C. Johnson & Son Administration Building tower. Still, it is a major monument to the life and work of America's greatest architect, who lived long enough to see the triumph of Modern design, in a form different from what he envisioned yet of which he himself had been the American pioneer.

Suggested Reading

Ambasz, Emilio. *The Architecture of Luis Barragan*. New York: The Museum of Modern Art, 1976.

Baldwin, Billy. *Billy Baldwin Remembers*. New York: Harcourt Brace Jovanovich, 1974.

Banham, Reyner. *The Architecture of the Well-Tempered Environment*. London: The Architectural Press, 1969. Chicago: University of Chicago Press, 1969.

Bony, Anne. *Les Années 50*. Paris: Editions du Regard, 1982.

Brown, Erica. *Sixty Years of Interior Design: The World of McMillen*. New York: Viking Press, 1982.

Cook, Jeffrey. *The Architecture of Bruce Goff*. New York: Harper & Row, 1978.

Darling, Sharon. *Chicago Furniture: Art, Craft, and Industry 1833–1983*. New York: W. W. Norton, 1983.

DeLong, David. *The Architecture of Bruce Goff: Buildings and Projects 1916–1974*. London and New York, 1977.

Design Quarterly. "Nelson/Eames/Girard/Propst: The Design Process at Herman Miller." Minneapolis: Walker Art Center, 1975.

Dixon, John Morris. "Goff on Goff." *Progressive Architecture*. December 1962.

Drexler, Arthur. *Charles Eames*. New York: The Museum of Modern Art, 1973.

Dreyfuss, Henry. *Designing for People: Human Factors in Design*. New York: Simon & Schuster, 1955.

Emery, Sherman, ed. 50th Anniversary Issue, *Interior Design*. April 1982.

Futagawa, Yukio. *Bruce Goff: Bavinger House and Price House*. Tokyo: ADA Edita Tokyo, 1975.

Gueft, Olga. "Two Decades of Interiors: 1940–1960," *Interiors*. November 1960.

Hennessey, William J. *Russel Wright: American Designer*. Cambridge: MIT Press, 1983.

Herdeg, Klaus. *The Decorated Diagram: Harvard Architecture and the Failure of the Bauhaus Legacy*. Cambridge: MIT Press, 1983.

Hiesinger, Kathryn B., and George H. Marcus, eds. *Design Since 1945*. Philadelphia: The Philadelphia Museum of Art, 1983.

Il Design Italiano Degli Anni '50. Editore: IGIS Spa, 1981.

Jacobus, John M., Jr. "Postwar Architecture, 1945–60," *American Art*. New York: Prentice-Hall, Harry N. Abrams, 1979.

Jeanneret, Charles-Edouard. *Le Corbusier: 1910–65*. Zurich: Les Editions d'Architecture Zurich, 1967.

Mang, Karl. *History of Modern Furniture*. New York: Harry N. Abrams, 1979.

McCoy, Esther. *The Second Generation*. Layton, Utah: Gibbs M. Smith, 1984.

Meadmore, Clement. *The Modern Chair*. New York: Van Nostrand Reinhold, 1975.

Pinkham, Roger, ed. *Oliver Messel*, catalogue of an exhibition. London: Victoria and Albert Museum, 1983.

Rae, Christine. *Knoll au Louvre*. New York: Knoll International, 1971.

Robsjohn-Gibbings, T. H. *Homes of the Brave*. New York: Alfred A. Knopf, 1954.

Robsjohn-Gibbings, T. H., with Carlton W. Pullin. *The Furniture of Classical Greece*. New York: Alfred A. Knopf, 1963.

Smith, C. Ray. "Model of Office Planning," *Progressive Architecture*. March 1962, pp. 151ff. Executive Offices, Cowles Magazines, Inc., by Knoll Planning Unit.

———. "Offices for Irwin Miller in Columbus, Indiana, by Alexander Girard," *Progressive Architecture*. October 1962.

The Architecture of Skidmore, Owings & Merrill, 1950–1962. New York: Frederick A. Praeger, 1963.

Notes

1. Edgar Kaufmann, Jr., "Interior Design: Architecture or Decoration?" *Progressive Architecture* (October 1962), p. 144.

2. C. Ray Smith, "Model of Office Planning," *Progressive Architecture* (March 1962), pp. 151ff.

3. Since the Good Design shows were seen not only for six months at the Museum of Modern Art but also for six months subsequently at the Merchandise Mart in Chicago, they had considerable influence on the store buyers and professional designers who visited the Mart and its showrooms.

4. Jeffrey Cook's critical appraisal of Bruce Goff's work in the encyclopedia *Contemporary Architects* (New York: St. Martin's Press, 1980), p. 292.

5. Russel Wright, in a 1976 speech to the Society of Industrial Designers, quoted by William J. Hennessey in his illuminating exhibition catalogue *Russel Wright: American Designer* (Cambridge: MIT Press, 1983), p. 65.

6. Ibid., p. 86.

7. The conversation pit, used by many designers during the 1950s (see p. 221), became a motif of the decade.

8. Not many designers knew about Barragan during the 1950s. However, Benjamin Baldwin, Ward Bennett, and several others of their generation and older generations did become influenced by his work because they wintered in Mexico.

9. In England, scholarly studies about the Victorian age included John Steegman's *Consort of Taste* in 1950, Sir Nikolaus Pevsner's *High Victorian Design* in 1951, H. S. Goodhart-Rendel's Slade Lectures in 1953, and Henry-Russell Hitchcock's *Early Victorian Architecture*, which was published first in England in 1954. The Victorian Society was founded in England in 1958, and was followed later by a sister organization in America.

10. Michael Taylor, quoted from *The Finest Rooms by America's Great Decorators*, ed. Katharine Tweed (New York: Viking Press, 1964), p. 158.

11. Alexander Girard, quoted in textile designer Jack Lenor Larsen's splendid appraisal of Girard's work in "Nelson/Eames/Girard/Propst: The Design Process at Herman Miller," *Design Quarterly 98/99* (Minneapolis: Walker Art Center, 1975), p. 31.

12. Larsen, loc. cit.

Chapter **8**

1960–1970: The Third Generation

In the 1960s the interior design field grew almost explosively. Along with a continuing building boom, adequate design work was available to support hundreds, perhaps thousands of professional and semiprofessional designers, of all degrees of creativity, in both residential and nonresidential design projects. Nonresidential design came to be known as contract design. Among the technical advances, synthetic fibers and permanent forming or shaping of manmade textiles continued to influence interior designers, both in the direction of simplicity and in the direction of excess.

Stylistically, a few vanguard Modern interior designers further refined and simplified the International Style into what became known as Minimal design. At the same time, the mainstream of interior designers and decorators who could see the possibilities of new business began to accept and adopt the Modern idiom. Also at the same time, however, a group of vanguard architects began to rebel against established Modern aesthetics and started a new—a perverse and contradictory—design approach. It was a complex and multidirectional decade.

The Architectural Establishment

For mainstream Modern designers at the beginning of the 1960s, total design was the objective for buildings and interiors. The Seagram Building by Mies van der Rohe and Philip Johnson (1958) had been recognized as the pinnacle of International-Style achievement in America.

The Four Seasons Restaurant

The Four Seasons Restaurant (see color plate 8), which had opened on the ground floor of the Seagram Building in 1959, was the most accessibly beautiful interior of the High Modern/International Style idiom. Designed by Philip Johnson with a team of consultants—including decorator William Pahlmann, lighting designer Richard Kelly, industrial designer Garth Huxtable, landscape architect Karl Linn, and graphic designer Emil Antonucci—the Four Seasons reached a balance of machine-made and living objects, of rectangular and free-form design that gave it relaxation and repose, movement and stability all at the same time.

The restaurant is planned as two principal rooms (see Figure 140A)—the main dining room and the bar—in the low block at the base of the tower; the two rooms are connected by a glass-enclosed passageway off the rear of the building lobby. There, art collector Philip Johnson hung a stage curtain painted by Picasso. The main dining room is walled on two sides by the bronze and glass curtain wall of the building, on a third side by rosewood paneling, and on the fourth by panels of rawhide—a cream-colored leather with a pale onyx-like texture. In the center of the space is a raised and gently circulating 20-foot-square pool sheathed in white marble; at the corners of the pool huge ficus trees spread their canopies. At each window module a planter basket is suspended on piano wire at head height to give the room a further sense of enclosure and focus.

The Bar and Grill room, however, is the real pinnacle of late-Miesian elegance (see Figure 140B). One enters up a carpeted stair to a grand space; it has a luxurious square bar to the right of the stair, a seating and planted seating area to the left, and tables with Brno chairs straight ahead. Beyond the table area is a raised mezzanine or gallery for more tables that gives the room multilevels of activity. Walls are of rosewood paneling; the ceiling is a gridded system that incorporates the heating, ventilating, and air-conditioning system as well as lighting designed by Richard Kelly. A discontinuous sculpture of narrow brass rods and steel wires by Richard Lippold is suspended over the bar.

At the curtain-wall windows small strands of aluminum chain, which are anodyzed brass and copper fabricated by Marie Nichols, are swagged to create large-scale Austrian shades of chainmail. Thoroughly consistent with the concept of the Seagram Building, the window covering also offers the unexpected effect of movement: The heating in winter activates the chains in a rippling movement from the bottom of the windows to the top; in summer the air-conditioning moves the chains from top to bottom.

Furniture made by Knoll Associates includes Mies's Brno and Barcelona chairs, and adaptations of Saarinen's Pedestal Furniture. All appointments were custom-designed by Johnson and his team of consultants. Johnson had taken the Miesian idiom to a new level of decorative elaboration. It was masterfully elegant and luxurious; it was third-generation Modern design.

Skidmore, Owings & Merrill and Davis Allen

Throughout the 1960s Skidmore, Owings & Merrill (SOM) continued to design interiors of the greatest refinement. Davis Allen had moved from SOM's Chicago office to become senior interior designer in SOM's New York office after his designs for the Inland Steel Building.

In the New York office he was responsible for the design of interiors for the Chase Manhattan Bank headquarters (see Figure 141), which in 1961 set the standard for corporate interiors for the decade; and for the interiors of the Beinecke Rare Book Library (1963) at Yale University; the Marine Midland Bank Building (1967) in New York; and the Texas Bank & Trust Company Building (1969) in Dallas. His interiors for the Mauna Kae Beach Hotel (1965) in Hawaii created a

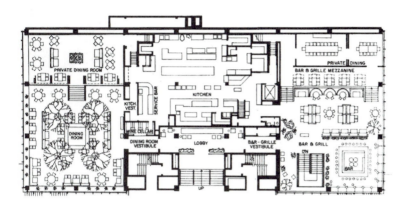

140A. Philip Johnson Associates. Plan, Four Seasons Restaurant. New York City. 1959. *Illustration from* Architectural Record *(November 1959).*

140B. Philip Johnson Associates. Bar and Grill room, Four Seasons Restaurant. New York City. 1959. *Photograph © Ezra Stoller/ESTO, 1959.*

new model for oriental regionalism with its combination of Modernism and country-style furnishings of willow and cane.

Beyond Mies: Girard's Colors and Crafts

In the early 1960s other Modernists developed approaches to Modern interior design beyond the Miesian idiom, but with a continuing goal of total design. In 1960 Alexander Girard, at perhaps the height of his career as an architect specializing in interior design and fabric design, designed La Fonda del Sol, a restaurant in the Rockefeller Center complex that offered South American cuisine.

141. Skidmore, Owings & Merrill. Chase Manhattan Bank headquarters. New York City. 1958–61. *Photograph by Alexandre Georges.*

Within the space, he created a bar in the form of an adobe building; it had a random pattern of windows, reminiscent of Le Corbusier's Chapel at Ronchamp, that were used as vitrines to display the folk-craft objects that Girard was collecting. The passage to the main dining room was through a cafeteria-like space with open-pit cooking tiled in vibrating patterns of tile and graphics that echoed the busyness of the cooking activities taking place there. In the main dining room diners were presented with a plan composed of arc-shaped alcoves—in the manner of Mies's Tugendhat House dining room—clustered around a central space; each alcove was upholstered in a different vibrantly colored or patterned fabric, and the chairs at the round tables were similarly multicolored with upholstery on their white plastic shells. The world of Op Art had come to interior design.

In 1961 Girard created the Textiles and Objects shop as a retail outlet in Manhattan for the Herman Miller furniture company. All white and glistening, with high-gloss enameled walls and ceiling, onto which specially designed silver-bowl lamp bulbs reflected light, the shop's plan (see Figure 142) offered free-flowing space in the manner of the Barcelona Pavilion, though at much tighter scale. Girard achieved that plan by suspending flat panels of his fabric designs from the ceiling in a maze effect (see Figure 143); the panels did not touch the white tile floor. Within the white envelope, the textiles—of brilliant and vibrating colors and of sheer transparent virtuosity—along with the objects—multicolored or shimmering metal folk handcraft from South America, India, and elsewhere—created a sensational expansion of the Miesian idiom. The imagery of folk crafts had been joined to industry.

In 1965, when Girard's corporate design program for Braniff International Airlines (see color plate 11) was introduced, it should have been no surprise to find all these elements combined into one package for a public commercial enterprise. But it was. Girard designed not only the airplane interiors with his blend of vibrating fabrics—each seat in a different pattern—but also the plane exteriors, which were each painted a brilliant solid color—yellow, purple, red, orange, or apple green. Girard also designed Braniff's ticketing offices and posters; and he coordinated a team of consultants who designed coordinated uniforms, plateware, and everything that customers identified with Braniff—even the baggage-pickup trucks on the field.

It was total environmental and graphic design—and significantly for industry and transportation—and it added multicolor, a folk-craft decorative theme, Op Art effects, and true elegance. This was a considerable achievement in view of the average thin theatricality of most commercial and industrial design of the day. In the early 1980s Alexander and Susan Girard gave their 100,000-piece folk-art collection to establish the Girard Wing of the Museum of International Folk Art in Santa Fe, New Mexico. Alexander Girard designed the wing and the exhibition of the collection.

Russel Wright's Shun Lee Dynasty Restaurant

Not entirely dissimilar in its remarkable combination of influences, the Shun Lee Dynasty Restaurant designed by Russel Wright opened in New York in 1966. It was Wright's last major commercial interior. The midtown Chinese restaurant, now demolished, was a dedicated Modernist's reinterpretation of Chinese tinsel glitter and flamboyant color. Chinese cultural elements were expressed in industrial materials as well as in common, unexpected Chinese artifacts.

Columns were covered in candy-apple vinyls, each side a different color—magenta pink, hot orange, royal blue, torrid purple, bright green, soft light blue, and chartreuse. Hot colors were on the entrance faces; cool colors led toward the exit. Inch-wide strips of gold vinyl tinsel composed curtains to divide alcoves for large tables. And an overhead wind chime, which also served as a focal chandelier, was composed of kappa shell, steel, and hundreds of Chinese toy animals, birds, dolls, fans, pom-poms, feather dusters, and coins of gold vinyl. All of this spun

142. Alexander Girard. Plan, Textiles and Objects Shop for Herman Miller Inc. New York City. 1961. *Illustration courtesy Herman Miller Inc.*

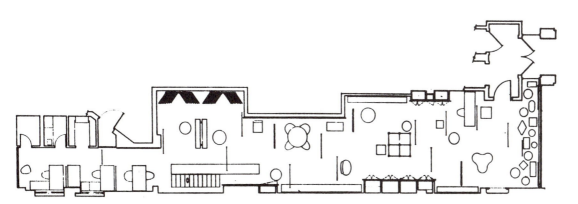

143. Alexander Girard. Textiles and Objects Shop for Herman Miller Inc. New York City. 1961. *Photograph by Todd Webb, courtesy Herman Miller Inc.*

around, swiveled, and tinkled in the air conditioning along with the gold-tinsel dividers and other elements. In addition, Russel Wright incorporated Chinese paper cutout animals and figures on window panels.

As might be expected from his career in designing dinnerware, Wright designed all the serving equipment and china. Black plates were provided for appetizers, turquoise for soups, burnt orange for entrees, and hot pink for desserts. Linen was gold- or lime-colored.

It all created a bright, shimmering, tinkling, Modern Chinese environment, a remarkable combination of modern materials and Chinese culture. As much as it expressed Russel Wright's interest in Chinese culture, it also spoke for the decade's reach for enrichment and for a greater humanistic regionalism beyond the machine aesthetic.

Saarinen's TWA Terminal

In 1962 Eero Saarinen's long-awaited sculptural TWA Terminal at JFK International Airport (then Idlewild Airport) in New York was finished (see Figure 144). Saarinen himself had died suddenly the year before. Cesar Pelli was the project designer for the terminal.

Sculptural furniture elements grow organically out of the floor. No distinction exists between architecture, interior design, and decoration. Only circulation graphics and other announcements stand as separate elements. Integral with the structure are signposts, seating units, counters, desks, and vertical units that integrate air-conditioning, heating, and lighting; all are both decorative and functional. Saarinen aimed for "the same integral character throughout the entire building so that all of the curvatures, all of the spaces, and all of the elements would have one consistent character." Sculptural forms synthesize the swift curves that were adopted "to catch the excitement of the trip."[1] Since more than two of these elements are seldom prominent from any single point, the overall space remains serene, as air flight at its ideal best.

144. Eero Saarinen & Associates. TWA Terminal, JFK International Airport. New York. 1962. *Photograph by Ezra Stoller Associates, courtesy TWA.*

Part of this effect in the TWA Terminal is due to the use of scale, part to a manipulation of color. The seemingly huge main space is 51 feet at its highest points, but this height is divided between two levels. A bridge bisects the main area and distinguishes the entrance lobby from the waiting room on the field side. Each space seems to have human scale, despite the vastness of the sculptural ceiling vaults. Color in the terminal, seemingly only off-white and charcoal, is withheld until, as one mounts the broad stair toward the field, a conversation-pit waiting lounge is gradually revealed—carpeted and upholstered in a rich red. The red seems to draw the pit-lounge together so that it coalesces, providing a calm and cozy oasis for travelers.

Furnishings in the terminal are composed of concrete, which was formed on the site, and of the same dime-size, white-with-gray-flecks ceramic tile finish that is used as the flooring. The functions of the furniture are, in some cases, multiple: Seating forms partitioning for some of the minor spaces, and it is used also to establish and control traffic patterns. The stairways from the mezzanine, for example, sweep down in flowing curves that double back to form the edges of a broader stair that leads down from the main waiting area. These same curves continue up the edges of lighting standards at the entrance to the baggage-claim area and the ticket lobby.

Counters and strip lighting emanate from the far side of the standards. The strip lighting (Stanley McCandless was the lighting consultant), which extends the length of the ticket lobbies, hangs free on wires above the counters. Both the standards and the bases of the counters are faced with the pervasive tile. Seating pieces are based on Saarinen's earlier Womb Chair and Sofa designs—upholstered pads rest in contoured niches. Everything bears witness to Saarinen's desire to have each element belong to "the same form-world."

Other Total Design Interiors

In 1964 Alvar Aalto completed his second project in the United States—the Edgar Kaufmann, Jr., Conference Rooms (see Figures 145A and B) at the Institute of International Education in New York City. There Aalto created a diagonally oriented small auditorium with adjacent conference rooms in the white birch–snowy forest imagery for which he had become renowned. He included a number of his other trademark motifs, notably the undulating ceiling, the vertically tiled walls, and the sculptural evocation of the Finnish woodland. Had he been headquartered in New York or Philadelphia, visibly and verbally more accessible to American designers, instead of being so distant in Helsinki, he might have been acclaimed as the most influential architect of the 1960s.

In 1965 Florence Knoll designed the executive offices in the CBS Building in the elegant Modern idiom she had so brilliantly refined with the Knoll Planning Unit. But here, for the board and waiting rooms, she included reproduction Louis XVI chairs in bleached wood and dark-brown leather. The rigid rules were being stretched.

Yet Modernism was being ever more broadly marketed to the general public—and with wide acceptance. Such stores as Design Research, which were design-directed by architect Benjamin Thompson, offered "good design" at reasonable prices—and with some invention. There the fabrics of Finland's Marimekko, with their bold superscale and bright flat colors, were introduced to the public. Design Research stores spread across the country, to be followed by other inexpensive

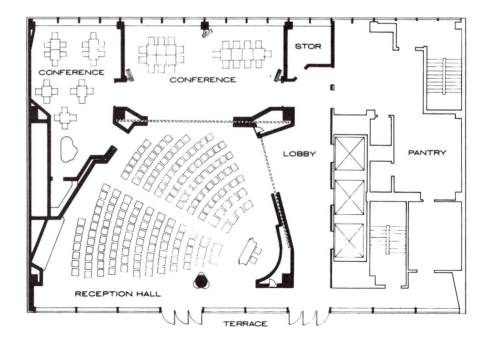

145A.   Alvar Aalto. Plan, Edgar Kaufmann, Jr., Conference Rooms. New York City. 1964. *Illustration from* Progressive Architecture (February 1965).

145B. Alvar Aalto. Edgar Kaufmann, Jr., Conference Rooms. New York City. 1964. *Photograph by Louis Reens, courtesy Institute of International Education.*

"good design" outlets such as Azuma and the Pottery Barn. It was all another evidence of the acceptance of Modernism.

Rudolph's Art and Architecture Interiors

Another total design structure had opened amid great fanfare in 1963—the Yale University Art and Architecture Building designed by Paul Rudolph. It was to become the most controversial building of the next twenty years.

Art and Architecture was a monumental building with great scale and powerful sculptural massing, constructed entirely of poured concrete that was finished with a rich, hitherto unseen ribbed texture, which was used consistently on both interior and exterior. Inside was an astonishing series of spatial varieties—changing levels, juxtaposed ceiling heights, small nooks adjacent to soaring spaces. The main drafting room for the architecture department (see Figure 146) was a vast two-story hall bridged by flying walkways, surrounded by balconies, providing low and middle-height spaces overlooking the central two-story hall. Skylighted wells rose two stories above, through the upper floors. The heating system fulfilled architects' dreams of integrating mechanical elements with structure—the main ducts were the hollow spaces in the four central piers at the corners of the drafting room.

Specially designed furniture, finished in brilliant orange, rested on flaming orange carpeting. Bare-bulb spotlights provided glittering illumination. Walls displayed ornamental details—plaster casts of Sullivan ornament and Assyrian friezes, of Greece and Rome—that prophesied the role of art in architecture for the next decade and the role of art history in architecture for the next two decades, at least. Such found Pop-like objects as cargo nets were used as window coverings. Murals, sculptures, and such poured-concrete details as the Modulor of Le Corbusier and feet-and-inch dimensions were integrated into the building. The detailing of the concrete revealed door bucks that were, instead of the common metal bucks, poured integrally into the structure.

It was one of the most creative and innovative structures—consistent in planning, structure, and detail, with the most complete integration of all the elements

146. Paul Rudolph. Architecture school drafting room, Yale University Art and Architecture Building. New Haven, Connecticut. 1963. *Photograph by Julius Shulman.*

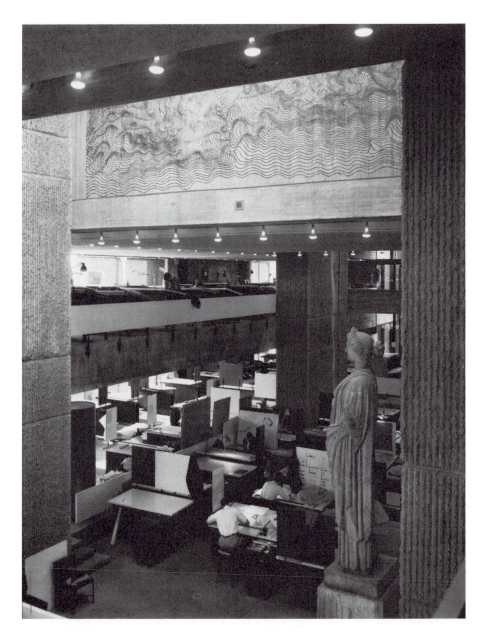

of architecture that had been seen in two decades, perhaps the most innovative and truly consistent building since Mies's Tugendhat House or Frank Lloyd Wright's Larkin Building. Mechanical systems, spaces, finishes, furnishings, and art program all proclaimed the Art and Architecture Building, to many observers, as most carefully designed and brilliantly inventive at every stage of the process and in every area of the building. It fulfilled a dream of the Modern movement as the total design building of its era. To some architects and designers it seemed like the second coming.

To the faculty and students who were using the building, however, it was another story—a failure, a nightmare, and a disaster. Several painters had moved out immediately, saying they could not work in the building; for them it had neither the traditionally desired illumination, nor a large freight elevator to move paintings up and down. Sculptors, moreover, were in the second basement under 7-foot ceilings and could not work on large vertical pieces; they too had no hoist to raise and lower their large and heavy materials. The print department, in the first basement, had no exhaust fans for their acid-reeking equipment; and the photography enlarger was in so low a space that it had to be laid horizontally and operated contrary to design.

Near the ground-floor entry to the Art and Architecture Building, a nautilus shell, cut in half with its delicate pinwheel of fins exposed, was embedded into the poured concrete, set into the monumental wall of massive concrete that rose crushingly eight stories above it. Observers dazzled by the virtuosity needed to preserve the delicate object throughout the process of pouring and curing the concrete may have also seen the feat as symbolic of the vanity of human wishes—fragility daringly exposed in the midst of irresistible force, the segment of pearly perfection innocently laid bare in the face of a rough and stony mass. Some of the faculty and students seemed to see the shell as a symbol of naive foolhardiness, inappropriateness, and something inevitably to be crushed—literally.

Within three years the interior was virtually unrecognizable—students had built squatter-like shacks as mini-environments—filled with cardboard, hanging bedsheets, and found objects, and covered with graffiti. In 1969 a mysterious, if not suspicious, fire tragically destroyed three upper floors of the building; and this was followed, even more tragically many felt, by an extensive rebuilding program, on which the original architect was never consulted.

A decade after the opening (1974–75), medical findings that asbestos was cancer-inducing caused a new scandal. The exposed asbestos ceilings, which had been installed throughout the building in the customary manner of the early 1960s, were torn out and new "improvements" made in what was, in effect, the third building program for Art and Architecture for a total of $1.5 million in slightly more than a decade. In this rebuilding, Rudolph's interior design concept was almost totally demolished.

Questioning the Modern Movement

Around 1963, then, the Modern movement began to be questioned. It was questioned not only by the general public, whose resistance to functional innovation and machine-made "coldness" had continued, but by professional designers as well. The Art and Architecture Building was not the only structure with problems. Louis Kahn's first great public acclaim from his Richards Medical Center laboratories in Philadelphia was simultaneously tarnished by the functional failures of its laboratories. Those failures were due to what the researchers considered small and inflexible spaces as well as to unshaded windows that, as in the Art and Architecture Building, caused "unbearable" glare and heat to build up. The High Modern movement began to seem suspect. Just as the public was coming to grips with Modern design, and the crusade for Modernism had been won, a professional segment began to question the very validity of the Modern movement. Indeed, from this time, we can date the beginning of what was ultimately seen as the failure of Modernism.

Integration of structural and mechanical systems, the consistent design of exterior and interior, along with the multiple and overlapping functions of these and other elements, were often achieved at the expense of efficient use and customary activity. Too often form followed only *design* function, not user function or activity function, and rarely psychological function. Innovation was more important to total designers than the cultural habits, traditions, and expectations of users or occupants of interiors and buildings. Brilliant as the best total design of the early 1960s was, the time had come to refocus design attention.

The Ford Foundation Building

Kevin Roche and John Dinkeloo completed the Ford Foundation Building in 1967, and Warren Platner achieved a new elegance in the design of its interiors (see

147. Roche, Dinkeloo Associates with Warren Platner. Executive office, Ford Foundation Building. New York City. 1967. *Photograph © Ezra Stoller/ESTO, 1967.*

Figure 147). At the center of the building is the celebrated 10-story landscaped atrium. In the surrounding offices, Platner designed elegant mahogany and bronze furniture, beige accordion-fold shades for the windows overlooking the atrium, and appointments of meticulous care and refinement. Even there, however, the level of elegance, the vast expenditure, and the degree of detail raised the question of conspicuous consumption, as Thorstein Veblen had earlier called such lavish spending.

Minimalism and Elegance

Earlier in the 1960s a group of vanguard designers of interiors developed a further refinement on the reductive or minimalistic approach of the International Style. Corresponding to a contemporaneous movement in sculpture by such Minimal sculptors as Sol LeWitt and Donald Judd, and influenced by the inspirational interiors of Mexican architect Luis Barragan, this new direction was to become a strong and widely accepted idiom in the 1970s. It was called Minimalism, or the Minimal school. Among the leaders were Benjamin Baldwin, Ward Bennett, and Nicos Zographos.

Their approach was to refine the Bauhaus principle "less is more" to its ultimate. For the Minimalists, "nothing was all." The Minimal approach could go almost unnoticed—especially by clients—since it looked effortless. Yet it was an elaborate undertaking, a kind of acrobatic prestidigital manipulation to conceal all elements into the smoothest, geometric forms that proclaimed the supremacy of technology and intellectual discipline. Whereas Bauhaus and 1930s designers ostensibly eliminated ornamentation, actually they had only simplified it. The Miesian idiom had restricted ornamentation to structural articulation. As one young student-architect said, "Even Mies had excess extrusions."

The Minimal style eliminated ornamentation even of this kind; it stripped nonessentials; minimized, miniaturized, or eliminated everything that might possibly be considered visually extraneous—joints, mechanical and electrical elements, reveals, moldings—and elements with duplicate functions. It produced simple white plaster boxes with broad expanses of plain surfaces—including bare floors, ceilings, and walls. Door and window openings were flush, frameless, and trimless—sliced severely into the planes. Window coverings were spare and ascetic.

These pure, "clean" envelopes depended on meticulous detailing to conceal functioning supportive systems. They were enriched only by natural-grown textures in deep wools, burl woods, veined marbles, and crisp Machine-Age furnishings that contrasted the natural-made with the products of industry. If there was an unrecognized antecedent of all this, it was the rarefied work of Jean-Michel Frank in the 1930s. The avowed aim was to focus on what is most variable in our environments: that is, on portable changeable objects, such as paintings, artworks, plants (often reduced to a single flower), and (ostensibly) people.

Ward Bennett

In 1961 Ward Bennett designed a suite of offices for L. J. Glickman in New York (see Figure 148). Bennett simplified the structure—furring out jogs in the walls and dropping the ceiling to conceal beams; he then unified the space with white walls and ceiling (including a white baseboard), buff-colored tile flooring, off-white draperies over a transparent interior partition, and white vertical blinds over

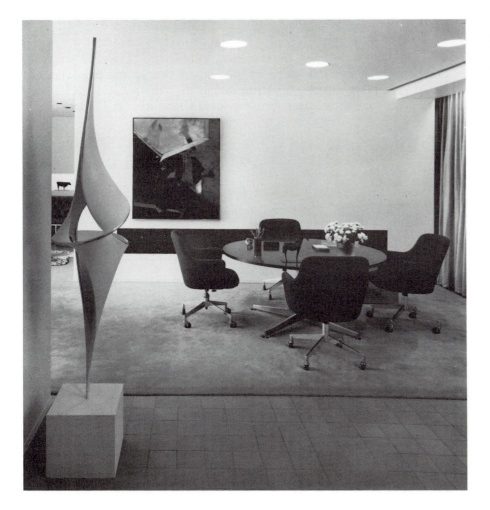

148. Ward Bennett. L. J. Glickman offices. New York City. 1961. *Photograph by Louis Reens.*

the window that afforded a view of the New York Public Library and its surrounding greenery. A sand-colored carpet was laid over the central work area, which also served as a dining area; it distinguished the functions of these areas from the entranceway and from a banquetted alcove for more relaxed conferences.

Within this background Bennett placed stainless-steel and richly grained elm-burl tables and cabinetwork of his own design. He lined the alcove with banquettes upholstered in natural glove leather, and at the desk and trestle table placed his Column-X chairs, upholstered in the clear blue that, Bennett felt, Braque often used. Notable was the unabashed inclusion of stainless-steel units for communication and controls of lighting and draperies; these Machine-Age units amid the more luxurious furnishings prefigured the contradictory juxtapositions of later Minimalism. Most of the furnishings were designed by Bennett, from built-ins and furniture to doorknobs, drawer pulls, and accessories.

The total effect was spare and cool, but it was the orchestration of the design within this minimal palette that was notable at the time: soft, warm textures against smooth, shiny surfaces; strong bright colors against a monochromatic beige-and-white background; patterns against plain materials; and the severe, machine-art statement of the communications and control equipment against the individualistic, romantic expressions of the artworks, which Bennett inspired the client to choose. The office was refined and graceful, yet patently masculine, owing to its spare—minimal—approach. From then on Ward Bennett produced a continually expanding line of chairs and tables of considerable elegance that soon became staples of twentieth-century interior design.

Benjamin Baldwin

Benjamin Baldwin was a leader in this idiom, with designs of rarefied simplicity yet uncommon humanism. Working virtually on his own, he was almost oriental in his purity and his connoisseur's discrimination. His combination of the Minimal approach with a sophisticated casualness produced utmost serenity. These qualities

149. Benjamin Baldwin. Own apartment. New York City. 1964. *Photograph by Louis Reens.*

made him sought-after as a collaborator by such architects as Edward Larrabee Barnes, for the Cowles residence in Wayzata, Minnesota (1964); I. M. Pei, for the Charles and Ann Tandy residence in Fort Worth, Texas (1970); and Louis Kahn, for the library at Philips Exeter Academy (1967–72) and subsequently for the Mellon Center for British Art at Yale University (1969–74).

In a Minimal apartment (see Figure 149) Benjamin Baldwin designed for his own use in New York City in 1964, the interplay of rectangular wall planes with paintings was the strong yet subtle design force. Broad, ceiling-height doors pivoted back against storage cores like unnoticeable walls; planes met without reveals; nearly invisible narrow-slatted, undraped venetian blinds served as the only window coverings; the sofa was a frameless, built-in nook, carpeted and filled with loose pillows. The alignment of the linear elements was meticulous, and furniture was kept to a minimum—yet as he changed it, the furniture could reflect eons of world culture in its eclectic sparseness.

His own house and garden in East Hampton, Long Island (1967), became a mecca for Minimalist designers (see Chapter 9). "My work in interior design expresses my opposition to the chaotic world man creates," he wrote. "It is a constant search for the calm tranquility one finds in nature. . . . In nature I find a sense of order—logical and lyrical—which I would like my work to express."[2]

Nicos Zographos

Also in the Minimal idiom, Nicos Zographos—a designer of both furniture and interiors—designed an office for the New York advertising agency Papert, Koenig, Lois (1966) that retained some functionalist structural articulation, but that distilled and refined it to an almost surreal essence.

Even the most luxurious executive spaces had no overlay of so-called elegance—no carpets, no draperies. In the office of partner George Lois (see Figure 150), bare wood floors, windows bare except for venetian blinds, and a column-mounted marble desk were enlivened by the sculptural effects of Marcel Breuer's Wassily chairs, cube occasional tables, and—seen through a floor-to-ceiling frameless smoked-glass partition—a tree next to the cylindrical plaster balustrade of a stair to the floor below. Zographos commented that "this design is romantic in its way: It is a throwback to the early days of the Bauhaus, but brought up to date."[3] These offices were startling for their evocation of 1920s Bauhaus imagery.

The Paradox of Minimalist Simplicity

That such opulence could be created from simplicity and that simplicity could be achieved by complex detailing are the paradoxes of the Miesian and Minimal idioms. As the boldest illustration of this effort, the invisible use of marble as the baseboard in SOM's Banque Lambert penthouse of 1965 in Brussels is the most elaborately minimal detail.

Designed by Jack Dunbar of SOM's New York office in 1965, white plaster walls appear to come down to the travertine floor line. But since a plaster base would be impractical for cleaning, the baseboard was actually white marble—white marble painted white to match the plaster wall. If the white paint chipped, went the thinking, then the white marble underneath would still appear continuous with the plaster walls until repainting. One further point about the baseboard demonstrated the difference between Miesian and Minimalist detailing: No reveal or scored line was used between plaster and marble to denote a change of materials; no spacer or recess connects baseboard to floor. It had been time for a change, at least for this refinement. SOM's chief New York designer, architect Gordon Bunshaft, said, "Maybe in the past we used to have too many notches."[4]

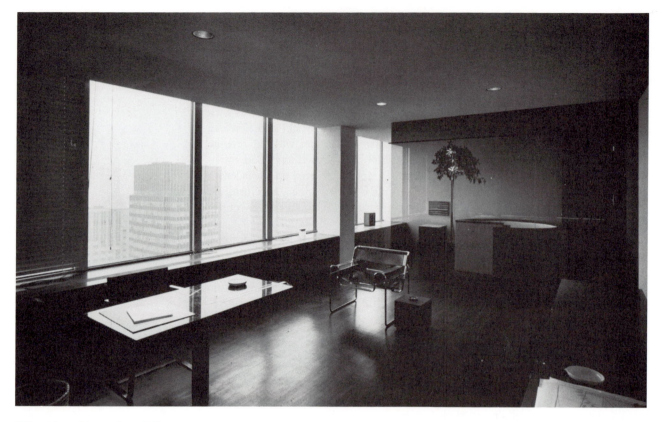

150. Nicos Zographos. Offices of Papert, Koenig, Lois, Inc. New York City. 1966. *Photograph by Carl Fischer.*

The purgative austerity of the post-Beaux-Arts period produced the Minimalist idiom, whose keynote word was "simplicity." What Minimalist designers aimed to provide was purer, clearer, cleaner visual scenes for our Athenian delectation. What they designed were simple geometric forms, "similar glass cages for dissimilar uses,"[5] isolated each from each, surrounded by as much space as possible, increasingly flatter, cleaner, textureless of elevation, accented only by some token artwork. This was the Minimalist refinement of Bauhaus goals—and perhaps the highest realization of them—in the 1960s.

The Residential Designers

For traditional interior designers, also, the scope of work increased during the 1960s. It encompassed corporate planning, the design of large office complexes, whole chains of hotels, and important public buildings as well as residential work in America and abroad for the very affluent. Many of these firms organized separate departments to do contract work—including McMillen Inc.

Decorators by and large continued the tradition of historicism and the application of printed and painted ornament—as the last vestige of the Beaux-Arts. At its most refined, decorating in America offered continuing elegance. Among many others, McMillen Inc. (see color plate 9) and Thedlow Inc. in New York City, and Michael Taylor and John Dickinson in California, worked a widely appealing kind of magic.

During the early 1960s Mrs. Henry Parish II was at work on refurbishing the White House (see Figure 151) for President and Mrs. Kennedy in a style far more appropriate than the mansion had seen for decades. Based on the idea of historical restoration, her scheme envisioned assembling American pieces to make the White House a museum-worthy display of late-eighteenth- and early-nineteenth-century

American interior design—the period when the house was built. About this time Albert Hadley joined her as partner to form Parish-Hadley.

Billy Baldwin

Billy Baldwin was at the peak of his career in the 1960s, designing houses and apartments, hotel suites, the Round Hill Club in Greenwich, Connecticut, and a hair salon for Mr. Kenneth in New York.

In 1963, for his own apartment (see color plate 10) Baldwin used high-gloss brown lacquered walls, a bare wood floor, and dark-brown raw-silk roman shades. A Korean lacquer screen was the background for cream-colored raw-silk upholstery, fur throws, feather arrangements in vases, and appointments of brass and bone, tortoiseshell and bamboo. The textural orchestration was rich and warming, refined and elegant; the apartment became a touchstone of the elegance of the decade. In another decade he would lighten the scheme further, in the use of both colors and textures.

Billy Baldwin had popularized Indian paisley walls, plaid rugs and upholstery, Matisse-inspired fabrics and wallpapers (see Figure 152), and pattern on pattern. He had decorated residences for Billy Rose, Mary Wells Lawrence, the Paul Mellons, Mollie Parnis, and Diana Vreeland. It was the last decade of his active career—he retired in 1972—but his influence was considerable.

Barbara D'Arcy

Barbara D'Arcy was jamming traffic with her model rooms, in every conceivable style, at Bloomingdale's. Not since William Pahlmann's model rooms in the 1930s and 1940s at Lord & Taylor had the public been so drawn.

Barbara D'Arcy's model rooms established a new popularity and merchandising viability for furniture and interior design. Detached from live-in clients, since they are residences without residents, her model room designs nevertheless opened the eyes of the public to the potential variety in interior design. They were regularly considered news by the daily papers, both for their commercial aspects and for the

152. Billy Baldwin. Living room with chintz pattern taken from a Matisse drawing; manufactured by Woodson Fabrics. New York City. Circa 1965. *Photograph by Horst from Billy Baldwin*, Billy Baldwin Decorates *(New York: Holt, Rinehart and Winston, 1972).*

stylistic flair that Barbara D'Arcy brought to them—sometimes Mediterranean in flavor with simulated hand-hewn beams; sometimes glitzy silver mylar spaceship imagery; sometimes pure Williamsburg historical tradition. D'Arcy presented a compendium of interior styles to reach out and appeal to as broad a market as possible.

The New Young Decorators

Other prominent American decorators of the decade included Ellen Lehman McCluskey, Melanie Kahane, Tom Lee, Joseph Braswell, and Inman Cook. In addition to those established decorators, a younger group of decorators began to be noticed. Among them were Edward Zajac, Richard Callahan, Angelo Donghia, Tom Britt, Robert Denning, and Vincent Fourcade. These new decorators, in their reduplicated historicism, seemed to echo the outrageousness of the decade—but with a sense of opulence and, even, magnificence.

Zajac & Callahan   Edward Zajac and Richard Callahan formed Zajac & Callahan in 1964 and began to demonstrate their eclectic and multilayered style. Edward Zajac (1932–) was born in Camden, New Jersey, and completed his design studies at the Parsons School in 1956. He first worked for McMillen Inc. for two years, then for Baldwin & Martin for seven years. Richard Callahan (1936–) was born in Manhasset, Long Island, and completed his design studies at the Parsons School in 1956, in the same class with Zajac. Callahan first worked with Jansen Inc. for three years and then with Valerian Rybar for four years.

During the 1960s, in addition to residences in New York and Dallas, they designed shops across the country for Splendiferous; Bendel's Fancy at Henri Bendel in New York; and apartments for the Albert Nippons, Mike Nichols, and Mr. and Mrs. Claude Giroux in Paris.

Angelo Donghia   Zajac & Callahan's Parsons classmate Angelo Donghia (1935–85), who had apprenticed with Yale Burge, won immediate acclaim for a model room with deep-blue gloss walls and white upholstered furniture. Donghia was to go on to become one of the prominent interior designers and furnishings designers of the next two decades.

Denning & Fourcade   The firm formed by Robert Denning and Vincent Fourcade also began to attract attention in the early 1960s. Robert Denning had worked with fashion and furnishings photographer Edgar D'Evia; Vincent Fourcade had moved from Paris to New York in the 1950s. Together they began an extraordinary new imagery: It was multilayered, multipatterned, becarpeted, and oversized, and appointed with clusters of bronzes and large oriental porcelains (see Figure 153). Their own offices were covered in oriental carpets—on floors and tables and as upholstery. They were to go on to do museum-quality work for some of the most affluent private clients in the next decade.

Other Designers   Other decorators began to catch up with the crusade of the Modern movement. They recognized the value of the increasing quantities of furniture in the Modern idiom and got into the mainstream of the age's office design—banishing ornamentation along with the clean sweep of the Modern idiom. They could do so because general merchandising had also begun to feature Modern design across the board. And "good design" shops such as Design Research, the Pottery Barn, and others were spreading industrial design and Modern design throughout the country. New furniture from Italy—including the designs of Carlo Scarpa, the Castiglione brothers, and others—was also beginning to have a profound influence on the vision of interior designers.

But just as this was happening, a small group of vanguard Modern architects was beginning to espouse decoration, ornamentation, and history. Once again, just when the two fields were veering toward a meeting of minds and directions, architecture and decorating went off in opposite directions. It seemed a frustrating if understandable event in light of the complex and contradictory expansions and investigations throughout the world during this decade.

153. Denning & Fourcade. Apartment for Vincent Fourcade. New York City. Circa 1960. *Photograph courtesy Denning & Fourcade.*

Design: Expansion and Revolution

An Expansion of Design Services

Throughout the 1960s, expansion was in the air—in the interior design field as well as in outer-space exploration. For interior designers this meant expansion of practice, expansion of contract work, and expansion in the use of materials and technology. The subcategorization of the design process accompanied an expansion in the number of consultant specialists available to interior design projects—lighting designers, acoustical designers, systems analysts, and many more. This expansion also included the closer alliance of interior design educators with the activities of the profession; the Interior Design Educators Council (IDEC) was founded in 1962 to achieve this goal. IDEC led to the creation of the Foundation for Interior Design Education Research (FIDER), which evaluates educational programs in interior design.

A Stylistic Revolution

The decade's expansionism soon led to a stylistic revolution as well. That change was generational and ideological before it was stylistic. Activism and involvement were the new passions, as well as the new passwords. Youth, now the majority of the population, assertively took part in the decisions and actions of the day. Social and political issues captured their concern—areas unrelated to formal or even nonformal design. Activism centered on the antiwar movement, on drugs and rock music, and on "doing your own thing."

The result was a design approach and a style based on the vision of the eighteen- to twenty-five-year-old age group. Economics made this possible, and the marketplace took advantage of, or played to, this new audience opportunity. All this led to a diversity of approaches in the design professions.

In the design fields this decade's revolution was initiated by architects and architecture students. Since many of these design revolutionaries were of a new generation with young practices, their innovations were demonstrated most strongly in interior designs. The 1960s design revolution was not an even, consistent movement with a single thrust—any more than any other twentieth-century design movement, since individuals of leadership and genius make up movements. Nor was there a unified view of style and technology. Architects and designers who were concerned about matters of form and style were usually not equally concerned about expansion of practice, about process as much as product, or about technology and materials. Nevertheless, the fundamental direction of growth and expansion was consistent in those concerned with practice and those concerned with vision.

Perhaps behind it all was the expansion of acceptable possibility and the expansion of scale that the decade's space exploration program brought about—or at least directly influenced. Space exploration was reaching for the moon, and throughout the decade youngsters especially believed that virtually anything was possible. The spokesmen and the leaders—Robert Venturi, Charles Moore, Philip Johnson, and Paul Rudolph—were as much as a decade older; but the newness of their rebellion and the adventuresomeness of their frontier gave it all a consistently youthful outlook and appearance.

This third generation of Modern architects and interior designers, who reflected these new attitudes in their theory and formal designs, was a new breed that rebelled against "the uptight formality of the past," which they believed had produced the uninspired, copybook curtain-wall towers. This new generation reacted against the unrelated nature of such freestanding buildings, since they stood on isolating podiums and plazas. They rebelled against static and fixed furniture and against refined preciousness—against the "design gestapo" regimentation of many established designers. Instead, vanguard designers in the 1960s showed greater interest in furniture systems that involved users and were adaptable to the psychological as well as the physical requirements of an environment and of activities.

The new designers rejected the uptight, packaged formality of the past—the Minimalist purity that had created monotonous, sterilized, easy-to-copy-badly pigeon crates and that seemed to negate the sumptuous and exquisite monuments produced in the idiom. They rebelled against the pure, clean, off-white and beige rectilinear designs that had been the established tradition for over a decade. To the designers of that tradition, tidy "tastefulness" had been the goal. To the new designer of the 1960s, tastefulness was a dirty word. Their new approach was an irreverent rebellion against the design establishment.

Paradoxically, then, around 1962—just when increasing numbers of traditional designers of residences and offices were adopting the Modern movement and espousing its taboos against historicism and decoration—along came a whole new school of vanguard architects who, in the rebellion of their generation to find something new for themselves, began to reject Modernism and overthrow its taboos. They espoused both historicism and ornamentation once again.

Supermannerism   Formally and stylistically, this rebellious vanguard presented a wider range of visual experience as candidates for our design vocabulary—it included more effects by which design could arrest our accustomed and habitually unseeing eyes. Also included, once again, were historical traditions such as decoration, applied pattern, and ornament. This revolution thereby aggressively adopted and espoused the very sacred taboos of the International Style. Areas previously considered undesigned and unworthy of designers' attentions, such as the influence of our commercial and roadside environments, were also part of this revolution. Among its new attitudes were permissiveness and chaos; whimsy and humor; synthetic and commercial allusions; ambiguity and invisibility; superscale, supergraphics, and superimposition. The relationships between this approach and Existentialism and the Theater of the Absurd are only beginning to be explored. During 1961–62, the two protagonists of this vanguard movement in architecture, Robert Venturi and Charles W. Moore, each designed houses that became the manifestos of their credo.

Robert Venturi

Born in Philadelphia, Robert Venturi (1925–) studied architecture at Princeton University, where he received his master's degree in architecture in 1950. Subsequently, he worked for Eero Saarinen and then for Louis Kahn. In 1958 he opened his own practice, first with partner William Short, and in 1964 with John Rauch; the firm became known as Venturi, Rauch & Scott-Brown when planner Denise Scott-Brown (Mrs. Venturi) became a partner.

The foremost design theorist of his generation, Robert Venturi made his thinking generally available with the publication of his book *Complexity and Contradiction in Architecture* by New York's Museum of Modern Art in 1966. He proclaimed in his opening chapter—"A Gentle Manifesto"—"I welcome the problems and exploit the uncertainties. By embracing contradiction as well as complexity, I aim for vitality as well as validity."[6]

Venturi also aimed to include in formal design a number of attitudes that he insisted prevailed in contemporary life, especially ambiguity and duality. He included contradictions as potentials of architecture, and acclaimed the inclusive dualities of "both/and" rather than "either/or," which had been the attitude of High Modernism. In his interior renovation of New York University's Institute of Fine Art, which is located in the Duke House of 1912, designed in the Louis XVI style by

Horace Trumbauer, Venturi included industrilly produced, non-high-style-design metal bookshelves juxtaposed to the Louis XVI woodwork. The metal shelving included "the undesigned," as Venturi deemed it, into his concept; and the juxtaposition with the classical detailing created a complex contradiction of "both/and" that was fundamental to Venturi's new vision of design.

The Chestnut Hill House   In 1962 Venturi designed a house in Chestnut Hill, Pennsylvania, outside Philadelphia for his mother. The house is a simple-looking building on a suburban lot. Its overall form is that of a gabled and chimneyed cottage, but Venturi twisted it around in plan and put the entrance on the gable side. Whimsically, the Palladian hallmark—the arched window—is alluded to by a broken arch of tacked-on wood trim. This and other details are historical allusions—typical of the allusions to Mannerist architecture that Venturi espoused—and they were used by Venturi ironically, sardonically, and perhaps perversely.

Inside the Chestnut Hill House the rectangular plan (see Figure 154A) is spiked with diagonals—at the entry, into other rooms, and at the fireplace and stair plans. The entry funnels circulation into the dining area, straightforwardly past the kitchen, and past the adjacent stair to the second floor. The stair and kitchen walls are inflected, to use Venturi's term, like directional signals to lead occupants and to accommodate their movement. In section, the dining room ceiling is a half barrel vault, echoing the arch motif above the main entry. Light streams in through oddly, distinctively placed monitors. Moldings are used decoratively; yet they are chopped off in a way that seems strange, but in fact recalls the sliced moldings of seventeenth- and eighteenth-century Mannerist and Baroque architecture. Above the bookcases in the living room (see Figure 154B), a valance of flat arches does not spring from the vertical supports of the bookcase.

Finally, the furnishings indicated a new attitude on the part of Modernists: Old furniture previously owned by the client was accepted—recycled—into the radical new design, was accommodated by the new design. In this way Venturi showed his intention to accept both the historical continuity and the activity patterns and desires of his client. Formerly, in the High Modern mode, the reuse of such furniture would have been considered an unfortunate allocation of the budget. Only new, consistent Modern furniture would have been acceptable to that total-design approach. Venturi expressed a new attitude—historical continuity; accommodation of the actual uses and desires of occupants; inconsistency as a fact of real life; and acceptance of common, undesigned items within a designed framework.

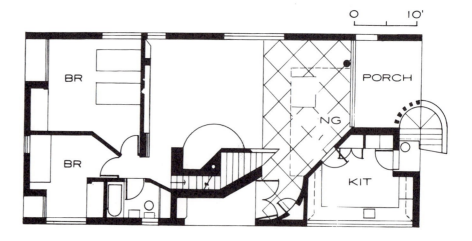

154A.   Venturi & Rauch. Plan, Venturi House. Chestnut Hill, Pennsylvania. 1962. *Illustration from* Progressive Architecture *(May 1965).*

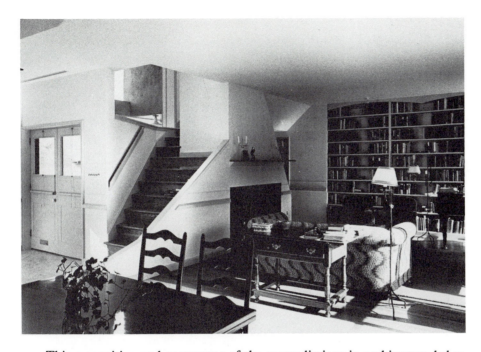

154B. Venturi & Rauch. Entry and living room, Venturi House. Chestnut Hill, Pennsylvania. 1962. *Photograph by Rollin R. La France.*

This recognition and acceptance of the contradictions in architecture led to his new and complex view of how the design professions could be more in step with the realities of actual use by people. But non-use by people was also demonstrated in a stair that led nowhere, in illustration of our alienation and frustration and, perhaps, of our continual reaching for the stars.

Charles W. Moore

One of the most facile and productive designers of his generation, Charles W. Moore (1925–) was born in Benton Harbor, Michigan. He received a bachelor's degree in architecture at the University of Michigan in 1947, and taught for two years before going to Korea with the U.S. Army Corps of Engineers. Thereafter he studied at Princeton University with Louis Kahn, taking a master's degree in 1956 and a doctorate in 1957. From 1957 to 1959 he taught at Princeton, and from 1960 to 1965 he taught at the University of California at Berkeley and practiced in the partnership Moore, Lyndon, Turnbull, Whitaker, which included two of his former students as partners. In 1965 he assumed the chairmanship of the Department of Architecture at Yale University, following Paul Rudolph.

He moved his practice to New Haven, Connecticut, and continued (with various partners and colleagues in San Francisco and Connecticut) to design and build over a hundred houses and numerous other structures in the next decade. In the activity of his fertile design facility and in his teaching, he brought a witty, colorful, and informal atmosphere to the complex attitudes of his generation. More than all the others, perhaps, Moore jangled the establishment by espousing the taboo that Modern design most vehemently rejected—decoration.

Moore's Orinda House In 1962 Charles Moore designed and built a house for himself in Orinda, California, that became another exemplar of the new design movement (see Figure 155A). The house has a simple rectangular plan and plain white wood siding; its roof is pyramidal, with a monitor or skylight running along the long ridge.

The outside is simple, although the enclosing walls are hung in sections on barn-door tracks so that they can be slid along to open up the house to the outside.

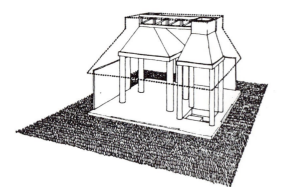

155A. Moore, Lyndon, Turnbull, Whitaker. Perspective section, Moore House. Orinda, California. 1962.

155B. Moore, Lyndon, Turnbull, Whitaker. Interior domed
bathing area. Moore House.
Orinda, California. 1962. *Photograph by Morley Baer.*

On this square structure no two façades are identical, yet it is so foursquare that
found-object molds for waterworks equipment, used as exterior sculptures, seem
almost free-form by contrast.

Inside, however, Moore's Orinda house was another story. Within the single
large space, which was painted pale hospital green or "eye-ease green," are two
pyramidal domes, each resting on four 10-foot-high Tuscan columns that were
salvaged and recycled from a San Francisco demolition. They define two square
areas—a living area or conversation pit under the larger dome and a sunken tub
and shower under the smaller (see Figure 155B). Because these two areas are off-
center and nonaligned, the smaller dome leans in toward the middle to reach into
the rectangular skylight; the larger dome leans toward one end of the skylight.
The domes are asymmetrical statements of the roof form. Like inverted funnels,
they pull light down onto the areas they define. They and their supporting columns
also compose rooms-within-rooms.

Around and between the domes, the space is open. During the day, sunlight
moves across the space, picking up the ceiling, the mauve and magenta paint on
the column capitals, the vibrant blue fascia, the soft putty-green walls, and the
dark floor.

The furnishings were casual, found, undesigned, accommodating pieces—
items collected on Moore's personal travels—Mexican pottery, Indian brass candlesticks, Peruvian rugs—and director's chairs, lamps with shades, ordinary found
objects. These things had association and meaning for him (and they also had a
quality of visual excellence because of his designer's eye)—things that Elsie de
Wolfe and the Modernists alike had banished from residential design.

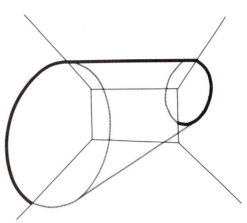

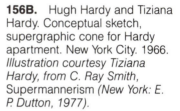

156A. Hugh Hardy and Tiziana Hardy. Supergraphic cone, Hardy apartment. New York City. 1966. *Photograph by Louis Reens.*

156B. Hugh Hardy and Tiziana Hardy. Conceptual sketch, supergraphic cone for Hardy apartment. New York City. 1966. *Illustration courtesy Tiziana Hardy, from C. Ray Smith,* Supermannerism *(New York: E. P. Dutton, 1977).*

This was the inclusive and accommodating view of this new generation of design revolutionaries. Besides bringing design closer in line with the understanding and desires of ordinary people—in a rejection of design for designers' sakes—the attitude was permissive, witty, and flagrantly flaunting historical allusion and ornamentation, the taboos of Modernism.

Other Designers

Hugh Hardy Another young architect, Hugh Hardy, demonstrated this more inclusive view with the recycling of a number of old buildings for new functions. Among them were some new theaters that had new kinds of audience-performer relationships—irregular, faceted, and unequal groupings of audience seating that offered what Hardy viewed as the corresponding vision of the day—random viewing, like television and the movies. It was a view of the live theater that aimed for the kind of overlaid vision, multiple vantage points, and all-around interaction that we see in flashbacks, crosscuts, and other film techniques.

Hardy's residential interiors (see Figures 156A and B) also showed a use of multiple vision and overlaid decoration; for example, mirrors overlaid with stripes, laissez-faire acceptance of reality (exposed electrical cables), painted and applied decoration, and other pranksterish tricks. Among the alleged "spatial investigations" were a number of fragments of geometric forms—circles and cones, predominantly—that Hardy and his partners in Hardy Holzman Pfeiffer Associates painted onto wall and ceiling surfaces. They were large-scale decorative stripes, which thumbed the nose at the taboo of Modernism against decoration. But as abstract painted fragments—which the best of them were—the viewer completed them mentally to make an even larger element. At their best, these decorations produced the effect of two simultaneously different visions for the viewer—one at human perspective, the other looking down from the skies. These came to be known as supergraphics, which were popularized in the last years of the 1960s.

157. Philip Johnson. Foyer, New York State Theater. New York City. 1964. *Photograph by Louis Reens.*

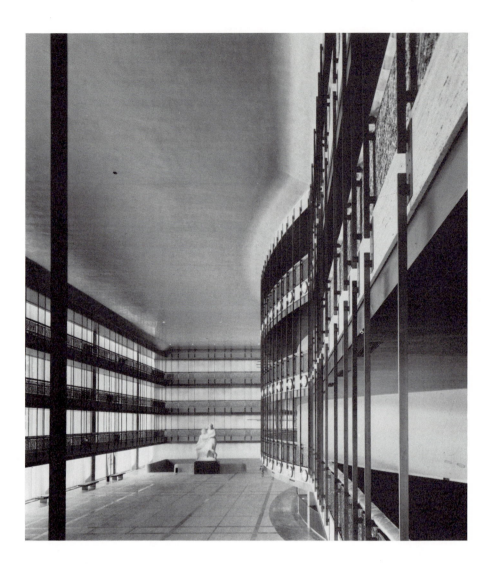

Barbara Stauffacher   Among the most flamboyant of these supergraphics were the painted stripes designed in 1967 by Barbara Stauffacher for Athletic Club Number One (see color plate 12), which was designed by Moore, Lyndon, Turnbull, Whitaker at Sea Ranch, in California. Part roadside caution stripes, part circulation graphics, part scale investigation, and all a decorative scheme to salvage a cut budget, these paintings were recognized as the ultimate overthrow of the Modernist taboo against decoration.

Philip Johnson

Philip Johnson had been prominent in the move away from the High Modern idiom. In 1964 he completed the New York State Theater at Lincoln Center—a design he intended to be the first monumental interior in the Pop Art idiom. Its auditorium was a reinterpretation of the nineteenth-century horseshoe auditorium—but in Pop materials—perforated metal, superscale lights, and Harry Bertoia–inspired metal lattice work. The foyer of the New York State Theater (see Figure 157) is one of the grandest and most handsome rooms in this idiom of breaking away from the Modern movement. Its surrounding balconies reminded some people of a jail, to which Johnson replied, "Yes, I saw it in a jail, and I liked it." Mies would not have understood the joke.

In 1966, with the wryest laugh of all, Johnson designed another handsome, classic room in the Miesian idiom, but sent it sky high. At first glance, the Founders Room (see Figure 158) atop Johnson's annex to the Museum of Modern Art in New York appears to be merely a domed version of the Miesian idiom that Johnson mastered so well. An exposed I-beam structure of modular bays apparently supports plaster Gothic vaults lighted with strips of exposed, unfrosted incandescent lamps. The immediate effect is a combination of Mies, Gothic, and a carnival midway of the Gay Nineties. But as the eye follows the steelwork downward, we see that the structure simply stops—a foot-and-a-half above the floor. It is, quite literally, a Miesian take-off—or lift-off. It gets off the ground because it has inverted the Miesian idiom by bringing it indoors and using it frankly as decoration. It was camp Mies.

A Diversity of Directions

By the mid-1960s, therefore, the Minimalist, purgative, exclusivist approach that had been the mainstream of the International Style was challenged by a counter-movement—one that waggishly, rebelliously raised an elaborately ornamented head—a decidedly un-minimal head. That movement was expansive, inclusive, and highly mannered. With cries of "shame," "ghastly chaos," and "trivial fad" ringing through the design establishment, a new breed of designer began to appear.

Their new approach espoused new attitudes toward design and living. It aimed to include speed and motion as well as monumental stillness; to include the boring as well as the interesting; nudity, profanity, and scandal as well as the polite and the decorous. The new approach also accepted additional formal devices: the diagonal as well as the rectangle and the square; and the influence of our often anonymous commercial environment on our designed environment. Just as early Modern designers discovered industrial factory buildings as a source of inspiration, designers in the 1960s spent time studying "roadside America," as Robert Venturi called it.

158. Philip Johnson. Founders Room, The Museum of Modern Art. New York City. 1967. *Photograph by Louis Reens.*

The diversity of directions—also called inclusiveness and pluralism—was indicated not only by these stylistic inclusions and expansions; it was also seen in the interest in structural process and construction technology—in prefabricated boxes to be used as housing units. The foremost example of this was Habitat, a hill-like town composed of prefabricated concrete boxes designed by Moshe Safdie for the Montreal Expo 67. These structural and architectural solutions, however, led to no advances in interior design.

Among expanded design services, financing was included, making the designer part of the client-entrepreneurial team. John Portman in 1967 completed the Hyatt Regency hotel in Atlanta, Georgia—not only as its architect, but as part-owner of the scheme, which he initiated. The "people-space" of the multistory, glass-enclosed atrium that was the center of the hotel scheme set a new vision for hotel design for the next two decades.

The interest in historicism on the part of this new generation of architects was also seen in the concurrent development of the preservation movement, which fought back against the demolition of our urban heritage by "urban renewal." That had destroyed countless treasures in the name of providing a clean sweep for Modern glass-and-metal towers surrounded by open plazas. As a consequence, the preservation movement encouraged an interest in restoration and recycling, that is, redesigning old buildings for other uses than the original use. In San Francisco the old Ghirardelli chocolate factory was preserved instead of being demolished. It was structurally restored and recycled into a new kind of urban shopping center that incorporated the history of the city into its merchandising program.

Recycling created some odd contradictions: Churches were turned into houses or discotheques, railroad stations became libraries, and the 1928 RKO Paramount movie house in Brooklyn, New York—perhaps the oddest example of recycling— became the gilded Baroque auditorium of Long Island University's basketball court and gymnasium. Soon it was recognized that the economies of preservation were more beneficial than had been thought, and the rationale of the preservation movement was established on financial bedrock.

By 1967 this new design movement based on diversity had recognized other Princeton architecture colleagues of Venturi, Moore, and Hardy. Along with their political activism, students also evidenced a new spirit of design activism—designing their own rooms, apartments, and houses as inventive experiments in the new attitudes that the movement proffered, and also building them, and getting them published well before they got out of design school.

In 1968 and 1969 this rebellion had been publicized enough so that it was reinterpreted in a popularized form that came to be known as Psychedelic. That version espoused the whiplash curve of the popularly rediscovered Art Nouveau, but expressed it in phosphorescent colors called Day-Glo. The vanguard of this rebellion was more interested in new attitudes such as the inclusion of Pop Art and of commercial and roadside imagery into the vision of academic architecture; in inversions of Modernist theories and approaches; in mannered manipulations of Bauhaus principles; and in tricks of scale and optical effects. This latter corresponded to the contemporaneous interest in Op Art. The rebellion was also interested in permissiveness, laissez-faire design, spontaneity, ambiguity, and chaos.

Office Landscape

In the field of office design, one significant development during the 1960s corresponded to the interests of this design revolution. That was the office design system called "office landscape," which seemed to exhibit many of the attitudes of the

159A. Conventional partitioned office layout proposed for du Pont's Freon Division. Wilmington, Delaware. 1966. *Illustration from* Progressive Architecture *(May 1968).*

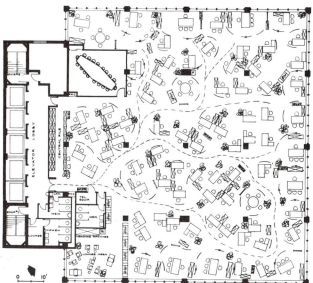

159B. Quickborner Team. Office landscape plan, du Pont's Freon Division. Wilmington, Delaware. 1967. *Illustration from* Progressive Architecture *(May 1968).*

rebellious vanguard and also appealed to a wide range of differently oriented mainstream interior designers.

Office landscape was adopted by a number of office designers who called themselves space planners. The assertion of the term was that office spaces would be planned rather than decorated, but the implication that no one had planned spaces before was embarrassing. Just as vanguard architects were opening up their design vocabulary, so too office landscape, a system of free-form furniture arrangement based on traffic, work flow, and communication, opened up the rigid rectangularity of previous office layout and design. To many the system looked like visual chaos (see Figures 159A and B).

Imported from Germany, where it was conceived by Eberhard and Wolfgang Schnelle, office landscape was adopted by major office planners and architects amid great controversy around the mid-1960s; it became the prevailing direction of office design for the next decade.

Office landscape was based on the idea of free-flowing communication and traffic between departments and working groups. It therefore eliminated barriers, such as the rigid rectangular-plan partitioning systems that had become so fixed a part of office design in the late 1950s and early 1960s—perhaps best achieved in the integrated partitioning and suspended-ceiling system designed by Skidmore, Owings & Merrill (SOM) for the Union Carbide Building (later Manufacturers Hanover Trust Building) (1961–62) on Park Avenue in New York. In office landscape planning, aisles became integrated with working spaces; major traffic flow was also merged with work areas to a degree to utilize workspace more intensively—thereby appealing to economy-minded clients. The large, open—that is, partitionless—bullpen office concept that had been the prevailing mode from the beginning of the century and earlier—the typing-factory image—was revived. But this time it had a scatter-pattern plan—and square-footage studies documented its economic advantages.

To compensate for the acoustical disadvantages of open offices, carpeting was assumed as an integral component. Carpeting had for centuries been a handmade craft and treasured artifact. But in the early 1960s, due to larger high-speed looms and to the tufting process, it became an economically available finishing material for virtually everywhere. It spread from the living room to the kitchen and bath. It was spread, almost like paint, in schools and playgrounds—which gave the carpet industry its new impetus. It became "wall-to-wall" everywhere. It even climbed the walls of many interiors, as in the foyer of Philip Johnson's New York State Theater and Saarinen and Mielziner's Beaumont Theater, both at Lincoln Center. Carpet was suddenly available, therefore, for banks, elevators, and offices.

Also to modulate the acoustics of open office landscape, large expanses of flat ceilings were lowered and hung with fins to break up reverberation; reflective-glass windows were hung with fabric curtains; and even the few remaining low and movable partitions that were required as divisions between work teams and for visual privacy—reaching to a maximum of 6 feet high and often arc-shaped in plan—were upholstered with fabric or carpeting so as not to be sound-reflective. Plantings also were adopted to aid in acoustical diffusion—as well as to provide a sculptural and alive quality. Finally, acoustical perfume, or white sound, could be added to diffuse any lingering acoustical annoyances.

It was a new functional order, this office landscape; but it was achieved physically—in planning terms, "formally"—with visual disorder. Its irregular arrangements looked like primitive, outrageous, free-form chaos. The controversy that greeted its use was vehement for the first several years, from 1965 to 1967. Historian Edgar Kaufmann, Jr., explained, however, that "Clustering is the pattern of human life; regularity is the pattern of theory."[7] To designers who espoused this new chaos, the results of office landscape were justified by the fact that the actual uses by people were the true and proper determinants of its organized—or disorganized—design.

Office landscape, like the approach of the third generation of Modern designers, justified itself on psychological grounds. This was something of a breakthrough at the time, although designers had been discussing the additional benefits of better environments and had been decrying the fact that adequate research had not been done in this area for some years. Office landscape justified its visual chaos and its chaos of movement by saying that when faces and movement are constantly visible, there is no distraction through single actions. The idea was that when everything is distracting, then nothing is more distracting than anything else. It was a psychological justification.

Among the design firms that advocated and adapted the office landscape system to American use was the Quickborner Team, which was the unit sent by the German originators to promote their work in this country. They designed the first installation of the system in this country for the du Pont Company's Freon Division (see Figure 160) in Wilmington, Delaware, in 1967; and in 1968 they followed that office landscape design with others for John Hancock Mutual Life Insurance Company in Boston, for Eastman Kodak in Rochester, and for the New York Port Authority at the World Trade Center in Manhattan. American designers who adapted the system included the Research and Design Institute (REDE) in Providence, Rhode Island; and the Space Design Group and Saphier Lerner Schindler in New York City—the principals of which firms were ardent public advocates for the system; as well as Designs for Business, ISD Inc., Duffy Inc., and others.

Manufacturers were not long in following their lead. Herman Miller, Robert Propst, along with George Nelson Associates, designed the first of the new-generation furniture along the lines of these psychological needs of workers. Called

Action Office, Propst's furniture line provided options for workers in the ways they could work—standing as well as seated, on high stools as well as on low soft chairs, at multi-tables instead of at single-unit desks.

Subsequently, the desk was superseded by the work station—which included desk, filing storage, bookshelves, pin-up boards, closets, and the like—as the unit that could be varied and expanded or contracted to suit the individual needs of each worker. Lighting, too, was incorporated into these units and, in the next decade, became a major focus of furniture designers and manufacturers.

Overall, the development of office design was indicative of three things: First, it demonstrated the greater interest in interiors that involve the user and are adaptable to both the physical and the psychological requirements of users. Second, it demonstrated the messy vitality—or energetic messiness—that was a keynote of the 1960s. Third, it demonstrated the growth of the interior design field in nonresidential areas, which became known as contract design. Like the term space planner, this was a questionable if not silly term, more indicative of a field in transition than of an actuality. Residential design had been commissioned by contracts at least since the early days of Elsie de Wolfe's and Frank Lloyd Wright's practices; so the distinction of nonresidential design from residential design by its business arrangements was not very distinct. Still, it did indicate that a greater segment of the interior design profession was beginning to be involved in nonresidential as well as residential design.

160. Quickborner Team. Office landscape, du Pont's Freon Division. Wilmington, Delaware. 1967. *Photograph by Louis Reens.*

This expansion of practice was accompanied by the overthrow of the Modern movement. Le Corbusier had died in 1965, Gropius and Mies in 1969. The door had been opened for a stylistic revolution—for anything-goes in design. Instead of the pure and the geometrical, the new generation proclaimed the fragmented and the layered; instead of total design the new generation now proclaimed the inconsistent, the ad hoc and spontaneous, the irregular and the incomplete. It was a new vision for the 1970s.

Suggested Reading

Baldwin, Billy. *Billy Baldwin Decorates*. New York: Holt, Rinehart and Winston, 1972.

———. *Billy Baldwin Remembers*. New York: Harcourt Brace Jovanovich, 1974.

Dreyfuss, Henry. *The Measure of Man*. New York: Whitney Library of Design, 1960.

Herdeg, Klaus. *The Decorated Diagram: Harvard Architecture and the Failure of the Bauhaus Legacy*. Cambridge: MIT Press, 1983.

Hicks, David. *David Hicks Living with Design*. New York: William Morrow, 1979.

Hiesinger, Kathryn B., and George H. Marcus, eds. *Design Since 1945*. Philadelphia: The Philadelphia Museum of Art, 1983.

Platner, Warren. *Ten by Platner*. New York: McGraw-Hill, 1975.

Scully, Vincent. *American Architecture and Urbanism*. New York: Frederick A. Praeger, 1969.

Smith, C. Ray. "Guest Apartment for Hallmark Cards by Alexander Girard," *Progressive Architecture*. February 1963.

———. *Supermannerism: New Attitudes in Post-Modern Architecture*. New York: E. P. Dutton, 1977.

Stern, Robert A. M. *New Directions in American Architecture*. New York: Braziller, 1969, 1974.

The Architecture of Skidmore, Owings & Merrill, 1963–73. New York: Architectural Book Publishing Company, 1974.

Tweed, Katharine, ed. *The Finest Rooms by America's Great Decorators*. New York: Viking Press, 1964.

Venturi, Robert. *Complexity and Contradiction in Architecture*. New York: The Museum of Modern Art, 1966.

Notes

1. Eero Saarinen, quoted from C. Ray Smith, "One Family of Forms," *Progressive Architecture* (October 1962), p. 158.

2. Benjamin Baldwin, quoted from an interview with C. Ray Smith, as recorded in "Minimal Interiors," *Progressive Architecture* (March 1967), p. 154.

3. Nicos Zographos, quoted from an interview with Smith, op. cit., p. 150.

4. Gordon Bunshaft, quoted from an interview with C. Ray Smith, as recorded in "SOM Details for the Minimal Age" *Progressive Architecture* (September 1967), p. 138.

5. Gordon Bunshaft, quoted in C. Ray Smith, *Supermannerism: New Attitudes in Post-Modern Architecture* (New York: E. P. Dutton, 1977), p. 68.

6. Robert Venturi, *Complexity and Contradiction in Architecture* (New York: The Museum of Modern Art, 1966), p. 22. This book has been generally recognized, as critic-historian Vincent Scully asserted at the time of its first publication, as the most important theoretical book on architecture since Le Corbusier's "Vers une Architecture" in 1923.

7. Edgar Kaufmann, Jr., speaking at a symposium on office landscape held at La Fonda del Sol restaurant in New York circa 1967. Quoted in Smith, *Supermannerism*, p. 125.

Chapter 9

1970–1980:
The Fourth Generation

After the vast space expansion of the 1960s, nothing, apparently, could get any bigger or more outgoing. The cyclic result was that the design professions, like so much of humanity, turned inward once again to smaller scale, to local and personal concerns and visions. Politically, the 1970s brought the end of American involvement in the Vietnam War, the reopening of China to the West, the emergence of Japan as a major industrial power, scandals in the White House, and the erosion of American primacy as international leader and police force. The reasons for this were both the ideological and humanistic goals of the decade and the general economic retrenchment.

Economically, the United States witnessed several periods of serious recession in the 1970s, bringing high unemployment and an end to the twenty-year-long building boom. Instead of vast urban schemes, the prevalent activity was piecemeal restoration and the refitting of new and old building elements together into a blend of new-old tradition and continuity. For many designers whose services were not fully engaged, it was a period of theorizing and of drawing. Yet the 1970s was also one of the worst periods of inflation in the country's history; it led to widespread real estate speculation. As a consequence, although there was less building construction than before, there was a great deal of interior design work in residences, apartments, lofts, and offices.

The oil embargo of 1974 began a series of energy crises that also shook the country's confidence. Energy costs for interiors rose sharply, bringing energy-conscious design to the forefront of design considerations throughout the decade. Because of this groundswell of concern for conservation—of energy resources, of endangered wildlife species—and for pollution—of the air and water, and of the landscape by solid wastes—the 1970s became known as the Environmental Decade. Environmental designers—as many called themselves—shared these concerns, focusing on underground and bermed buildings, on solar energy, heat loss, and a new technology to deal with this new concern. Preservation and recycling, with energy-consciousness, were therefore mainstay activities for designers of interiors.

Design Pluralism

The 1970s were characterized by a multiplicity of design approaches: The inclusiveness of the 1960s was more widespread than ever, and was called Pluralism. The single approach of the Modern crusade was rejected in favor of a multiplicity of approaches, possibilities, and directions. No longer was there a concerted design crusade even within the architecture community. The "failure" of Modernism was proclaimed by critics of widely different ages (see Blake, 1977; Jencks, 1977). The new appeals were to accustomed function, to a respectful humanism, and to the continuity of historical context.

The decade showed convincingly that each generation has singled out idiosyncratic incidents and elements from the work of the preceding generation and has developed it into major features. The diagonals, inflections, and violin curves of the 1920s and 1930s that had begun to be explored in the 1960s were adopted as pivotal motifs of the 1970s. The tentative interests that were new in the 1950s—historicism, classicism, decoration, and the vernacular—had grown beyond platforms of rebellion, which they had been in the 1960s, to become, in the 1970s, the general interests of the profession. It was not surprising that a popular revival of the 1940s and 1950s began at this time. Other directions, adopted primarily by architects, were Structuralism, Constructivism, and Italian Rationalism and neo-Rationalism. Although they did not have much broad visible influence on the design of interiors, except for those interiors in the buildings designed by the architects who espoused such directions, it could be expected that Structuralism, Constructivism, and Rationalism would be stronger in the 1980s.

A New Humanism

The focus on designing for the needs of people, which was expressed so frequently during the 1960s, gained even more sharpness in the 1970s. Some of it was real; some was mere lip service. But it was clearly on the minds of many designers. At mid-decade Charles Moore, Donlyn Lyndon, and Gerald Allen proclaimed this new humanism in "The Order of Dreams"—a chapter in their *The Place of Houses*. They wrote:

> The dreams which accompany all human actions should be nurtured by the places in which people live. . . . The Order of Dreams demands that you . . . open up the full range of your own responses to the world, your own concerns. It demands that you acknowledge and display the pretenses which you habor . . . that you imagine your house in the ways your daydreams and memories suggest, and that you envision the special places that might correspond to them. . . .[1]

It was a new kind of proclamation for the humanism and the plurality of the times.

Historicism

At the beginning of the 1970s, for a brief moment, it seemed as if the divergent paths of the different interior design professions were beginning to come together in the explorations of vanguard designers. Historicism, of one kind or another, was a common thread, albeit adopted for different ideologies. A wide array of historical influences, design work, and personalities came to attention. In the continuing rediscovery of Art Deco, the work of Eileen Gray from the 1920s and 1930s came to greater recognition than during her lifetime. The preservation movement, with recycling and renovation as its most prevalent activities, was a pervasive aspect of historicism.

The Return to Ornamentation

A new generation of architects, in their continuing rebellion against mid-century International Style, rejected Modernism's taboo against historicism and applied ornament. They brashly adopted, headlong, a new kind of flattened, silhouetted, outlined ornamentation. First brightly painted on in multiple colors, this ornamentation soon sported simplified three-dimensional classical motifs. This new generation of architecture began to call itself Post-Modern around 1974. Traditional decorators, still using the highly molded forms of classicism, may have wondered what was new about all this, but they nevertheless began to share a common ground with architects who were designing such interiors.

Contextualism

Along with historicism came a renewed commitment to and respect for the context, location, and adjacencies of one building to another, one space to another. Architects called it contextualism (see Figure 161). They said it restored "meaning" to urbanism and to architecture, which had been lost during the purgative clean-up of Modernism's taboos. Indeed, both contextualism and the historicism that designers were adopting ever more eagerly at this time were also first justified as "returning lost meanings."

Minimalism

Other designers of interiors continued to explore the Minimal approach. Their work also showed a tendency toward enrichment. It was found sometimes through a return to natural rustic materials and sometimes to the Modern furniture classics of the 1920s. By 1970 the use of a chair design from 1920 was, for the young generation, a historical recall.

Industrial Pop

The straightforward expression of all building elements, which had been the goal of the functionalists since the 1920s, was popularized in the 1970s. Designers exposed structural systems, air-conditioning ducts, sprinkler systems, lighting troffers, alarm systems—whatever existed—as honest, expressible design elements. Often each subsystem was differently polished or painted—sometimes differently color-coded for clarity of expression and for decorative effect. By the end of the decade the mirror-polished duct and the mirror-polished steel round column were literal glosses on this imagery.

In this direction, the firm of Hardy Holzman Pfeiffer Associates led daringly in the design of public interiors such as Orchestra Hall in Minneapolis (1974),

161. Susana Torre. Reception room, Old Pension Building. Washington, D. C. 1978. *Photograph by Norman McGrath.*

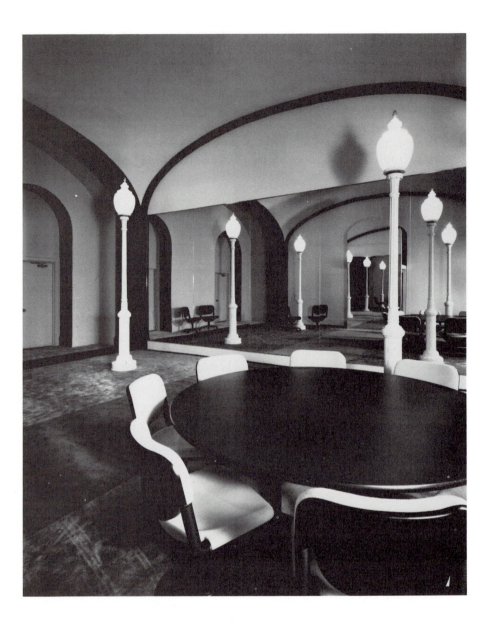

Boettcher Concert Hall in Denver (1979), and the Columbus Occupatioinal Health Center (1973) (see Figure 162).

The Pompidou Center in Paris, completed in 1977, raised this long-established direction to international attention. Designed by architects Piano & Rogers, the Pompidou Center was an ultimate expression of this kind of functionalism in that it put the structural and mechanical systems on the exterior as a kind of superscale, tinker-toy decoration.

Some of the new generation of Minimalists also pursued this approach, using high-gloss and highly polished ducts and other building elements. Also popular were pipes and wire shelving, lighting with coiled electrical cables, and other items originally made for commercial, industrial, or construction uses. They were used in offices, restaurants, and residences. They were adopted as a last stylistic symbol of the Industrial Revolution, of High Modernism, and of their final acceptance in the chic living room of everyman, it was said. A campaign of serious intent since before World War I, these components became high-style fashion and were journalistically categorized as High-Tech.

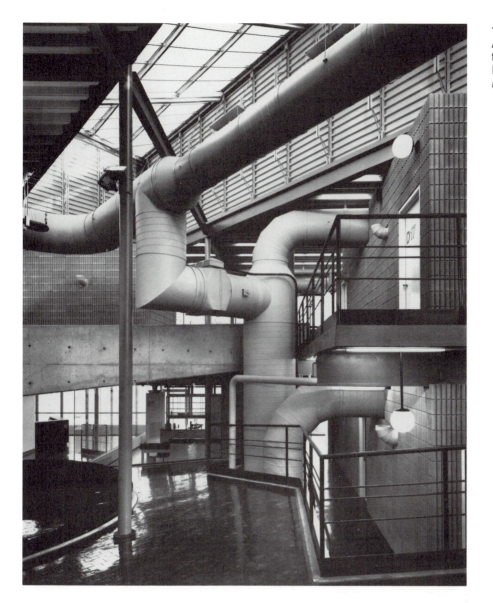

162. Hardy Holzman Pfeiffer Associates. Columbus Occupational Health Center. Columbus, Indiana. 1973. *Photograph by Norman McGrath.*

Country Vernacular

The 1970s also saw widespread interest in Country Vernacular and in Arts and Crafts and Mission style furniture. It was something of a resurgence of the Peasant Vernacular of the 1930s, but Americanized. Residential subdivisions and shopping malls were designed as farm-like, barn-like spaces, with exposed wood beams and trusses, woodsy textures, and nostalgic cracker-barrel imagery (see Figure 163). It was a popularization of the California Vernacular idiom pioneered in the 1960s by the recycling of San Francisco's Ghirardelli Square and by architects Moore, Venturi, and Hardy. It also owed something to a 1940s revival of natural materials and to the perennial yearning for the country, the primitive, the provincial, and the peasant look.

More people began to collect old and new patchwork quilts, wicker and willow woven baskets, old farm implements, dried flowers and herbs, and other country items. For architects it was another approach to contextualism. For designers of all ideologies, it was a popular field from which to assemble decorative objects to give patina and texture to interiors.

163.   Haines Lundberg Waehler. Offices of Haines Lundberg Waehler, Architects/Engineers/Planners. Basking Ridge, New Jersey. 1979. *Photograph by Ashod Kassabian, courtesy Haines Lundberg Waehler.*

Late Modern

Still, the common language or mainstream of corporate and commercial interior design continued to be the modular, clean-lined internationalism that had developed around 1960 (see Figure 164). Some observers called it Late Modern.

Throughout the 1970s all these directions were not only explored simultaneously, but accepted as part of the pluralism (recognized also as confusion) of the design fields. There was an air of rather dilettantish excitement—as at a scholars' convention—yet the designs were sophisticated and refined, elegantly formed and colored. It was, perhaps, the Rococo of the Modern movement.

Restoration and Recycling

Historical preservation of buildings and interiors became a mainstream design activity in the 1970s. Changes in federal tax laws allowed greater tax credits and

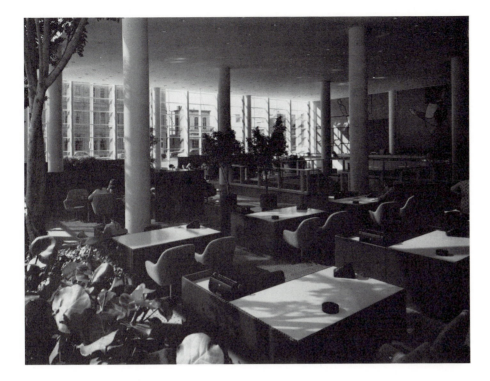

164. Skidmore, Owings & Merrill. First Bank of Wisconsin. Madison, Wisconsin. 1974. *Photograph © Ezra Stoller/ESTO. 1974.*

accelerated depreciation for commercial preservation and restoration. Because of the economic recessions and inflation, as construction costs and interest rates soared during the 1970s, restoration was recognized as a sometimes more economical approach than building anew.

Preserved, restored, or recycled were such interiors as the original Senate Chamber in the U.S. Capitol; Frank Furness's Pennsylvania Academy of the Fine Arts in Philadelphia; the Cooper Union in New York; the Oak Room at the Plaza Hotel in New York; the 1931 Timothy Pfleuger–designed Paramount Theater of the Arts in Oakland, California; the recycling of the Andrew Carnegie mansion into the Cooper-Hewitt Museum; the recycling of McKim, Mead & White's Villard houses into the Helmsley Palace Hotel in New York; as well as the Chicago Public Library, the Minnesota State Capitol, and countless more across the country. Crucial to this work was the discovery of available craftsmen such as the Rambusch Studios and the muralist Richard Haas, who helped in different ways to solve the problems posed by restoration.

One paradox in this seemingly enlightened new opinion came to light, however; many people began to adopt a respect for the old as a wholesale axiom. For them, "old" came to mean "good." It was again necessary, if treacherous, to distinguish the age of an old building or interior from its quality.

Hotel Design

The design of new hotels with large central atrium spaces—larger than the skylighted palm courts of the older hotels by being almost the full height of the building—continued to be one of the major goals of hotel design in the 1970s. Beginning with the Atlanta Hyatt Regency Hotel in the late 1960s, architect John Portman produced a series of hotels with atriums: Among them was the Hyatt Regency Hotel in San Francisco (1973), with its pyramidal ziggurat effect, its vast sculpture, hanging plants, and exposed glass-walled and midway-lighted elevators that ran up and down in the atrium like space capsules.

165.   Johnson/Burgee Architects. Guest room, Marquette Inn. IDS Center. Minneapolis, Minnesota. 1974. *Photograph by Phillip MacMillan James & Associates.*

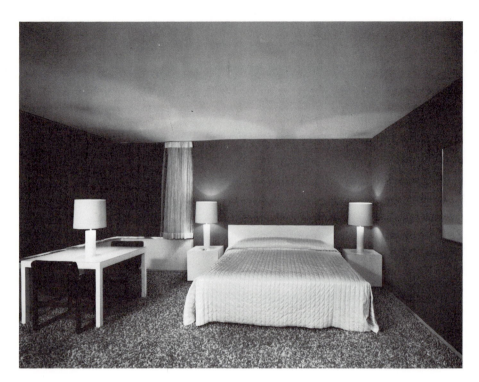

The atrium as an indoor room was recalled to modern usage. Its earlier incarnation had been during the 1880s and 1890s in department stores. In the 1960s Kevin Roche's Ford Foundation Building in New York offered a garden atrium amenity for the surrounding offices. Cesar Pelli's town-square atrium for Columbus, Indiana, during this time also showed the value of large indoor rooms to urban life. As much as any other interior spaces, these glassed atriums indicated the new humanism, the new concern for occupants and passersby. They offered places to sit and chat, places where people could look at splashing water and colorful flowers, or could watch people and the activity of the constantly moving elevators.

Architects Philip Johnson and John Burgee showed how the atrium could be an effective town square with their Crystal Court at IDS Center in Minneapolis, Minnesota, and at Pennzoil Place in Houston, Texas. As part of IDS Center, Johnson/Burgee designed the interiors of a new hotel, the Marquette Inn (1974) (they worked with an associate firm of architects on the overall building). The interiors were unique among hotel designs by being in the Modern idiom. Not only were the public spaces stylish, original, and comfortable, but they were beautifully detailed within a commercial budget. The zigzag lighted corridors alone made the hotel innovative, but the uncompromisingly modern guest rooms (see Figure 165) were a distinctive mixture of Pop and Minimalism. There was something of this same mixture in the New York restaurant Genghiz Khan's Bicycle, designed by Gamal El Zoghby with plastic laminate and vinyl furniture that was integrated with the overall interior.

Store Design and Display

Designers were more and more active in department-store and boutique design during the 1970s. Display design had another surge of inspiration in the cartoon-like tableaux that were created with mannequins in store windows. Robert Currie drew crowds with his theater-like scenes in the windows of Henri Bendel and elsewhere. He was followed by Candy Praz at Bloomingdale's and by others across the country. All owed a debt to the long tradition of Gene Moore's windows for Tiffany & Co. and for other firms. This new store and window display seemed like a new concern for human response.

Product Design

The involvement of interior designers as designers of products for furnishing was markedly increased in the 1970s. In addition to specialist product designers, many prominent designers of interiors found their ways into designing products for what had been called "the home furnishings industry." It was a great improvement over the "decorator colors" slogan of the previous decades. In the tradition of "designer name" labels for wearing apparel, interior designers attached their names to furniture and fabrics, sheets and towels, carpeting and rugs, and a broad spectrum of products for interiors.

Corporate Office Design

The mainstream of commercial interior design—office planning—continued to provide business and design opportunities for a wide range of design professionals. The marketing of design services was organized by large space-planning firms as a structured and separately staffed program. A quick marketing growth brought the California firm of Gensler Associates to the position of largest interior design firm in the country. Stylistically, offices were invested with a wide range of options, from supergraphic murals and photomontages to Post-Modernist historical allusions and the full pluralism of the decade.

Workstations

Workstations and their new lighting requirements became a major technical concern. It had been only thirty years since all mechanical systems had been incor-

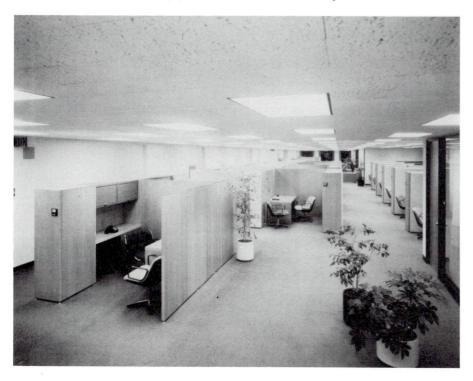

166. ISD Inc. Stephens Plus System workstations by Knoll International, installed in offices of Atlantic Richfield. Philadelphia, Pennsylvania. 1975. *Photograph courtesy Knoll International.*

porated into suspended ceilings. By the mid-1970s, after office-landscape systems had liberated the furniture plan from the regimentation of the building grid, those same office-landscape systems began to let lighting break out of the ceiling grid and become more related to movable work tasks. The new goal was for task lighting that was in balance with ambient lighting.

First had come the redefinition of the office as a workstation—a low-partitioned (58 to 74 inches high) enclosure that was, ostensibly, easily movable and that incorporated desk/table surfaces and drawer/shelf storage, usually hung from the partitions. By the mid-1970s furniture manufacturers were producing more and more of these systems (see Figure 166).

The separation of these open-plan mini-rooms from the overall ambience revealed the need for a separation in the way the two were lighted. Task lighting needed to be brighter than the lighting in ambient corridors. The new lighting, although it took many different forms—fixtures, optics, and lamps—consisted of indirect up lighting for general illumination and direct down lighting for work activities. Both were being incorporated into the design of the workstation itself. The economic advantages were the elimination of the modular illuminated ceiling and virtually all ceiling troffers, along with a consequent saving in electricity as well as savings in taxes for building elements versus movable furniture. Once again in the 1970s, adaptability to change and a concentration on people and their activities were the humanistic goals.

Lighting design at last reached a recognized position among design professions. More and more lighting designers not only practiced, but were consulted by the designers of interiors. The first textbook for architects and interior designers on the subject of interior lighting was written in this period by James L. Nuckolls (see Suggested Reading).

The New York Five

The prominent leaders of the decade's fourth generation of Modern designers were a group of young architects who became known as the New York Five: Richard Meier, Charles Gwathmey, Michael Graves, Peter Eisenman, and John Hejduk. Their work became known through the publication in 1972 of the book *Five Architects*. The first three became influential on interior design in the 1970s; the latter two were more concerned with conceptual architecture, structuralism, and teaching. Fundamental to their early work was the influence of and inspiration from the white architecture of the 1920s, especially Le Corbusier's Purism. Le Corbusier's investigations provided their model—the language that they continued to develop. In this regard, the work of the Five was the most prominent example of the decade's new historicism.

Richard Meier

Meier began to be known in professional circles in the mid-1960s for his Smith House in Rowayton, Connecticut (1964), and for his Salzman House in East Hampton, Long Island (1969); but his work was neither publicly prominent nor influential on interior design until the 1970s. Then his explosions of the Corbusian idiom, including ever larger and more complicated violin curves and ocean-liner railings, became broadly influential on the decade's design direction.

Richard Meier (1934–) was born in Newark, New Jersey, and studied architecture at Cornell University. He began his career working for Frank Grad Architects in New Jersey; for Davis, Brody & Wisniewski in New York; then for Skidmore, Owings & Merrill and Marcel Breuer. He opened his own practice in 1963

167. Richard Meier. Salzman House. East Hampton, Long Island. 1969. *Photograph © Ezra Stoller/ESTO, 1969.*

in New York and since then has designed numerous houses and housing units, shops, health and educational facilities, clubs, galleries, and other buildings.

Meier's Salzman House (see Figure 167) had built-in furniture (albeit upholstered in tiger-skin plush by the clients) and Mies- and Corbusier-inspired furnishings, with crisp tables in plastic laminate and glass tops, with white-lacquered cabinets for the music system and bar storage. But except for furniture essentials, paintings, and animal-skin upholstery, the architecture of the house—its structural columns, bridges, and ocean-liner railings—was the only decoration used.

Late in the 1970s Meier designed a library reading room within Frank Lloyd Wright's Guggenheim Museum. It was a model of respect for the context of the room, and presented new furniture designs by Meier as well. This led to the production of his furniture designs by Knoll International.

Charles Gwathmey

From the beginning of his career Charles Gwathmey extended the Corbusian idiom of large-scale cylinders, angles, and the open-free plan by, at first, sheathing those forms in shingles. Architecture historian Vincent Scully acclaimed this work as adapting the International Style of Le Corbusier to the New England context.

Charles Gwathmey (1938–) was born in Charlotte, North Carolina. He studied architecture at the University of Pennsylvania under Louis Kahn and Robert

168. Gwathmey Siegel & Associates, Architects. Shezan Restaurant. New York City. 1976. *Photograph by Norman McGrath.*

Venturi and then at Yale University under Paul Rudolph and James Stirling. He began his architecture practice in New York in partnership with Richard Henderson and, since 1971, has been in partnership with Robert Siegel. The firm has designed numerous residences, educational and commercial buildings, and interiors of many kinds. By the end of the decade, Gwathmey was designing furnishings for major production.

Along with his partners, Gwathmey designed a number of interiors—for houses, apartments, and galleries—that reflected the Corbusian influence in the sculptural modeling of white plaster, in ship railings, and in direct quotations of Le Corbusier's work. In an apartment for actress Faye Dunaway in New York (1970), Gwathmey's firm reinterpreted a bathroom in Le Corbusier's Villa Savoye of 1929–31 (see Chapter 4). Later in the decade Gwathmey and his partner, Robert Siegel, began to be represented by furniture and carpet designs that further reiterated Corbusian themes and motifs.

His reconstruction after a fire at Whig Hall at Princeton University in 1972 brilliantly demonstrated the inclusion of the Corbusian free-plan Domino and large-scale Corbusian forms within a nineteenth-century Greek revival temple. His design of Pearl's Restaurant (1974) and Shezan Restaurant (1976) (see Figure 168), both in New York City, demonstrated how the materials of Internationalism— glass block, polished metal acoustical ceiling tiles, travertine, and oak—could be manipulated to achieve an unexpected elegance within commercial spaces.

Michael Graves

Of the Five, it was Michael Graves who was to contribute the most to interior design in the 1970s. His influence was first through a symbolic use of colors that aimed to give "meanings"; and later through his mannered classical ornamentation, delicate pastel colors, and furniture designs.

Michael Graves (1934–) was born in Indianapolis, Indiana, and studied architecture at the University of Cincinnati and at Harvard University. Then, at the

American Academy in Rome, he became especially interested in the work of Borromini and spent days drawing everything by Borromini that he could. It was then that his celebrated drawing technique was developed. In 1962 he settled in Princeton, New Jersey, where he has practiced architecture and taught at Princeton University ever since.

By the end of the 1970s his designs included a dozen or more houses and house additions, half a dozen museums and galleries, several medical facilities, offices for an investment group, and the beginning of a series of showrooms for Sunar (see color plate 15) that would provide direct exposure to his work for a vast number of young designers and of potential clients. In all of these projects, his use of color and ornament was liberal and remarkable.

The principal feature of Michael Graves's work is an art-historical approach—especially a Cubist simultaneity of images, meanings, and inspirations or derivations. He is concerned with multiple layers of space, of structure, and of symbolism. The relationships of his interiors and architecture to their physical sites and cultural backgrounds—questions of contextual continuity—are primary concerns for Graves. His is architectural storytelling. He relates base, wall, and ceiling to ground, horizon, and sky or to foot, body, and head. His is anthropomorphic symbolism rather than machine symbolism. It rejects abstraction in favor of the representational, the humanistic, the communicative.[2]

In the 1970s Michael Graves assumed the mantle as the leading young philosopher-theorist-aesthetician of the day. His designs and drawings, the latter of which became among the most celebrated by architects in our time, showed classical manipulations and Mannerist inventions, along with delicacy of colors and original juxtapositions of scale and texture, of form and structural reference. All these factors made him one of the leading influences on and inspirations for young designers in the 1970s (see Figure 169).

By the end of the decade Graves was attacking the very precept of twentieth-century space. Along with other Post-Modernists, he maintained:

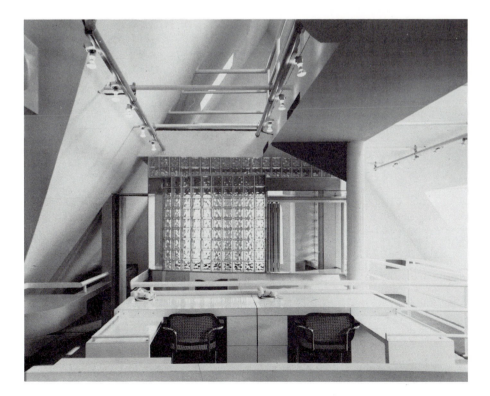

169. Michael Graves. Gunwyn Ventures Office. Princeton, New Jersey. 1972. *Photograph by Norman McGrath.*

[In the open-free plan, Modernism] lost the divisions that gave us privacy, that gave us hierarchy of rooms. If you look at the Tugendhat house you see a De Stijl–like arrangement without hierarchy. I don't think that is our culture's rule system. I think it is wrong and inappropriate for all of us all of the time to make a homogeneous world of space. Rooms are all we have; space is within the room. Without the room we have no walls, and without walls you don't need architects or designers.[3]

It was the Post-Modernists' indictment of Modernism, but it did not preclude their historical reverence for and revival of the white architecture of the 1920s.

Early in the 1970s Graves experimented with a system of colors used for symbolic content. He called it color metaphor. Graves's use of color was an example of the influence of French and Russian Structuralism on 1970s design. Structuralism in design was an analogy with Structuralism in linguistics, which had sought meanings in the underlying nature of language and its fundamental structure. Graves, along with Peter Eisenman early in the 1970s, was concerned with meanings expressed by forms arranged as an architectural language. Graves's experiments and his correlations with nature were part of this investigation.

His color use—in additions to houses, in offices, and in the medical offices for Ear, Nose, and Throat Associates (see Figure 170) in Fort Wayne, Indiana (1971)—aimed for a "metaphorical landscape." That is, colors themselves offered connotations or "cultural references": Blue symbolized sky or water; yellow signified sunlight; green connoted the leaves of plant life; and Etruscan red meant "wall."

Graves's design for the ENT interiors followed this analogy: Sunlight streaks in by means of the low yellow partitions of the central nurses' station; overhead, the green-painted air-conditioning ducts suggest a canopy of leaves; above them is a track from which spotlights are hung—painted blue to suggest a halo of sky. In each treatment room at ENT Graves himself painted a cubistic mural of the surrounding landscape that reiterates these color analogies.

It was, in fact, the compounding of these multiple images, metaphors, and meanings that gave Graves's work its depth and richness, both intellectually and

170. Michael Graves. Nurses' station in medical offices for Ear, Nose, and Throat Associates. Fort Wayne, Indiana. 1971. *Photograph by Balthazar Korab.*

visually. The expression of this full imagination of aesthetic metaphors, connotations, and multiple meanings made his interior designs and his architecture vital and stimulating in the early 1970s and brought him to international stature. Later, he moved away from color reference and changed his way of conceiving space.

The Post-Modernists

Around 1973 or 1974 a small vanguard group of architects adopted the term Post-Modern to explain their work. For them, it meant manipulating and applying the tradition of history—especially classical architecture and classical decoration, but also including any other historical reference that attracted them at the moment. Historical allusion and mannered classicism were the keystones of what they called Post-Modernism. What all this led to was a rage of classical recalls and motifs that was as mannered as the mannerism of the 1960s had been. The Post-Modernists claimed that this direction provided multiple levels of meaning for people who had been deprived of humanistic content by the Modern movement. In this approach, they were reaching out beyond the abstraction of the Modern movement toward a representational architecture with more communicational content.

The term Post-Modern had long been used by the art world to designate the change of sensibilities that occurred around 1950, when Abstract Expressionism and the second generation of Modern designers had led the rebellion against the rigid abstraction of Modernism. The Post-Modernists of the 1970s used the term more specifically to denote their particular brand of historical inclusion and manipulation of historical elements.

The third generation of Modernists, who had begun to shake the foundations of Modernism in the 1960s—such as Robert Venturi and Charles Moore—continued their allusions and quotations from architecture history. Although they resisted the term, they had to accept being called Post-Modernists. Philip Johnson dared direct imitation—or "quotation"—in his design of New York University's Bobst Library floor, which repeated, identically, the marble flooring pattern in the sanctuary of Palladio's church of San Giorgio Maggiore in Venice (see Figure 171). Years before, Johnson had maintained, "You cannot not know history."

In the late 1970s, even more publicly, he gained the spotlight in this activity for his design, with partner John Burgee, of the AT&T building in New York with its broken-pediment roofscape. That histrionic motif scandalized many observers from all classes of understanding. It came to be called "a Chippendale broken pediment," though the broken pediment had had a longer lineage in the history of ideas—certainly before Chippendale, most obviously in the work of Inigo Jones and Grinling Gibbons. To the public, Chippendale was the most known. It was an age that took travesty seriously.

A younger generation of Post-Modernists also investigated historical allusion. The most prominent and vociferous spokesmen for this generation and for this direction from about 1974 onward were Robert A. M. Stern and the writer-architect Charles Jencks. They led the campaign for the term Post-Modern to denote the sleuthing out of new historical models.

Among the periods and architects that the Post-Modernists revived for adaptation were Sir Edwin Lutyens, Georgian periods, Alvar Aalto, Paul Cret, Josef Hoffmann, the lattices and grids of the Wiener Werkstaette and the Shingle Style, along with other sources. The forms and ornamentation of these designers and periods were adapted to a system of classical ornamentation for our day.

It therefore became a popular, elegant half-joke to design classicized furniture. Also influential to architects and to Minimalist designers of interiors was Post-Metabolism (the Japanese correspondent of Post-Modernism) in Japan led by Arata Isozaki, Kisho Kurokawa, and Fumihiko Maki, as well as a younger generation.

171. Philip Johnson and Richard Foster. Palladio-inspired marble floor pattern. Elmer Holmes Bobst Library, New York University, New York City. 1973. *Photograph courtesy Philip Johnson & Richard Foster, Architects*

Robert A. M. Stern

His activities as critic, architect, and historian; his single-minded dedication to work; and his perseverance of the Post-Modernist ideal made Robert A. M. Stern one of the prominent spokesmen and advocates for the movement. Born in New York City, Robert A. M. Stern (1938–) studied history at Columbia University, then architecture at Yale University, where he came under the influence of Philip Johnson, Vincent Scully, Robert Venturi, and Paul Rudolph. He began working in New York as organizer of programs for the Architectural League. He worked in the office of Richard Meier for a few months, then with the New York City Housing and Development Administration; and in 1969 established his own architecture practice with his Yale classmate John S. Hagmann. In 1977 the partnership was dissolved and Stern formed Robert A. M. Stern, Architects. During those years he designed apartment renovations, showrooms, educational facilities, and houses—the latter numbering twenty major renovations and complete new works in that decade.

His work in the 1970s demonstrated his advocacy of Post-Modernism. He created spaces that were explosions of shapes—twists, literally, on the images of Le Corbusier, Robert Venturi, and Art Deco. His spaces were formed of flat paneled walls, curving walls, diagonals, layers of screens—and they were illumi-

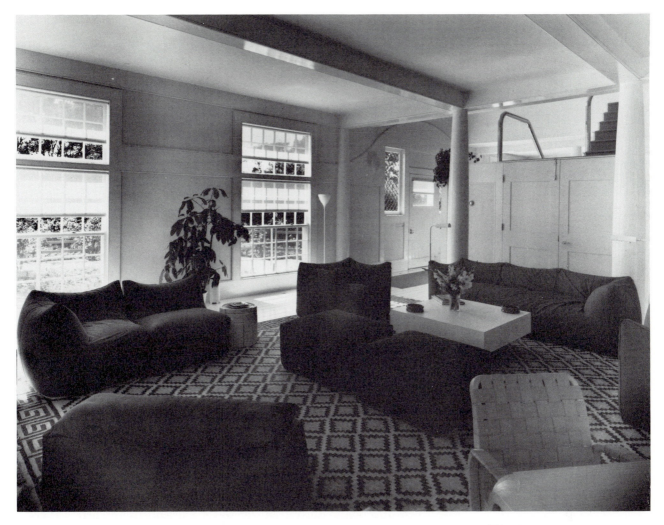

172. Robert A. M. Stern. Living room. East Hampton, Long Island.1976–77. *Photograph by Ed Stoecklein, courtesy Robert A. M. Stern, Architects.*

nated by Aalto-esque skylights over fireplaces, over unexpected setbacks of ceiling, and from side ports.

As a proponent of applied ornament and historicism, he decorated with architectural elements in a wide range of historical styles—with Palladian pilasters and arched windows, with Gothic string courses, and Georgian paneling. He included Shingle-Style inglenooks, Art Deco cabinetwork, parallel lines, and indirect lighting coves. Like his lounge at Columbia University Law School, one of Stern's houses in East Hampton, Long Island, gained white pilasters, wide borders to achieve paneling, small-paned windows, and cream-colored walls (see Figure 172). Both decorative schemes returned the interiors to the vintage of their original structures. With other contemporary Post-Modernists, he felt that such interior treatments could, unlike the abstract industrialism of Modernism, communicate to people once again.

The Italian Influence

Throughout the 1970s the influence of Italian designers was stronger than it had been since around 1950. Furniture designs from Milan continued to electrify professionals and laymen alike. In 1972 New York's Museum of Modern Art produced a lavish exhibition and catalogue by Emilio Ambasz, "Italy: The New Domestic Landscape." From Italy also came the influence of neo-Rationalism and neo-Pur-

173. Massimo Vignelli and Lella Vignelli. St. Peter's Lutheran Church. New York City. 1977. *Photograph by George Cserna.*

ism, which were led by Aldo Rossi, Massimo Scolari, and Mario Botta. Their work gave a new direction to Surrealism—or was it Existentialism? There was also a revival of interest in the work of the 1920s Italian Modernist-Rationalist Giuseppe Terragni. Among the most prominent of the Italian furniture designers were Mario Bellini, Ettore Sottsass, Jr., and the Castiglione brothers.

Meanwhile, since the mid-1960s, the Italian design team of Massimo and Lella Vignelli had maintained an outpost of Italian design in New York. They continued to expand beyond their graphic designs into product and interior designs. Among their designs were furnishings and household objects—including popular tableware in multicolored plastic—and the interior of St. Peter's Lutheran Church in New York (see Figure 173).

Emilio Ambasz

Emilio Ambasz developed a design practice in the United States and in Italy. Born in Argentina, architect Emilio Ambasz (1943–) studied architecture at Princeton University and subsequently taught there as well as at Carnegie-Mellon University in Pittsburgh and in Ulm, Germany, before being appointed curator of design at the Museum of Modern Art in 1969. He left the museum to form his own practice in 1977.

In Italy, with Giancarlo Piretti, he designed a series of chairs that automatically adjusted to a variety of seating systems while providing proper orthopedic and posture support. This Vertebra Seating System was produced in America by Kreuger.

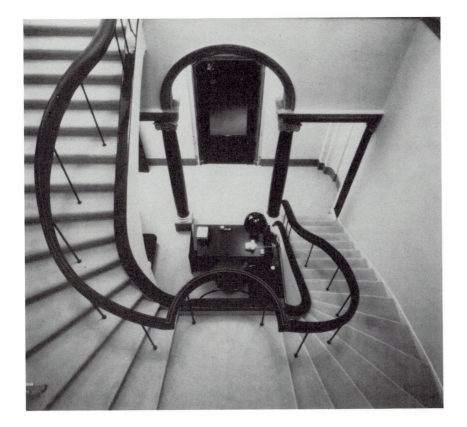

174. Emilio Ambasz. Banque Bruxelles Lambert. Milan, Italy. 1979. *Photograph by Santi Caleca.*

At the end of the decade Ambasz and Piretti completed a branch bank in Milan for the Banque Bruxelles Lambert (see Figure 174). It combined preservation with Post-Modern inclusions and the tradition of decorating craftsmanship—a multicoated paint schedule, varied furniture specification and coloring, and decorative detailing. The paint scheme for the walls began with a layer of heliotrope color, was next sprayed with clouds of white paint, and finally a light spray of gray and brown speckles. The effect was deep, like traditional lacquers, and yet overall creamy white. The carpet also achieved this delicate multicolored effect with yarn dyed lilac at the base and light beige at the carpet surface. The bank interior is poetic and inventive, especially in its imaginatively inventive stair railing, which not only turns from a vertical rail to a horizontal one at mid-stair level, but also meanders from the stair edge into the stair tread area.

The Late Modernists

Among those mainstream designers who continued to refine the Miesian idiom from the 1960s were the interior design departments of the large architecture firms, the large space-planning firms, and many independent architects and interior designers. Several designers became newly prominent during the 1970s for their work in this area.

Skidmore, Owings & Merrill (SOM), across the country and now around the world, continued to produce new and fresh variations on corporate and institutional interior design. In SOM's Chicago office Bruce Graham, with senior interior designer George Larson, brought a new image to banking with his red-lacquered workstations—the system Davis Allen designed for G. F. Business Equipment—at the First Bank of Wisconsin in 1975 (see Figure 164).

175. Skidmore, Owings & Merrill/Davis Allen. Conference/dining room of Alexander & Alexander. New York City. 1978. *Photograph by Jaime Ardiles-Arce.*

Davis Allen

In 1974, after nearly twenty-five years of designing interiors and custom furniture designs for SOM projects, New York senior interior designer Davis Allen was finally permitted by SOM to have his name assigned to a line of furniture he had designed that was to be mass-marketed. Called the Davis Allen Collection by G. F. Business Equipment, the furniture, through its publicity, began to bring the recognition that should have been accorded to Davis Allen for the past fifteen years. Allen had been the chief interior designer at SOM's New York office since the late 1950s. He had been the interior designer of the Chase Manhattan Bank Headquarters, and it had been due to him that the interiors by SOM in project after project steadily grew in refinement, sophistication of systems, appeal of textural juxtaposition, and range of artworks.

Among his major projects during the 1970s were a suite of offices for Gianni Agnelli in Paris (completed in 1975); the headquarters of a major grain company in New York (completed in 1976); and the headquarters of Alexander & Alexander in New York (completed in 1978) (see Figure 175). All were interiors projects with vast budgets, costly materials, ingenious artworks programs, and palatial planning and detailing. In the evolution of Modernism and in the revolutions against it, the interiors of SOM were less in the forefront than they had been in the 1960s, when such work was the mainstream center of interior design; but it was, in the 1970s, a corpus of work that showed continual refinement, invention, and elegance. Davis Allen was the virtually unknown hero of this operation.

Powell/Kleinschmidt

From the Chicago office of SOM in 1976 sprang the new interior design firm of Powell/Kleinschmidt in Chicago. Donald D. Powell (1933–) was born in North Dakota and studied architecture at the University of Minnesota, where he received his B.Arch. in 1956. He joined SOM's Chicago office in 1962 as a senior designer of interiors and became an associate partner in 1968. His knowledge of virtually every dimension of Mies's furniture designs and other details of the Miesian canon was impressive.

Robert D. Kleinschmidt (1939–) was born in Chicago and studied architecture at the University of Illinois, receiving his B.Arch. in 1963, and at Columbia University, earning his M.Sc. in architecture in 1964. He joined SOM's Chicago office in 1964 and became an associate partner in 1973.

From 1966 to 1976 Donald D. Powell and Robert D. Kleinschmidt had been interior designers in the Chicago office of SOM. There, their work on SOM's Sears Bank and Trust Company in Chicago (1974) brought a golden richness to bank offices.

Their work for SOM's Banco di Roma in Chicago of the same year showed their ability to take the SOM idiom into permissiveness, ambiguity, and reflection. Based on the building's rotated square columns, the bank design manipulates rotated squares and diagonals along with mirror surfaces and rich colors of burgundy, plum, rust, and eggplant.

By the end of the decade their independent work included banking facilities, educational and cultural institutions, residential units, restoration work, showrooms, banks, and office complexes. In this they showed a meticulous and colorful approach—influenced by color-field painting—and humanized in the direction of the decade. Basic to their approach was the goal of total design—the consideration of all the elements that comprise the total environment. They aimed to challenge manufacturers to respond with new technology.

Charles Pfister

From the San Francisco office of Skidmore, Owings & Merrill, the designs of Charles Pfister began to be noticed in the early 1970s. Born in Santa Rosa, California, Charles Pfister (1939–) studied architecture at the University of California at Berkeley and worked independently in San Francisco for a brief period before joining SOM's San Francisco office in 1965. He became an associate partner of that firm in 1974 and continued as director of interior design in the San Francisco office until 1981. In that year he formed his own practice.

Pfister was first recognized for the interior design of SOM's headquarters for the Weyerhaeuser Corporation in Tacoma, Washington, in 1971. There, with SOM design partner Edward C. Bassett, he designed 300,000 square feet of office landscape—the largest installation of the concept in this country at that time. The entire five-level building was planned and furnished as an open landscape (see Figure 176), including the office of the president. Islands of rectilinear workstation groups, rather than totally free-form arrangements, composed the plan.

Pfister also designed the furniture system, which was the first new landscape system produced in this country. This oak panel system was produced by Knoll as the Stephens System, because SOM designers were then not permitted to have their names on their furniture designs. Acoustically, the open space was modulated by an acoustical-tile ceiling with gray sound added for privacy and by partitions that were acoustically treated on both sides. Carpeted throughout—one floor each planned as blue, gray, amethyst, and camel—and filled with Colombian upholstery fabrics by Jack Lenor Larsen, the interiors were richly warm in contrast to the rugged landscape visible everywhere through expansive glass walls. It was for this project that Pfister designed his first seating pieces, also produced by Knoll, a sofa and lounge group modified from a tuxedo sofa and made modular—a single lounge chair, a settee, or a three-cushion (or longer) sofa.

In the mid-1970s Pfister designed a tubular metal chair for the offices of the fashion designer Halston; it was produced by Metropolitan Furniture. In addition

176. Skidmore, Owings & Merrill/Charles Pfister. Weyerhaeuser headquarters. Tacoma, Washington. 1971. *Photograph © Ezra Stoller/ESTO, 1971.*

to his continuing series of interior designs for SOM, Pfister designed a line of radius corner tables for Knoll; and by 1980 he was designing the executive offices of Swid/Cogan in New York.

Warren Platner

Throughout the 1970s Warren Platner produced elegant designs in the Late-Modern idiom that were also expansive and flamboyant. His Grill restaurant in the TWA Terminal at Kennedy Airport in New York, completed in 1970 with Kevin Roche, John Dinkeloo & Associates, was an enrichment of the building's sculptural forms with heady colors and textures.

His American Restaurant in Kansas City, Missouri, completed in 1974 in Edward Larrabee Barnes's building, combined window walls that were covered with floor-to-ceiling louvered shutters—a kind of New Orleans effect—with Perpendicular Gothic fan vaultings lighted with midway lights in each fan (see Figure 177). Superscale mirror-brass lighting fixtures—a scaled-down version of the Castiglione brothers' Arco Lamp of 1965—arched over banquettes to provide downlight on tables. It showed the historical pluralism of the decade.

In 1976 the Windows on the World restaurant atop the World Trade Center in New York was opened with interiors by Warren Platner. There, Platner produced a design both modern enough to be sympathetic with the building and intricate enough to be competitive with the view from the 110th floor. Terraced floors made the view uninterrupted from the inner levels. Highly polished, large-scale brass railings and lighting fixtures gave glitter to the elaborately textured spaces with their carpeted ceiling-high nooks and banquettes and other elaborations.

Platner's designs for offices, educational institutions, clubs, and residences at this time were less flamboyant, and all displayed balanced full-range orchestration of textures, a blown-up scale, and inventive if multitudinous detailing.

177. Warren Platner Associates. American Restaurant. Kansas City, Missouri. 1974. *Photograph by Alexandre Georges, courtesy Warren Platner Associates.*

Paul Rudolph

During the 1970s Paul Rudolph maintained a lower profile than he had during the previous two decades, but he regularly continued to design large and small projects with his usual invention and detail in interiors. He demonstrated his fertile imagination and his zeal for innovation at every scale of total design, from siting and materials to furnishings and inventive detail. His chapel for Tuskegee Institute in Alabama (see Figure 178) at the end of the 1960s was a continuation of these themes and an exploration of the motifs of Ronchamp in flat rather than molded planes and with imaginative lighting and integral coloring.

Among his significant interiors during the 1970s were the lobby of the Borroughs Wellcome building in Durham, North Carolina (1972), which integrated the horizontal effect of 1920s architecture with diagonals; an unpublished house in Fort Worth, Texas (1979); and several churches and chapels. The chapel in Boston's Health Services Center (see Figure 179) is a poured-in-place concrete sculpture within a much larger complex that utilizes the corrugated concrete texture Rudolph had devised a decade before. A totality in its consistency of forms and details, the chapel is one of the high points of Rudolph's interior work.

178. Paul Rudolph. Chapel, Tuskegee Institute. Tuskegee, Alabama. 1969. *Photograph © Ezra Stoller/ESTO, 1969.*

179. Paul Rudolph. Chapel, Health Services Center. Boston, Massachusetts. 1971. *Photograph by Robert Perron.*

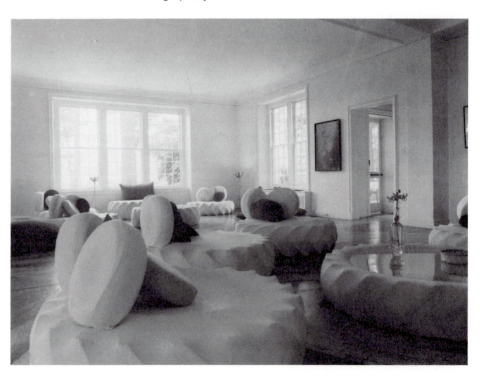

180. Paul Rudolph. Living room, Elman residence. Great Barrington, Massachusetts. 1975. *Photograph by Robert Perron.*

181. Louis Kahn. Mellon Center for British Art, Yale University. New Haven, Connecticut. Circa 1976. *Photograph by R. D. Smith, courtesy Center for British Art.*

In addition to these major works and numerous residential projects during the 1970s, Rudolph also made one of the great jokes on the dream of the Industrial Revolution and on Industrial Pop: In the living room of the Elman residence in Great Barrington, Massachusetts (1974), Rudolph the functionalist painted the concrete floor as a colorful circulation diagram to emphasize the possibilities of the awkward five-door room (see Figure 180). His colors were pale-blue stripes winding into swirls of concentration, symbolically, at the whirlwind centers of conversation. On top of those swirls he located what was the most superscale Pop furniture of its day—tractor tires covered in stretch fabric with upright cushion backs to serve as seating and with glass tops to serve as tables. It was Pop Country Vernacular as well as Industrial Pop—and it was also one of the most forceful demonstrations of the battle between innovation and tradition.

Louis Kahn

Among the other established masters of the 1970s, Louis Kahn completed his library for the Exeter school in New Hampshire in 1972 with furniture designed and specified by Benjamin Baldwin. Like the Mellon Center for British Art at Yale (completed after Kahn's death in 1974), interior walls and paneling were in a rich warm wood that contrasted ingeniously with the exposed concrete (see Figure 181). Furnishings, again, were specified by Benjamin Baldwin, who, by this time, had become interiors consultant to some of the most renowned American architects. These interiors, along with those of Kahn's Kimball Art Museum in Fort Worth, Texas, showed that raw concrete, natural wood, and superb detailing could create as finished and elegant an interior as any lacquered space.

The Minimalists

The Minimalism of the 1960s came to general public attention in the 1970s. Prominent was the work of the older generation of Minimalists: Benjamin Baldwin,

Ward Bennett, and William Machado with Norman Diekman. In addition, the work of a number of architects was more commonly recognized as sharing this Minimalist intent: Edward Larrabee Barnes; I. M. Pei & Partners; Skidmore, Owings & Merrill; Kevin Roche; Cesar Pelli; and Hugh Stubbins. They were joined by a new younger generation of Minimalist designers.

Among the purest of the older generation's work was I. M. Pei & Partners' National Airlines Terminal, a design from the 1960s that was completed at Kennedy Airport in New York in 1970. Robert Lym was Pei's director of interior design in charge of this and other Minimalist designs by Pei & Partners.

Benjamin Baldwin

Benjamin Baldwin's work in the 1970s, which included interiors for architects Louis Kahn, I. M. Pei, and Edward Larrabee Barnes, also included furniture designs produced by Larsen Furniture. Beginning with the chair Baldwin had designed for the Ritz Bar in Boston in 1967, he went on to create a line of new designs.

During the 1970s designers traveled to see the house and garden Baldwin had built for himself in East Hampton, Long Island, in the late 1960s and which he was constantly refining. It showed his Minimal detailing and his sensitivity to juxtapositions of scale, of texture, and of house to garden. In addition, his inclusion of a somewhat Japanese refined rusticity pointed a new direction for the decade.

The house (see Figure 182 and color plate 14) is a small and modest Long Island barn-like structure perched above the brick foundations of a former house; the foundations have been turned into a garden. Inside the house an exposed wood structure—reminiscent of both barn construction and traditional Japanese houses—divides the two floors into three bays. In the middle is a living area with glass doors opening onto gardens on both sides of the house. The two end bays, which are windowless, are open to this central interior space, separated from it only by

182. Benjamin Baldwin. Own house. East Hampton, Long Island. Circa 1978. *Photograph by Jon Naar.*

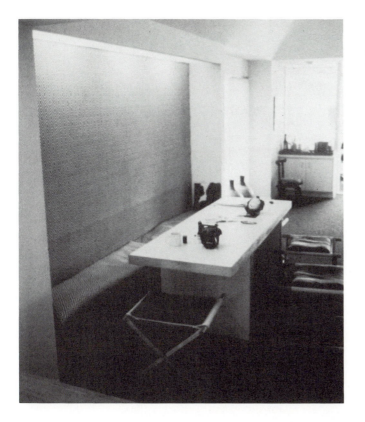

183. Benjamin Baldwin. Dining room, own house. Sarasota, Florida. 1979. *Photograph by C. Ray Smith.*

the exposed wood columns and by pull-up bamboo-strip roller blinds. In one end bay is a kitchen, which is surrounded by white floor-to-ceiling doors to storage cabinets and in the center of which is a 6-foot-square island counter topped in 4-inch-thick butcher block. It is luxuriously spacious and appropriately rustic in juxtaposition to the kitchen equipment. The other end bay was originally a lounge area with a central platform covered in dark-gray industrial carpeting, with a fireplace at the center of the end wall, and with gold-and-black eighteenth-century Japanese screens at each side of the room.

Originally, the middle living-room bay contained a choice selection of furnishings—a Venetian Louis XV chair, a nickel-steel footrest, a small stainless-steel and glass table, and a standing lamp by Giacometti. It was a tour of cultures and ages through four furnishings, as he had in Chicago in the 1950s. Subsequently, these furnishings were changed to reflect the decade's interest in low, sculptural, modular seating; still later, that seating was moved into the end bay in front of the fireplace, and the middle bay acquired a sumptuously spacious, superscale library table and chairs; they doubled for conversation, reading, and dining.

Baldwin's East Hampton house typified his ideal of interior design as "tranquil, calm, and serene." It was echoed by his winter house in Sarasota, Florida, designed in the 1970s. There, the banquetted dining nook (see Figure 183) and the plaster details combined Minimal sculpture with calm rusticity.

Ward Bennett

During the same period, Ward Bennett designed a house for himself at Springs, Long Island, in 1973. It combined Minimal Purism as a Miesian pavilion with country and Japanese overtones. The square wood house has a central skylighted space that is surrounded by modular bays, some open to and some separate from the central living space (see Figure 184). An exposed structure of wood is juxta-

184. Ward Bennett. Own house. Springs, Long Island. 1973. *Photograph © Peter Aaron/ESTO, 1978.*

posed with glass walls, huge plants, an industrially carpeted fireplace inglenook of Miesian character, a Mexican white-string hammock, and a collection of Ward Bennett's elegant furniture designs. The house has a high pitch of refinement, even within the rustic structural system, and the combination of the two is superbly orchestrated.

A New Generation of Minimalists

Among the younger designers who espoused and continued the direction of Minimalism in the 1970s were Joseph D'Urso, Bray-Schaible, Scott Bromley and Robin Jacobsen, Peter Andes, Michael Kalil, James Maguire, Dennis Jenkins, Juan Montoya, and a number of others. They were inspired by the work of Luis Barragan (see Chapter 7), which was publicized by the Museum of Modern Art's 1972 exhibition directed by Emilio Ambasz and by Ambasz's book (see Suggested Reading).

So widely publicized was the use of industrial and industrial-looking products—in interiors, out of normal context—by this younger generation that it became known, in some circles, as "High-Tech" design. After seventy years industrial mass production had become popularized to the widest possible audience. In other circles the work of this generation of Minimalists was categorized as "the platform school."

A few corporate-office interiors of the 1970s were designed in the Minimal idiom. Notable were the offices designed for RCA Corporate Headquarters in New York by Ford & Earl's New York office, headed by James P. Maguire with a team of Marlys Hann and Ziva Gruber. Sleek, flat, trimless planes of white, red, and charcoal-brown were enlivened by polished-metal frames of the plug-in furniture system. But it was the residential work in this idiom that drew the most attention.

Joseph Paul D'Urso   Combining a spartan Minimal envelope with industrial furnishings and materials, Joseph Paul D'Urso achieved a rich style in which chairs from the early Modern industrial period served as silhouetted sculptures.

Born in Newark, New Jersey, Joseph Paul D'Urso (1943–) got his B.F.A. in interior design at Pratt Institute and won a New York chapter AID scholarship award on his graduation in 1965. He then traveled and spent two years studying in England—first at the Royal College of Art in London, then as a fellow at the Manchester College of Art and Design, where he earned a master's degree in art from the Manchester Polytechnic Institute. In 1968 he began his independent practice in New York for the design, first, of residential interiors, and then of furnishings and larger interior projects. Since 1968 he has taught at Pratt Institute. His work was highly influential during the 1970s. His interiors were radically stripped—stark white walls, offset by platforms and steps often covered in dark-gray industrial carpeting, furnished with industrially produced chairs, tables, doors, track lighting, and vertical blinds. With this limited palette, D'Urso created interiors that nevertheless had a strong and expansive sense of scale, a crisp sculptural disposition of furnishings, and true richness and elegance. Punctuated by a single red flower, his uncompromising interiors often achieved an air of refined magic.

At mid-decade D'Urso designed an apartment for shoe designer Reed Evins in an undistinguished New York apartment building. He accepted the givens—low ceilings, wide rooms—without attempting to hide them or create something that was not there. He then opened the space further by painting walls and ceiling glossy white, and by installing integral platforms—a continuous one (6 feet 6 inches wide by 11 inches high) for seating along the 28-foot window wall and two 5-inch-high platforms stacked at one end of the first platform as a bed base. The sleeping area was defined by pull-back vertical venetian blinds, as was the 28-foot-long window wall. Gray industrial carpeting, track lighting, and a hospital door to the kitchen completed the minimal envelope. At the long platform stood a 10-foot-6-inch-long three-pedestal-base table with a glossy black rubber top banded in polished stainless steel. Complementing this spare and ascetic environment was a

185.   Joseph Paul D'Urso. Calvin Klein Menswear showroom. New York City, 1979. *Photograph courtesy D'Urso Designs Inc.*

chaise designed by Le Corbusier—the only conventional furniture except for the mattress; it also served as a sculpture. Paintings and flowers, along with the lights of the city, provided the only color. The apartment was similar to one that D'Urso designed at this time for couturier Calvin Klein.

About the same time, D'Urso also designed a showroom for Calvin Klein Accessories, for women, that had bare high-gloss white walls, gridded windows of glass block, dark-gray industrial carpeting, lines of exposed fluorescent tube lighting between the beams, exposed white-enameled air-conditioning ducts, and polished-metal pipe fixtures for fabric display. White plastic-laminate-topped black-based pedestal tables and black chairs completed his severe industrial image, in which the colorful handbags and belts, and an occasional bright-red door and flowers, enlivened the space. It was a summation of Industrial Pop and what came to be called High-Tech.

Bray-Schaible   The partnership of Robert Bray and Michael Schaible has produced interiors that have all the spartan purity of Minimalism, but also incorporate a decorative, less rigorous and doctrinaire approach.

Robert Bray (1942–) was born in Ardmore, Oklahoma, and studied architectural engineering at Oklahoma State University. Michael Schaible (1940–) was born in Oakley, Kansas. He received a B.F.A. from the University of Colorado and attended the Università di Firenze per Stranieri. They were classmates at the Parsons School of Design and began their careers working for the large space-planning firms of Ford & Earl Design Associates and Saphier, Lerner, Schindler Environetics, where most of their experience was in corporate work.

The work of Bray and Schaible is cool, clean, and elegant with an impression of spaciousness. This effect is produced by long, unbroken lines—by broad, open, and uncluttered planes—wide platforms and broad table surfaces set off against clearly defined floor areas and an almost seamless and uninterrupted background.

That seamless background is the signature of Bray-Schaible's craft: smoothed to the bone, cleared of all intruding blemishes—such as trim and baseboards, handles and knobs, light switches and electric outlets, air conditioning and light tracks (see Figure 186). Their interiors are usually pale, often vanilla-colored envelopes composed of eggshell-enameled walls, bleached wood floors or beige carpeting, off-white accordion-pleated window shades, and pale-toned stone used as flooring, fireplaces, tabletops, and serving credenzas. These envelopes are crisp, spare, and ascetic. They would be almost slick and cold if the designers did not enrich them sumptuously, as they do, differently for each client. In the 1970s they investigated rooms-within-rooms, layering, and historical allusions and quotations. Plushes and velvets, suedes and natural glove leathers, needlepoint carpets, and museum-quality artworks and objects embellished and personalized their concepts.[4]

Bray and Schaible opened their practice in 1969 with the design of a flower shop that was all glossy black enamel, aluminum shelving, glass shelves, mirrors, and spotlights on the flowers. The flower lighting became a restaurant tradition by the end of the next decade. In 1974 they designed the interiors of the First National bank of Hialeah, Florida (see Figure 187), rigorously carrying through on the inside the planar horizontality of the speculative building exterior. Each plane meets the next at a sharp edge: Floors butt directly against walls, partitions, and counters; walls butt directly against ceilings and soffits—like a fine line drawing. It was a model of hidden details that achieve simplicity. The planar effect and the horizontality again recall the white architecture of the 1920s. The tellers' counter has a half-round metal lighting troffer hung above head level from airplane cables mounted in the 60-foot-high, atrium-like ceiling. Other work of Bray-Schaible has included residential interiors, corporate installations, and complete house designs that include both planning and architecture.

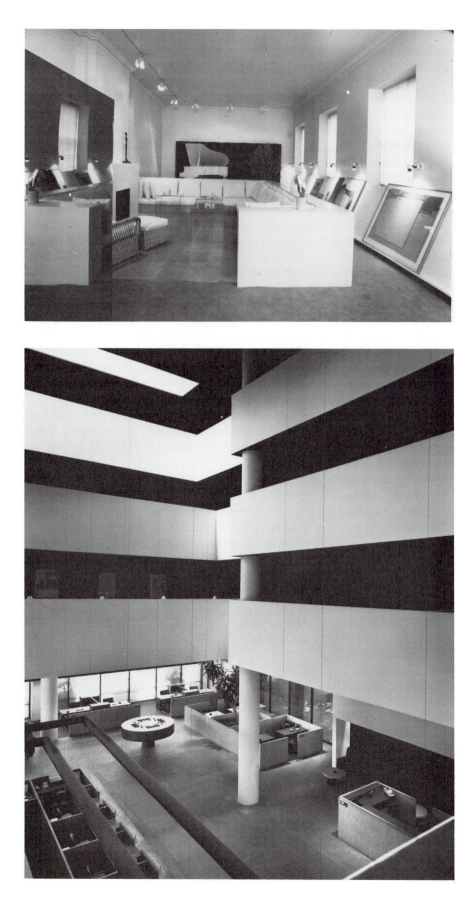

186. Bray-Schaible. Dina Cerruti Schmidt apartment. New York City. 1978. *Photograph © Wulf Brackrock for Jahres Zeiten Verlag.*

187. Bray-Schaible. First National Bank, Hialeah, Florida. 1974. *Photograph by Norman McGrath.*

Peter Andes Peter Andes was among those who pushed Minimalism to its barest, most reductive limits. Born in Lancaster, Pennsylvania, Andes (1935–) studied architecture at Yale University under Paul Rudolph's chairmanship. In the 1960s he worked in New York for Florence Knoll's Planning Unit, for which he was a project designer of interiors in New York—he worked on the CBS Building executive offices—and abroad, in Japan and Australia, where he designed the offices of the Bank of New South Wales; and in Mexico City, where he designed the interiors of the Camino Real Hotel. There he came to know Luis Barragan and Mathias Goeritz, who changed his vision.

Returning to New York in the 1970s, Andes pursued the most elemental interiors he could produce—furniture was eliminated wherever possible; platforms served as benches, banquettes, and bedsteads. All floor-related built-ins were covered in dark-gray industrial carpeting; walls were painted white or off-white; window coverings were aluminum venetian blinds. Mirrors and plants were additions to this palette to reinforce the element of repetition. His approach to elimination of detail included leaving existing room defects or moldings in place, accepting them as part of the recycling process. For one New York apartment (see Figure 188) he employed this vocabulary with tricks of enormous scale: The bed platform was 36 inches high; the venetian blinds covered the entire window wall. It was difficult to determine how large things in the apartment were.

For another apartment Andes repeated this black-and-white vocabulary, enriching it with glossy white trim and flat off-white walls. He furnished it with thirty 3-foot-square stacking cushions and 2-foot-square throw pillows, all in dark-gray suiting cloth with Turkish corners; these made up the portable, flexible, and Minimal seating. The scale trick of the larger-than-normal cushions was disorienting. Stacking white plastic tables, stacking ashtrays—and, in the dining room, stacking chairs, plateware, and glasses—completed the system of multiple function and repetition.

These appointments emphasized the extreme effects that the repetition of a minimal number of elements can produce—this work has been called "The Emperor's New Furniture."[5] By the late 1970s Andes was devoting himself to recycling lofts for residential use, doing the actual construction with his partner to learn more about the craft of this interior sculpture and the potential of minimalizing it further.

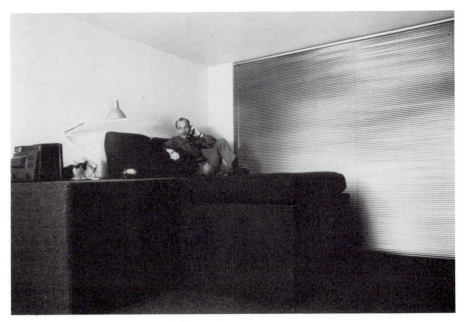

188. Peter Andes. Own apartment. New York City. Circa 1970. *Photograph by Jon Naar.*

The Residential Designers

More and more contract work was being done by traditional decorating firms. Billy Baldwin retired in 1972, leaving his firm to his partner, Arthur Smith. In his book *Billy Baldwin Remembers* he wrote about the interiors and people he most remembered. He spent the last decade of his life on Nantucket island, off Massachusetts, and died in 1984. William Pahlmann, after completing a large commission for Texas A&M University in 1976, retired to live in Mexico. Then in the 1970s, a new group of residential designers came to prominence.

David Hicks

From England to America, in 1968, had come the designs of David Hicks—carpets and fabrics patterned with all-over squares, plaids, and other small-scale geometric shapes. Billy Baldwin wrote that Hicks had "revolutionized the floors of the world with his small patterned and striped carpeting."[6]

Hicks had begun his career as an interior designer in London in 1955, and in 1960 his first carpet designs were produced. Fabric designs followed in 1964. They were immediately popular with American designers. Hicks's bathroom designs with tubs set in the center also influenced American designers in the 1970s. He had liked the straightforwardness with which Americans hung large contemporary paintings unframed, and began using English contemporary abstracts unframed, in rooms filled with eighteenth-century furniture. It was a fresh liberation of the sometimes stiff approach to formality taken in English interior design up to that time. The French liked it and called it "Le Style Anglais." By 1979 Hicks had published seven books about his design approach.

Albert Hadley

In the 1970s Parish-Hadley redesigned the Southampton, Long Island, summer house that William Paley of CBS had bought from Eleanor McMillen Brown, bringing another circle of connections between McMillen and Parish-Hadley. Hadley also designed and completed in three weeks, as originally required, a library-study for Mrs. Vincent Astor in New York that showed his inventiveness.

The herringbone-pattern flooring, which was scraped and restained in alternating zigzags three floorboards wide of dark and light, began a revival of stained and painted floor patterns. The wall paneling of this room was marbleized on a cream-color ground. The frames of some of the eighteenth-century French furniture were lightened and painted; upholsteries were in tones of yellows and creams. A silk fabric with an irregular black-and-white stripe, designed by Hammet & Morrow, reinforced the flooring pattern. One calfskin upholstery was stenciled to look like leopard. Draperies were of a crewel pattern. The entire composition was a personal mixture of disparate elements with a variety of scales and textures, yet complete unity.

About the same time, Albert Hadley designed a larger, more formal library for Mrs. Vincent Astor in New York that won praise. Paneled in red-lacquered wood with polished-brass trim for delineation, the library had a Bessarabian rug of red medallions with cream-and-brown flowers resting on *parquet de Versailles*. A red-and-green chintz striped with dark brown was the upholstery for the overstuffed seating. One bergère was painted white and upholstered in natural suede. An antique ikat silk was draped over one table; a coffee table was of brown lacquer. Billy Baldwin wrote, "Albert Hadley has made Mrs. Vincent Astor's red lacquer library a timeless triumph. He is a decorator with inspired ideas and great knowledge of the past."[7]

Michael Taylor

In San Francisco, the 1970s saw Michael Taylor at a peak of his career with combinations of the sophisticated and the rustic. His long use of wicker furniture, quarry-tile flooring, desert plants, and desert colors was extended by a series of furniture designed of large-scale logs—stripped and bleached but with branch stubs and knot holes retained. It was an updating of late-nineteenth-century Adirondack furniture at superscale and in 1940s California imagery—somewhere between adobe construction and cowboy bunkhouse. These pieces were made by Mimi London and Dixie Marquis, who later went on to design their own line in this idiom.

A penthouse apartment by Taylor for writer Pat Montandon in San Francisco at the end of the 1970s was spectacular at the start because of its view through 25-foot-high floor-to-ceiling glass walls. Michael Taylor transformed it into a floating white-looking aerie that was nevertheless warm and rich. He floored the space with travertine, installed a French sandstone mantelpiece, and mirrored the chimney breast and the wall opposite the windows. He then filled the space with ceiling-high ficus trees, retained the Belgian tapestry that was already there, and furnished his space with Taylor-designed cast-stone seating units that were piled with pale-beige cotton basketweave pillows. He added bleached Régence chairs upholstered in yellow-beige and tables of cast-stone that he designed, as well as rattan and stone, shell, and large-scale sculptural objects.

John Dickinson

The designs of San Francisco's John Dickinson were acclaimed for their oddly spare, peculiarly selective historical references, and the distinctive manner in which these inspirations were assembled. In his own San Francisco house, he had assembled a wide assortment of primarily nineteenth-century objects and recreations within a framework of white that was outlined or punctuated with black and softened by natural wood tones.

His living room had a bare floor, white tongue-and-groove siding on the walls, and a white ceiling; nineteenth-century iron furniture was upholstered in white. One wall displayed a collection of ironstone platters hung above a Dickinson-designed console that looked like a stripped late-nineteenth-century country table that had been cut in half. Brass kerosene lamps, Art Nouveau bronze tree-trunk lamps, and opaline globes that recalled barbershop poles served as the quasi-nostalgic lighting. Decorative elements included a group of farm tools—a scythe, a rake, two hoes—that had been enameled white, along with an armoire painted in trompe l'oeil to look like an 1870s townhouse. In the bedroom Dickinson recreated an 1870–90s look with a bamboo-turned four-poster bed that was undraped, like the windows, which were framed in dark wood tones like the tongue-and-groove wainscoting. All these rested on leopard-skin-patterned carpeting. The updated and America-inspired historicism were symptomatic of the decade.

At mid-decade, Dickinson designed a virtually all-white entertainment room in a San Francisco house by architect Julia Morgan. Beyond the dark redwood-paneled woodwork of Julia Morgan's design, Dickinson painted matte-white walls with glossy white woodwork and moldings of pearl gray, pale apricot, and chamois color. A thick white wool rug of octagonal shape rests on a dark-stained wood floor. White Belgian cotton canvas is used for Roman shades and upholsteries—even those on backless benches, the frames of which are covered in natural linen velvet. Pull-up chairs have white epoxy-lacquer finishes. The juxtaposition of the all-white scheme with rustic coffee tables designed by Dickinson to look like packing crates was evocative of both Syrie Maugham and the 1940s.

In 1979 John Dickinson designed a San Francisco residence in a renovated 1930s building with contextual respect for its surroundings. Dickinson designed all the furnishings, including the occasional tables that suggested African animal legs. Minimalism was the overall effect because of the pale, monochromatic scheme, but there was an echo of Robsjohn-Gibbings in the long banquettes and large-scale chairs.

John Dickinson demonstrated a special flair for mixing then-undiscovered periods of late-nineteenth-century style with furniture of his own design and inspiration. His range of white-on-white combined with tawny "unfinished" wood textures showed a notable sensitivity to the orchestration of both textures and colors. His untimely death in 1982 deprived the world of interior design of a master of style who had just come into his own.

Zajac & Callahan

In the 1970s Zajac & Callahan designed interiors ranging from Paris and London to Dallas and San Francisco. They continued to design virtually every element of their interiors—all newly made furniture except for the fabrics—upholstered pieces, tables, desks, lamps, mirrors, and screens. They often sculpted models of elements such as moldings to serve as prototypes. Other pieces were either antiques or signed by artist-craftsmen. They were intrigued by uncommon styles—Swedish Louis XV and Irish Chippendale, which was in direct descent from Ruby Ross Wood—as well as textures from other cultures, Japanese lacquers especially.

One New York apartment living room by Zajac & Callahan was richly expressive of the decade's multidirectional historicism (see Figure 189). Within a multi-

189. Zajac & Callahan. Apartment. New York City. 1975. *Photograph by Alexandre Georges.*

textured terracotta-red envelope was a gray-and-gold subscheme. Walls were striped with battens, were given twig-moldings like Adirondack furniture, and were strié-lacquered in four coats of rust-red. Windows were covered with Madagascar-inspired lattice screens lacquered the same terracotta-red. To compose the gold-and-gray secondary colors, floors were painted the pattern of Chopin's house in Warsaw—pale-beige graining and small blue-gray squares; a tobacco-gold Louis XV marble mantelpiece was lined with beige and gray tiles. Bleached pigskin Louis XVI chairs with trapunto cushions and tufted backs along with tables of cream-colored plastic laminate and lacquer inlaid with cane continued the gray-and-gold subscheme. A coffee table was by Giacometti.

Lighting included Lucite lamps of their own design and exposed-bulb reflector lamps. At one end of the room was a long library table with raised candle-stand-top legs; it was piled high with another smaller table and with plant stands holding a collection of oriental vases, jardinieres, and convex mirror reflectors framed with gilded fern leaves by French designer Line Vautrin. In the middle of the room, atop a tall fluted column, stood a Turkish bust. It was another of the decade's extraordinary exercises in mannerism and scale.

In another apartment, Zajac & Callahan demonstrated their ability to work with a more subdued palette—beiges, ochres, and siennas with accents of black, white, red, and blue—but the range of their textures was expansive. Glossy surfaces (Lucite and lacquer, silver and chrome, stone and steel, crystal and glass) were offset against rough textures (wools, wickers, woods, canes, and crackle lacquer as well as a glazed red-linen finish on a Chinese reproduction coffee table). In all of this, one pattern with variations—the basketweave—was used throughout. Typical as this was of the decade's multidirectional historicism, it was highly original in expression.

Denning & Fourcade

Along with many residential designs in the 1970s, Robert Denning designed a New York restaurant—Gertrude's. Though he designed it with some of his firm's trademarks, it was restrained by the heavy commercial traffic of the interior. Masters of the pattern-on-pattern, texture-on-texture, object-on-object technique of superimposition, Denning & Fourcade sheathed the walls in apricot-painted rough-hewn wood and with cut-and-painted mirrors in a sunburst pattern. A polished pressed-metal ceiling with a sunburst pattern reflected the pink-bulb light from steel-and-brass Neoclassical wall sconces that had fringed shades. (The latter had become one of Denning & Fourcade's trademarks.) Blue-and-green Chinese porcelain bowls, carafes, and ashtrays accented the blue tablecloths.

It was a scheme slightly more rustic than the suave Madison Avenue shop that the firm designed for Diane Von Furstenberg's line of cosmetics about the same time. The extreme of their pattern-on-pattern manipulation was in an apartment for Diane Von Furstenberg (see Figure 190). Denning & Fourcade also did highly controlled historical recreations of great country houses during the 1970s.

Mark Hampton

The designs of Mark Hampton first came to attention in the 1970s for his refreshed recreations of the eighteenth-century spirit. He worked in both informal and highly formal veins. Seven-coated lacquer walls, marbleized woodwork and moldings, huge coromandel screens, patterned wallpapers with elaborate borders—scallops, swags, and pennants—were typical of his work in residences.

Born in Plainfield, Indiana, Mark Hampton (1940–) attended De Pauw University and the London School of Economics. He received an M.F.A. from New York University's Institute of Fine Arts. He began his design career as David

190. Denning & Fourcade. Dining room, Diane Von Furstenberg apartment. New York City. 1975. *Phaotograph by Norman McGrath*

Hicks's American representative, then worked for Mrs. Henry Parish II and as an associate of McMillen Inc. for the next six years. He opened his own practice in New York in 1976 and has since designed numerous residences as well as yachts, railroad cars, and offices.

John Saladino

John Saladino's designs came to national prominence in the 1970s for what he called "interior design as fine art" or "fantasies made real."

Born in Kansas City, Missouri, John Saladino (1939–) began his career not as a designer, but as a painter—first at Notre Dame University, where he received a B.F.A. in art history, and then at Yale University, where he received an M.F.A. in painting under Josef Albers. He then worked in Italy for architect Piero Sartogo (see Chapter 10) and returned to New York, where from 1963 to 1969 he worked with large space-planning firms—Saphier, Lerner, Schindler, and J.F.N. Associates. After a brief partnership with J. P. Maggio, he started his own practice in

New York in 1972. During the 1970s he designed numerous residences, offices, and pieces of furniture; the latter were put into production by Dunbar.

Saladino's designs combine Late Modern with traditional historical decorating and with Country Vernacular. His designs merge the elegant urbanity of the Machine Age with the domestic simplicity of country life. He blends the sleekness of Modern forms and detailing with the sensuousness of an art-oriented eye. "Oriented" is a key word for his style. He uses the colors and textures of oriental art—the aubergine of Japanese ceramic glazes, the celadon green of Chinese glazes, the mauve-pinks of the plum blossom—and actual artworks from the Orient in large measure. He is also fond of the simple materials that are associated with the Orient—wicker, bamboo, and unfinished wood.[8]

Against these elements, John Saladino sets the shapes and forms of the most refined Modern purity—frill-less corners, crisp and shimmering reflective sur-

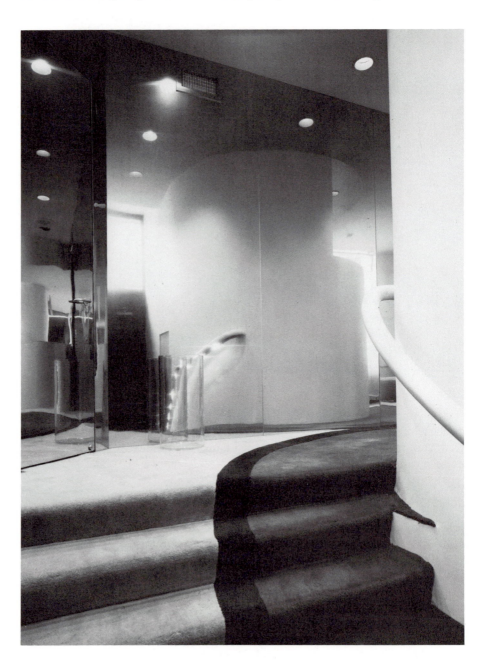

191. John Saladino. Physician's offices. New York City. 1974. *Photograph by James Mathews, courtesy John Saladino.*

faces, chunky sofas, and whimsical Post-Modern table bases, as well as built-in furniture and accessories of elegant precision and convenience. There is an air of simplicity and refinement about his work, an air of control and minimalism. Yet, overall, his interiors exhibit a painterly use of color that is delicate and sensuous.

His work has included residences, corporate offices, doctors' offices, and other interiors. One doctor's office designed in the mid-1970s combined crisp Art Deco–like carpet borders with mistily shimmering brushed-steel panels (see Figure 191) and a corridor of vibrant colors arranged progressionally—blue to yellow, to orange, to cream—that were run in diagonal bands around floor, walls, and ceiling.

His orchestrations of texture—stainless steel and wicker, wood and stone, velvet and plastic laminate—were balanced and rich. By the end of the decade he was using fabrics in quilted patterns, in flat hanging panels, in loose wind-wafted panels, and in a casual crumpled texture. In 1979 Saladino designed offices for the Almay cosmetics firm with a color palette derived not from the Post-Modern idiom, but contextually related to the tints and textures of the firm's products—pale apricot, peach, and similar tones covered the walls and upholsteries. Other interiors by Saladino sported lavender and pale blue, magenta and peach, cream and beige. It was a rich dessert of colors, textures, materials, and periods that he served.

Licensing for Interior Designers

In 1972 NSID and AID formed a joint committee to develop a common qualification examination and investigate licensing for interior designers. The National Council for Interior Design Qualification (NCIDQ) was the result. NCIDQ is governed by representatives of numerous organizations concerned with the profession of designing interiors: the American Society of Interior Designers, the Interior Design Educators Council, the Institute of Business Designers, the National Home Fashions League, and the Interior Designers of Canada.

The NCIDQ examination, which was developed with the aid of the Psychological Corporation and Educational Testing Service, was first given in 1974. It is designed to establish the core of interior design knowledge that is required to practice as a professional interior designer. The NCIDQ examination is also considered an essential first step in state-mandated legal licensing.

Throughout the decade these organizations continued to investigate licensing and examinations that would qualify interior designers. Throughout the decade, also, an interorganizational committee worked with the American Institute of Architects on a mutually agreed-upon standard contract for interior design services. In 1975 AID and NSID were consolidated as the American Society of Interior Designers—ASID. These activities, it was hoped, signaled the beginning of consolidation for the entire range of design professionals.

Suggested Reading

Abercrombie, Stanley. "The 70s Recap: Highlighting Events of the Decade," *AIA Journal.* January 1980, pp. 38–50.

Ambasz, Emilio. *Italy: The New Domestic Landscape.* New York: The Museum of Modern Art, 1972.

———. *The Architecture of Luis Barragan.* New York: The Museum of Modern Art, 1976.

Baird, George, and Charles Jencks. *Meaning in Architecture.* New York: Braziller, 1979.

Barthes, Roland. *Elements of Semiology.* New York: Hill & Wang, 1979.

Blake, Peter. *Form Follows Fiasco.* Boston: Little, Brown, 1977.

Broadbent, Bunt, and Charles Jencks. *Signs, Symbols and Architecture.* New York: John Wiley, 1980.

Drexler, Arthur. *Transformations in Modern Architecture*. New York: The Museum of Modern Art, 1979.

Filler, Martin. "The Plain, the Fancy, the Real, and the Unreal," *Progressive Architecture*. September 1977.

Five Architects: Eisenman, Graves, Gwathmey, Hejduk, Meier. 2nd ed. New York: Oxford University Press, 1975.

Charles Gwathmey & Robert Siegel: Residential Works, 1966–1977. New York: Architectural Book Publishing Co., 1977.

Jencks, Charles. *The Language of Post-Modern Architecture*. New York: Rizzoli, 1977.

———. *Late-Modern Architecture*. New York: Rizzoli, 1980.

Kron, Joan, and Susan Slesin. *High-Tech*. New York: Clarkson N. Potter, 1978.

Lévi-Strauss, Claude. *Myth and Meaning*. New York: Schocken Books, 1979.

Meier, Richard. *Richard Meier, Architect*. New York: Oxford University Press, 1976.

Meyer, Ursula. *Conceptual Art*. New York: E. P. Dutton, 1972.

Moore, Charles, and Gerald Allen. *Dimensions*. New York: Architectural Record Books, 1977.

Moore, Charles, Donlyn Lyndon, and Gerald Allen. *The Place of Houses*. New York: Holt, Rinehart and Winston, 1974.

Nuckolls, James L. *Interior Lighting for Environmental Designers*, 2d ed. New York: John Wiley, 1983.

Platner, Warren. *Ten by Platner*. New York: McGraw-Hill, 1975.

Ross, Michael Franklin. *Beyond Metabolism*. New York: Architectural Record Books, 1978.

Smith, C. Ray. "Alexander Girard's Offices for Irwin Miller," *Interiors*. February 1975, p. 60.

———, and Ruth Miller Fitzgibbons. "Workstations with Up and Down Lighting," *Interiors*. September 1975.

Stephens, Suzanne. "Playing with a Full Decade," *Progressive Architecture*. December 1979, p. 49.

Venturi, Robert, Denise Scott-Brown, and Stephen Izenour. *Learning from Las Vegas*. Cambridge: MIT Press, 1972.

Wheeler, Karen, and Peter Arnell, eds. *Michael Graves: Buildings and Projects, 1966–1981*. New York: Rizzoli, 1983.

Notes

1. Charles Moore, Donlyn Lyndon, and Gerald Allen, *The Place of Houses* (New York: Holt, Rinehart and Winston, 1974), pp. 124, 127. This book is a superb analysis of how to look at houses as well as a pioneering return to the importance of user response in interior design.

2. Adapted from C. Ray Smith's appraisal of Michael Graves's work in the encyclopedia *Contemporary Architects* (New York: St. Martin's Press, 1980), p. 305.

3. Michael Graves, quoted from an interview with C. Ray Smith and Allen Tate in New York City on November 3, 1982.

4. Adapted from C. Ray Smith's articles on the work of Bray-Schaible in *Architectural Digest* (November 1979 and October 1981).

5. This is the title of an article discussing this apartment design, written by C. Ray Smith as Editor of *Interiors* magazine (October 1974), p. 116R.

6. Billy Baldwin, quoted in *20th Century Decorating, Architecture, and Gardens*, ed. Mary Jane Pool (New York: Holt, Rinehart and Winston, 1980), p. 10.

7. Ibid., p. 11. See *House & Garden* (October 1985), pp. 136–39.

8. Adapted from C. Ray Smith's article on the work of John Saladino in *Avenue* magazine (March 1978), pp. 46–52.

Chapter **10**

1980 to the Present: Today and Its Challenges

In the first half of the 1980s the interior design profession was still in transition, but its growth since the beginning of the century had been great. Professional interior design was being provided for medical facilities and schools, for hotels and restaurants, for commercial and institutional facilities, for retail sales boutiques and department stores, for theaters and museums, for offices and residences. Few types of interior spaces, in fact, were *not* being given careful professional attention. In addition, this interior design work by American designers was located not only within the United States; American designers of interiors were practicing around the world.

Employment for professional designers was at last available in numerous situations: as independent self-employed designers; as employees in interior design departments of large architecture or interior design firms; in the in-house design divisions of large corporations, large hospitals, and large hotel chains; in the interior design departments of department stores, retail and wholesale furnishings outlets; and in government agencies. More and more architecture firms began to establish their own departments of interior design. Other architects increasingly commissioned office-planning and other interior design firms to work with them on the interiors of their buildings. Interior design had grown to a $5-billion-a-year business.

Professional groups concerned with interior design were working steadily toward professional licensing and registration. The Foundation for Interior Design Education Research (FIDER) continued to develop national guidelines for interior design education. FIDER is now recognized by the federal government as the accrediting organization for educational programs in interior design. The National Council for Interior Design Qualification (NCIDQ) continued to promote its two-day examination to qualify members of professional organizations. In the early 1980s Alabama and Connecticut established legal licensing; there, use of the designation "interior designer" as a professional designation is restricted to those who have passed the two-day NCIDQ examination. Such legalities are intended to lead to required registration of professional interior designers in every state of the country. The aim is to make the profession as legally responsible (and respectable) as medicine and the law.

Designers of interiors from several different professions—architects, space planners, and interior designers—and from several different organizations whose members practice interior design—AIA, ASID, IBD—continued to sit jointly on the Interiors Committee of the American Institute of Architects to devise standard contract documents for all interior design professionals, as well as to conduct programs that would improve understanding, coordination, and management of interior design projects.

Directions at Mid-Decade

Energy and Conservation

Energy continued to be a prominent concern of interior designers, as it was for the rest of society; and the demands of the technology for energy conservation similarly increased demands on professional designers of interiors. Advances in other technologies—in office, medical, industrial, retailing, and even residential environments—created continuing needs for postgraduate professional education.

It became clear to most Americans that the Computer/Electronic Age was here. Designers of interiors were concerned with accommodating computers in offices and residences, with wide-screen television installations, and with other electronic devices. Whatever the degree of contribution to the process of design computers made, it was irrefutable that, as assists in doing repeat work—drafting, detailing, and the like—computers could increase speed, accuracy, and efficiency by many hours. Countless articles discussed the subject; but they focused primarily on the equipment, without due attention to making the new electronic environments satisfying or attractive to users or occupants. Among other notable technical advances that affected the field was the introduction of flat wiring in electrical systems. In construction technology, metal studs along with plasterboard and gypsumboard sheets had almost wiped out the plasterers' trade.

Professional journals as well as newspaper reporting on the interior design field all had undergone a considerable increase in numbers and quantity of reporting as well as quality. More of the complete range of interior design was presented by the journals—including historical interiors that had remained intact since their creation, restorations of the historical monuments of interior design, especially those from the 1920s and 1930s, as well as the new, the vanguard, and the stately homes from the eighteenth and early nineteenth centuries.

A Pluralism of Approaches

In the early 1980s the widest possible range of directions, approaches, styles, talents, and interests was at work in interior design. "Inclusiveness" and the "pluralism" of approaches were the terms used by analysts of this phenomenon, which was also labeled "confusion." This situation was expanded and complicated by unexpected combinations of one or more of the pluralistic possibilities; these combinations produced images of duality, multiplicity, and, sometimes, discontinuity. Historical eclecticism and mannered ornamentation were the single direction shared by most of the interior design professions—both in architecture and in decorating.

Post-Modernism was still the polemic idiom of the day, though there was little agreement on what it was. The prevailing definition or understanding was that it meant historicism and ornamentation, especially mannered classicism—games with classical ornament and scale. The AT&T Building in New York by Philip Johnson and John Burgee, Architects, with its superscale broken-pediment roofscape became the symbol of this school. Post-Modern interior designers seemed most indebted to the classically derived interior designs of Michael Graves. The Country "look," this time based on North American vernacular, furnishings, and folk art, for a short time held out hope of a new feeling for straightforward national realism; but American Country interiors soon gave way to the old Arts and Crafts romanticism.

The preservation movement began to focus more on treasured historical interiors. There were continuing revivals of neo-Deco and new revivals of neo-1950s. There were recalls and comments on art movements throughout the century— Abstract interiors, Conceptual interiors, and Constructivist interiors. There were also numerous recalls of early-twentieth-century designers, such as Hoffmann and Loos; and of later designers ranging from Aalto and Asplund, to Barragan, to SITE Inc.; and even recalls of Robert Venturi. Among the stylistic ventures of the first half of the 1980s were such combinations as Post-Modernism with Country; Minimalism within historical restoration; Country with Minimal; and so on.

As in every decade, there were vanguard innovative interiors, a few of which were truly innovative and others of which proffered imagery that was more meaningful to the designer than the concern for the client's activities or desires. In the middle were compromises and combinations that showed a confusion or uneasy compatibility of styles or ideas, muddled middle minds, and the like. And at the low end of the scale were shallow, glib glosses on style and function, on pretension and aspiration, that deserved the pejorative epithet "glitzy."

Preservation and Recycling

Preservation and recycling were accepted rationales for historicism and historical revivals, which were practiced by vanguard architects as well as traditional decorators. Lofts and other spaces from old industrial buildings were recycled into offices, shopping centers, residences, and any number of other functions for which they were not originally designed. It was beginning to look as if there might be a general recognition of the value of saving whatever old that was good and of preserving our design heritage. Since 1976, when laws began to make restoration economically advantageous, commercial organizations had begun to jump on the preservation train. Hotels, movie houses, and other commercial establishments began to capitalize on their historical advantages.

By the mid-1980s approximately one hundred major old hotels across the country had been restored instead of "renovated" to some contemporary state. Among them were Denver's Brown Palace Hotel of 1893, New York City's Plaza Hotel of 1907, Boston's Copley Plaza of 1912, Dallas's Adolphus Hotel of 1912, Seattle's Four Seasons Olympic Hotel of 1923, and Memphis's Peabody Hotel of 1925. In 1980 the Los Angeles Biltmore of 1923 was restored by Phyllis Lambert and Gene Summers, who furnished some of the old suites with Mies van der Rohe's classic furniture from the 1920s. In 1981 the Arizona Biltmore of 1929, designed by Albert Chase McArthur with the consultation of Frank Lloyd Wright, was restored to its original appearance. Also in 1981 the Villard houses in New York were saved and incorporated into the contrastingly overblown Helmsley Palace Hotel as its most elegantly designed reception rooms.

All this activity made clear the need for restoration designers who knew their history as well as the techniques for preservation and restoration.

Historical Revivals

The historicism of the decade was continued both as pure, academic restoration or recreation of period rooms, primarily eighteenth and nineteenth century as well as revivals with inclusions of twentieth-century mannerism such as scale manipulations. Architects continued to recall the work of early-twentieth-century architects. Cesar Pelli was designing mid-Victorian wall treatments for New York's Battery Park City complex that recalled London's Houses of Parliament and evoked

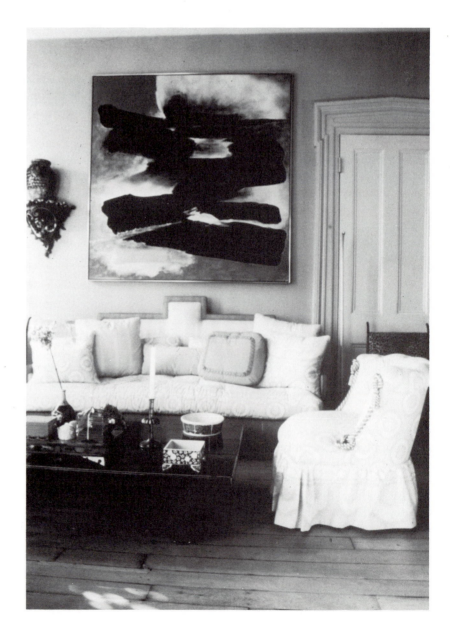

192. Zajac & Callahan. Apartment. New York City. 1983. *Photograph courtesy Zajac & Callahan Inc.*

again the spirit of the Great Exhibition at the Crystal Palace. Parish-Hadley and McMillen were doing more and more corporate and institutional work. The sixty-year career of Eleanor McMillen Brown was celebrated in a book published in 1982.

Albert Hadley redesigned the apartment of Mrs. Nelson Rockefeller after the death of her husband, rearranging the original Jean-Michel Frank furnishings (see Chapter 5). Mrs. Rockefeller needed a smaller apartment and, with Hadley's designing, she consolidated her collection into fewer rooms. The original living room, designed in 1937 by Wallace Harrison and Jean-Michel Frank (as "Louis XV—but modern," Nelson Rockefeller had said), was recast in the former dining room. Relocated were Jean-Michel Frank chairs; Christian Berard rugs and upholstered furniture; Giacometti's gilded consoles, sconces, and andirons; and a museum-quality collection of artworks. It was a fortuitous recycling—as well as an extension of the 1930s spirit—that was the essence of the history-oriented 1980s.

Historical revivalism also brought back some unexpected period styles: Zajac & Callahan manipulated 1880s frills for a Victorian house in Philadelphia. One apartment in New York by Zajac & Callahan exhibited a combination of the most recherché and unlikely—but beautiful—pieces of furniture, sculpture, painting,

193. Powell/Kleinschmidt. Apartment. One Magnificent Mile. Chicago, Illinois. 1984. *Photograph © Tony Soluri, 1984.*

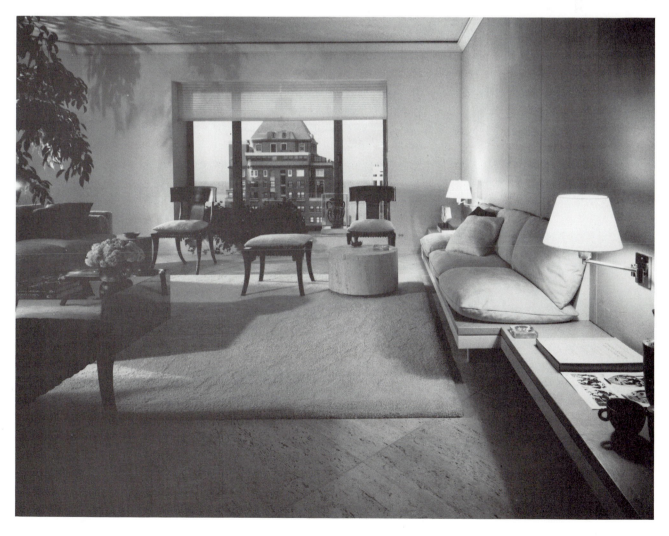

and decorative objects in a fresh and radiantly personal arrangement and atmosphere (see Figure 192). Powell Kleinschmidt in Chicago continued variations on the Miesian idiom, updating it with colors that recalled color-field painting (see Figure 193). Sufficient time has not yet elapsed to determine whether this should be called Miesian revival, Miesian survival, or Late Modern. Furniture revivals, or survivals, included the furniture designs of Mies, Le Corbusier, Breuer, Aalto, Josef Hoffmann, and Eliel Saarinen; there was also a collectors' and commercial revival of Stickley and other Mission furnishings.

John Saladino was at a peak of popularity for his special color sense in blending mauves, pinks, apricots, ivories, pale grays, and taupes (it was the ice-cream palette of the decade); and for his sensitive juxtapositions of furniture—Machine Age, historical, Peasant, and his own soft and seductive, often channel-quilted upholstered pieces (see Figure 194).

Mark Hampton was doing more restoration design with his work on Gracie Mansion, New York City's mayoral residence (see Figure 195) and on Blair House in Washington, D.C.

194. John Saladino. Apartment. New York City. 1984. *Photograph © Peter Aaron/ESTO, 1984, courtesy Condé-Nast Publications, Inc.*

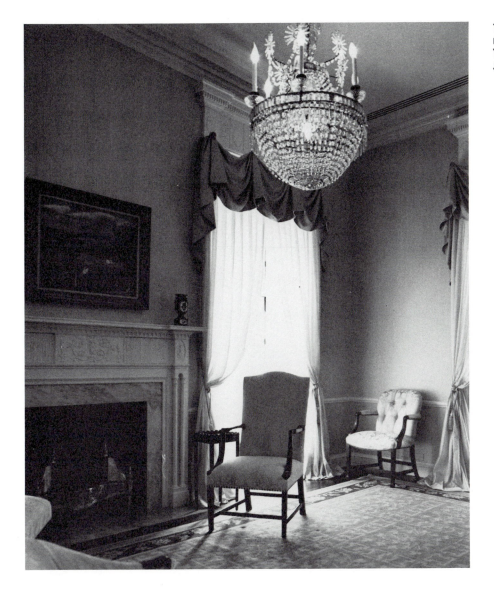

195. Mark Hampton. Restored room, Gracie Mansion. New York City. 1984. *Photograph © Stan Ries, 1984.*

Minimalism

A continued interest in stripped interiors with industrial-looking furnishings was also strong in the 1980s. A working-out of the goals of the Deutscher Werkbund since 1907, this approach also had overtones of prefab, found, and Pop. Among the designers working in the Minimal idiom were those continuing from the 1960s and 1970s—Benjamin Baldwin, Ward Bennett, William Machado, Joseph D'Urso, Bray-Schaible (see Figure 196), Robin Jacobsen and Scott Bromley, Norman Diekman, and Peter Andes (see Figure 197)—as well as a new generation from the 1980s who combined Minimalism with other influences.

In 1981 Benjamin Baldwin designed the interiors of the new Americana Hotel in Fort Worth, Texas, in his simple, Minimal idiom. Baldwin engaged Roger Ferri as assistant to design the ballroom and restaurant of the hotel. Ferri's large-scale sculptural elements were additions to the Minimal concept and were his first opportunity to adapt his plant-form concepts to commercial interiors.

Exemplary of the combinations, Joseph Paul D'Urso in 1983 redesigned the interiors of a turn-of-the-century house in Southampton, Long Island, as a com-

196. Bray-Schaible. Residence. New York City. 1982.
Photograph by François Hallard.

197. Peter Andes Apartment.
New York City. 1980. *Photograph by Norman McGrath.*

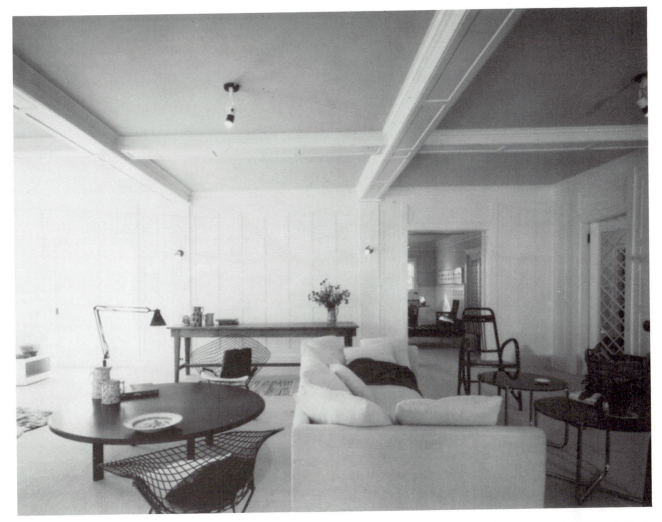

198. Joseph Paul D'Urso. Residence. Southhampton, Long Island. 1982–83. *Photograph by Rick Barnes, courtesy D'Urso Designs Inc.*

bination of Industrial Minimalism with historical preservation (see Figure 198). The woodwork in the paneled and pilastered living room and dining room with their diamond-paned windows was restored and painted white; the ceilings were painted pale mauve; the dining room walls above the white wainscoting were painted a pale pink; and beige sisal carpeting was used throughout. Against this background D'Urso located white upholstered sofas and window seats with white cushions, and black tables and black metal chairs, and black-and-white industrial-looking lighting fixtures. Between these extremes he located furniture in natural wood tones that continued the palette of the sisal carpeting. The interplay of old and new, handcraft and industry, black and white, painted and natural, and of two versions of the diamond motif made a special synthesis of the decade's interests.

Post-Modernism

Post-Modern designers and architects continued to work out their manipulations of stripped classical ornamentation—what might better be called "mannered classicism"—in ice-cream colors (pale apricot, vanilla, and black raspberry). Although a definition of Post-Modernism had still not been broadly agreed upon, it was becoming clear that its primary components were historicism, classical ornamen-

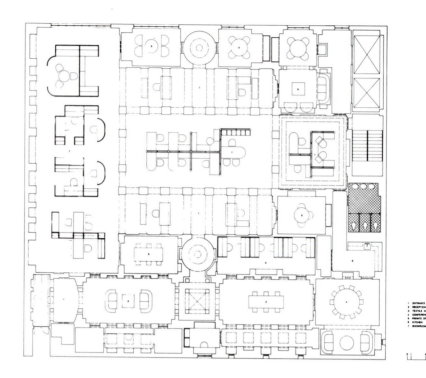

199. Michael Graves. Plan, Sunar showroom. New York City. 1981. *Illustration courtesy Sunar/Hauserman.*

tation, color, a pluralism of approaches, and sometimes simultaneity of multiple approaches, meanings, messages, historical inspiration, and emotional content.

Michael Graves designed a series of eight showrooms in different cities for the Sunar furniture company, beginning in 1979. Their impact on other designers was immediate. Graves's technique of displaying fabrics as loosely draped and flowing yard goods, first thought so outrageous and inappropriate by many designers and display designers, was soon emulated widely. His muted, delicate, and seductive color palette—apricot, gray, French blue, taupe, ochre—was adopted by mainstream, established designers as well as by the vanguard young. Graves's concept for these showrooms was of contained, separate rooms, rather than flowing space; a hierarchical sequence of those rooms; and a three-part division of walls into base, middle, and top or, as Graves stresses the anthropomorphic classical backbround, "foot, body, and head."

In his second New York showroom for Sunar (1981), Graves integrated the working areas into the showroom space, forming both in his classically derived vocabulary—columns and capitals, pediments and vaulted ceilings, flutings and marbleizing (see Figure 199). In the third Chicago Sunar showroom (1982), colors were more somber and monumental; softly draped fabrics complemented hard surfaces in crisp forms; and Graves's Deco-Streamlined indirect lighting was subtle and captivating (see color plate 15). For Sunar, also, Graves began to design furniture in his personal vein of classical allusion.

Voorsanger & Mills, Architects, interpreted this direction (1982–84) with their designs for the New York restaurants Le Cygne and Nightfalls, with their offices for the New York chapter of the American Institute of Architects, and with the Janovic-Plaza paint store. And they had good company in the work of numerous other designers.

The architect-historian Robert A. M. Stern continued his multiple role of promoting Post-Modernism, rediscovering neglected designers and architects of the 1920s and 1930s, and designing buildings and interiors in the Post-Modern idiom with its multiple historical influences. One indoor swimming pool in a New Jersey residence (1982) was entered by Deco-Grecian stairs and was supported by columns that recreated the metal palm-tree capitals of John Nash's Brighton Pavilion of 1815–21. (In 1979, the influential architect Hans Hollein in Austria had called upon the same historical reference in a travel office in Vienna.) Elsewhere in the same residence, the furniture recreated the work of Mies and Le Corbusier and offered layered screens, Deco lighting effects, and at least one caryatid-decorated fireplace.

His other residential interiors, often within houses that were sensitive assemblies of motifs and elements from Shingle-Style buildings, showed the influence of Sir Edwin Lutyens, Stanford White, and other turn-of-the-century architects and designers. One of Stern's offices, for Dr. Herbert E. Walker, subtly reinterpreted the classicism of Stanford White. It contained furniture selected and specified by Peter Andes, that reinterpreted the classical-contemporary furniture that clients would recognize as being in the accepted idiom of other doctors' offices. Stern's showroom for Shaw-Walker furniture company in Chicago (1982) (see Figure 200) showed his manipulation of Hoffmann-inspired motifs—especially the grid—as integrated with Post-Modern circulation and the Post-Modern visual vocabulary.

Other Post-Modern designers indicated that "interiors as narrative" was their concept of the decade's direction. The theory was that designs should be reflective,

200.   Robert A. M. Stern, Architects. Showroom for Shaw-Walker. Chicago. 1982. *Photograph © Peter Aaron/ESTO. 1982.*

expressive of their locale or content, of the client's background or history, or of some other interrelationship. Diana Agrest & Mario Gandelsonas, Architects, designed their Pink House as a discussion of the many kinds and uses of doors. "Contextualism" was the term used to denote this design attention and this basis for design. Some office designers adopted murals as a major communication technique for this aim: Photo murals in a variety of large-scale techniques and trompe l'oeil murals—some of them billboard size and building size by painter Richard Haas—became prevalent.

Abstract Interiors

A number of furniture and fashion showrooms as well as a few designers' own apartments were designed with homage to twentieth-century art movements such as Constructivism, Dadaism, or Surrealism. Abstract forms and bizarre selection and placement of furnishings suggested Magritte and other formalist dissociations.

Vignelli Associates designed several showrooms in this vein, including one in Los Angeles in 1982 for the E. F. Hauserman Company, makers of partitioning systems and furniture. Their concept was to relate the story of Hauserman's wall-partition systems to the artwork of Dan Flavin with light and color. Flavin's work depends on lighting walls with colored fluorescent tubes. The Vignellis made this the envelope for the display of Hauserman's partitioning systems (see Figure 201). For their design of the Italcenter in Chicago (1982), a showroom for a consortium

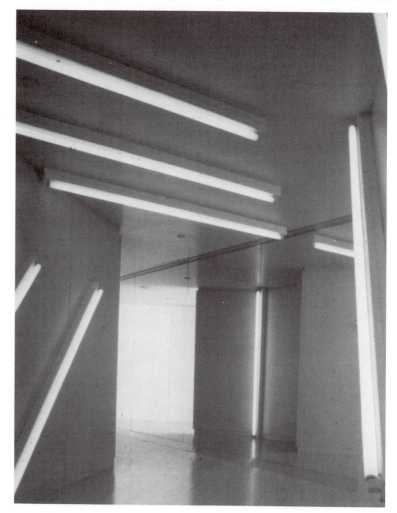

201. Vignelli Associates with Dan Flavin. E. F. Hauserman showroom. Los Angeles, California. 1982. *Photograph by Toshi Yoshimi, courtesy Vignelli Associates.*

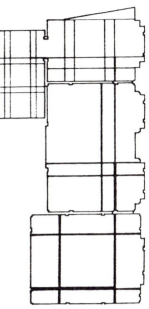

202A. Sartogo & Schwarting. Grid diagram, apartment. New York City. 1981. *Illustration courtesy Design Collaborative.*

202B. Sartogo & Schwarting. Apartment. New York City. 1981. *Photograph by Norman McGrath.*

of Italian furniture manufacturers, the Vignellis designed a series of low partition-like walls, finished to look like superscale stone texture, that were offset by a grid screen and massive sculptural forms such as an 8-foot-diameter sphere, a cylinder, and a pyramid, finished in the same texture but in different colors. It was a surreal landscape reminiscent of de Chirico, with motifs of Post-Modernism—the broken wavy line, the stepped wall, and the diagonal.

Conceptualism

Interiors as Conceptual Art was the approach of architects Piero Sartogo and Jon Michael Schwarting. Their apartments for a client in New York (1981) (see Figures 202A and B) and in Rome (1982), along with their Italian Trade Center in New York (1982) (see Figure 203), were elaborate conceptual overlays of this type. For the apartment in New York (see Figures 202A and B) Sartogo and Schwarting's concept was like a progressional nautilus shell. From room to room a series of columns and grids got larger but fewer. For the apartment in Rome, Sartogo's concept was that an identical plan of the apartment had been superimposed on the original one but a foot or so off alignment with the original. By painting the colors of each room along the lines of the imaginary, superimposed plan, the actual walls were considered as nonexistent; but looking along the juncture of the paint lines made it look as though the imaginary walls had been made real.

For the Italian Trade Center on Park Avenue, Sartogo and Schwarting envisioned an imaginary plan of the L-shaped space rotated over the actual plan; the intersections were indicated by changes of color and material. The effect was of one space that worked like two (see Figure 203).

203. Sartogo & Schwarting. Italian Trade Center. New York City. 1982. *Photograph by Norman McGrath.*

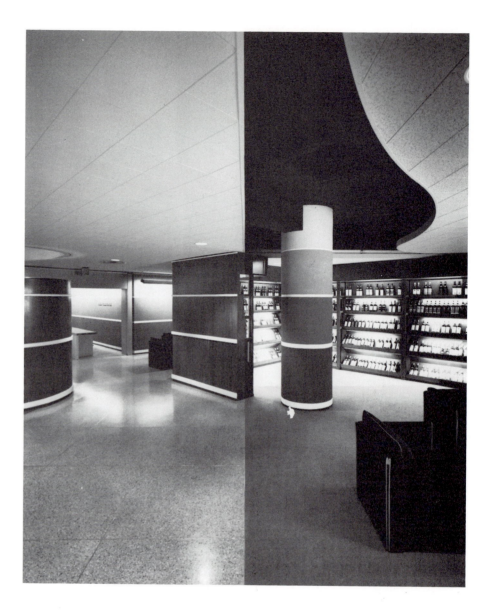

Mainstream Vanguard

Among interior designs by established architects, I. M. Pei's East Wing of the National Gallery of Art in Washington, D.C. (1980), showed the angular lengths to which establishment architects could go in their attempts to compose new interior imagery. Paul Rudolph continued to work out Futurist-Expressionist themes with vertigo-defying glass floors, glass bridges, and a transparent elevator in his own remodeled New York apartment (1980–85).

Other Combinations

A new school of young architects—including Friday Architects in Philadelphia, Arquitectonica in Miami, Taft Architects in Houston, and other firms—produced interiors as well as buildings that were a mix of Russian Constructivism, Art Deco, and 1950s motifs. Among their favorite motifs was the grid—as derived from Japanese traditional architecture, from Vienna in the 1900s—Loos, Hoffmann, et al.—and from Barragan and the 1950s.

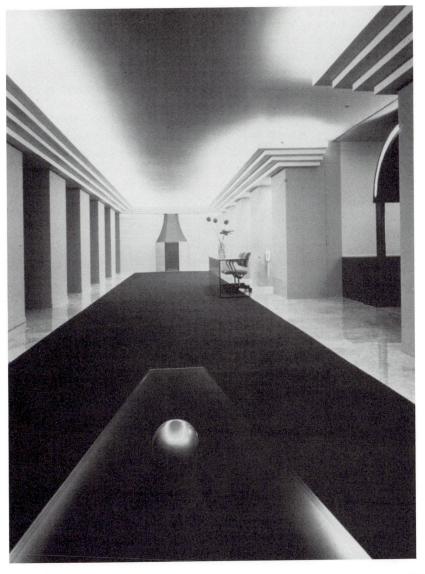

204. Arata Isozaki. E. F. Hauserman showroom. Chicago, Illinois. 1982. *Photograph by Barbara Karant, Sadin/Karant.*

Perhaps the paradigm of all these combined influences was devised by the poetic Japanese architect Arata Isozaki. Among his many attention-gathering interiors, he designed a showroom for E. F. Hauserman in Chicago (1982) (see Figure 204) that was the American introduction to his multiplicity of historical recalls— Post-Modern classicism, Streamlining, turn-of-the-century Vienna, Japanese traditions, Romanesque barrel vaults, Palladio, Mies, Kahn, and a list of other influences. No American designer combined so many inspirational devices in a single interior.

Problems of the Profession

Innovation

One critical question about the profession of interior design continually recurs throughout this history: If the most innovative designs have interested us as the significant contributions to the design world, why have those designs been received with less broad acceptance than (1) traditional designs, (2) ingrained eighteenth-century models, or (3) anonymously designed commercial products? The question is not about rivalry between designers or between the different design professions; it is more to the deep concern of all designers: Why are design innovation and progress not generally acceptable or desired?

Part of Modernist thinking has held that innovation is the ultimate goal—innovation of functional process as well as of formal shape. Modernists have felt that if designers or architects analyzed and thought carefully enough, they might, after six or eight months, devise a design that could be better than anything the world had ever seen for that purpose before. If you build a better mousetrap, the maxim goes, the world will beat a path to your door. By extension, if a good, thoughtful designer worked out a more efficient toilet, which also revolutionized the process of using it, then humankind ought to accept this innovative work of genius, perhaps even seek it out. It has not worked out that way.

The continued resistance to Modern design has made it increasingly clear that humankind cannot be swayed to give up a functional process that it has developed over a million years. Our race cannot easily reject a cultural tradition and adopt something that has just been worked out. Perhaps the battle between innovation and tradition, as between futurism and historicism, is ingrained.

Part of the answer to this question about innovation may be related to the desire for comfort. Why have the designs of innovators often been so uncomfortable? From Frank Lloyd Wright's furniture to Paul Rudolph's, from some of Le Corbusier's and Mies's to Richard Meier's? The question is strained by how many traditionally tried, proved, and accepted models from the past two centuries can be emulated. Those models have been approved of as comfortable by a majority of users.

Only on rare occasions have twentieth-century design innovators achieved comfort comparable to that of the most traditional furnishings. Charles Eames and, more recently, Donald Pettit, Charles Pollock, and Richard Schultz, have produced chairs that have been accepted as both handsome and truly comfortable. This question of comfort remains the core of the battle between the two schools of interior design—traditionalism and innovation—comfort to the body, and comfort to the accustomed eye. Was this question also raised in the eighteenth century? "We know what we like" really means "We like what we know."

Publishing Furniture Plans and Dates

Due to the concentration on surface and visual effects by both the majority of decorators and the shelter publications, furniture plans and sections are seldom presented along with the photographs of interior design projects. Without them, we cannot know whether innovative or even interesting placements of furniture, changes in level, or broader issues are addressed. Do we have any understanding of the plan of Jean-Michel Frank's salon for the de Noailleses? Or of Billy Baldwin's apartment for Cole Porter? For the profession to record its accomplishments, for individual designers to show the true strengths of their concepts, the plans and sections must be made an essential part of recorded presentations.

Dates are another essential element that is generally lacking in interior design records. Since early twentieth-century decorators did not have to file registered plans or other legal documents, there are numerous missing dates for design and construction. Can we ever know the dates of innovation in furniture finishing or other crafts endeavors? Furthermore, it is said that because of vanity many of the early "blue-haired lady decorators" would never let their birthdates be known. Ruby Ross Wood is a prime example. Nor have any of the books by the major decorators tried to provide more precise chronologies about their careers than specifying the decades—as opposed to the years—in which their projects were designed and installed. Establishing the facts is difficult enough in this situation; analyzing the time lags within this chronology is, at this stage of the profession, sometimes impossible.

The inclusion of more precise dates for interior design projects—more precise than assuming six months prior to a publication of the project—will be a greater requirement as the profession grows more professional. In later contract work, from the 1950s onward, this problem begins to vanish. But in residential work it lingers in the would-be perennially up-to-date pages of general-press journalism.

Getting Together

Will the different professions of interior design ever get together? The separation early in the 1900s of the architect-designer, who traditionally orchestrated a team of artists and artisans, from the decorator-designer, who served as art-and-object consultant and orchestrator of the assembly of those objects, set the two professions on divergent paths. Then in the 1960s, when many interior designers began to adopt the Modern idiom, the paths seemed to converge—except for the fact that vanguard designers were already turning away from Modernism to Post-Modernism.

Can the interior design professions ever come together at a single stylistic meeting point and agreement? Or are they destined to be—quite properly, numerous critics claim—separate and distinct because they focus on completely different things—architecture on ideas, space, and structure; interiors on vision and touch? Or are the professions merely different sides of the same coin, so that one cannot exist without the other? Architect-designer Warren Platner is said to have commented that the reason for architecture is interiors. Perhaps the overview of interior design history in this book will offer a new viewpoint.

Philosophy/Theory/Ideology

Why is there no aesthetic theory of interior design from interiors specialists? Why is it all from architects? Interior designers show no signs of having deep, overall philosophies about their work. They have generalized approaches that are governed by strong and individual points of view, and they have strong likes and dislikes. But those are not complete, developed philosophies. Interior designers seem not to develop complete systems of thought or ideology that stretch out to the intellectual frontiers of their work; they seem to have no cerebral methodologies that are all-pervasive—from overall approach to the most minute detail.

Architects, clearly, are not like that, have never been throughout history. The history of architecture is filled with critical works on architectural philosophy—from Vitruvius to Alberti and Serlio, from Viollet-le-Duc to Frank Lloyd Wright, from Le Corbusier to Camillo Sitte. Architects continue to write books about design theory and history. Decorators and interior designers seem only to write books for popular consumption to increase their fame or clientele.

Architects thrive on theories and philosophies—at times it seems as if they need such theories to keep their expanded visions expanded; at other times it seems as if theorizing and philosophy are all that architects have to concentrate on. Architects constantly take sides in great debates—which change from year to year—and these ideological issues seemingly condition their work, pervade it, and make it appear indivisible from those philosophies—if sometimes in contradiction. Louis Kahn mesmerized listeners at lecture after lecture with his mystical and mythical aesthetic philosophy; his was an almost complete mythology, as detailed in word and thought as it was in sketch and line.

It is not that all architects are verbal about their design philosophies. The practice of architecture and the professing of theory are not mutually dependent.

But the high points in the history of architecture do seem to have been made largely by those who have achieved high points of architectural theory. The same cannot be said for interior design and interior design theory. Some critics say that this difference in interest in design theory is due to the fact that architecture is, indeed, about ideas, whereas interiors are about vision and touch. This matter invites designers' convictions.

Design Morality

Today, the consideration of design morality relates not to the handmade versus the machine-made object. That battle was won long ago. Rather it concerns the original/individual item versus the mass-produced reproduction—in addition to design piracy, of course. This consideration of originality is complicated by the many stages of industrial production. The unique hand-carved chair is an original object; the hand-carved chair that is reproduced in multiples is considered a copy. A prototype chair intended for industrial production by Mies or Eames was a unique and original object; the chairs produced in multiples by industry are—originals or copies? This is the contemporary moral dilemma in design.

An analogy with culinary craft may be illuminating on this subject: To cook from scratch is the goal of purist chefs; opening a can or package of something already processed is rejected as unoriginal. Yet sugar and flour have already been processed, and serving fresh oysters is, essentially, a matter of opening a package and providing originality only in a sauce. Perhaps we should look at design for production—for reproduction—as a multistage process in which originality can be injected at any stage—in the conceptual stage, in the final form, in the material, in the process itself, or even in the final garnish or presentation.

Conclusions

As we look at the history of twentieth-century interior design as laid out in some detail, we recognize cycles of design emphasis, those continuous swings of the pendulum from one side to the other. But we also see the many different pendulums that constitute the totality of design choices:

- historical versus futurist
- classical versus romantic
- functional versus aesthetic
- geometric regularity versus biomorphic irregularity
- symmetrical versus asymmetrical
- clean versus messy
- vital versus static
- simple versus elaborate
- peasant versus palatial
- elaborated versus refined/purgative/stripped
- colorful versus monochromatic
- calm repose versus agitated excitement
- total/consistent/integral versus fragmented/layered/inconsistent

These seem to run in cycles of interest. The twentieth century has seen the ultimate aesthetic expression of the Industrial Revolution in its celebration of the imagery of the machine. Our century has also seen the working out of the Futurist vision of speed and light, of dematerialization and the ephemeral. What can we learn from an overview of these cycles or swings of the pendulum?

One fact seems clear: The great mistake is the tendency not to respect the existing, original conditions—client requirements, site, period, or original design. This leads to confusion of fashions in the cycles of design emphasis. Fashions become confused with the kind of timelessness that the best design must aim for.

Elaboration versus Refinement

In our century, also, each design revolution seems to be praised for its overthrow of the excesses of the past and its refinement of current design tastes. Refinement, along with white or light colors, seems to get the highest vote of praise in our age. Elsie de Wolfe simplified the Victorian interior; Jean-Michel Frank distilled the classical vision of the 1930s.

Yet, if everything that is good is simple and refined, what can be said positively for elaboration? And if everything that is good continues to be refined, will there ultimately be anything left to refine? Perhaps what is not explained by history is the disintegration of simplicity by popularization. What is initially refined by a vanguard visionary, then accepted and adapted by his or her colleagues, never stays as it was invented. Each adapter adds his or her own personality; each addition de-simplifies. Then, to be mass-producible and marketable, it must be changed—adapted to the available technology, modified to meet what the sales organization understands of marketable taste, then changed again by the inevitable copyists. As William Morris said, "There is always someone who is willing to debase a design to make it cheaper and sell it at a greater profit." In this way, it seems, both products and styles become elaborated rather than further refined. Soon, again, it will be time for another design revolution of refinement.

Time Lags

These cycles have come faster and faster, in our century, due to rapid transportation and to the instantaneous communications systems we have devised. Between 1921 and 1923, Mies van der Rohe drew his first visionary schemes of towers with all glass-and-metal curtain walls. It took thirty years for the available technology to catch up until such a building was made possible—in Mies's 1951 Lake Shore Drive Apartments in Chicago. In the next ten years, manufacturers of curtain-wall systems proliferated to accommodate the designs and demands of countless architects following in that idiom. By about 1961 professional critics were already calling such structures "boring"—just when the general public was beginning to see enough examples of glass architecture to become familiar with the idiom. Still, since then—now over twenty years—the glass-and-metal curtain wall has been the mainstream of building construction and technology around the world.

Meanwhile, of course, other cycles of design revolution have been going on, overlaid on this pyramid of acceptance that trickles down from the visionary designer to the profession and then to acceptance by the mass of population. And there are cycles that "trickle up" from nonacademic design circles—Peasant and Vernacular styles, Pop and Rock—to become high-style idioms. In this regard we cannot overlook the towering influence, throughout the century, of Picasso's and Matisse's Peasant or Primitive style on the field of interior design. Yet these simple styles by high-style artists further complicate the picture. All of these complicate our understanding of the cycles of design and the time lags inherent in those cycles.

Clients

In most books on design there seems to be so much to discuss about the problems, solutions, goals, techniques, and inventions of designers that several critical topics are usually omitted. One of these topics is the central role played by designers of fabrics and by upholsterers, drapers, and the many other contractors who build interiors. Another of these topics is the client. That is the case of this book also. A mass of information, sensitivity, and credit is due to every mention of the Vicomte and Vicomtesse de Noailles, the Mexican art patron Carlos de Bestigui, Nelson Rockefeller, Pauline Potter Baroness Philippe de Rothchild, Linda and Cole Porter, the Gilbert Millers, J. Irwin Miller, and countless other clients who made the work of the interior designers discussed in this history possible. The role of clients in the making of interiors is pivotal. For without the client, both the financing and the function are missing. It has often been rightly said that every great work of design requires a great client as well as a great architect or designer.

Interior design, as we must constantly bear in mind, is an applied art, not a fine art. It has a program of requirements—requirements for physical function, requirements for psychological function—that are or should be part of the goal of a designer. And it is a joint venture of client and designer that must set, pursue, modify, and express those goals. Both collaborators can foil the success. The designer can ignore the client's requirements and make a fine-art interior, with no regard for the client's requirements. The client can withhold understanding, agreement, cooperation, or funding, making it impossible for an interior designer to achieve the vision, the concept that he or she sees as fitting for that set of requirements, location, and the rest.

As much as an interior designer must maintain a personal vision—parameters, perseverance, and control to achieve the concept, and, ultimately, the total work of art—so too a client must maintain a commitment to the designer's talent and professionalism, as well as a commitment to the budget and the timetable. As much as the designer must maintain his or her vision, so must he or she also maintain a commitment to the functional and psychological requirements of the client, to the budget, and to the schedule.

In any work there are only three first and basic goals: to do the best job we can, to do it within the budget, and to do it on time. A failure in any one of these goals is a failure short of whatever perfection of professionalism a designer can have in mind in doing the best job he or she can do. Meeting these goals and creating appropriate and fitting interiors with a new and personal magic are the goals to which all designers of interiors aspire.

Glossary

aubergine a purple-black color; the color of eggplant skin

chaise longue (not "lounge") a chair with a long seat that one can stretch one's legs out on

chaise percée a chair with a hole in the seat and a cabinet below to conceal a chamber pot

Churrigueresque an elaborately ornamented genre of Spanish and Mexican baroque, named for José de Churriguera (1650–1725)

classical (1) formal, stately, and composed; (2) based on Greek and Roman antiquities; (3) based on any ancient civilization, such as Egyptian, Mayan, Greek, Roman, and so forth.

Cromwellian the period of Puritan revolt in England (1642–1660), named for Oliver Cromwell, when comparatively austere and undecorated furniture was adopted. American Colonial Puritans also adopted the style. Simplified rope-turnings on gate-leg tables and on square-backed, Spanish-inspired leather-upholstered chairs were produced chiefly in walnut, white oak, and maple.

Day-Glo a series of vivid phosphorescent colors popularized in the 1960s

distressing a technique of aging and weathering furniture and other objects to give them patina—such as streaks and gouges, dents and worm-holes

door buck the frame built into a wall to support and enclose a door

fenestration the placement and treatment of windows in building design

furred out/furred down the building-out of a wall surface to meet a desired contour

intarsia wood inlaid with ivory, metal, or other materials

knock-down the name given to furniture that can be assembled and disassembled for production and for shipping

lambrequin a horizontal drapery, such as a valance or pelmet, hanging on a fireplace shelf in the Victorian period; or, the drapery around the top of a bed

parquet de Versailles a pattern of wood flooring popularized at the Palace of Versailles

plenum a space in a wall or ceiling used for air supply or return

silver-bowl lamp a lamp bulb that is silvered on its hemispherical end to produce a reflector

spline a strip connecting or covering a long flat joint between elements, such as two panels

strié a stripe-like texture or pattern in paint or fabric

tête-de-nègre a rich red-cast chocolate brown; a color popularized in France

valance a horizontal hanging or pelmet over a window or other opening

Victorian common lumping of all nineteenth-century periods from 1840 to 1900, during the reign of Queen Victoria.

Pronunciation Guide

Andes   AN-deez

Au Quatrième   oh kah-tree-EHM

Bauhaus   rhymes with out-house

Beaux-Arts   bohz-arh

Berlage   BEAR-lah-geh

Bijvoet   BYE-foot

Breuer   BROY-er

Castiglione   cas-teel-YOH-neh

Chareau   sha-ROH

Chiattone   key-ah-TOH-neh

Cret   kray

De Stijl   in Dutch, somewhere between deh shtyle and deh shtale; in English, deh style

Der Blaue Reiter   rhymes with dare-POWER-writer

Déscartes   day-CART

Deutscher Werkbund   DOYT-sher verk-boond

Die Bruecke   dee BROOK-eh

ensembliers   on-SAHM-blee-ay

Errazuris   ehr-RAH-tsoo-ree

Foucault   foo-COH

Fourcade   foor-KAHD

Gesamtkunstwerk   Geh-ZAHMT-koonst-verk

Ghirardelli   gear-arh-DELL-ee

Gris, Juan   gree, wahn

Hejduk   HAY-duck

La Jolla   lah HOY-ah

Labrouste   lah-BROOST

Loos   lohs

Lutyens   LUTCH-ens

Maire   my-REH

Mairea   my-RAY-ah

Maugham   mawm

Mauna Kae   moh-nah KAY-uh

Mielziner   mill-ZEEN-er

Mies van der Rohe   mees van dehr ROH-eh

Muthesius   moo-TAY-zee-oos

Neutra   NOY-trah

Noialles   noh-EYE

parti   par-TEE

Pei   pay

Pfister   FEES-ter

Poughkeepsie   poh-KIP-see

Quitandinha   key-tahn-DEEN-yah

Rietveld   REET-velt

Sachlichkeit   ZAHK-lick-kite

Scheebart   SHAY-bart

Schnelle   SHNEL-leh

Stoclet   stock-LAY

Syon   ZIGH-un

Taliesin   tally-ESS-in

Terragni   tear-RAHN-yee

trompe l'oeil   trahmp LUH-ee or tromp LOY

Versailles   vehr-SIGH

Vignelli   veen-YELL-ee

Wasmuth   VAHS-muht

Weyerhaeuser   wear-HOW-zer

Wiener Werkstaette   VEEN-er VERK-shtet-teh

Zajac   zay-JACK

Index of Names

Index of Topics